BROADCAST NEWS HANDBOOK

WRITING, REPORTING & PRODUCING IN A CONVERGING MEDIA WORLD

Fifth Edition

C. A. Tuggle
University of North Carolina at Chapel Hill

Forrest Carr
News Director
KGUN Tucson, AZ

Suzanne Huffman
Texas Christian University

The McGraw·Hill Companies

Connect
Learn
Succeed™

BROADCAST NEWS HANDBOOK: WRITING, REPORTING, AND PRODUCING IN THE AGE OF SOCIAL MEDIA, FIFTH EDITION

1 2 3 4 5 6 7 8 9 0 DOC/DOC 1 0 9 8 7 6 5 4 3

ISBN 978-0-07-352622-5
MHID 0-07-3526223
Vice President & General Manager: *Michael Ryan*
Executive Director of Development: *Lisa Pinto*
Managing Director: *David Patterson*
Brand Manager: *Susan Gouijnstook*
Marketing Specialist: *Alexandra Schultz*
Managing Development Editor: *Penina Braffman*
Editorial Coordinator: *Adina Lonn*
Director, Content Production: *Terri Schiesl*
Project Manager: *Judi David*
Buyer: *Jennifer Pickel*
Media Project Manager: *Sridevi Palani*
Cover Designer: *Studio Montage, St. Louis, MO*
Cover Image: *Forrest Carr*
Compositor: *MPS Limited*
Typeface: *10/12 Palatino*
Printer: *R. R. Donnelley*

Library of Congress Cataloging-in-Publication Data
Tuggle, C. A.
    Broadcast news handbook : writing, reporting and producing in a converging media world / C. A. Tuggle, University of North Carolina at Chapel Hill, Forrest Carr, News Director KGUN, Tucson, AZ, Suzanne Huffman, Texas Christian University. —Fifth edition.
        pages cm
    Includes bibliographical references and index.
    ISBN 978-0-07-352622-5 (alk. paper)
    1. Television broadcasting of news—Handbooks, manuals, etc. I. Carr, Forrest.
II. Huffman, Suzanne. III. Title.
PN4784.T4T76 2013
070.4'3—dc23   2012036405

www.mhhe.com

DEDICATIONS

From C. A. Tuggle
To my wife, Tracey, and children, Brynne, Bethany, and Jenny, and to the memory of my father, T. B. Tuggle, my inspiration to always do my best.

From Forrest Carr
To the memory of Bruce Breslow, a good friend and the finest photo-journalist I have ever known.

From Suzanne Huffman
To my husband, August F. Schilling III, and to my parents, Carrol Statton Huffman and Margaret Anne Byrd Huffman.

ABOUT THE AUTHORS

Dr. C. A. Tuggle began teaching at the university level in 1994 after a 16-year career in local television news and media relations. He spent the majority of his career at WFLA-TV, the NBC affiliate in Tampa. He has held numerous newsroom positions, but spent the bulk of his career reporting and producing. He covered both news and sports, including six Super Bowls. Tuggle earned undergraduate and master's degrees from the University of Florida in Gainesville, and his Ph.D. from the University of Alabama in Tuscaloosa. He is currently teaching electronic communication at the University of North Carolina at Chapel Hill. His research has appeared in nearly a dozen scholarly journals and trade publications, and centers on television news practices and procedures. He regularly conducts writing workshops for local stations, professional and academic groups, and high school journalists. He has overseen student newscasts at three universities and his students have won numerous regional and national awards, including six Emmys and best student radio newscast and best student television newscast in the nation in each of four other competitions. In addition, he helped mentor more than 50 interns during his professional career.

Forrest Carr began his broadcast news career in 1980 as a radio reporter but quickly switched to television, starting as a copy writer and fill-in reporter before working his way into newscast producing and eventually into management. After working in the Memphis, San Antonio and Tampa markets, in 1997 he joined KGUN9-TV in Tucson, Arizona for his first news director's job. During his tenure there, KGUN9 made waves locally and nationally with Viewer Advocacy Journalism, an innovative viewer-oriented coverage philosophy expressed in its one-of-a-kind statement of principles, "The Viewers' Bill of Rights." Carr returned to Media General's converged Tampa news operation in 2001 as news director for WFLA-TV, a position he held for 4 years. After serving terms as news director at WFTX-TV in Fort Myers and KRQE-TV/KASA-TV in Albuquerque, Carr returned to KGUN9-TV as news director in 2009. Carr has won or shared credit in more than 90 professional awards and was a 2002 Poynter Ethics Fellow.

Dr. Suzanne Huffman is a professor of journalism in the Schieffer School of Journalism at Texas Christian University in Fort Worth, Texas. She earned her B.A. at TCU, her M.A. from the University of Iowa, and her Ph.D. from the University of Missouri at Columbia. She has reported, anchored, and produced news at commercial television stations in Tampa, Florida; Santa Maria, California; and Cedar Rapids, Iowa. Dr. Huffman taught at three other universities before joining the TCU faculty, and her former students occupy newsroom positions throughout the South and Southwest. Her academic research centers on the practice of broadcast journalism and her research articles have been published in *Journal of Broadcasting & Electronic Media* and other academic journals. Dr. Huffman is co-author with Dr. Judith Sylvester at Louisiana State University of *Women Journalists at Ground Zero: Covering Crisis,* published by Rowman & Littlefield in 2002, about the experiences of women journalists who covered the 9/11 terrorist attacks on the United States. She is also co-author with Dr. Sylvester of *Reporting from the Front: The Media and the Military,* published by Rowman & Littlefield in 2005, about the experiences of journalists who were embedded with U.S. troops in the 2003 U.S.-led invasion of Iraq.

CONTENTS

Bob Dotson

Senior Correspondent
"NBC Nightly News"

My grandmother always worried about my life's work. The first time she got a chance to see one of my stories on "NBC Nightly News," I called to see what she thought.

"Did you like my story on Tom's show tonight?" I asked.

There was a long pause on the other end of the line. Then she said, "Bobby, I think you should learn a trade."

"A trade?"

"Yes, they're not going to keep paying you for two minutes of work a day."

Well, they have. For nearly four decades I've been traveling the world on someone else's nickel. I've been in more motel rooms than the Gideon Bible.

And it's been a wonderful life.

The ticket to that life begins on the pages that follow. They contain the nuts and bolts of our business—the basics that hold us all together. This book will help you master our complex and challenging profession. It will also refresh your memory in the years ahead, so keep it handy.

I went to college back when the earth was cooling. Every technical thing I learned about is now in a museum. But the things you'll find on these pages are timeless. They're lessons that will last a lifetime.

So, read on. Have a good life. Call your grandmother.

PREFACE

Dave Cupp
University of North Carolina at Chapel Hill

For most of human history, information never traveled from one location to another any faster than a man could run, a horse could gallop, or wind could blow a ship across a sea. If you were an ancient ruler, you might arrange for a series of mountaintop bonfires to signal that a distant battle had been won or lost, but for details beyond the basic outcome you'd face an agonizing wait. During times both ancient and modern, of course, few issues could be of greater importance than the fate of your own soldiers in battle.

The frustrating delay in exchanging information eased in 1837 when Samuel F. B. Morse invented the telegraph. Utilizing Morse's invention, an operator could tap a key in a series of coded dots and dashes representing letters of the alphabet. Using this code, he could spell out words and convey complex information rapidly to a counterpart in any distant city where a telegraph cable went. As the United States expanded so did the web of cables, and one even traversed the ocean. In 1858, just 21 years after Morse invented the telegraph, an operator sent the first transatlantic message using his code.

A few years later, President Abraham Lincoln relied on a steady stream of telegraph messages to monitor the progress of Civil War battles. This was a far cry from the wartime reality of 1776, when weeks were stretching into months before news reached King George that those upstart American colonists had won their revolution by defeating his vaunted British troops at Yorktown.

President Lincoln wasn't the only person with access to a steady supply of fresh information about the progress of the Civil War. The telegraph enabled newspapers to bring daily battle updates to the nation at large, and at the same time another new technology brought the ugly reality of warfare home to average citizens in an unprecedented and emotional way.

Photographer Matthew Brady sent a corps of photographers into the field to document the Civil War. In 1862, he shocked the residents of New York City by displaying graphic photographs of bloated battlefield corpses from Antietam. This marked the first time that most people had witnessed wartime carnage. Observers found the images deeply disturbing in the same way that, a century later, their descendents would be shaken by the powerful, uncensored images of the Vietnam War that filled their television screens each evening.

The decades after the Civil War saw a series of inventions that would free information from the bonds of telegraph wires and send those Morse dots and dashes out through the ether. In 1886, Heinrich Hertz demonstrated the nature of radio waves. Nine years later,

Guglielmo Marconi transmitted radio signals for short distances. In 1898, the *Dublin Daily Express* received radio-telegraph coverage of the Kingstown Regatta. As the 20th century dawned, even operators on ships at sea were able to communicate with each other using wireless telegraphy. In 1912, Morse messages relayed word of the CQD and SOS calls from the sinking *Titanic* to stunned people around the world. But even as those distress calls were being deciphered, such coded radio transmissions were on the verge of being replaced by another innovative technology.

In 1906, the wireless operator of the S.S. *Kroonland* was startled when his headset crackled to life without the familiar dits and dahs that always comprised the messages he received. Instead, he heard music and a person reciting poetry. It was a Christmas surprise from inventor Reginald Fessenden, who had made the first voice "broadcast" in his Pittsburgh laboratory back in 1901. At the time, even that use of the term itself was a novelty. When the 20th century opened, people used the word "broadcasting" to describe the way farmers scattered seeds far and wide in their fields.

Fessenden wasn't alone in exploring radio transmission of the human voice. Even before the 1800s drew to a close, inventor Lee DeForest had been studying high-frequency radio waves, and in 1907 he received a patent for the first three-electrode vacuum tube for amplifying radio signals. Two years later in San Jose, California, Charles "Doc" Harrold began broadcasting the first regularly scheduled news reports using what he called a "wireless telephone." During the next decade, hobbyists and inventors continued to experiment. They transmitted radio waves from balloons, bathyspheres and even from an airplane.

World War I stopped development temporarily, but already businessmen were starting to recognize the potential of this new technology. In 1915, young David Sarnoff of American Marconi sent out his "Radio Music Box" memorandum, envisioning a world in which radio could provide entertainment and information for millions of people. In 1922, Sarnoff's first "radiola" went on the market. Two years later came the broadcasts of the Republican and Democratic conventions. Calvin Coolidge won the election, and in 1925, for the first time ever, Americans heard the inauguration of a president in their own homes. Later that year Americans were riveted by radio coverage of what came to be called the Scopes Monkey Trial, and in 1926, the National Broadcasting Company established the first radio network, 24 stations strong.

In 1927 radios brought proud Americans the voice of their hero, Charles Lindbergh, home from his historic flight across the Atlantic Ocean. In 1933, at the height of the Great Depression, radio enabled worried Americans to hear the voice of President Franklin Roosevelt; not giving them a speech, but calling them "my friends" and reassuring them in a series of fireside chats. Roosevelt was perhaps the first politician to recognize the unique ability of broadcasting to not only reach people by the millions, but also to forge an intimate, one-on-one connection with each listener.

By the end of the 1930s, the world was once again sliding into war. On a nightly basis during the Blitz, German bombers pounded London, and CBS's Edward R. Murrow brought the conflict home to Americans. Murrow pioneered the journalistic concept of painting a series of small word pictures in his news stories that would humanize and illustrate the big picture that listeners needed to understand. Writer Archibald MacLeish said that, in the process, Murrow had "accomplished one of the great miracles of the world. You destroyed a superstition . . . the superstition that what is done beyond 3,000 miles of water is not really done at all. You burned the city of London in our houses, and we felt the flames that burned it. You laid the dead of London at our doors."

Five days later, the Japanese bombed Pearl Harbor, and for the rest of the war radio brought details of the worldwide conflict into the homes of Americans. The next war would come a decade later in Korea, and this time Americans would not only hear the sounds of warfare, but would also see it for themselves through the marvel of television.

Today, not many people remember the names of the inventors who brought us television. They include Vladimir Zworykin, who developed the "iconoscope" for the electronic scanning of pictures in 1923, and Philo T. Farnsworth, who developed the orthicon tube in 1930. FDR would become the first president to appear on television as he ceremonially opened the 1939 World's Fair.

Just as the development of radio had slowed because of what people called "The Great War," World War II delayed the progress of television. The delay ended as peace arrived, followed by the economic boom of the 1950s. Television sets became the focal points of the living rooms of America, their screens filled with entertainment and news programming that had migrated from radio to this new medium. When America went to war again, this time in Korea, TV went along. Edward R. Murrow described his coverage of this new conflict as using a "Thousand Pound Pencil." The film cameras, tripods and sound equipment his "See It Now" crews used were bulky, and the Christmas broadcasts they produced were slow in reaching viewers— but for the first time, those reports brought the combined sights and sounds of American soldiers in a war zone into the homes of millions of Americans.

For daily news, though, most members of those American families still turned to newspapers. For broadcast information, they were still more likely to turn to their radios. Evening network television newscasts at the time were only 15 minutes long. In 1963, though, two things happened. Evening TV newscasts expanded to a half-hour—and a gunman killed President John Kennedy in Dallas. Two days later, his accused assassin was murdered in front of a live network television camera, and the next day Americans by the millions gathered around their television sets to watch, in real time, the funeral and burial of the charismatic young president they had lost. This national shared experience of grief marked a pivot point for television news—which by the end of the decade would go on to become the dominant information source for Americans.

As the years passed, television technology evolved and improved. Bulky film equipment disappeared, replaced by portable videotape gear that could, and did, go almost anywhere. Simultaneously, communication satellites enhanced the ability of broadcasters to go live from nearly any location. Just as live television images had united Americans in grief by taking them to Dallas and Washington in 1963, live television images united Americans in celebration in 1969 by allowing them to essentially set foot on the moon along with astronaut Neil Armstrong.

Other television coverage of the 1960s brought violent, deeply disturbing images into American homes and shaped viewers' perceptions of historic events. Television news visuals included ugly attacks on civil rights protesters in the South, disturbing stories of warfare, atrocities and protests related to the Vietnam War, and grim coverage of the assassinations of Dr. Martin Luther King Jr. and Robert Kennedy.

By the end of the decade, television news had the figurative power to destroy a politician. In 1968, when Walter Cronkite offered his on-air opinion that America could not win the war in Vietnam, President Lyndon Johnson said if he had lost Cronkite, he had lost Middle America. One month later, Johnson announced he wouldn't run for re-election. Television news could also make a politician. During his own 1968 presidential run, Robert Kennedy said he'd rather have "30 seconds on an evening news program than coverage in every newspaper in the world."

Part of the power of those evening newscasts stemmed from the fact that there were so few of them. Three networks—CBS, NBC and ABC—set the national broadcast news agenda. They also heavily influenced local television news coverage, which was dominated by stations affiliated with the three networks. During the last few decades of the 20th century, though, network dominance was eroded by the continuing march of technology. Television had always been a broadcast medium. Now, though, viewers could opt for cable delivery services or satellite reception.

In 1980, entrepreneur Ted Turner combined these new technologies to create the world's first Cable News Network—CNN. Broadcasters initially scoffed, referring to Turner's shoestring operation as Chicken

Noodle News. They stopped scoffing on January 17, 1991, when America's first war in Iraq began with a bombardment of Baghdad. The traditional networks had all their reporters stationed with American troops. CNN had personnel positioned in a Baghdad hotel room, equipped with satellite telephones and other state-of-the-art equipment, providing live coverage from the receiving end of the aerial assault. CNN's ability to cover both sides in the war made it unique, and brought it both viewers and credibility.

Television cameras had once allowed Americans to ride along on rockets to the moon. During the first Iraq war, they allowed Americans to ride along on cruise missiles as they approached enemy targets. CNN became the first of many competing services to offer additional news and entertainment choices to viewers, eventually leading to the broad variety of options available today on broadcast, on satellite, on cable, and online.

The first time Americans gathered around their televisions to communally experience a national tragedy came on November 22, 1963, with the Kennedy assassination. Another time for such a communal gathering in front of TV sets came on September 11, 2001, with the terrorist attacks on the World Trade Center and the Pentagon. If a tragedy of a similar magnitude occurred today, millions of Americans would certainly turn on their TVs, but millions more would reach for an array of other electronic devices that now link them to information and to each other.

As the 21st century arrived, the equipment evolution that has always driven the development of electronic journalism accelerated. Today's television is digital, and video has become more compelling thanks to the shift to High Definition. But young consumers seeking information are now more likely to reach for smart phones, tablets or laptop computers than they are to seek out televisions, radios or newspapers. Network and local broadcasters find themselves adjusting to the rise of the Internet, the expansion of Wi-Fi, and the evolution of e-mail, texting, Facebook and Twitter. The audience is evolving too. Once it consisted of passive viewers. Now it includes active participants, who want to contribute their own content and engage in a give-and-take regarding the issues they care about.

During the early decades of the 20th century, inventors created a series of devices that would change the basic ways people communicated with one another. The first electronic journalists took advantage of these new technologies to develop powerful new forms of storytelling and information sharing. In the process, they helped millions of people make sense of the world around them.

Today the world remains as confusing as ever, and new technologies are proliferating at an unprecedented rate, once again changing the basic ways we communicate with one another. Today's electronic journalists are looking for ways to take advantage of these new technologies and develop powerful new forms of storytelling and information sharing. In this book, they'll find a strong and sophisticated foundation to build their efforts upon.

—D. Cupp

The Importance of Writing

A university professor once noted that a student told him she decided to study broadcast journalism rather than print journalism because she didn't like to write that much. It is, of course, a misconception that there isn't much writing in broadcast journalism. Anchors and reporters don't just stand (or sit) in front of a camera or microphone and pour forth interesting information. To understand the real world of broadcast journalism is to learn the step-by-step process involved. Good writing is at the heart of that process.

Our Approach

With *Broadcast News Handbook,* our goal is to teach aspiring broadcast or cross-platform journalists how to write, how to craft the language, and how to be effective storytellers using all the technology available to them without letting technology drive the process. Together, we have more than 50 years of broadcast journalism experience. In the final two decades of the 20th century, we saw many technological advancements that affected how news is covered: videotape, microwave and satellite technology, digital editing, and the list could go on. Technology has changed and will continue to change. But the need to be an effective storyteller hasn't changed, and won't. Regardless of what the tools are, those who can use those tools well to impart interesting information will always have a place in journalism. Foremost among those tools is the language itself. We don't buy into Marshall McLuhan's contention that "the medium is the message." We think the message is the message and the medium is simply a means to get that message to an audience. Technology and journalism are intimately connected in radio, television, and online applications, but content must always drive which stories we select for coverage and how we cover them.

Who Will Benefit from the Book

We've tried to construct a text that will be useful to beginning broadcast journalism students as well as to those who have advanced in their college training and education and even to those who have entered the workforce. We believe the practical "how-to" sections of this text and the real-world advice will serve students and early career professionals well. We hope the book becomes a resource for students as they progress through their studies and for working journalists as they further their careers in the information business. We believe this book could also be a valuable resource for news workers and managers in traditional print and broadcast newsrooms as they face the need to cross-train.

Special Features of the Book

The three authors have decades of broadcast news experience. Between us, we've held every newsroom position there is. We approach this book from the perspective of what worked for us, as reporters, producers, and managers, and what we know will work for others. We believe the practical tips and guidelines we've included will not only help you break into the highly competitive world of broadcast news, but will also help you advance while remaining true to the ideals that led you to pursue a journalism career.

Although the book uses three different "voices," and although each author approaches the material from his or her unique perspective, we are frankly somewhat surprised at the cohesion that has emerged during the process of writing this book. There might be minor differences in our approaches, but there is unanimity about how the product of broadcast journalists should look and the steps necessary to get to that point.

- To help readers understand and remember those steps, we've included a DOs and DON'Ts box at the end of most chapters as a quick study guide and desk reference.

- Words in **bold** are defined in the glossary.

- Producing and writing are so closely tied together in broadcast news that a writing book would be incomplete without a thorough look at producing. The member of the team who's a working news director wrote the producing chapter. As with other chapters in the book, the producing chapter is filled with practical tips—both about how to become an effective producer and how to make yourself stand out in the producer ranks.

- Broadcast writers write stories to be heard, not read. Therefore, we place emphasis on the performance aspect of radio and TV reporting.

- Although the book contains a wealth of information about how we do certain things, we've also included a chapter titled "Why We Fight"—a close look at the ethical component of the broadcast news business. We believe strongly in the power of the media, and with power comes responsibility. We work in and teach about one of the most important aspects of a democracy—media that are free from government control. Protecting rights as we deal with the public's right to know is a vital part of journalism.

- The book ends with three very important appendixes. Appendix A is a look at some problem words that good writers must master. Language is our foremost tool, and we need to know how to use that tool extremely well. Material used in the grammar and word precision quizzes that accompany this text comes from the appendix.

In general, the book advances from the characteristics of broadcast writing to the story selection process and writing tips that apply to all broadcast story forms. Interviewing and writing for radio chapters introduce us to the vital role of sound bites and natural sound. The book then presents three distinct television story forms: VOs, VO/SOTs, and packages.

Supplements for the Fifth Edition

An Online Learning Center to accompany the new edition (http://www.mhhe.com/tuggle5e) includes additional teaching and learning resources. Student material includes student exercises and videos. Password-protected material for instructors includes an instructor's manual, professional scripts, and professional resources. Please contact your McGraw-Hill sales representative for the access information.

CourseSmart This text is available as a CourseSmart eBook. CourseSmart is a new way to find and buy eTextbooks. At CourseSmart you can save up to 50% off the cost of a print textbook, reduce your impact on the environment, and gain access to powerful Web tools for learning. CourseSmart has the largest selection of eTextbooks available anywhere, offering thousands of the most commonly adopted textbooks from a wide variety of higher education publishers. CourseSmart eTextbooks are available in one standard online reader with full text search, notes and highlighting, and e-mail tools for sharing notes between classmates. For further details contact your sales representative or go to www.coursesmart.com

Final Thoughts

Throughout, we acknowledge that radio and TV news is a business, but also stress that it's more than that. It's a calling, both work and passion, and a means to document and be a part of history as it's made. We hope we've imparted some of our passion for the craft of broadcast writing through this text.

ACKNOWLEDGMENTS

The authors thank a number of people for their assistance in bringing this project into being. First we would like to thank the following institutions, employers, friends and former colleagues who supplied script samples:

At KGUN9-TV in Tucson, Arizona:

General Manager Julie Brinks and former General Manager Karen Rice, for permission to use station material.

At KRQE-TV in Albuquerque, New Mexico:

General Manager Bill Anderson for permission to use station material.

At WFLA-TV in Tampa, Florida:

Former General Manager Eric Land and former Media General Broadcast Division Director of News Dan Bradley, for permission to use station scripts, and former Assistant News director Kathryn Bonfield and former sports producer Dave Cook for their assistance in selecting them.

At KGUN9-TV in Tucson, Arizona:

Former General Manager Karen Rice, for permission to use station material scripts.

At The Tampa Tribune in Tampa, Florida:

Former Senior Vice President and Executive Editor Gil Thelen, for permission to use story excerpts.

At TBO.com in Tampa, Florida:

Former General Manager Kirk Read, for permission to use copy excerpts.

Photographer Cliff McBride

At McGraw-Hill, Managing Editor Penina Braffman, Developmental Editor Craig Leonard, and Project Manager Judi David have been exceedingly helpful in getting the fifth edition and all of the elements associated with it ready for publication and distribution. We look forward to working with them on subsequent editions. Thanks also to Marketing Specialist Alexandra Schultz.

Additionally, Forrest Carr would like to acknowledge:

Bob Steele of the Poynter Institute for Media Studies, for invaluable guidance in the preparation of the ethics portion of this book.

Al Tompkins, Jill Geisler and Lillian Dunlap, also of the Poynter, for their assistance, leadership and inspiration on the subject of ethics.

The Poynter Ethics Fellows for their advice and support through the years.

The RTNDA's *Communicator* magazine, in which earlier versions of some of this material first appeared.

The many readers of *Communicator* and *Shoptalk* who have shown steadfast support and encouragement through the years.

KRQE.com New Media Content Provider Bill Diven, for his enthusiastic assistance in the preparation of the chapter about Web writing.

LIN TV, for keeping the faith and providing a great place for broadcast and Web journalists to work, at a time when such faith and commitment is in short supply industrywide.

Lee Enterprises, Inc., the former owners of KGUN9-TV, whose corporate mission and vision created an environment in which viewer-oriented journalism could thrive.

Former KGUN9-TV General Manager Ray Depa, for being one of the world's great bosses. At the Tampa Tribune and TBO.com: present and former employees Donna Reed, Morris Kennedy, Pat Minarcin, Malanda Saxton, Jim Riley, Peter Howard, Clarisa Gerlach and Adrian Phillips, for their invaluable assistance in the preparation of this manuscript.

At WFLA-TV: The late Dana Tomlins for her great graphics work and support through the years; Julie Cowan, for additional graphics help; Investigative Reporter Steve Andrews, for his example and inspiration on the subjects of journalism, writing, editing and ethics and, above all, for showing that it is possible to be an aggressive reporter and still treat people with professionalism and respect.

At the Tampa law firm of Thomas & LoCicero: Gregg Thomas, Carol LoCicero, and Susan Tollotson Bunch, whose many years of friendship, guidance, and assistance made the chapter about legal issues possible.

And, finally, Forrest's wife Deborah, who has allowed him to disappear into his study for long periods. Whether she has found this to be a burden or a blessing, she's graciously kept to herself.

Characteristics of Broadcast News Writing

Writing is easy. After all, most of us learned to do it by the time we graduated from kindergarten. However, good writing is difficult. Sometimes it's very difficult. If it weren't, most of us would be novelists. So what is it that distinguishes writers from good writers? In very simple terms, it's the ability to craft the language, not just use it. In this book we'll help you learn how to craft the language for a broadcast audience—to tell stories in ways that will grab attention, impart information, and leave television news viewers or radio news listeners with the impression of having been at the event themselves. But before we can get to that, we need to lay some groundwork. First, let's point out some of the differences between broadcast writing and most of the writing you've done during your formal education and look at some general characteristics of broadcast style.

We Get Only One Opportunity to Make Ourselves Understood

Chances are you've written a number of essays in your time; you might have even written for the school newspaper. In both cases, you were writing for the eye. In broadcast, you'll write for the ear. When your English teacher read through one of your essays, the teacher had the opportunity to go back and reread sections that weren't immediately clear. Readers of newspapers, magazines, and other printed material have the same opportunity. Broadcast audiences don't. (Most people, we assume, don't record the evening news to go back and look at it later unless they or family members or friends were part of the news that day.) So, we have to make every sentence we write very clear so audience members understand what we're talking about after having heard it only once.

Additionally, even if something looks good on the page, we don't know how it will sound until we read it out loud. You should read every broadcast script aloud so you can hear how it will sound when someone speaks the words on-air. Writing for the ear is one of the biggest differences between print and broadcast writing, but there are others.

Story Structure Is Different

Although print writers seem to be moving away from rigid adherence to the inverted pyramid style, it remains the basis of many newspaper stories, especially hard news stories. With inverted pyramid style, stories begin with the most important facts and continue with facts of lesser and lesser importance. Writers do this primarily to make it possible for editors to shorten stories without affecting the most important information. You might have noticed that some newspaper stories seem to end rather abruptly. Most likely, that was the work of an editor trying to fit a 450-word story into a 400-word space.

In broadcast writing, we don't use the inverted pyramid style. On the contrary, we write television and radio news stories in such a way that the viewers would definitely notice something was missing if we "trimmed from the bottom" because we don't build stories in descending order of the facts. Also, the end of longer broadcast news stories should either contain a summary statement or leave the viewers with something to think about, and that might be lost if viewers started to tune out toward the end. So we need to hold their attention throughout the story. Note that a summary statement isn't necessarily intended to indicate that we know all we're going to know about that story. Often, we don't know the resolution of stories for days or even months after the event occurs. Frequently, the summary statement is to let the viewers or listeners know that the story is a continuing one and that we'll follow it to its conclusion.

For specific examples, please see Chapters 7, 8 and 9.

Broadcast Writers Use Conversational Tone

This doesn't mean speak as you would on the basketball court or at a club with your friends, but broadcast writing is a bit less formal than print writing. You might have already noticed that we've written this book using contractions. That's one of the main things that separate broadcast and print writing. More about contractions in a bit. When you write for television or radio news, the goal is to tell a story to someone who knows less about what happened than you do. You want to impress this person, but you don't want to make that desire obvious. The way to impress without appearing that you're trying to impress is to use common words but use them very well. Many of us have used some words incorrectly for so long that they sound wrong when we use them the right way. Sound confusing? Just think what the viewers and listeners might be going through. Some of them know when you use a word incorrectly or try to talk above their heads; others just have a feeling that something is amiss. In either case, you, the writer, have distracted the audience members momentarily. One of the things to avoid in broadcast is anything that distracts the viewers or listeners. There are already too many things fighting against us for their attention for us to be fighting against ourselves.

We mentioned that broadcast writing is less formal than print writing is, but it's more formal than how we speak to one another. When we talk, we don't often think about rules of grammar, sentence construction, and the like. But when we write, we have to think about those things. Why? Because for now, television and radio news flows one way only with no immediate interaction between audience members and reporters or anchors. (Social media have us almost at that point, but not quite yet.) Just as viewers and listeners have nothing they can reread to make sure they understand it, likewise, they're unable to ask the person speaking what he or she meant by what that person just said. More about conversational writing in Chapter 3.

Writing for Broadcast Includes Using Contractions

You don't want the anchor (one day it could be you) to sound stiff or as though she's talking down to the audience. One way to avoid this is to use contractions, because contractions are a big part of sounding conversational. But, as with most "rules" in broadcast writing, there are exceptions, and you shouldn't use contractions in every instance. For example, if you want to place emphasis on something, a contraction is *not* as strong as using both words. Additionally, some contractions don't roll off the tongue very smoothly and you should avoid those. Some examples are "that'll" for that will, "it'll" for it will, and "there'll" for there will. Avoid those three and any others that just don't sound right to you when you read the script out loud. You should also be careful with contractions that sound like plurals. If you say, "The plan's giving her reason for hope," it's unclear at first whether you're talking about one plan or more than one. Television and radio audiences know only what they hear; they can't see the apostrophe. But for the most part, write with contractions.

In Broadcast Writing, We Use Short, Declarative Sentences

This is closely related to using conversational tone. This doesn't mean that all sentences should be simple sentences along the lines of "See Dick run," but we should stick to sentence construction that makes it very evident who and what we're writing about. Hence, we rarely use complex sentences because it's very easy for our meaning to get lost in the shuffle. Broadcast writers also keep the subject and the verb as close to each other as possible. For example, "This morning, police arrested a suspect" is easier to follow and sounds better than "Police this morning arrested a suspect." We also don't often deal with complex stories as part of everyday coverage. They're difficult to tell and difficult to follow, so they require extra development. Even in fairly straightforward stories, it's better to present a few well-developed facts than lots of little bits of information. The viewers are apt to get lost (in more ways than one) if you hit them with too much information in a short amount of time.

Active Voice Is the Choice of Broadcasters

Simply put, active voice is someone doing something and passive voice is something being done to someone or something. Here are examples of both:

Active. The governor gave a speech.

Passive. A speech was given by the governor.

There are occasions in which passive voice actually sounds better, but they're fairly rare. Write in active voice unless the sentence sounds strange when you read it aloud. If that's the case, try it in passive voice to see if it sounds better. But you'll rarely go wrong using active voice. The key to constructing sentences in active voice is to make sure the action is preceded by the actor, and that there *is* an actor mentioned. In the active voice example above, the actor is the governor; his action was giving a speech. Broadcast writing is full of passive voice because writers don't follow this simple rule. "The gunman was arrested" is the worst kind of passive-voice construction because not only did the writer fail to put the actor first, *there is no actor mentioned.* Active voice helps us with another broadcast writing guideline: keeping the subject and verb together. We'll look more closely at active voice and its importance in Chapter 3.

Broadcast Writers Use Present or Future Tense When Appropriate

Some writing coaches and textbook writers advise the use of present tense at all times, but that just doesn't make sense. If there's a reference to World War II in your story, you certainly wouldn't write about that as if it were currently taking place. However, you should use present tense as often as you can. Remember, we want to give today's news, not yesterday's news. Also, don't use more than one tense in the same sentence; for example, you wouldn't write "Police arrest a Carrville man and charged him with arson." You could place both verbs in the past tense, but your best bet is to use the present tense by telling us what's happening now; for example, "A Carrville man is in jail tonight." There will be more about tense in Chapter 3.

We Write Broadcast Stories in Today Language

The word "yesterday" isn't allowed in the lead sentence of broadcast news stories. If something happened yesterday (or last week) and nothing new has developed, why would we include that story on the evening news? But using today language doesn't necessarily mean using the word "today." For example, "Police are continuing to investigate" indicates that something is going on today without us having to use the word "today." Further, today language doesn't mean we can't update something that happened yesterday. It might even be necessary to use the word "yesterday" somewhere in the story. After all, if that's when the event occurred, we can't change that. Just don't use "yesterday" in the opening sentence.

Also, keep in mind the news program on which your story will appear. Starting a story that's part of the 9 P.M. update or the 11 P.M. newscast with "this morning" indicates that either nothing has happened since this morning or we aren't out there digging for the latest information. In a world of round-the-clock news channels and program interruptions to bring viewers and listeners the latest news live from the scene, failing to "freshen" stories for subsequent newscasts is a major failing indeed.

How to Deal with Dates and Days of the Week

Although we don't want to use the word "yesterday" in the lead sentences of our stories, if something happened yesterday, you'll have to use the word at some point in the piece. *When* something happened is important, and we can't say it happened today if it didn't. If you make time references in a story, use these guidelines: Use the words "yesterday" and "tomorrow" if the event in question is only one day in the past or one day in the future. If it's more than one day distant, give the day of the week. Dates aren't necessary unless the event happened more than a week ago or will happen more than a week from now. For example: The bill became law yesterday. The trial begins tomorrow. The concert will be Sunday. (Note: If you write *next* Sunday, you leave a question as to whether you mean a few days from now or a week and a few days from now. Delete the word "next" if you mean the Sunday to follow, and put the date if it's a Sunday that's more than a week away.) If you use a date, it's acceptable to write it in shorthand form rather than writing in full, such as 2nd, 4th, 21st, and so on.

Some news operations use the day of the week rather than the words "yesterday," "today," or "tomorrow." CNN does this frequently because a piece might run on Wednesday evening and again on Thursday morning, or it might already be Thursday somewhere in the world. If you refer to today and the piece runs again on Thursday, it's now a different day. So, keep in mind when your story will run when deciding how to refer to the day that something happened. Wednesday could be yesterday, today, or tomorrow, depending on what you're talking about. But it will always be Wednesday. So, although we prefer the words "yesterday," "today," and "tomorrow," there are cases in which you'd use the day of the week instead.

Broadcast Writers Use Last Names and Put Titles First

Except on first reference or when more than one person with the same name is part of the story, use the last name only. Hence, the first reference to a person in the story would be to Bill Smith, but use Smith in all subsequent references to that person. If Bill's brother Tom is also part of the story, it might be necessary to use the full names of both men on all references to avoid confusion. Some writers like to use the first name only, but the only time you can get away with that is when the person you're talking about is a child. It would sound strange to refer to 6-year-old Tommy Jones as Jones. So when you're referring to children, it's OK to use the first name alone on subsequent references.

When you use a title, place it in front of the name. Again, this is to avoid confusion and keep the sentence flowing smoothly. It sounds better to say "Former Midville Mayor Jane Brown says . . ." than to say "Jane Brown, former mayor of Midville, says. . . ." But please, if some government official you talk to has a title like "Texas Railroad Commission Pipeline Regulatory Division Engineer," shorten the title to something the viewers or listeners can digest. For TV, you're going to have to do that to get it to fit on the screen for a **super** (graphics information superimposed over the video) anyway.

There's some disagreement among television news writers about the need to verbally identify the people whose on-camera quotes we use because we'll show their names and titles in supers on the lower third of the screen. However, a number of studies have shown that many people don't watch the news closely from beginning to end.[1] Often, people are preparing dinner, dealing with the kids, getting ready for bed, or talking about work that day as they watch or listen to a news program. The viewer might even be in another room during parts of the newscast. So it isn't advisable to depend on a super as the only means of identifying a speaker.

Additionally, even with those viewers who watch the news program intently, supers don't always suffice. Any producer or show director who has been involved with television news for any length of time will tell you that when mayhem reigns in the control room (and that isn't uncommon), getting supers on the air falls far down the list of priorities. Therefore, we suggest verbally identifying on-camera sources the first time they're about to appear, if you consider that identification pertinent to the story. We'll have more about introducing sound bites in Chapter 8 about **voice-over/sound on tape (VO/SOT).**

In Broadcast Writing We Use Phonetic Spelling and Avoid Foreign Names When Possible

Although broadcast writers are supposed to spell correctly under most circumstances, there are times when spelling a word correctly might result in the anchor pronouncing it incorrectly on the air. Therefore,

---

1. See, for example, *Study of Media and Markets: Television Attentiveness & Special Events* (1994), Simmons Market Research Bureau; R. Neuman (1991), *The Future of the Mass Audience,* Cambridge, United Kingdom: Cambridge University Press.

you should spell any uncommon word the way it sounds. This presents some special problems for closed-captioned television, but most newsroom computer systems make it possible to deal with those concerns. Viewers tend to phone the station en masse when an anchor or reporter mispronounces the name of a person or place, especially if most of them know the correct pronunciation. One of the goals of writers is to keep this from happening by spelling those names phonetically. We don't need to spell "Davis" or "Miami" phonetically, but there's no predicting how "Sarmiento" or "Kazakhstan" will come out of someone's mouth unless you indicate that the anchor should pronounce those names Sahr-me-in-toe and Kahz-ahk-stan.

You should also spell some fairly common words phonetically because they have two pronunciations. On more than one occasion, an anchor or field reporter has been known to pronounce "bass" the way it should be pronounced in reference to a fish, when actually the word was being used in reference to a low tone on the musical scale. When that happens, it's embarrassing for the person whose face is on-screen and for the news operation as a whole. In such an instance, write "base drum." Although the word isn't spelled correctly, the overwhelming majority of viewers don't see the words but hear them only, and it's certainly not good for the news operation's credibility for one of its anchors or reporters to say "bass drum" (as in a drum that holds fish). Several other words are spelled the same but pronounced differently. Watch out for them. One note of warning: If seeing a misspelled word distracts your anchor, you might want to spell the word correctly, review the script with the anchor, and hope that he or she pronounces the word the way it's supposed to be pronounced. Audience members always seem to notice even the slightest double-take by someone on-camera.

In reference to hard-to-pronounce names, sometimes we can do without using a foreign name at all. It might be important to mention the name of the French president, but if we're referring to the French undersecretary of defense, using the title might be enough for the viewers to understand that person's role in the story without having to deal with a difficult foreign name. However, when the name is important to the story, if you think there's a chance the anchor will mispronounce it, spell it phonetically whether it's a foreign name or not.

When you're not concerned that the anchor will mispronounce a word, spell it correctly. Also, don't count on a spell-check program to catch your mistakes. The computer doesn't know whether you were writing "tired" or "tried" and will accept "tired" when you meant "tried" because, to the computer, you spelled the word correctly. It's just not the word you intended to use. Computers are great tools, but they can't match the human mind on some things, such as editing copy. At least not yet.

Broadcast Writers Avoid Most Abbreviations and Are Careful with Acronyms

In broadcast writing, avoid almost all abbreviations. The fairly common abbreviation "St." can mean either street or saint. News anchors have plenty to think about without having to figure out which one it's supposed to be. We don't use some abbreviations simply because we don't need them. This is the case with courtesy titles such as Mr., Ms., and Mrs. Generally, a person's marital status isn't important to the story. One exception to the no-courtesy-title rule is with heads of state and their spouses. It's appropriate to refer to President Obama or Mr. Obama, or Mr. Cameron or Prime Minister Cameron. Likewise, the spouses of those particular heads of state would be Mrs. Obama or Mrs. Cameron.

It might be important to identify someone as doctor, but when it is, spell out the word rather than use the abbreviation. "Dr." is short for both doctor and drive. The same is the case with president (you wouldn't want an anchor to say pres, so don't write it that way), senator, or representative. (Note: Such titles aren't courtesy titles. They're earned titles. There's a difference between the two.)

Some agencies and entities are better known by the acronyms or abbreviations that identify them than by their full names. For example, F-B-I is more widely used than is Federal Bureau of Investigation. But notice how we write F-B-I. When you want the anchor to pronounce each letter, place hyphens between them. This is also true with A-M and P-M in references to time.

Other abbreviations that are acceptable on first reference are C-I-A, N-C-A-A (but if you want the anchor to say N-C-double-A, write it that way), N-B-C, C-B-S, A-B-C, C-N-N, and so on. Let your guide be the way you're accustomed to hearing it. Almost no one says American Broadcasting Companies in conversation, and most probably don't even know what E-S-P-N stands for. For local or regional groups that might not be familiar to all the viewers, give the entire name on first reference, then go to the abbreviations. For example, the group Save Our Cumberland Mountains might be called SOCUM on second reference.

In Broadcast Writing, Keep Hyphenated Words on the Same Line

We should hyphenate any words we want the anchor to read together. In addition, all parts of the hyphenation should appear on the same line. There could be a brief delay as the words are rolling up on an electronic prompter. It looks silly when an anchor gets out half a hyphenation but has to wait for the other half to appear. For the same reason, a sentence shouldn't carry from one page to another.

Hyphenation is called for when we use two or more words as a unit to describe something. "A long-running trial" could come out sounding as if we're talking about a lengthy trial about running (a long running trial) without the hyphenation.

Broadcast Writers Don't Use Symbols

Unlike print writers, we don't use any symbols in broadcast. We should spell out all references to dollars, cents, percentages, and other such words. We also don't use the number sign, the "at" sign, the ampersand (symbol for the word "and") or any other symbol you can come up with. We should even spell out "point" in "one-point-two million dollars." If we included symbols in scripts, it could cause the news reader to pause momentarily trying to figure out exactly what we wrote. That, of course, would break the flow of the story and might even make the anchor look or sound foolish.

In Broadcast Writing, There Are Different Guidelines for Dealing with Numbers

Quite often, the precise amount or number of something is unimportant in broadcast. Certainly, if 163 people die in an airplane crash, the number is important. But it's better to say a budget of nearly two million dollars than to say a budget of one million—865 thousand dollars. Additionally, filling a story with too many figures and statistics brings the flow of the story to a screeching halt and sends the viewers scrambling for their remotes. Most of the time, round off numbers.

When you write numbers in broadcast, it's important to make them easy to read. Here are some simple guidelines.

Numbers 1 through 9—write out the word (some news operations prefer that you write out the words through eleven)

Numbers 10 through 999—use numerals

Numbers higher than 999—use a combination of words and numerals. For example: 37,915,776. Write: 37 million—915 thousand—776.

Write phone numbers and years using all numbers because that's how we're accustomed to seeing them. For example: 610-555-0201, 1776, 1492.

Often, Addresses and Ages Aren't Important in Broadcast Writing

Chances are most of the viewers in a given market wouldn't know where 1600 Eagle Street is, but they might be familiar with a certain section of town. Hence, it's better to refer to an area or point out landmarks close to the place where an event occurred instead of giving a street address. Likewise, a person's age usually isn't important unless we're talking about a 10-year-old college graduate or a 73-year-old snow-skiing champion. However, there are exceptions. When a local person dies, it might be necessary to give the age and an address so relatives of other people with the same name as the dead person aren't alarmed for no reason. Also, when someone meets an untimely death, the age adds some context, as when a 28-year-old dies of a heart attack. Remember, in broadcast writing there are few rules that came down from the mountain on stone tablets—only guidelines.

Making Corrections to Copy

The standard markings print writers and editors use to indicate changes in a script can be very confusing to an anchor trying to read a story on the air. Someone has to change the hard copy version of the script and change the script in the computer. Most newsroom systems send the script directly to the prompter, and if you don't make the corrections electronically, the anchor will be seeing an uncorrected version of the script. When the director and the anchor are looking at different versions of a script, that can create big problems. Producers should make any corrections that are necessary on the computer, send the revised story to the prompter, and print out another copy for distribution to the anchors and all other news personnel who get copies.

Broadcast Writing Is Punctuated Differently

The most common form of punctuation in broadcast writing is the ellipsis. The longer the ellipsis, the longer the pause. We often use the ellipsis for effect. Additionally, we underline on hard copy the words the anchor should emphasize. Hence, the anchor could read this short sentence three different ways:

Sue loves you.

Sue loves you.

Sue loves you.

The way you write the sentence is the way the anchor will say it.

Other than the ellipsis, question marks, and periods, we use few punctuation marks in broadcast. Remember, broadcast writing is meant to be heard, not read by the audience. You should write copy to make it as easy to read as possible. The easier it is for an anchor to read, the easier it will be for audience members to listen to the copy.

We Handle Quotations Differently in Broadcast

In broadcast writing, we rarely use direct quotations in the script, but normally paraphrase instead. Most people don't speak as succinctly as we're supposed to write, so we paraphrase what they've said in as few words as possible, being careful, of course, not to change the meaning. In those few instances when a writer feels compelled to use a direct quotation, it's important to make the sentence flow as smoothly as possible, as is always the case in broadcast writing. For example:

> THE PRESIDENT SAID . . . I WON'T SIGN THE BILL UNLESS IT'S AMENDED
> TO INCLUDE PROVISIONS FOR LOWERING THE DEFICIT . . . MISTER OBAMA
> ADDED THAT HE DOESN'T EXPECT THE REPUBLICAN MAJORITY IN THE
> HOUSE TO ADD THOSE PROVISIONS.

Setting off the direct quote with an ellipsis tells the anchor (and the listener or viewer) that what the anchor is about to say stands apart from what the anchor has said up to this point and from what the anchor will say afterward. However, if you sense the audience members might be confused, set off the quote by adding "in his words" after "the president said." Definitely avoid these pitfalls: "The president said, quote," and "end quote" at the conclusion of the sentence.

Again, however, we rarely quote in text. If what someone has to say is important enough for us to quote that person, we'll get a taped comment or will write out the comment on a graphic. In a visual medium such as television it's better to see and hear the person who makes the comment rather than quote the person in the script, unless we have a supporting graphic. The same is true for radio, except, of course, the visual part.

Broadcast Writers Are Careful with Pronouns

Pronouns are acceptable in broadcast writing, but only if there's no question about to whom the pronoun refers. Clarity is vitally important to broadcast news, and pronouns can create a problem in that regard. For example: "The police officer tackled the fleeing robber. He's a former football player." In this sentence, it's unclear to whom the pronoun refers, the officer or the robber. It's likely the writer used "he" to refer to the officer, the person who did the tackling. However, there's room for doubt, and that's something broadcasters can't afford to raise in viewers' minds. In this example, it's best to delete "he" and restate the noun.

Broadcast Writers Use Attribution Before Statements

If we don't tell the viewers or listeners beforehand who made a particular comment, stated a fact, or offered an opinion, it sounds as though those things are coming from our anchor. For example, "Sally Johnson extorted thousands of dollars from X-Y-Z Bank during a three-year period, according to bank officials" sounds as though we're making an accusation until the viewer hears the end of the sentence. Inverting the sentence takes care of that. "According to bank officials, Sally Johnson extorted thousands of dollars from X-Y-Z Bank during a three-year period" lets the viewers or listeners know right away that bank officials are making the charge, not the members of the news team.

Almost everything we know about a particular story comes from someone else and we should attribute it. Exceptions would be that an event is taking place somewhere, at a certain time, costing a certain amount. There's no need to attribute common facts, but most other information can't stand without the writer needing to tell the audience its origin. Words and phrases such as "accused of," "convicted of," or "charged with" help us in this regard. If we say someone is a convicted murderer, it's obvious the person was convicted by a jury, but even in that circumstance, we don't know for sure the person did the crime. Plenty of people have been on Death Row for years and the courts later found them to be innocent. Hence, we advise against saying someone did something unless a television news crew captured the event on video and there's no doubt the person we're talking about is the person we see on the video.

Conclusion

Someone once asked former network anchor David Brinkley if he considered himself a journalist or a broadcaster. Brinkley replied that there's no difference because good writing is good writing. In a sense, that's true. If you can write good print copy, you can easily make the transition to broadcast writing. But, as you've seen, there are some differences between the two regarding how we arrive at good writing. The guidelines listed above don't change the language, but do slightly alter how we use it. We've designed all the guidelines to make the copy easier to read and, therefore, easier to listen to. Remember, the key in broadcast writing is *don't make viewers or listeners work to get their information.* As a writer, you should do all the work so the audience members don't have to do any. Otherwise, they'll turn to a newscast (or other programming) that requires less effort.

General DOs and DON'Ts

Do	Don't
• Be clear and concise.	• Forget that you know more about stories than audience members do.
• Make life easy for the anchor.	
• Write like people talk (to a degree).	
• Be careful with pronouns.	• Depend on the computer to catch mistakes.
• Attribute.	• Fail to make corrections on the prompter as well as on hard copy.

Questions

1. In broadcast writing, why is it important to be conversational?

2. If print writers use inverted pyramid style, how would you describe the style broadcast writers use?

3. Why is it so important to avoid using a lot of pronouns in broadcast writing?

4. How do you handle attribution when you're writing a broadcast story?

5. What are two important characteristics of a well-structured broadcast sentence?

6. Describe active voice and why you should use it when writing a broadcast story.

CHAPTER TWO

C. A. Tuggle

Selecting Stories and Starting to Write

In radio and television newsrooms across the country, some of the youngest people in the operation are writing stories and making decisions about which stories should be included in the newscast and in which form. It isn't uncommon for associate producers and assignments desk personnel to start right out of college, even in some of the largest markets in the country. So you could be helping to make major decisions sooner than you think.

In this chapter, we'll look at the factors assignments managers and producers consider when deciding which stories are worthy of inclusion in radio and television news programs, and we'll start to get down to the nitty-gritty of writing for broadcast news. We'll look more at the joys of producing live news in a later chapter.

A highly respected network news anchor once noted that the script for a half-hour news program wouldn't fill the front page of a major newspaper. Most television and

Taken by Claudia Rupcich, web managing editor at WSET

A typical newsroom assignments board. Notice the emphasis on live reporting.

Taken by Claudia Rupcich, web managing editor at WSET

Newsroom of WSET, Lynchburg, VA.

radio stations air more than 30 minutes of news a day, but the point remains the same: Newspapers have a lot more room for stories than broadcast news operations have time for stories. Hence, there are fewer stories on television and radio news programs than in newspapers, and most broadcast stories are shorter than most newspaper stories are.

Television news stories might last for only 10 or 15 seconds and rarely run longer than a minute-and-a-half to two minutes. Radio newscasters face similar time constraints. So, broadcasters have to be very choosy when it comes to deciding which stories make it on the news. There are several factors that influence what's been called the **"gatekeeping** process"—deciding which stories to select from the hundreds or even thousands that are possible on a given day.

Newsworthiness

Newsworthiness is a highly subjective matter, but people in the news business must decide every day which stories are the most deserving of coverage. Excluding weather and sports, news operations report only 15 to 20 stories in a 30-minute television newscast. Even 24-hour radio news programs are limited regarding the number of stories they can broadcast. The decision regarding which stories are included and which are rejected is based on what those in the newsroom think those in their living rooms or cars are most likely to watch or listen to. Attracting viewers is undeniably part of the equation. Because of that, those involved in the news business strive to present what some call **infotainment**—information presented in an entertaining way.

Some critics have charged that television news is too entertainment-oriented—stressing flash and trash over substance—and some of the criticism is warranted. But news programs must compete for attention with other television programs, the Internet, movie rentals, and a myriad of other choices. Hence, the finest information in the world is of little value if no one is watching or listening. If broadcast news is guilty of turning the equation around and producing **entermation**—entertainment with only a dash of information—then all the criticism we could heap on those who think entertainment is the first mission of news is deserved. But presenting information in a way that will make your station stand out (while maintaining fairness and accuracy) is simply good business. We think well-told stories are informative, interesting, and entertaining, and we hope you'll embrace higher ideals while recognizing that we work in the information *business.*

Before writers, editors, videographers, and others involved in news gathering can begin the process of telling stories in compelling ways, someone has to decide which stories to cover. The assignments manager, show producers, the executive producer, and other newsroom managers are often the ones who make these coverage decisions, with input from reporters and other personnel. The decisions are based on a nebulous concept called "news judgment," but there are ways to make the process more objective than relying on a "gut feeling." Many of the factors television and radio news workers take into account when selecting stories are the same criteria used by newspaper editors, but others are different.

Proximity

Where an event occurs is important. If a six-car pileup delays traffic on a major local thoroughfare for hours, that's likely to make the news. If the same accident occurred elsewhere in the state, it's unlikely the story would air on your market's local news program. An old maxim in television news says that one local death is worth (in terms of news interest) five elsewhere in the state, 20 elsewhere in the country, and hundreds elsewhere in the world. It might sound cold, but we assume what happens locally is more important to local viewers than what happens elsewhere. Of course, there are many other factors that influence the decision to include those stories that happen in other places, such as how the deaths occurred, the prominence of the people involved, and other factors. But all other things being equal, local stories take precedence over stories from elsewhere.

In the earliest days of broadcast news, proximity was of paramount importance for a very practical reason. If something happened far from the station, it was simply impossible to get to the scene and cover it, drive back, process film or edit audiotape, and get the story on the air. Therefore, news operations were geographically limited by the technology. That changed dramatically with the introduction of electronic news-gathering and satellite news-gathering technology. Online file-sharing options continue to shrink the time needed and expense involved with getting distant material into your system. Now it's possible to get video and/or audio from almost anywhere in the world and to get it pretty quickly. What some have called "a river of video" is there for the picking from any number of organizations that supply video to local television stations for a fee, or from cooperating stations that might even be affiliated with different networks. Many cooperatives (called consortia; one would be a **consortium**) exist in both radio and TV, and some stations belong to four or five of them. So, proximity might not be as important as it once was because a local station's reach extends so much farther, but it's still pretty important.

Timeliness

Some news observers contend that timeliness is even more important on today's local news scene than it was in earlier days because of the technology. We can cover local stories live and with very little time needed to get a microwave truck operating or Internet link established once the news crew arrives on the scene. Local stations can arrange to get a live report from another part of the region or the world and can get that on the air just as quickly as the local news operation in that area can. A story involving a live report in Los Angeles can be on the air live in Miami (and plenty of other places) simultaneously and within minutes of news managers learning of it.

All this has led some news outfits to operate as if something that happened this morning is no longer news at 6 P.M. So local news has gone from not being able to get something on the air at 6 P.M. if it occurred after 4 P.M. to being able to get something on the air if it happens during the newscast. Many news workers across the country believe timeliness has taken on too much importance in television news. A nationwide survey of news directors and senior reporters conducted in the late 1990s indicated that many respondents in both groups think plenty of local news operations give far too much attention to stories that happen to occur close to or during the news hour. Stories news operations might have covered briefly (if at all) had they occurred earlier in the day are afforded live coverage early in the news programs (both "going live" and placing a story early in the newscast indicate the story is important) simply because they lend themselves to live coverage.[1] So timeliness is an important factor, but news managers have to guard against letting timeliness outweigh all other factors and their good news judgment. But even in the dark ages of television news, timeliness was important. No one wanted to present information that viewers had already read in the newspaper.

Impact

Clearly, one of the things news managers consider when deciding which stories to cover is which ones will have an impact on the greatest number of listeners or viewers, whether directly or indirectly. A cure for cancer, the abolition of the income tax, or the surprise resignation of the city's mayor would certainly affect almost everyone in the audience to one degree or another.

You have to go after the big stories, and go after them hard, because this is a competitive business and nobody wants to get beat on the big story of the day. Many producer job ads now ask for evidence of that producer's "owning" the top story. But the pursuit of the big story often leads producers and other managers to lose sight of the rest of the show. When the big story breaks, you have to immediately start thinking about not only how you'll cover it, but

---

1. C. A. Tuggle and S. Huffman (1999), "Live News Reporting: Professional Judgment or Technological Pressure? A National Survey of Television News Directors and Senior Reporters," *Journal of Broadcasting & Electronic Media, 43*(4), pp. 492–505.

also how you'll shuffle everything else. Remember, you still have other stories that deserve quality treatment, and for some of your viewers, one of those stories might be the most important one of the day. The story about a third grader using the Heimlich maneuver to save his teacher's life deserves a featured place in the newscast. Sometimes station personnel go crazy trying to "own" the top story, but the idea is to put together a winning newscast, not just beat your competitors on the top story of the day.

Emotional stories can also affect large numbers of viewers. A story about a young child battling a life-threatening disease, a "good Samaritan" story in which a person does something good for another with no tangible reward, or the death of a celebrity who millions found interesting are all examples of emotional stories that attract attention and have an impact on the audience.

The number of people involved in an event also affects whether it receives coverage. When a rock concert fills a large stadium, it's apparent a lot of people are interested enough to pay good money to hear the musical group and gives an indication that many viewers might be interested in a story about the concert, even if they couldn't attend for some reason.

Prominence

One of the things that makes stories about celebrities of interest is their prominence. A person's standing in society or recognizability plays a role in making stories about that person newsworthy. For example, should your instructor be involved in a minor car accident, it's unlikely that story would make the evening news. However, should the governor be in town on the same day and be involved in the same fender bender, then we have a story. It's not that your instructor isn't an important person, but many more people know who the governor is, and something minor that happens to her is of more interest than something minor that happens to most of us "average" people. So, when the president's daughters get a dog, we hear about it on network news.

The same is true with athletes, rock singers, movie stars, and other entertainers. They're among the country's most widely known residents, and even mundane things that happen to them are of interest to some people. If that weren't true, something else would quickly replace tabloid newspapers and television shows. What producers and assignments editors have to do is avoid letting a person's celebrity be the *only* factor they consider when deciding if a story is newsworthy: The shows about what's happening in Hollywood come on *after* the news.

Conflict

Disagreement makes for good copy and even better video. Confrontations between protesters and police are interesting because the viewers don't know what might happen next. A shouting match at the city council meeting is likely to draw coverage, but the passage of uncontested ordinances probably wouldn't. Good broadcast writers know how to highlight conflict *without* embellishing it. However, showing conflict simply for the sake of showing it isn't good decision making. Unless we provide some context, we've done the viewers a disservice. As with all the other factors that go into deciding whether something is newsworthy, conflict shouldn't stand alone. Otherwise, we'd show 30 minutes of bar fights every night, and viewers might confuse the news with a national talk show known for violent outbursts from the guests.

Unusual or "Human Interest" Stories

Stories about "average" people are interesting if those people do unusual things. A story about a college student who collects the pictorial covers of a popular sports magazine becomes more interesting when the viewers learn that the student has nearly 1,000 magazine covers and that all are signed by the athletes pictured on the covers. If a local person has a few unpaid parking tickets, that might not be of interest, but if he had 200 unpaid tickets and police threw him into jail, that would probably attract some attention.

Also, many television news producers seek out interesting and unusual stories to place at the end of news blocks or at the end of the program. These stories are typically called **kickers** and involve something amusing or cute, such as a water-skiing squirrel or a ladder-climbing dog. Such stories aren't likely to have an impact on anyone's life, but they do give the viewers a little bit of relief from what some complain is too often 30 minutes of death, destruction, and corruption.

Simplicity

News decision makers often dismiss complex stories as "print stories." It isn't because such stories are necessarily uninteresting, but it takes time to tell complex stories, and because they're complex, they're also difficult for viewers or listeners to follow. A minor change in the tax law might affect a large number of viewers, but such a story would likely receive minimal attention on television or radio because the details would be difficult to present and absorb. Some say that television news is little more than a headline service. In many ways, that's probably right. But other than occasional investigative pieces, local news isn't designed to offer a lot of detail about stories, and news workers might even alienate a portion of the audience if they tried to pack too much detail into short stories. However, we can tell complex (even seemingly nonvisual) stories on TV news. So don't dismiss stories automatically if they don't seem simple: Make them simple. Relate difficult concepts to common things, such as comparing information flowing through a computer chip with highway traffic. This gives viewers a concrete representation of an abstract idea. Also, remember graphics. They help with pacing and are a very good way to relay information for which you have no video.

Can We Get Good Video and Natural Sound?

Television is a visual medium, so pictures (and the audio that goes with them) are worth thousands of words. To be sure, stories sometimes make the news when there's no video to accompany them, but such stories would be very short and would probably include a promise from the anchor to bring pictures to the viewers as soon as the video becomes available. But in many cases, a story for which video wasn't available wouldn't make the news. Frequently, producers drop a story when video is available but simply isn't very compelling. Maybe this shouldn't be a part of the equation, but it is. Again, however, we strongly suggest that decision makers consider all factors when deciding whether to air a story, and not drop it simply because of a lack of video. The most important question to ask is, "Is this story important to our viewers or listeners?" There is no quick and easy answer. It takes thought, research, and intuition. Consider carefully and decide wisely. What we select for presentation and how we present it are vitally important.

There's one other thing to consider related to visuals. Television news operations use file footage extensively. The station might not be able to get video of a famous entertainer being arrested for soliciting prostitution, but would probably have clips of his television show on hand to illustrate the story. The video we use affects the way we write a story, of course. More about the importance of writing from available video and incorporating natural sound in Chapter 7.

What Else Is Happening?

One of the most difficult things to deal with in television and radio news is that producers have a set amount of time to fill, regardless of what's happening in the world. Of course, for a huge story news managers can choose to stay on the air beyond the normal end time of the news program, but in most circumstances, the news ends at an appointed time and certainly never before that time arrives. One television news operation used to end its program by having the anchor say, "And that's all the news we have time for."

So, in a typical 30-minute TV news program or 5-minute hourly radio update, there's room for only a certain number of stories. Whether we include a particular story in that mix sometimes depends on what else we're covering. Coverage of a plane crash might knock out other stories that on slower news days would be included. One day the news might be 90 percent local and the next day be only 70 percent local because major stories are happening elsewhere and not much is happening locally. Holidays, which are often very slow news days because businesses and institutions are closed, bring out all the standard holiday stories because there's little or no breaking news to cover. With TV, on those days when a lot is happening, it's not unusual for the producer to trim the time allotted for weather and sports (rarely commercials, though) in order to free up more time for all the news. So the decision of whether a story makes it on the news can depend on other stories against which the story must "compete" for attention.

What Are the Viewers/Listeners Talking About?

If the weathercaster is predicting snow to fall in an area that rarely receives snow, many viewers or listeners are likely to watch or listen to the news program to find out what the chances are. If a widely known celebrity is set to visit the area, members of the audience are likely to be curious about the appearance and plans to accommodate the person. News managers use focus groups and other research methods to try to figure out what the viewers are interested in and what they might want to know. Often, though, a good gauge of what the viewers are talking about is what everyone in the newsroom and in other departments is talking about or experiencing.

The Role of News Philosophy in Story Selection

In some modern newsrooms, traditional news judgment values aren't the only factors at work in the story selection process. *News philosophy* might also play a role—sometimes, a huge one. What is news philosophy? Essentially it's a set of values the station uses to emphasize some types of stories instead of other types. The philosophy might be unwritten and informal. It might be written and quite formal. In some cases it might be not only unwritten, but also unspoken, simply a part of the newsroom management culture that causes decision makers to put their thumbs on the scale when weighing certain types of stories against others. If no station in a market has a unique news philosophy, then each station's coverage will look about the same. Each will cover car crashes, chases, murders, fires, city council meetings, civil rights disputes, consumer investigations, and so on, in about the same proportion, and will tend to choose similar leads for their newscasts every day. But in the modern competitive environment, it's not unusual at all for one or more stations to make a concerted effort to deviate from a traditional "middle-of-the-road" news philosophy and stand out with a unique coverage profile. For instance, one station might fancy itself as the hard-nosed, investigative station. Its managers tend to choose, lead with, and promote stories that are investigative in nature. Another station might portray itself as the consumer advocate station. Its managers will choose, lead with, and market consumer stories. Another might be the "tabloid" station, choosing to emphasize chases, murders, and celebrity news. Managers will expect news producers and reporters working at a station with a unique news philosophy to know that philosophy and help execute it. (Hint: Learn all you can about a station's news philosophy before taking a job there. Such advance knowledge might help you land the job—or lead you to turn it down if the station's approach to news conflicts with your personal values.)

A Final Note about Gatekeeping

Many factors play a role in the gatekeeping process in television and radio news. There's no way to say whether one is more important than another, because there are often several at work at the same time. Also, one of the factors listed above might sway news managers to include a certain story, but another factor might prove to be the most important in the decision behind whether or not to include a different story.

For television producers and assignments managers, paying close attention to which stories are included each evening is important for a number of reasons. Since 1964, Roper surveys have shown that most Americans get most of their news from television and would believe the television version of a story if other media had different accounts of the same event. Even though more and more people are getting news from the Internet and on mobile devices, the Pew Research Center reports that there has been no overall decline in the percentage of people who get news from television, so the other platforms are supplementing, not supplanting, TV as a place to go for news. Some have questioned the accuracy of these polls and whether the way the questions are worded leads respondents to answer in certain ways. But if these polls are even close to being an accurate reflection of how Americans get their news, those of us in broadcast news have a big responsibility to include the most important stories in the limited time available.

Additionally, a long line of research has shown that the media (television in particular) often set the agenda for what's considered important. Researchers McCombs and Shaw noted that the media might not tell us what to think but are remarkably successful at telling us what to think about.[2] The other side of that coin is that when they don't include stories, television news decision makers are saying, in essence, that those stories aren't as important. People become interested in pursuing careers in television or radio news for a number of reasons. One can only hope that being part of one of the most important conduits of information in the information age is a major reason young people become interested in the field.

---

2. M. McCombs and D. Shaw (1993), "The Evolution of Agenda Setting Research: Twenty-Five Years in the Marketplace of Ideas," *Journal of Communication,* 43(2), pp. 58–67.

The Page F Test

Deciding which stories to include in the newscast is only part of the battle. The next step is to present those stories in the most clear, concise way possible, and that goes back to writing. As is the case with our friends working on other media platforms, we must answer the five Ws: who, what, when, where, and why. When possible, we also have to answer the one H: how. Another letter of the alphabet sums up the need to make our stories meaningful and interesting to our audience, the S: so what? To get started in your quest to do all of this, we suggest that you write a script, go ahead and get something on the page, and then apply the Page F test to it. Then have someone else (usually a producer) do the same thing. If it doesn't pass all five parts of the test, then you need to do some rewriting. Even the best writers in history were rarely completely pleased with the first draft of their work. The five parts of the Page F test are:

P—Are the words precise?

A—Is the story accurate?

G—Is every element germane?

E—Are all actors treated equitably?

F—Does the story flow?

Precise Words

We're sure you've heard people who are struggling in their attempts to learn English say it's not an easy language to pick up. There are a number of reasons for this. First of all, the English language uses a lot of slang and cliches. It is also full of words that sound alike but have different meanings. There are also lots of words that someone might think mean the same thing, but there are actually subtle (and not-so-subtle) differences between them. For example, do you know the difference between anxious and eager? If you ever come across two words that mean exactly the same thing, rid your vocabulary of one of them. Why would we need both?

Toward the end of this book you'll find an appendix containing words and phrases Americans often misuse. Textbook readers tend to read only what they have to read and skip appendixes. We strongly encourage you not to do that in this case. The section about word usage is very important because you'll never be a very good writer if you don't use words correctly. You might be able to fool most of the people most of the time, but it's likely someone in the audience will catch every word usage mistake you make. How credible will you be as a purveyor of information in the minds of people who've caught you misusing words? You might even be surprised at how many words you think you know how to use correctly that you actually use incorrectly. So, the first part of the Page F test is to make sure each word you use means exactly what you think it means.

Accuracy

Many people who teach or practice journalism will tell you that if what you write isn't accurate, your credibility and that of the news operation is sure to suffer sooner or later. Even if every word you use is precise, your story might not be true. All of us were kids at one time (believe it or not), and we know that there are shades of untruth. Often, you can get away with something really bad by admitting to something a bit less heinous. But that's not the way it is in journalism. We must tell the truth, the whole truth, and nothing but the truth. The viewers count on us to tell them what went on as best we can without letting our own biases interfere. They also count on us to do the legwork necessary to ensure that what we report is actually what happened.

Of course, very few newspaper writers or broadcast journalists set out to deceive the public. But if we pass on something as fact without doing any digging to find out if it's true, our laziness serves the same purpose. People want to trust what they hear on the news. Unfortunately, they've been given a lot of reasons in the past several years not to.

Germane Information

In addition to being accurate, what we write has to be germane; it must be relevant to the story. All broadcast writers have a common enemy: a lack of time. A rush to get things on the air can lead to factual errors, and because of the limited time we have to tell stories, the information we choose to include must be the most important information. Is the age, sex, marital status, or race of a person germane? Does the information add understanding, or does it just take up space? If a presidential candidate is caught in an affair, is that germane? It might be relevant in a story about the candidate's character and might not be in a story about the candidate's stance regarding a flat-rate income tax.

Part of the failure to include only relevant information comes from the writer's *inability to decide what the story is about*. Many broadcast news stories today are a little bit of this followed by a little bit of that, with no theme running through the story. Report about one thing. Is your story about the huge crowds at the auto show or the newest technology on display? We're not saying you can't mention the technology, because that's probably one of the things that attracted the huge crowds. But decide what the theme of the piece is and concentrate on that. So, before you write a single word of copy, *make a one-sentence commitment to the story so you know what to write about.* This is an item we can't stress too much.

Have We Treated All Groups Equitably?

Treating groups differently can take many different forms. Using sexist language is one of them. Not only might certain terms alienate members of the audience (and every news director will tell you we need all the viewers or listeners we can get), but they aren't very precise. Words such as "fireman," "policeman," and "congressman" are throwbacks to a time when women didn't occupy those roles. Many of us still tend to think of certain jobs as being filled by men (doctors, for example) and others by women (such as nurses). Of course, men and women fill roles today that were once the exclusive domain of the other sex. So don't let archaic thinking slip into your writing.

Now, don't get us wrong. We're not talking about being politically correct, which has come to mean "don't do or say anything that has the remotest chance of offending someone." Hence, old people are referred to as "chronologically challenged," short people are "vertically challenged," and corrupt people are "morally challenged." If someone is corrupt (and we have proof), then the person is corrupt. But a firefighter isn't necessarily a fire*man.*

Also, in terms of being equitable, there are almost always two sides (or more) to an issue. If you devote two-thirds of your story to one side of the issue and only a third to the other side, one group thinks you're siding with the other. It's especially important to make sure to talk to both sides regarding issues that generate intense feelings, even if one side seems to be in the minority. It could be that most people agree with the second position but just aren't very vocal about it. Don't let the number of activists involved sway your thinking about which is the most widely held opinion about an issue.

Does the Story Flow?

Even if your words are precise, your story is accurate, the information is germane, and you've treated everyone as equitably as possible, you still might not have a very good piece if it doesn't flow. Each thought must flow logically into another. If you don't work to make the sentences flow, you can catch the viewers off guard when you introduce new information without showing its relationship to the information you've already presented.

"Tie-writing" is the term used to describe how we get stories to flow. We have to tie one thought to the next, and that one to what follows it, and so forth. One place within stories that this often doesn't occur is going into and coming out of sound bites. We'll address this particular concern in Chapter 9.

Conclusion

A lot goes into making a good piece of broadcast copy. In addition to the points of style we've already covered about how to write broadcast copy, we also have to be concerned with the content, what we write. We don't have the luxury of being able to spend hours on a piece of copy to make sure it's the best we can make it; at times it's a luxury to be able to review it once. So much of what we do in terms of self-correction has to happen almost automatically. That begins to be the case only when we've written a lot. We trust that sooner rather than later you'll grasp how to deal with various story forms and broadcast writing guidelines as you continue writing—a lot.

DOs and DON'Ts When Starting to Write

Do

- Think like a viewer.
- Be precise, accurate, germane, and equitable, with flow.
- Decide what the story is about before you start writing it.

Don't

- Let your own biases come into play.
- Let the entertainment part supersede the information part.
- Disregard the need for strong grammar and word precision skills.

Questions

1. What does it mean to be the "gatekeeper"?
2. Define "infotainment" and "entermation" and explain the differences between them.
3. Before you write a single word, what should you do, and why?
4. What are the six main questions you need to ask yourself about the "newsworthiness" of a story?
5. Describe the "Page F Test" and how to use it when you're writing a broadcast story.
6. What is "news philosophy"? Describe what role it might play in the story selection process.

Writing Great Leads and Other Helpful Tips

It's a truism that "everyone knows a story written for television or radio must be conversational." But casual observation of the news in any media market shows the skill of turning that truism into reality isn't so common. In this section, we'll use several guiding principles and some examples to show how to write conversationally while also doing a good job of delivering the news.

A well-written story contains three basic ingredients:

- The writer captures the essence of the story in the lead.

- The copy itself doesn't sound like you've *written* it at all. It sounds, in fact, like one side of a conversation, exactly as if the anchor or reporter is talking to someone, rather than *at* someone.

- The writer presents the facts in narrative storytelling format.

In writing copy, you must always keep in mind our basic mission in broadcast news: Relay needed information to the viewer or listener, making yourself clear *on the first attempt*. Remember, you get only one pass at it.

The Art of the Lead

A story "lead" is, quite simply, its first sentence. Arguably, it's also the story's single most important element. In broadcasting, the lead accomplishes much the same task as a headline in the print world. For the consumer, it's the "point of purchase." The viewer or listener will decide whether to pay attention to the story on the basis of the strength of the lead in much the same way a reader decides whether to scan through a given newspaper story on the basis of the headline. However, there's one huge difference between print and broadcast customers. If the print customer doesn't like a story headline, he or she probably won't put down the newspaper but will simply skip to the next story. A television viewer faced with the same situation is likely to pick up a remote and zap the entire newscast into oblivion. The state of oblivion is arguably a good place to visit on occasion, but who wants to live there? To avoid such a fate, when writing a lead:

- Grab the viewer's or listener's attention right away by capturing the essence of the story.
- Don't make the lead hard to digest by loading it down with too many facts! Instead, write a "nonfactual lead."
- Don't write a lead that sounds dated or stale.

In addition, you should apply the same rules and techniques in the lead that pertain to copywriting in general, including:

- Write in active voice.
- Use narrative storytelling technique.
- When appropriate, use creative techniques to make the copy sparkle. But don't overdo it!
- Write conversationally! Employ the **"Mom Rule."**

We'll explore each of these points in the pages ahead, beginning with the most important point of all.

Writing Conversationally: The "Mom Rule"

In the print world if a reader doesn't understand a sentence, paragraph, or story on the first attempt, he or she can go back and reread it. That's not an option in broadcasting. As mentioned, we must get it right the first time. To accomplish that, we must write the way people *listen,* a technique sometimes referred to as "writing for the ear." And to do *that,* we must write the way people *talk.* An easy way to prepare yourself for that is to remember the Mom Rule. Ask yourself: If I were sitting down at the dinner table to tell this story to my mom, what would I say? We hope you'd want to speak in sentences that are grammatically correct but not rigidly formal. You'd be friendly and conversational, using short, declarative sentences. You'd get to the point right off the bat. Apply that same rule when you're speaking to the viewer or listener. Visualize the copy as your part of a conversation with someone standing right in front of you. Keep your sentences short: Take a breath! Make your tone friendly and informal, but not so informal as to be chatty, gushy, or silly.

The Mom Rule doesn't apply just to writing leads; it also applies to general copywriting. We'll talk more about the Mom Rule and see how to apply it in some of the examples that follow.

Capturing the Viewer's Attention: The Essence of the Story

The most basic definition of a newsworthy story is one that the viewers or listeners find beneficial or valuable. Remember, they're making a decision about your story (whether you like it or not) during the lead. Here's something you might find helpful: Imagine every single viewer or listener is tuned in to the same radio station. Its call letters are WII-FM, or "What's In It for Me?" If your lead doesn't answer that question *immediately,* you might lose the viewer or listener.

The lead is, in essence, a sales pitch. Make it a good one. The sale is important to you: no sale, no viewer; no viewer, no ratings; no ratings, no revenue; no revenue, no paycheck. To close the sale, you must immediately convince the viewer of the value or benefit of the story. Sometimes this is obvious and easy for the writer to do; often, it's far from it. One thing is clear: **In order to capture in your lead the essence of what makes your story newsworthy, you must know it yourself.**

Here's an example, loosely based on an actual news story. The scenario: Three weeks ago in Miami (for the purpose of this exercise, assume that this is a city in your state but not in your market) police arrested Kathy Newsmaker and charged her with involuntary manslaughter for the death of her baby. Kathy had left the child locked inside her car while she went inside to speak to a neighbor for "just a moment." But she was gone for more than an hour, and when she returned, the child had died from exposure to the severe heat inside the car. You've previously carried stories about this in your local newscast. Now today, just before airtime, a story crosses your newswire stating that the state attorney has decided to drop all charges against

Kathy, saying her investigation shows that Kathy is a loving mother and that the baby's death was simply a tragic accident.

Your mission: to write a lead to this story that captures its essence and makes a connection to the viewer, without resorting to lurid writing or tabloid-style sensationalism.

This is similar to the lead that actually aired on one Florida TV station:

> TODAY IN MIAMI THE STATE ATTORNEY ANNOUNCED SHE WON'T PURSUE A
> MURDER CASE AGAINST 38-YEAR-OLD MOTHER KATHY NEWSMAKER.

Among its other sins this lead inspires a response along the lines of "So what? Who's she?" The lead does key on what happened today, but doesn't even come close to capturing the essence of what makes this story newsworthy.

Now let's apply the Mom Rule. When you open your mouth to tell Mom about this story, you won't agonize about how to begin. You'll just start talking, and you'll start with the fact that has the greatest impact on you: "Mom, can you believe it? That Miami woman who left her baby in the car got off!" What you've just expressed is the same factor that makes this story newsworthy to the average viewer: the expectation that Kathy would pay a price for her mistake, and the surprise that she won't. To be meaningful and relevant to the viewer, then, your lead must address that same issue.

It would be convenient if you could write a lead such as this:

> A LOT OF MIAMI RESIDENTS ARE SHOCKED AND OUTRAGED TONIGHT: A WOMAN
> ACCUSED OF LETTING HER BABY DIE IN A LOCKED CAR HAS WALKED FREE.

However, because this story is just breaking and no one has had an opportunity to react to it, you can't honestly say anyone is shocked and outraged. Instead, you have to focus on the *development*, which might (or might not) later lead to those outraged feelings, and get to the point right off the bat:

> A MIAMI WOMAN WHO WENT TO JAIL FOR LEAVING HER BABY LOCKED IN A HOT
> CAR IS FREE TONIGHT. THE STATE ATTORNEY SAYS THE CHILD'S DEATH WAS
> NOTHING MORE THAN A TRAGIC ACCIDENT.

There's also another way to do this. You can write *specifically* to the viewer's unspoken expectations:

> YOU MIGHT THINK IF A BABY DIES WHILE LEFT LOCKED INSIDE A HOT
> CAR . . . SOMEONE WOULD GO TO JAIL. BUT IN ONE MIAMI CASE . . .
> YOU'D BE WRONG.

This last example has the advantage of being much more conversational, and because it speaks directly to the viewers' or listeners' emotions, it will be relevant to a wider circle of people. Some traditional journalists might feel this direct viewer connection "crosses the line" toward being an editorial. However, one of the great strengths of broadcasting's conversational style of writing is that it gives the opportunity to make a personal emotional connection with the news consumer. Showcasing the relevance of a story by referencing the viewer's expectations in this manner is perfectly appropriate.

Present or Future Tense—without "TV Speak"

A very common lead style is use of the simple declarative sentence. Most producers, writers, and reporters have it drilled into them that they should never write such a sentence in past tense. The reason this rule is so universal in broadcasting is simple: If it's happening now, or will be happening soon, then it's news. If it happened hours ago, it's old news and fading fast into obscurity. Yesterday's news doesn't hold a great deal of value except to historians, otherwise no one would use yesterday's newspaper to line parrot cages. A dated newscast has even less value; you can't even wrap fish with it. The easiest way to telegraph to your audience that your newscast is fresh, new, and therefore valuable is to showcase what's happening *now* or what *will be happening* in the near future—using present and future tense, respectively.

Now here's where many broadcast news writers go astray. Many a producer will start with a past-tense lead. Then, fearing the wrath of news managers, the producer simply changes the tense of the verb from past to present. The result is a nonconversational, mangled, bastardized form of English known as "forced present tense" or "TV speak." It's about as pleasant as fingernails screeching across a chalkboard.

Example Scenario

You're working in the Tucson market and are writing about a local bank robbery. The scenario: A gunman held up a bank and got away with some cash. After running out the door, for no apparent reason the gunman shot at a passerby on the sidewalk. The passerby, Otis Armstrong, was about to step into the bank to cash a check. When the gunman fired the shot, Otis dived to the sidewalk and wasn't hurt. Police say it was a miracle the bullet missed Armstrong, and officers credited him for his quick reflexes in ducking for cover. The bank is processing the security film and will release it in the morning.

A traditional, unimaginative past-tense lead might read something like this:

[handwritten: There w]

A TUCSON BANK WAS ROBBED THIS MORNING . . . AND THE GUNMAN GOT AWAY.

[handwritten: This morning ~the~ ~gun~ ~Tucson~ Bank A gunman]

But wait! It's past tense! So the producer, suffering from a sudden, acute attack of *mediocritus unimaginitivus*, simply changes "was" to "is" and "got" to "gets," and comes up with:

A TUCSON BANK IS ROBBED THIS MORNING . . . AND THE GUNMAN GETS AWAY.

The above sentence is indeed in the present tense, but the problem is that it doesn't sound natural. In fact, it's ridiculous. It's written in TV speak. The writer made a half-hearted attempt to follow the present-tense rule, but in doing so gave no thought or creativity to the effort and simply changed the tense without regard to how it would sound. Think about it. When was the last time you sat down to dinner with your mom and said, "Hey, Mom, a bank is robbed this morning"? The answer is "never." No one talks that way. This style of writing might be appropriate for a tease, but not for the story itself. In "fixing" the past-tense lead, the writer actually has made the situation much worse, violating the first rule of broadcast copywriting, "be conversational." The best way to fix it is to start over, from scratch. Ask yourself three questions:

1. Who are the participants in this story?
2. What are they doing now?
3. What will they be doing later—tonight, tomorrow, or next week?

The answers to these questions will tell you how to rewrite the lead.

In this particular example, who's in the cast of characters? The list includes:

- Police
- The employees developing the security film
- The bank teller who was robbed
- Witnesses
- The gunman
- Otis Armstrong
- The viewing/listening public (never forget the viewers and listeners!)

A list of things happening right now might include:

- Police are looking for the gunman.
- The gunman presumably is trying to avoid capture.
- The victim is telling his story to friends and in general is glad to be alive.
- Police are investigating the incident.
- The bank is processing its security camera pictures.

A similar list of things that will happen in the future regarding this story might include:

- The gunman will or will not be caught.
- The bank will release its security photos.
- The bank will reopen tomorrow with business as usual.

A good writer can fashion any and all of these facts into a present- or future-tense lead. The best and most effective lead will also be the one that focuses on the most interesting human element. In this case, who in the cast of characters has the most interesting and colorful story to tell?

Present-Tense Examples

1. ONE TUCSON MAN IS RECOVERING FROM A FRIGHTFUL EXPERIENCE THIS AFTERNOON.

2. THIS HAS TURNED OUT TO BE A DAY ONE TUCSON MAN WON'T SOON FORGET.

Future-Tense Examples

1. WHEN OTIS ARMSTRONG RETURNS TO WORK TOMORROW . . . HE'LL HAVE ONE AMAZING STORY TO TELL HIS FRIENDS.

2. POLICE HOPE EVIDENCE TO BE RELEASED TOMORROW WILL HELP THEM CATCH A CROOK.

3. OTIS ARMSTRONG'S GRANDCHILDREN WILL BE HEARING ABOUT THIS DAY FOR YEARS.

Finally, just to show that even the past tense can on occasion be effective if it's written conversationally and employs narrative storytelling:

ONE SECOND OTIS ARMSTRONG WAS WALKING DOWN THE STREET WITHOUT A CARE IN THE WORLD . . . THE NEXT . . . HE WAS DIVING FOR COVER.

The Narrative Lead

As we just saw in the example above, though the prohibition against past-tense leads works as a general rule, there are some perfectly acceptable uses of past tense. Sometimes the best way to write a lead is to jump right into the story in narrative fashion. Such narrative leads don't always have to be in the present or future tense.

Example 1

THEY CAME EXPECTING FOOD . . . FASHION . . . AND FUN. BUT FOR THOUSANDS OF PEOPLE WHO TURNED OUT FOR THE ANNUAL POETRY IN THE PARK EVENT . . . THIS HAS TURNED OUT TO BE A DAY OF DISAPPOINTMENT.

Example 2

JOHN SMITH ALWAYS WANTED TO BE A POLICE OFFICER. HE NEVER EXPECTED TO
BE CALLED A HERO. BUT UNLESS SEVERAL HUNDRED OF TAMPA'S FINEST HAVE
IT WRONG . . . THAT'S EXACTLY WHAT HE IS.

Example 3

THE FIRST THOUGHT THAT RAN THROUGH HIS MIND WAS THAT IT COULDN'T
BE HAPPENING. BUT IT WAS. AND WHAT FRED JONES DID NEXT ON A RAINY
HIGHWAY ONE NIGHT LAST SPRING WOULD CHANGE SEVERAL LIVES . . .
INCLUDING HIS OWN. TONIGHT RIP REED BRINGS US THE STORY OF AN
ORDINARY MAN . . . WHO FOUND EXTRAORDINARY COURAGE.

Leads such as Example 3 that begin with a specific incident or
thought are sometimes referred to as "anecdotal."

Connecting with the Viewer or Listener

The electronic media are very personal. They provide a unique opportunity to make a direct connection with the end user, and in fact work best
when they make such a connection and make it effectively. One powerful way to do that is to simply ask a question of the viewer or listener.

Example 4

HAVE YOU EVER WONDERED WHY KEYPADS ON DRIVE-UP A-T-MS ARE WRITTEN
IN BRAILLE?

Example 5

HOW MUCH TIME DID YOU SPEND STUCK IN TRAFFIC THIS MORNING?

One key advantage of the rhetorical question is that it often makes
a direct connection through use of the word "you," a very personal
pronoun. Like any good seasoning, however, the rhetorical question is
best if not overused.

Another good way to make a direct connection is to directly challenge the viewer's or listener's expectations.

Example 6

YOU MIGHT THINK IT'S NOT EASY TO GET AWAY WITH MURDER. BUT THAT'S NOT
THE CASE IN BLAMVILLE. DETECTIVES THERE HAVE SOLVED FEWER THAN HALF
OF LAST YEAR'S KILLINGS.

Finally, you can make a direct connection by writing a statement
that appeals directly to the viewer's or listener's personal experiences.

A statement of this type is frequently conditional, beginning with the word "if."

Example 7

IF YOU'VE EVER DRIVEN ON THE INTERSTATE AND HAVE FOUND YOURSELF SANDWICHED BETWEEN TWO SEMIS ... YOU KNOW HOW FRIGHTENING BIG RIGS CAN BE.

The danger of this kind of lead, of course, is that it might not appeal to viewers or listeners who haven't had the experience it references. Example 7 would be a very valid lead for residents of Los Angeles, but perhaps less valid for the subway riders of Manhattan. The key is to reference experiences that touch large numbers of viewers. In order for this to work, topic doesn't necessarily have to affect the viewer *directly*. For instance, the subject of prostate cancer doesn't directly affect women, but it's likely to affect some of their loved ones.

Keeping It Short: The Nonfactual Lead

How many facts should your lead contain? Here's a startling thought for you: The best broadcast leads might contain no *specific facts at all*.

Many writers are tempted to launch into the body of their story right out of the starting gate. Thus we might see a lead like this:

A TRANSPUDDLE AIRLINES 737 WITH 57 PASSENGERS ON BOARD DISAPPEARED FROM RADAR SHORTLY AFTER TAKEOFF FROM BUENOS AIRES THIS MORNING . . . SPARKING A MAJOR SEARCH BY THE ARGENTINE AIR FORCE.

It has too many facts. We don't need to know in the very first breath how many passengers are on the manifest, the airline company involved, the circumstances surrounding the disappearance, the location, and who's conducting the search. This sentence has so many facts competing for attention the viewer can't possibly remember them all. *Keep it simple:* Save the details for the body of the story. Again, ask yourself: How would I say this to my mom? Would I sit down and say, "Hey, Mom! A Transpuddle Airlines 737 with 57 passengers on board disappeared from radar shortly after takeoff from Buenos Aires this morning, sparking a major search by the Argentine Air Force"? Probably not. If so, you've been watching too much bad TV news. Chances are you might say something more like, "Hey, Mom! Did you hear about that plane crash in Argentina?" Your lead should get the viewer's or listener's attention in a very similar fashion:

WE HAVE BREAKING NEWS OUT OF ARGENTINA THIS AFTERNOON: A MASSIVE
SEARCH IS UNDER WAY FOR A MISSING JETLINER.

Such a lead also serves a preview function. In essence you're saying, "Listen up. You're about to hear a story about a plane crash." With
this style, when you do begin presenting the facts, the viewer or listener is prepared to accept them, instead of being clobbered over the
head without warning.

Beyond the Lead: General Copywriting Tips

"Selling the story," though critically important, isn't the only purpose
of the lead. It must also set up and support certain tasks and styles to
be accomplished in the body of the story. The lead must begin the
"preview and review" function. It must support the narrative storytelling technique. And, like all copy throughout the newscast, the
voice should be active, not passive.

Preview, View, and Review

Your mission, as stated, is to be clear the first time. The best way to
reach any destination is to have a clear road map. When you're writing
copy, that road map consists of a framework providing a clear beginning, middle, and end to the story. We call this "preview, view, and
review," or the "Tell 'em what you're going to tell 'em, tell 'em, then
tell 'em what you told 'em" rule. Exactly how to accomplish this in
practical terms varies widely from story to story. A nonfactual lead
written according to the guidelines we've discussed will serve as a
preview for the story. In the jetliner example above, the lead makes it
clear we're about to hear a story about a missing jetliner. The body of
the story should contain all the pertinent facts. Wrap up with a line
that summarizes the current status of the story or looks ahead to what
might happen next, such as:

AUTHORITIES SAY THE SEARCH FOR THE MISSING JETLINER WILL CONTINUE
THROUGH THE NIGHT.

Or,

WE DON'T KNOW WHETHER ANY OF THE MISSING PASSENGERS IS AMERICAN.

Or,

THE AIRLINE IS NOW IN THE PROCESS OF CONTACTING RELATIVES OF MISSING
PASSENGERS.

Each of these sentences serves to reinforce the idea that the jetliner is missing and that concern about it is ongoing.

For a major story involving one or more **sidebars,** it's usually a good idea to write a copy story to run after the final sidebar summarizing and recapping the situation.

Narrative Storytelling

To know how to tell a story, *you must first know what the story is.* The basic definition of any story is simply this: It's something interesting, remarkable, or unusual that happened to somebody. Sounds simple enough, right? But casually glancing at or listening to many local newscasts will show that some reporters don't stop to define their stories before they sit down to write. The resulting product is confusing, incoherent, and unfocused. To prevent yourself from falling into this trap, ask yourself this simple question: What is the story about? If you can't answer that question *in one sentence,* you need to rethink your report and narrow the focus. In doing so, define the "something" that happened (the "what, when, where, and why") and the "someone" at the center of the story (the first "W," the "who").

Usually, the best way to relate a story is to tell it the way it happened, in chronological order, preferably through the eyes of a central character (the "someone"). It's the same age-old style writers use in most fairy tales and novels. "Once upon a time there was a fair maiden who lived in the forest. And then yah da yah da yah da happened. And then they lived happily ever after." Narrative storytelling works because the events unfold in their natural order in a fashion that's easy to follow and comprehend. The challenges you face in your writing and the principles you'll use to approach them are not much different from what Charles Dickens, Mark Twain, or Margaret Mitchell faced. Your task, too, is to tell a story, to spin a yarn, to engage your customers in a narrative exercise that will leave them with a firm understanding of the events you're trying to relate *as if they had lived it themselves.*

But wait! When writing for TV, news directors, chief photographers, and some consultants will insist that the "best pictures should go first." Is this good advice? Not always. Putting the best pictures first doesn't always make the best story and can, in fact, make the story harder to follow. Here's an example. On one particular day in the Tampa market, all the TV stations were competing to cover a hostage situation. Two teens had broken into a house where an elderly man lived. The police SWAT team surrounded the house. The police broke a window and threw in a telephone. The teens refused to negotiate. Eventually, police fired tear gas through the windows, broke down the door, stormed the house, and dragged the hostage takers out by their hair in full view of TV cameras. Later, police found the home owner dead. Some reporters opened their stories in a very predictable way:

They began with the dramatic video of police breaking down the door and storming the house. One reporter chose a different route. He began with video of the police surrounding the house. Then he told the story in **narrative style,** revealing a new fact with each sentence as it had actually occurred, allowing the drama to unfold for the viewer as it had unfolded in real life. The story won an Emmy award in spot news reporting that year. The judges found it clear and compelling. Chances are the viewers did, too.

But as with all rules, there are exceptions. Sometimes narrative storytelling principles conflict with other concerns. In most newsrooms, for instance, it's important for stories in the late evening newscast to begin with the freshest, most updated video. When such a conflict arises, go ahead and put the new pictures first, but then immediately cut to an earlier part of the story and pick it up from there in the proper chronological order. Here's an example:

(Open with natural sound, flames)

> THESE TOWERING FLAMES WERE A FIREFIGHTER'S NIGHTMARE. FOR HOURS THIS AFTERNOON . . . THE MEN AND WOMEN OF FIRE COMPANY 33 BATTLED THE RAGING FIRE. THEY BRAVED SEARING 120-DEGREE HEAT. BUT FAR MORE DANGEROUS THAN THAT . . . WAS THE SULFURIC ACID IN THE BURNING TANK TRUCK. THIS ORDEAL BEGAN FOUR HOURS EARLIER . . . AT THE U-SAVE GROCERY STORE ON BRUCE B DOWNS BOULEVARD. THAT'S WHERE TRUCK DRIVER MACK SIMPSON BLUNDERED INTO A HIGH-SPEED POLICE CHASE.

If you have to break from the chronology, try not to deviate from it more than once. In a story the length of a typical TV package, your viewers or listeners can probably handle one clearly defined flashback or flash-forward, but don't ask them to follow you through a whole series of them.

When writing your story, it's crucial that you not only relate the events in chronological order, but also pick a strong central character. The best and most memorable stories are those told through the eyes of a person to whom we can all relate. In Chapter 9, about packages, we refer to this as the diamond approach. That's why in the bank robbery story outlined earlier in this chapter, passerby Otis Armstrong makes a good choice for the central character—what happened to him could have happened to any of us.

A final point about narrative storytelling: Although the traditional "five W's" are very important, don't forget the "S"—the "so what?" Make sure your story contains context, perspective, and meaning. In the bank robbery, is the bank taking any extra steps to improve safety? How many other bank robberies have taken place at that branch? In that neighborhood? Are bank robberies on the rise? Are your deposits safe? Does your story show what the robbery means to the news consumer?

Write in Active Voice

As you might remember from Ms. Grundy's elementary school grammar class, a sentence is in active voice when the person or thing expressing an action is the subject of the sentence. It's in passive voice when the person or thing *receiving* the action is the subject of the sentence. There are several reasons why passive voice isn't well suited for news copy. For one, passive voice just doesn't sparkle. It's drab, stodgy, and usually cumbersome. Two or three back-to-back passive sentences can kill a story dead.

Which of the following examples sounds crisper and more memorable to you?

Example A

JOHN WAS SHOT BY FRED. FRED WAS QUICKLY ARRESTED BY POLICE. THE QUICK RESPONSE BY POLICE WAS PRAISED BY THE MAYOR.

Example B

FRED SHOT JOHN. POLICE QUICKLY ARRESTED HIM. THE MAYOR PUBLICLY THANKED THE OFFICERS FOR THEIR QUICK RESPONSE.

We hope you chose Example B. Use of passive voice can make copy sound dishwater dull. But the real sin of passive writing is that it makes your story more difficult to comprehend. Passive voice makes the narrative storytelling technique difficult or impossible to carry out because it interferes with attempts to present the story in chronological order. It shows the target of the action before presenting the person or thing that initiated the action. We discover the result before seeing the cause, the exact opposite of the way it happened in real life. In our example of Fred doing evil to John, in real life the first thing that happens is that Fred acts, pulling the trigger, and then John falls with a gunshot wound. But if you write it in passive voice—"JOHN WAS SHOT BY FRED"— then you're showing us the second action first (John being shot), the first action second (Fred pulling the trigger), and then trying to go back and piece it all together. It's confusing. Put enough passive sentences in your story and you'll make it an incomprehensible quagmire.

Finally, passive voice leads journalists to adopt lazy habits in pursuing the facts. It allows them to omit major information—such as who did it. For example, "JOHN WAS SHOT." Who did it? Maybe the reporter knows, maybe not. But if you write this sentence in the active voice, it's *not possible* for you ignore the "whodunit" question. You can write "Fred shot John" or even "Someone shot John," but it's impossible to write an active-voice sentence without some reference to the person or thing responsible for the action.

So how do you fix a passive sentence? The most common advice is to follow the classic "SVO" format: subject, verb, object. In an active-voice sentence, the subject *always* will be the person or thing doing or expressing the action, and the object will be the person or thing *receiving* the action.

Perhaps an easier way to remember to put the "act" in "active voice" is through use of the acronym "ACT," as follows:

$$ACT = actor \rightarrow commission \rightarrow target$$

First, identify the "commission"—the verb you'll use to describe the action. Next, identify the "actor"—the person or thing committing the action—and write that down. Then, write the appropriate conjugation of the verb to the right of the "actor." Finally, identify the "target," the person or thing receiving the action (if there is one; not all active-voice sentences must contain an object) and write that to the right of the verb. Using our example, the "commission" was a shooting. The actor who did it was Fred. The target of the action was John, whom the bullet hit. Actor = Fred. Commission = Shot. Target = John. Fred shot John.

It seems simple, but the challenge of converting a passive sentence to active stumps some people because in many passive sentences, *the actor is missing*. Consider the following passive sentence: "Thousands of dollars' worth of bills and coins were dropped along a two-mile stretch of highway." To fix it, the first thing you have to do is to identify the missing actor. In some cases this might require a little journalism, but usually it will be obvious. Suppose we know that an armored truck with a broken door dropped the money. The fix is easy: "The armored truck dropped thousands of dollars in bills and coins along a two-mile stretch of highway." Actor = truck. Commission = dropped. Target = thousands (of dollars). But what if we really don't know where the money came from? You have two choices. One, you can pick a "generic" actor, such as "someone" or "something." Or, you can abandon the sentence structure altogether and approach the statement from another angle, such as: "Sometime this morning, thousands of dollars in bills and coins appeared along a two-mile stretch of highway." The common denominator is that in every case we'll choose an actor and start our sentence or phrase with it.

Sensitivity

Let's face it: We live in a "politically correct" world. Most newsrooms have changed dramatically in recent years. Behavior that would get you canned today was common yesterday. We've all had to learn to be more sensitive in our personal and professional behavior, to think before we speak, and to filter copy for potential offensiveness before putting it on the air. Whatever your political views might be, this new sensitivity isn't a bad thing. If your copy makes a connection to 90 percent of your audience but alienates 10 percent of it because you've inadvertently offended someone, then it's 10 percent less effective than it should be. Why accept that, if you can reach more people by deleting offensive wording? It's certainly true that good journalism occasionally offends people, but here's a good rule of thumb: Never offend anyone *by accident.* If you're going to do it, then make sure you're doing it on purpose and for a very good reason. On every other occasion, potentially offensive copy is simply an accidental roadblock to good communication.

Your own gut instinct, if you listen to it, will tell you about 75 percent of the time whether copy is offensive. The rest of the time, you must rely on feedback from co-workers and, most especially, from members of the public. Listen to what they have to say, and apply the New Golden Rule: Treat Others as They Want to Be Treated. Each case is different, of course. But to the extent that it's possible and practical for you to follow it, do so. Your copy will be that much more effective.

Basic Creative Techniques

You don't have to use a lot of creative writing techniques to write good copy for television or radio. In fact, normally you should be suspicious and wary of too much creativity. Colorful adjectives and flowery prose, if you don't use them properly, can make a story sound contrived, hyped, and trite. Even so, some creative techniques, when you use them in moderation, can add to the story and make it more understandable and memorable.

Alliteration

Alliteration is the practice of taking a number of words beginning with the same consonant and grouping them together in the same sentence or phrase. For example:

POLICE ARE PLANNING TO PUT A PERSISTENT PURSE SNATCHER IN THE POKEY.

This technique has the virtue of making your sentence instantly memorable and even entertaining. The danger is that it's also a very easy technique to overdo and abuse. It's fairly safe to use with light stories but riskier with hard news. In either case, use it with moderation.

Repetition

As a general rule, writers try to avoid using the same words again and again in close proximity. The idea is to find synonyms to keep the copy from sounding dull and unimaginative, which is why most writers keep a well-thumbed thesaurus close by. However, there is a place for repetition. Good writers can use repetitive words, phrases, or patterns to drive home a concept or point. Typically this means constructing two or more successive sentences around the same word or phrase in a repetitive pattern.

Example 1

HE WAS ANGRY. HIS BEST FRIEND WAS ANGRY. IT SEEMED EVERYONE HE KNEW WAS ANGRY.

Example 2

FOR YEARS FRED JONES STUDIED WAR. HE LIVED WAR AND BREATHED WAR. BUT ON THIS DAY HE TURNED HIS BACK ON WAR FOREVER.

Example 3

JANE SMITH POUNDED THE PODIUM AND DEMANDED RESPECT. SHE POUNDED IT AGAIN AND DEMANDED JUSTICE. SHE RAISED HER FIST TO POUND IT A THIRD TIME, BUT INSTEAD TURNED AND LEFT WITHOUT ANOTHER WORD.

It's also possible to use repetitive patterns that don't involve repeating any particular word. To achieve the desired effect, the structure of both sentences must be similar.

Example 4

LAST YEAR HE WOULD HAVE PACED THE ROOM ... WRINGING HIS HANDS IN PANIC AND SELF-DOUBT. BUT NOW HE SAT AT THE KEYBOARD, PUNCHING THE KEYS WITH CLARITY AND CONFIDENCE. COUNSELING AND THERAPY HAD MADE THE DIFFERENCE.

In the above example, notice how parts of the first sentence correspond to parts of the second, as follows:

Last year = But now
paced the room = sat at the keyboard
wringing his hands = punching the keys
in panic = with clarity
and self-doubt = and confidence

Parallel Writing with Wordplay

As you might remember from your high school English class, parallel form is the act of expressing two or more ideas by using phrases or sentences of similar construction. All four examples above are forms of parallel writing. Combine that concept with a little wordplay and you now have a creative technique that can help you get a point across in a more memorable fashion. For our purposes, then, parallel writing with wordplay is the act of linking two (or more) ideas in order to compare or contrast them, using a pun or a double meaning of one word to link them.

Example 1

IN IOWA . . . TEMPERS ARE RISING ALONG WITH THE WATERS.

This is a play off the word "rising," one verb used to place two very different but linked concepts into parallel: the act of land being flooded and people getting angry about it.

Example 2

THE SKYRISE APARTMENTS CAME WITH A SKY-HIGH COST TO THE ENVIRONMENT.

This is a play off the word "sky" or, more specifically, a play off the concept of "rising to the sky." Again, it places two very different but linked concepts into parallel: the act of building an apartment complex and the act of damaging the environment.

This technique isn't available or effective in every situation. The key is to look for two parallel actions that you can then link together with a common verb, phrase, or concept.

The Rule of Threes

The idea behind the Rule of Threes is that people remember ideas more easily if they're presented in groups of three. Examples abound in everyday conversation: "reading, writing and 'rithmetic," "earth, wind and fire," "Tom, Dick and Harry," "wind, sea and rain," "morning, noon and night," "blood, sweat and tears," to name a few.

The Rule of Threes is especially effective when you use it in conjunction with parallel writing. This involves using a group of three words or phrases to draw a comparison or contrast to a second group of three words or phrases. The danger is this technique, like alliteration, is more difficult to bring off properly and more likely to sound contrived. When it works right, however, it can be effective. For example:

DONALD SMITH SWEARS HE BEGAN HIS DAY LIKE ANY OTHER. HE CLAIMS HE
WOKE UP . . . SHAVED . . . AND HEADED OFF TO WORK. BUT THE F-B-I TELLS
IT DIFFERENTLY. IT CLAIMS HE WOKE UP . . . PUT ON A FAKE BEARD . . . AND
HEADED OFF TO ROB A BANK.

(Rule of Threes: waking, shaving and heading off.)

> INSTEAD OF SPENDING THEIR DAY IN SCHOOL LEARNING READING . . .
> WRITING . . . AND 'RITHMETIC . . . POLICE SAY THESE GANG MEMBERS
> SPENT IT IN A CAR RIDING . . . RACING . . . AND ROBBING.

(Combines alliteration and parallels three expected activities with three unexpected ones.)

Simile

A simile is the technique of comparing one thing to another, typically using the words "like" or "as."

Example 1

THE TORNADO TOSSED THE CARS AROUND LIKE TONKA TOYS.

Example 2

THE BOLT HIT WITH A BLAST AS LOUD AS A CANNON.

Metaphorical Writing

This is the technique of using a physical situation, thing, or activity to symbolically describe something else. A metaphor takes a comparison further than a simile does, by presenting one concept in terms of another.

Example 1

THE ATTORNEY GENERAL SAYS THE PONZEE MINING COMPANY WAS INDEED DIGGING FOR GOLD ... BUT IN THE WRONG PLACE ... THE POCKETBOOKS OF ITS INVESTORS.

Example 2

THE COMPANY NEVER FINISHED THE POOL. AND THE DARINS WEREN'T THE ONLY FAMILY TO GET SOAKED. THE A-G SAYS NOT ONE OF THE FIRM'S DOZEN OR SO CONTRACTS HELD WATER.

The root of most creativity is simple word association. When writing, take a minute to throw out all words and phrases you think are associated with the principal activity involved in the story. In Example 1 above, the subject is a mining company; "digging for gold" is one of many concepts one might expect to associate with that particular activity (so is "the shaft," but let's not get carried away). Similarly, in Example 2 the concepts of "holding water" and "getting soaked" are easy associations with the words "pool" and "water."

Exaggeration

This is known in literary circles as "hyperbole." A bit of well-placed exaggeration serves to paint your subject in vivid and therefore more memorable terms. This is another one that's easy to overdo; be judicious. It works best with light stories such as kickers. Examples: "Roach the size of a Rolls-Royce"; "Killer rabbit"; "Kamikaze pelican."

Human Terms

Stories dealing with large numbers often get lost on the average listener or viewer simply because he or she can't relate to them. It's your challenge to translate those numbers into terms people can understand. This might take a little quick arithmetic on your part, but the results are well worth it. For instance, suppose you're doing a story about oil exports and find that gasoline usage has gone down by a million gallons a year. What does one gallon of gasoline mean to you personally? How much gasoline do you burn each week? About 20 gallons? At that rate it would take you 50,000 weeks to burn a million gallons—that's 962 years! Now you get the picture—and you can put it in just those terms for the viewer or listener:

> IF YOU BURN ABOUT 20 GALLONS OF GASOLINE A WEEK ... A MILLION
> GALLONS WOULD LAST YOU 962 YEARS.

Personification

Personification is the technique of assigning human attributes or actions to things or concepts that aren't human. Examples include "Winter's icy breath," "hand of fate," "nature smiled," and so forth. Be *very* careful with this one. Many of the common uses deriving from this technique are so shopworn they've passed into the land of the hoary cliché. Also, be careful not to assign human characteristics to inanimate objects by mistake; see the beginning of Appendix A for more about this.

Exercise

At this point, we're going to use some of the principles we've discussed to take apart and fix a poorly written story.

Here's an example of how not to write:

> AN APPARENT ONE-CAR ACCIDENT HAS CLAIMED THE LIFE OF A LOCAL MAN.
> POLICE SAY FOR SOME REASON A RED 1987 FORD TAURUS DRIVEN BY 38-YEAR-
> OLD JOHN SMITH OF 1237 GONER ROAD IN TUCSON WENT OUT OF CONTROL ON

PRESTON LANE . . . FLIPPED . . . ROLLED DOWN AN EMBANKMENT . . . AND
LANDED UPSIDE DOWN IN A DRAINAGE DITCH FILLED WITH WATER FROM LAST
NIGHT'S STORMS. APPARENTLY THE DRIVER WASN'T KILLED BY THE IMPACT BUT
RATHER DROWNED AFTER BEING TRAPPED IN THE WRECKAGE. IT HAPPENED
ABOUT SIX THIS MORNING. THE WRECK WAS WITNESSED BY ANOTHER
MOTORIST. THE CAUSE OF THE MISHAP IS BEING INVESTIGATED BY POLICE.

The second sentence alone is so filled with facts, adjectives, and dependent clauses that in one breath, the writer is telling the viewer: where the facts came from (attribution); the name of the driver; the age of the driver; the driver's hometown; the driver's address; the make of the vehicle involved; the model of the vehicle involved; the year of manufacture of the vehicle involved; the color of the vehicle involved; the name of the street involved; that police don't know the cause of the accident; that the car flipped and rolled; that it landed in a drainage ditch; that it landed upside down; that the ditch was full of water; and that it rained last night. That's 16 facts in one sentence!

And excessive length isn't this sentence's only sin. It also begins and ends in passive voice. In grammatical terms, the subject of this sentence is the 1987 Ford Taurus, but in fact the subject of the story is John Smith, and the story is about how our subject met his untimely end. Because the subject of the sentence doesn't match the subject of the story, the viewer or listener is hard-pressed to figure out which is which, and thus finds it harder to understand what's going on.

Though this copy is technically accurate and grammatically correct (other than the use of passive voice), its style is atrocious. Yet copy just like it airs on TV and radio stations every day (we took this from an actual example of a story that aired). How can we fix it?

For one thing, the second sentence is so loaded with facts that we can break it up into an entire paragraph, and that's what you should set out to do. The writer should give each major fact its own sentence, rather than attempting to convey several major facts in a single sentence.

Again, apply the Mom Rule. How would you relate this story if you were telling it to her? Chances are you'd say something like, "Hey, did you hear about the guy who ran off the road into a drainage ditch last night and drowned?" Why would you start that way? Because the fate of a guy who died unexpectedly while doing nothing more offensive than driving down the road is the single most interesting and memorable aspect of the story. It's something that could have happened to anybody—which is precisely what makes this story newsworthy. The lead to your story therefore should accomplish the same purpose as the opening gambit to your conversation with Mom.

After you'd captured your mom's attention with that opening line, chances are she'd respond with a question like "No! What happened?" At this point, you'd likely continue your story, starting at the beginning and continuing in chronological order until you reached the end of your story—the outcome of which you'd have already revealed in your opening remark. Your news copy has to accomplish essentially the same thing. Here's one way to do it, applying the above rules:

> LAST NIGHT'S STORMS ARE PARTIALLY TO BLAME FOR A TRAFFIC DEATH THIS
> MORNING. A TUCSON MAN DROWNED WHEN HIS CAR RAN OFF THE ROAD INTO
> A FLOODED DITCH. IT HAPPENED ABOUT SIX THIS MORNING ON PRESTON
> LANE. ACCORDING TO POLICE . . . THE CAR WENT OUT OF CONTROL . . . VEERED
> OFF THE ROAD . . . FLIPPED . . . AND ROLLED. IT LANDED UPSIDE DOWN IN
> A DRAINAGE DITCH STILL FILLED WITH RUNOFF FROM LAST NIGHT'S
> THUNDERSTORMS. THE DRIVER DROWNED. ANOTHER MOTORIST SAW THE
> WHOLE THING HAPPEN . . . BUT THE CAUSE OF THE CRASH REMAINS A
> MYSTERY. POLICE HAVE IDENTIFIED THE VICTIM. HE'S 38-YEAR-OLD JOHN
> SMITH OF 1237 GONER ROAD IN TUCSON.

This particular version of the story has most of the facts of the first. The sentences are short and conversational, and each contains a smaller number of facts. Every sentence is in active voice, with action following the subject rather than vice versa. Note that it doesn't contain many of the creative techniques outlined earlier; they aren't necessary in this instance. The story is much easier to understand in one take than the previous version was, and its style much more closely matches the form a conversation about the same event would likely take.

Conclusion

The single most important point to remember in writing a lead for a broadcast audience is that you must capture the attention of your viewers or listeners on the first attempt. To do this your leads must be conversational and fresh, and they must capture the essence of the story. The most effective tools in your box are short, declarative, active-voice sentences and a narrative storytelling style. Consider using creative techniques to make your copy memorable and effective, but remember that the goal of your copy is clarity and brevity, not creativity. *Don't overdo it.*

DOs and DON'Ts for Writing Leads and Other Copy

Do	Don't
• Write a fresh, updated lead.	• Write a stale, dated lead.
• "Sell" the story.	• Start writing until you decide what the story is about.
• Use preview and review.	
• Use the "Mom Rule."	
• Make stories relevant to listeners and viewers; remember WII-FM.	• Put too many facts in a lead.
	• Write in "TV speak."
• Use active voice.	• Break from chronology more than once.

Questions

1. Explain the "Mom Rule."

2. In what way is the lead sentence a sales pitch?

3. What is "TV Speak" and why should we avoid it?

4. What is a minimum number of facts you can have in a lead, and why?

5. Explain "preview," "view," and "review."

6. What's the broadcaster's correlary to what you learned in third grade English class related to subject-verb-object?

Deadly Copy Mistakes and How to Avoid Them

Four Words That Kill Good Broadcast Copy

"Allegedly"

> **Question:** When is it safe to "call names" on the air?
>
> **Answer:** Hardly ever. Not even if you say "allegedly." On-air name calling is what funds Caribbean vacations for libel lawyers.

The words "alleged" and "allegedly" are the most abused and misused words in television news. Why? Because too many writers believe the words stand as shields protecting them from litigation and freeing them to make statements they couldn't otherwise make. Unfortunately, this feeling of protection is a delusion. According to Gregg Thomas, a First Amendment expert and partner in the law firm of Thomas, LoCicero & Bralow, the word "has no value." Thomas says reporters who liberally sprinkle the word "allegedly" into their copy are practicing "condom journalism."

"The word is vastly overused," he says, "because somebody feels it has some prophylactic effect" and allows writers to "avoid responsibility for making a declarative statement." But the word doesn't impress judges or juries. "It offers no protection whatsoever," Thomas says.

Name-calling is one area in which writing in a conversational style—the way people really talk—can get you into serious trouble. Why? Because when it comes to general conversations about people arrested, charged, or convicted of heinous crimes, members of the public tend to assume the person involved is guilty and speak about him or her accordingly. As a journalist, you don't have that option—not even if you couch your name-calling in the word "allegedly" or its cousins.

Example

Let's say you're writing a story about a high-profile child molestation case in which the defendant, John Doe, to the surprise of many, was able to come up with enough cash to make bail. A casual conversation with Mom about this incident might go something like this:

CAN YOU BELIEVE IT? THAT CHILD MOLESTER GOT OUT!

A casual conversation with close friends might be even more direct:

CAN YOU BELIEVE IT? THAT DIRTBAG DOE GOT OUT!

As you sit down to write your own lead, you're faced with a problem. One, you want to write in the same conversational style, but you realize (we hope) that you can't use the word "dirtbag" or any like it. Also, you want to be careful not to convict the defendant on the air. So, you write something like this:

JOHN DOE . . . THE ALLEGED CHILD MOLESTER . . . IS OUT OF JAIL.

There are several problems. One, the sentence isn't conversational; aside from professional journalists, few people use the word "alleged" in casual conversation. Two, it's sleazy; in this sentence, through use of the word "alleged," we're calling Doe a really ugly name without attribution, without allowing him to face his accusers. Three, what if Doe didn't do it? If your facts aren't straight, the word "alleged" will give you about as much protection as an umbrella in a hurricane. Because you didn't make an attribution, a jury is more likely to decide that you were simply careless with the facts—and jurors might even attribute the accusation to you *personally*.

The problem is that whenever you call some specific individual a name—such as "criminal," "killer," "child molester," "embezzler," and the like—essentially you're drawing a conclusion. If the facts overwhelmingly support that conclusion, you're probably safe. But if the facts are at all in dispute—as they almost always are in criminal cases—that's another matter.

There's another problem with the word "allegedly." It's a lazy person's word that cheats the audience of details. It's a shortcut around the facts. Strike the word, and insert the facts. Let's take the case of John Doe, the alleged child molester, and the example lead "JOHN DOE, THE ALLEGED CHILD MOLESTER, IS OUT OF JAIL TODAY."

Which of the following conclusions can we comfortably and safely draw from that sentence?

1. The defendant's name is John Doe.
2. John Doe got out of jail today.
3. Police have charged Doe—or, at very least, have charged him in the past—with molesting at least one child.

Answer: only 1 and 2. If you also drew conclusion number 3, you're not alone. Probably a good portion of the audience would have drawn the same conclusion. However, you can't draw that conclusion from the lead as presented, and it's a good example of why the words "allege" and "allegedly" are so dangerous. The lead doesn't make plain who's making the allegations or give any hint as to how strong the case might be. Who says Doe is a child molester? Police? His neighbors? Sidewalk graffiti? From the lead presented above, any of the following could be true:

- The DA's office brought the charges; it's a strong case, and prosecutors are angry Doe is out.
- An individual police officer made the arrest and filled out a complaint, but the DA hasn't had a chance to study the paperwork and has no idea whether there's a case.
- Doe's next-door neighbor made the complaint and swore out a warrant for Doe's arrest, but the DA hasn't yet been able to substantiate her allegation.
- Doe is under indictment.
- Doe isn't under indictment; the grand jury hasn't heard the case yet.
- The DA privately believes there's no case and told the magistrate that he or she wouldn't be opposed to letting Doe out on bond and, in fact, plans to drop the charges after the publicity dies down.

If police have indeed charged Doe with the crime of molestation, then you're safe. But if not, you're potentially in trouble. Even if police haven't charged Doe, you might get away with the above copy—for one story. But what happens when the 11 P.M. producer rewrites your copy for his or her newscast? He or she might draw a false conclusion from the sloppy copy you wrote. Thus you might get a lead story for 11 P.M. reading, "JOHN DOE . . . A MAN POLICE SAY IS A CHILD MOLESTER . . . IS FREE TONIGHT." This sentence is now completely divorced from the truth, and you and your employer are in trouble.

Here's another way to look at it. As mentioned, your job is to write to the facts. Take this sentence: "DOE ALLEGEDLY MOLESTED A THREE-YEAR-OLD GIRL WHO LIVES NEXT DOOR." Which fact are you trying to present here? That Doe did it? Or that someone says he did? Unless you were there personally, you can't say whether Doe did it. Therefore, you can only say that someone *says* he did. Your story, then, is about the *allegation*, not about the act of molestation. Let us say it again: You're writing about an accusation, not a crime. This is a crucial point, and it's paramount that you remember it to clarify your thinking and writing about the matter. The molestation is, for all you know, fictional. Stick to the facts, and the fact is someone is accusing John Doe of molesting someone. Don't structure your sentence as if Doe actually did it, with only the word "allegedly" making the difference between someone's accusation and an on-air conviction. Structure your sentence and story around the accusation itself. Tell us who's making the accusation, then delve as much as you can into the quality and soundness of that accusation. Bring out the players: Tell us who they are, what they have to say, and how likely they are to be telling the truth. Forget the words "alleged" and "allegedly." Tell the audience what you know, with specific attribution: "SEVEN NEIGHBORS ACCUSED HIM OF MOLESTING THEIR CHILDREN. BUT TONIGHT JOHN DOE IS A FREE MAN."

Dropping the word "allegedly" will accomplish three very important goals. First, it will force you to write a much clearer, more concise story. Second, your story will be much more conversational in style and therefore more understandable and memorable. And last, but certainly not least, it will stick to the facts and therefore be true. As any lawyer will tell you, the only *absolute* defense in a libel case is the truth. By taking a little extra time to present the facts, you'll be doing a better job with your audience and you will be less likely to get into trouble. The word "allegedly" stands in the way and serves no purpose. Lose it.

The threat of legal action shouldn't be your only motivation for dropping the word "allegedly." Regardless of whether you get sued, the abuses this word invites simply aren't fair to the person named. The Sixth Amendment of the U.S. Constitution gives every person the right to face his or her accuser. Journalists sometimes short-circuit the spirit of the law by hiding behind the word "allegedly." Drop the word. Come out from behind cover. Spell out who the accusers are with specific attribution. It's the fair and socially responsible thing to do.

If none of the above arguments convinces you, consider this point: As a beginning producer or reporter, you're much more likely to land a job and advance up the career ladder if your résumé reel doesn't contain eight uses of the nonconversational word "allegedly" within one 90-second period (which, so far, stands as a record among tapes this author has reviewed personally).

"Suspects"

If "alleged" is the single most abused word, then "suspects" has to be a close second. A suspect is a specific, *named* individual who is charged, jailed, or wanted in connection with a specific act. There's no such thing as an "unknown suspect." It's an oxymoron, a self-contradictory phrase describing something that doesn't exist. For a person to be a suspect, police or investigators have to know who he or she is. They must have a specific name in mind or on paper.

If someone holds up a bank but police have no idea who the person is, you can refer to the perpetrator as a man, woman, bandit, robber, gunman, gunwoman, street person, or whatever (but please don't use the word "perpetrator"). Note that in this case you *can* use red-letter, name-calling words such as "bandit" and "robber"; you're not calling anyone names on the air because *you haven't named anyone.* But if the robber is unknown, you can't refer to him or her as a suspect. The reason is simple: If police don't yet suspect anyone, there is no suspect!

You're not convicting anyone on the air if you write words like "WITNESSES SAY THE GUNMAN FIRED TWO SHOTS . . . KILLING THE VICTIM INSTANTLY," even if police have named a suspect. But you can't substitute the word "SUSPECT" for "GUNMAN" without careful and proper attribution. If there's a dead body with a bullet hole in it, and if it was a case of murder, then there was a gunman, and you can write about him and even speculate about him. What the gunman did or didn't do isn't the dispute in this case. The dispute, and the issue to be addressed in court, is whether the suspect was the gunman.

Bottom line: If there was a crime, then there was a criminal. You can write about him or her generically and call the person any names you want, provided of course that your story is factual. But you have to be extremely cautious when you begin saying a *specific individual* was the bad guy. "Bandit," "robber," "killer," and the like are generic terms not describing any specific individual. "Suspect" is a specific term describing a specific individual, an individual who has rights and, presumably, a lawyer just aching to sue you. But if the specific individual is unknown, there is no suspect.

Thus you can't write a sentence such as "THE SUSPECT IS ON THE LOOSE" if police have no idea who the bad guy is. Instead, you have to write "THE BANDIT IS ON THE LOOSE."

Conversely, you can write "THE SUSPECT IS IN JAIL." But you can't write "THE BANDIT IS IN JAIL" without careful attributions unless you've never been sued and are curious to see what it's like.

A final point about attribution: The only truly safe stories are those that attribute the facts and accusations to an official source, such as police officers, fire officials, or prosecutors. In most cases journalists have a qualified privilege to quote government officials and official documents. Generally speaking, you can't be sued for reporting what a police officer or prosecutor says, even if it later turns out the official was wrong or even lying. But the further you get away from official sources, the more dangerous the game becomes. Handle witness accounts very carefully when reporting accusations against individuals. In libel terms, *their* speech is *your* speech. If a witness makes an untrue libelous statement, *you* are liable and can be sued, just as if you'd said it yourself. (We'll have much more about the legal aspects of copywriting later in this book.)

"Apparently"

Consider the following sentence:

APPARENTLY SMITH LOST CONTROL OF HIS CAR . . . WHICH RAN INTO A DITCH.

The only thing apparent here is that the writer doesn't have a clue what really happened. Did the steering fail? Did the driver swerve to avoid a moose? Was it a mob hit staged to look like an accident? Did the driver commit suicide? Who knows? The only thing we know for sure is that we don't know. In this case, the writer is using the word "apparently" to camouflage the fact that he or she has no facts and is just making a guess about what really happened.

Remember, it's *permissible* not to have the answers. In such cases, 'fess up. Tell the viewers or listeners you don't know. Explain what you do know, and outline the current speculation about what might have happened. Here's a fix of the above sentence using those guidelines:

THE CAR RAN OFF THE ROAD AND CRASHED IN A DITCH. BECAUSE ROAD CONDITIONS WERE DRY . . . POLICE ARE AT A LOSS TO EXPLAIN IT.

Or,

THE ROAD WAS DRY AT THE TIME. POLICE ARE NOW CHECKING TO SEE WHETHER THE CAR'S STEERING FAILED.

"Undetermined"

The fourth most worthless word in broadcast news is "undetermined" in connection with a bank robbery or other theft. One, it's not conversational. When have you ever turned to someone and said, "The robber got away with an undetermined amount of cash"?

Two, it's not factual—or at least, it's not always factual—and it leaves the viewer with a false assumption that someone will determine the amount of money missing later. Guess what, folks. Often officials know *exactly* how much money the bandit got away with, for the simple reason that he probably has a "bait bag" with a dye bomb inside it. If they don't know, they'll find out very quickly. But believe this: *They might never tell you how much cash the bandit got.* There's a good reason for this: Revealing the amount of cash the bandit took is the worst form of advertising for the bank. The bandit might have escaped with a nice wad of cash. If the bank reveals the amount, it's essentially throwing out a challenge for other robbers to try to match or surpass the previous robber's haul.

As a matter of policy involving the public's safety, it makes sense for news operations to support this concept of not revealing the amount taken in bank robberies and other armed robberies. The exceptions are cases in which the robber got very little, or a whole lot, such as Brinks holdups running into the millions, in which case the amount taken will be well publicized.

Therefore, drop the word "undetermined." It adds nothing and isn't conversational. If you believe it's crucial to make some reference to the cash amount—and there's some indication that (1) the amount is relevant, (2) police really don't know how much the bandit took and are trying to find out, and (3) they're going to share this information with you—then you should write specifically to that point. For example:

POLICE DON'T KNOW HOW MUCH CASH THE BANDIT GOT . . . BUT THEY
DON'T THINK IT'S MUCH. THE BANK IS COUNTING ITS LOSSES AND HOPES
TO HAVE THE ANSWER BY TONIGHT.

Summary—Example of a Completely Worthless Sentence

THE UNKNOWN SUSPECT ALLEGEDLY POINTED A GUN AT THE TELLER . . .
DEMANDED MONEY . . . AND APPARENTLY ESCAPED WITH AN
UNDETERMINED AMOUNT OF CASH.

Questions

1. Why don't the words "alleged" or "allegedly" offer any legal protection to journalists?
2. What does it take for there to be a "suspect"?

3. What else is important to consider when writing about a suspect's actions?

4. Which words can you use instead of "suspect," and if you use them, what must you be careful of?

5. Writers use the word "apparently" as a replacement for what?

6. What does the word "undetermined" really mean?

CHAPTER FIVE

Suzanne Huffman and C. A. Tuggle

Interviewing: Getting the Facts and the Feelings

Interviewing members of your community, important people visiting your community, or newsmakers you travel to visit is a vital part of the broadcast writing and reporting process. Interviews provide background information for your story, and they provide sound bites for your package or VO/SOT, or the radio equivalent of those television news story forms. It's important to remember that one of the unique strengths of broadcast news is its ability to transmit the experience of what happens at the scene of an event to members of your audience. The people you interview and what they say are key parts of that process.

Interviews are essentially conversations with members of your community or those who have something to say that your viewers or listeners would find important or interesting. And when your story is broadcast, you share those conversations with your audience. So you want to let the people you interview tell about what's happening. Let them tell the story themselves from their point of view, to the degree they can. You want to let their personalities come through so people watching or listening will feel something for them. The average person wasn't at the scene of the story and doesn't know what happened. Through your interviews, you can take the viewers or listeners to the scene to experience what happened and understand it through the words of those who were there.

The people you interview are the people whose voices audience members will hear in your newscast. So remember to talk and listen to a diversity of "regular" people in your community. Don't rely entirely on the experts, the officials, the usual voices. As a reporter, you can give voice to the voiceless in your community by interviewing them for your stories.

Those you choose to interview and the tone you take when you interview them will also contribute to the image your audience will have of you as a reporter and of your station as a local business. It's often the case, particularly with beginning reporters in smaller markets, that the reporters are young, single, from someplace else, and looking to move on to a larger market as soon as possible. This is the opposite of what's true of many of the members of the viewing or listening audience, who tend to be older, married with children and a mortgage, born in the community, and who plan to stay in this town that's their home and workplace. So stop and think and ask who's in your audience, what their lives are like, and what their concerns and interests are.

Thinking Ahead

When you're thinking about which people to interview, ask yourself: "How do I make this story real for my viewers and listeners? How do I make a difference in my community? And how do I tell this story clearly and in a compelling way?" You don't want to get in an interviewing rut, going to the same experts and officials time after time, although this is easy and quick and sometimes unavoidable. Take some time to be thoughtful and creative in choosing whom to interview. Some interview subjects are given to you, not chosen, as in news conferences and emergency situations. But other situations offer you more opportunities to choose from among a broad spectrum of people.

If water rates are going up, you might think in terms of interviewing the people who come to the window at city hall to pay their bills, or the person who receives the water bill payments at the window, or the person who answers the phone and listens to comments from local residents about the rate increase. You might ask that person what people are saying to her when they pay their water bills. If the story is about the economy, you might first ask your neighbors, colleagues, and social media friends "Do you know anybody who's out of work, who's been laid off, or who's looking for work?" People who are out of a job and looking for work will have firsthand knowledge about the state of the economy as it affects their lives. These individuals can add depth, perspective, and context to your story, which "official sources" might not be able to provide.

Interviews with affected individuals "humanize" your stories. For example, if the welfare allowance for a woman with two children goes up from $388 a month to $401 a month, a mother of two can put a human face on the story by telling you what $13 more a month will buy.

Being Prepared

You want to prepare for your interview by learning as much as possible about your subject in advance. That means research. Read what you can about the subject so you'll be familiar with it. Ask other people in your newsroom and station what's important to ask about the subject. Brainstorm with them, to the extent that time constraints allow. The person you'll spend the most time with on any given TV story is your photographer. He or she can help you prepare by suggesting questions and offering perspective. Talk with your photographer as you plan each story, and work together as a team.

You want to have some idea what you're going to ask and in what order before you go out on a story. Prepare at least a few questions, and write them down to use as a memory jog if you get nervous or draw a blank. You don't want to be "married" to these questions and follow them blindly in spite of what the interviewee says, but you do want to have a focus beforehand for your story. Too often, students and young professionals go into an interview with a list of questions and essentially read them to their interviewees. When that happens, it *isn't* a conversation. But a list can be helpful, because you don't want to be fishing around and asking questions about everything in the hope of getting a usable sound bite. Interviews have a dual purpose. They're a way for the reporter or writer to gather information, and they're a way to gather usable sound bites. Do the information-gathering part of the interview before you start recording or capturing.

In the information-gathering part of the interview, what people tell you provides details and even language you can use in your story. NBC correspondent Bob Dotson was one of the many reporters who covered the Union, South Carolina, story about Susan Smith, who drove her car into a lake with her two young sons strapped into the back seat. One of the recovery divers told Dotson the first thing the diver saw in the submerged car was "a tiny hand pressed against glass." Dotson used that detail and those words at the top of his report.

When you're writing your TV news package or radio wrap, you'll be weaving together the words in your narration track with natural sound and with sound bites (and video in the case of television) you've gathered in the field. So the writing for your story actually begins in the field as the crew is recording interviews and natural sound. Before you go out into the field, you want to be prepared and know your subject so that you'll know what you're talking about and asking about.

If your interview is part of a spot news story, and there's no time to prepare, you'll be drawing on the base of knowledge you've accumulated from reading your local newspaper, reading newsmagazines and books, surfing the Internet, meeting people in your community, and keeping up with their topics of concern and conversation. So always pay attention to what's in the news, and pay attention to what the controversies and disagreements and issues are within your community. These are daily habits you want to cultivate. They'll serve you well over time. Remember, in spot news situations, reporters have no time to prepare—just react.

Interviewing is equal parts art, craft, and science. And the first question you ask can dictate the entire experience. If people are offended by what you ask them or by the tone in which you ask it, it will color the whole interview. If people feel they know and can trust you, things will go more smoothly. So, people skills are essential. Tell the person up front who you are, which station you represent, and what you're doing. For example, "I'm Jane Smith from Channel 2. We're doing a story about the heat. We'd like to talk with you about how it's affecting your company, family, business, health"—whatever the focus of your story is. Don't tell the interviewee beforehand what the specific questions will be. That leads to rehearsed answers. Just tell him or her the topic of the questions. Use a professional and conversational tone of voice.

You must also remember to ask questions the person can answer in short phrases or in a few sentences—something *other* than yes or no. What made the Chris Farley interview skits on "Saturday Night Live" (and now on YouTube) so hilarious was Farley's own bumbling, nervous attempt at being an interviewer. He would ask long rambling "do you remember when" questions. All his interviewees could answer was yes or no. We learn nothing from such interviews.

Knowing the Mechanics of Interviewing

Remember to look straight in the eyes of the person you're interviewing and maintain eye contact with him or her. Strong eye contact seems to help divert the person's attention away from the equipment, which makes for a less nervous interviewee. Don't fidget with your notes or with your hair or wave the microphone around. When possible, use a clip-on microphone. When interviewing for TV, ask the person you're interviewing to look at you, not at the camera. Your back will be to the photographer, who will get a shot over your shoulder of the interviewee's face. Stand very close to the camera. Never chew gum. If you shoot your own interviews as a one-person band, set up the camera, frame the interviewee, and then stand right next to the camera so the person you're interviewing will be looking slightly to one side rather than right into the camera lens.

The microphone should point toward the interviewee and be about six inches below his or her mouth in normal situations. In a situation in which there's loud ambient noise, such as a cheering crowd at a football game, put the microphone closer. (Clip-on mics don't work well in these situations.) As you ask your questions, point the mic at yourself and record your own questions because you might want to use them in the edited piece. However, be sure to have the mic directed at the interviewee for all of his or her comments. If the mic is moving back toward the interviewee as he or she begins to answer, the audio might not be usable.

As often as possible, conduct the interview at the scene of the event or in the setting of the story, whether in a factory or a classroom or an orange grove. Be sure to find out your interviewee's full name, how to spell it, and how to pronounce it correctly. Write down his or her phone number in case you need to call back later. If the person is an "official," get a title.

In the interview itself, you want to be direct, clear, straightforward, empathetic, and respectful. You want to be frank, sincere, and courteous. You want to ask precise, specific questions, one at a time. You want to show interest in what the person is saying by looking directly at him or her. And you want to actively listen to what the person is saying to you. That's the only way you can come up with logical follow-up questions. In many ways, this kind of active listening is really watching, for you must pay attention to any nods of the head, frowns, clenching of the teeth, or tightening of the facial muscles that might tell more about the interviewee's true reactions than what he or she is saying to you. Also keep in mind that people sometimes lie or "shade" the truth.

Your questions should be direct, simple, and open-ended. Asking people open-ended questions allows them to show what they know. You want to get them talking by asking questions that start with why, how, and what. Ask them, "What is the proposal designed to accomplish?" Or "What is your understanding of how the accident happened?" Or "Why do you love your hobby?" Or "How does the agency's report fall short?"

You must also understand what the interviewees mean by what they say, and you might need to ask for clarification to make sure. You might need to say, "What do you mean when you say . . . ?" Or "Tell me a little bit more about that." Or "Give me an example of that."

Ask questions that cause the person to think, to reflect, to search and, if necessary, to clear up any discrepancies in earlier statements he or she might have made about the same subject. Challenge the interviewee to respond to different viewpoints or to answer critics by asking, "How do you respond to Councilman White, who says this is only a short-term fix and won't solve the problem long-term?" Or "Why are you so determined to push this legislation through when there's so much opposition to it from the teachers' union?" Attribute challenges such as these so that it doesn't sound like you're the one making them.

You might also need to ask the people you interview to summarize what they've just said in one or two sentences, especially if they tend to ramble on or talk in long run-on sentences. You might need to interrupt them and re-ask the question if they go way off track. You need short answers—sound bites—you can use in your story. Because you'll be recording/capturing your interview, and you or someone else will be editing it later, you can ask the question a second time if the interviewee flubs up the answer the first time. Or you can ask the question another way. Or you can ask it a third time. Take the time to get the most understandable, succinct statement you can. After you've asked all of your questions, ask if there's anything the interviewee would like to add. Then wait. For television interviews, also ask the photographer if there's anything else he or she would like to ask. Remember, you and the photographer are a team.

Leave some editing "space" during the interview. Let the person you're interviewing finish answering each question, then pause for a couple of seconds before you ask the next question or interrupt the speaker in some way. This can be tough to learn, but it becomes important in the editing booth when you're working on a deadline. You don't want to "step on" the sound bites. Also, don't listen out loud by saying "OK" or "Uh-huh" in response to everything your interviewee says. You don't want to sound as if you're agreeing (or disagreeing) with what the person is saying. If you're off-camera, you can slightly nod or tilt your head to confirm to the person you're interviewing that you're listening and paying attention.

You want to stay in control of the interview and not let yourself be used. This is particularly important in live situations. One California TV reporter, interviewing a member of the Hell's Angels motorcycle gang, live, was shocked when the biker grabbed the microphone and began swearing during the 6 o'clock news. In hindsight, perhaps the reporter should have anticipated such an outcome. But once the biker had the microphone in his hand, the reporter was helpless to end the interview. It was up to the director and producer in the control room to end it instead and for the anchor to apologize. Remember, you hold the microphone. You stay in control. There are other, less extreme situations to watch out for. At times, politicians and others who are accustomed to being interviewed frequently won't answer the question you ask; instead they'll respond with something they want you to use in your story. You might ask the governor what the state is doing to curb illegal immigration, and the answer he gives you might be that he's working hard to provide tax relief for home owners this year (a part of his campaign platform). So pay close attention to what he's actually telling you. If you think a politician is avoiding a question, ask it again. And again. Then ask him why he's avoiding the question.

If you're writing a 90-second TV story, you'll be looking for sound bites that run about 10 seconds in length; that's about one sentence long. If you're writing a documentary, you'll be looking for sound bites that might run 20 seconds in length; that's about two or three sentences long. Radio sound bites range from about 5 to 15 seconds in length and are usually in the lower end of that range. Sometimes you'll be looking for a long series of quick sound bites from your interview subjects. If you're interviewing college students about where they'll be traveling for spring break, you might just ask them that one question, "Where are you going for spring break?" When the sound bites are edited together into the final piece, the answers will then be: "Cancun . . . Austin . . . home to Miami . . . London . . . Phoenix . . . I'm staying here to study." In this case, one- or two-word answers are all you're looking for.

If your station has cameras or audio recorders with time code, it's helpful to set your watch and the camera or recorder time to real time, so that you can just glance at your watch and make a note of the time when you hear a sound bite you're pretty sure you'll want to use. This makes the editing process go more smoothly and quickly. It's particularly important when you're working on a daily deadline or when you're covering a trial, for example. You might wind up with several hours of recorded/captured material.

It's also helpful for television reporters to carry audio recorders with them to their interviews. This way, reporters can pick out their sound bites by listening to the audio while they're riding back to the station or to wherever they plan to edit. When choosing a sound bite, remember to listen to the phrasing of the sentence. You want to cut the sound bite at the end of a phrase or the end of a sentence when the voice falls. You don't want to cut someone off midsentence, when the voice is rising.

Because you or someone else will most likely be editing these interviews later, it will be important for your photographer to shoot some cutaways of you (in TV interviews) when the interview is finished. These are essentially shots of you listening to your interviewee. When the photographer is shooting these, re-ask your interviewee one or two of your questions so that you can look at her knowledgeably and listen attentively. Hold the mic as you did for the actual interview. Don't nod your head, shake your head, laugh, smile, or talk while the photographer is shooting these cutaways. Just listen attentively. The editor will use the cutaways in the editing process, and you want him or her to show you listening, not agreeing or disagreeing or laughing at what your interviewee is saying.

You'll conduct most interviews with both you and your interviewee standing or with both of you seated. The point is you want your eyes to be on the same level. If you're interviewing a person in a wheelchair, you should sit in a chair. If you're interviewing children, be extra patient with them, and get down to their eye level by sitting in a chair or getting down on your knees. If you're interviewing an NBA center, you might need to stand on a step stool or have him sit while you stand!

Dressing Appropriately

Let caution and restraint be your wardrobe watchwords. It's very important that you dress modestly and professionally, especially if you're on TV. The only logo you should ever display on your clothing while on the job is that of your station or network. Also, safe and traditional styles are much wiser selections than are fashion-forward and true-to-the-trend choices. Be sure you're not attracting too much attention for what you wear; you want viewers to concentrate on what you say.

If you're going to interview a U.S. senator in her Washington, D.C., office, wear a suit. If you're going to interview a West Texas rancher, jeans and boots would be appropriate. If you're doing a live television report outside in Minnesota in the winter, you might want to wear as much clothing as you can scrounge up. Sometimes, informal attire for celebrities can give the interview a casual feel, and conversely, semi-formal attire for people not usually the subject of interviews might be viewed as a sign of respect. Wear something sensible to work every day, and keep a pair of khaki slacks and some hiking boots in a suitcase by your desk for those times you're sent at a moment's notice to cover a fire or flood or chemical spill.

For both men and women, jewelry should be kept to a minimum. Necklaces, bracelets, and large earrings can be distracting if they reflect light, and they can clang against microphones. Also, busy patterns and pastels tend to create havoc for sensitive cameras.

Though this advice speaks primarily to the on-camera talent among you, please know that radio reporters, photographers, and other field personnel also have standards to meet. Wear clean clothes, without logos, suitable to step into a place of worship if you have to get a quick sound bite from a clergy member.

"Managing" the Interviewee

The camera or audio recorder intimidates many who aren't accustomed to it. And most "regular" people have never been interviewed or been on-camera before. You might need to put your interviewees at ease and "warm them up" by asking a few easy questions to begin interviews. You don't want to start immediately with the toughest question you have, the one most likely to end the interview when you're in confrontational situations. The photographer or sound tech can use this "warm-up" time to double-check that the microphone is working and to help the interviewee get comfortable.

In the case of TV, remind the person you're interviewing to look at you during the interview and to ignore the camera and crew as best he or she can. It will then be up to you to be fair with this person and to establish your own rapport with him. No one wants to look "bad" during an interview or to stumble over words or to lose composure. No one appreciates leading questions. No one wants you to put words in her mouth. And no one likes to feel as though he's been "tricked" by the media. If the interviewee is in a tough spot, she might be anticipating a tough question, so don't wait *too* long to ask it. Often, people will rise to the occasion when you ask them really pointed questions. You don't have to ask hard questions in nasty, vitriolic ways. Overly aggressive, rude, dishonest reporters have left some members of the public with a wary attitude toward the media, and they might be defensive until they get to know you individually as a member of the media in your market. Winning their trust can take some time.

Keep in mind also that not everyone wants to be interviewed and not everyone is good at it. And, because of company policy, some employees are essentially forbidden from talking with members of the media, and they'll be putting their jobs on the line if they talk to you. That's a powerful deterrent for them.

Your goal as a reporter is to inform the people in your community, not to panic or titillate or mislead them. When you're working on your story, you're working to answer the basic journalistic questions of who, what, when, where, why, and how. When you're in the field and conducting interviews, you want to find out all the information you can about the story you're writing. If this is a conflict story, you want to identify spokespersons for all sides of the issue and talk with as many of them as possible.

But keep in mind that you absolutely do *not* want to turn your photographer's gear into a hundred-pound pencil and notepad. You're going to have to listen to this recording later and log all of it, and you don't need or want 60 minutes of interview for two quick, 10-second sound bites. Many questions are for background information, and you can take written notes about those off-camera: information such as how old the person is or how long she's worked for the company. But others are for sound bites, and you want those to be sharply focused, narrow questions done on-camera. You want to ask: "What did you see?" "What did you hear?" "What did you think?" "What did you feel?" "What led you to make that decision?" "What will you accomplish with this new program?" "What bothers you about that?" "How did you . . . ?" "What was it like to be . . . ?" These questions are open-ended and don't presuppose an answer. In contrast, it isn't informative to ask someone, "Isn't it about time we begin to clamp down on these violators?" That leads to a one-word yes or no answer and makes it appear the interviewer already has an opinion about the matter.

If at all possible, you want to avoid questions that result in yes or no answers. For example, if you ask someone, "Is it hot enough today?" his answer might be yes or no. But if you say to him, "The weather's so hot today, how would you describe it?" you'll get a sound bite you can probably use. This is especially true when interviewing children. If you ask a child, "Are you having a good time in preschool?" her answer might be yes or no or simply a nod of the head. But if you ask her, "What do you like best about preschool?" you'll get an answer such as "playing with computers" or "coloring in my coloring book" or "playing with my friends." In some cases, such as stonewalling by a politician or local official, if yes and no are the only answers the individual will provide, it can be effective to edit a string of them together into one long sound bite. Next time, the politician might give you more of an answer.

Also, some people will avoid you because they have something to hide. One controversial style of interviewing is the "ambush," wherein a reporter runs up to someone as he's leaving his home for work, for example, and starts firing questions unannounced. This might be all you can do if the person consistently refuses to agree to a scheduled interview, but it catches the person off guard and the answers might not be particularly informative.

Telling Their Stories

Reporters can relay details more succinctly than "average" people can, because reporters are trained storytellers. What reporters can't relay as effectively are the thoughts, feelings, attitudes, and reactions of the people they interview. That's what sound bites are for. Your interviews are a way to get at what's in a person's mind, expressed in his or her own words. As often as possible you want to look for people who are *telling* this story, rather than people who are telling *about* this story. In other words, look for eyewitnesses you can interview. Look for those people who are directly affected by an action or event. Look for those who can provide the color, the details. Then let these people tell you what they went through, what it was like, what they see as the problem. (We'll have more about this in Chapter 9 as we look at the diamond approach to structuring a package.)

As a reporter, you're the one who can best summarize the *objective* information in the narration track and stand-up of your story. Those you interview are the ones who can best tell the *subjective* information about how they felt, about what they experienced, about how they live on $401 a month. They can tell you the ideas, the reactions, the opinions, the feelings, the fears, the challenges. One of your top priorities as a reporter is to seek subjective sound.

Being Sensitive

Beware of asking "how do you feel" questions when interviewing those in shock or in grief. Members of the audience often *know* how the grief-stricken feel. They can see how the person feels by looking at her face in your video clips, or by remembering a tragedy in their own lives. You'll appear immature at best and insensitive at worst for not knowing how it feels to lose a family member or neighbor or friend to a violent or sudden death. Think of something more informative to ask. "Give sorrow words," said Shakespeare, and many in grief can articulate their loss. But they and those around them might be in a daze, struggling to retain their composure and to understand what you're asking. Kindness and tact and patience will serve you well in these situations. You might want to approach someone in this situation without the camera or recorder. Any crew members with you can stand back a bit while you go up to introduce yourself. You might say, "What's happened is awful. And we're sorry to bother you right now. But we'd like to talk with you about what's happened."

Most people will do it, if you approach them in the right way. It's actually easier to get a "yes" response in person than by phone, so go ahead and approach people in this situation in person. If the person's son has been killed in an automobile accident, you might say, "We're so sorry about what happened. We'd like to talk with you about your son. What was he like? What did he like to do? We'd like to tell our audience what he was like as a person. Do you have any pictures you could share with us?" Or "What happened is a tragedy and I know you must be devastated." Sometimes people will just pick up on such a statement and start talking about what their son was like. If they're comfortable with you, they'll open up. But keep in mind that people know their rights—they know they don't have to talk with you—and if you're standing on their private property, they know they can ask you to leave and expect you to comply.

Be sensitive to people and their situations. Many spot news stories are tragic, traumatic. They involve fires, murders, fatal accidents. Your interviewees are human, and you're in their faces with a microphone and maybe a camera, too. This is their family or livelihood you're asking about. This is their home or business you're in. People are perceptive. If you're sincere and caring, your interviewees will pick up on that. If you're merely feigning sympathy, they'll pick up on that, too. The interviews you've already conducted will have shaped your reputation as a reporter in the community. People will remember you from your previous work. Many will feel they know you and might already like and trust you. Of course, if this is your first interview, you're just starting to build your reputation in the market. How you handle those first few tough interviews will go a long way toward setting your reputation with the viewers or listeners in the market you're in.

Dealing with Death

WRAL's (Raleigh, NC) Tara Lynn knows, as journalists, we all handle death differently. Some days, you simply handle it. Others, you don't. You knock on the door of a family that just lost a loved one and hope your sincerity comes through, all the while trying not to feel like a vulture salivating over tears in an interview that everybody "back in the building" (and even you) knows will be a "home run" interview.

On one such occasion, a young lady had a fight with her sister, demanded to get out of the car and was hit and killed while walking in the middle of a busy street. Tara braced herself to go to the family's home. She had a bad feeling in the pit of her stomach and knew she probably wouldn't handle this assignment very well, because the girl who died was just a few years younger than Tara was.

She knocked on the door. An older gentleman answered. She explained who she was and said she wanted to give the family the opportunity to talk and share memories of the daughter. When he declined, she tried the next avenue, "Does the family have any special

Taken by Jeff Reeves Photography

WRAL's Tara Lynn reports about how people were enjoying an early start to spring.

photos of her you'd like to share?" The man called a woman to the door. Tara again explained who she was, and could tell she was getting a little emotional at this point. The woman told Tara she didn't think it was a good time right now and asked what the reporter's "angle" was. Tara simply told her she was reporting about the accident and wanted to give the family a chance to speak about who this young lady was and share memories of her. At that time, the uncle of the victim walked up to the house and said, "I'll talk to my brother about this," in an angry voice. He stormed in and Tara started to say good-bye, asking the woman if she could give her a hug and asking her to give Tara's condolences to the family. She had tears brimming in her eyes at this point. As she was walking down the stairs, the uncle came back out, "What do you want to know?" he asked in a demanding voice.

Tara couldn't speak. She simply waved him off and heard the woman she was talking with say, "It's okay."

She walked back to the live truck sobbing and continued to cry for a while. What was different about that day than another time she had to knock on a grieving family's door? She doesn't know. Sometimes you handle it and sometimes you don't.

There's a fine balance between empathizing with the people you encounter on a daily basis and not allowing every story to rock you to your core. Just remember, it's not always easy; it's okay to be emotional; it's okay to walk away without an interview and know that you walked away with your integrity.

Make a Human Connection

Carly Swain is a reporter at WITN-7 in New Bern, North Carolina. She says when you're in school to study journalism, your primary goal is to land a job as an anchor, producer, or reporter. But once you get that job, sometimes after only a few weeks in the field, you might discover that you've lost a bit of your humanity.

Somewhere between the autopsy photos at a murder trial and talking to a mother who just lost a child in a wreck, you go home to find what dominates your thoughts isn't the story you told, but that you nearly missed your slot. That's the wake-up call she doesn't want and has yet to have because of one thing her favorite professor told her in college: "Don't just be a reporter. Be a human being." That lesson hit home for her all the more in April of 2011. Her station's satellite truck was set up on the property of a flattened home-care facility, which housed people with physical and mental disabilities. Crews had been there for days, with live shots starting at 5 A.M. and running through the 11 P.M. news. One afternoon, the facility's operator, Ava Morris, came back to see her property; she pointed out where she herself had uncovered two bodies of the patients she called "my babies." Morris agreed to do an interview. She and Carly walked around the property,

Taken by Bob Mackowski

Reporter Carly Swain interviews and consoles tornado victim Ava Morris.

perched on the crumbling foundation, and when Morris told her story, she wept. Her heart was so open and broken, laid out in front of a camera crew, and in that moment, also laid out in front of the young reporter.

Carly learned the importance of simple comforts from her mother, and a hug only seemed right. She held the older woman, both of them shaking, for a couple of minutes. Nearly all of that encounter made air time. It was a strikingly human moment that prompted the station's viewers to ask what they could do for Ava and her lost "babies." Immediately, plans were in place for an on-air fundraiser that later earned upward of $30,000 for the Red Cross in Bertie County. And it was all because Ava Morris shared her story and a reporter with only a couple of years' experience on the job remembered one of the most important lessons she learned in school and reacted naturally to a human-to-human connection.

Show Some Class

Some students must have missed class the day their professor gave the "be a human being" lecture. Being sensitive isn't just for interviews. After a tornado touched down in the viewing area of WMBF (Myrtle Beach, SC) where Brandon Herring works, his station sent a team of reporters and the chief meteorologist to cover the story.

Fortunately, there were no deaths or serious injuries, but there was lots of damage to homes, schools, and so on. Some of the worst damage was to a home the tornado lifted off its foundation and tore apart.

The homeowners graciously allowed the news crew to set up a live shot in the front yard as they worked to find anything salvageable.

Eventually, a crew from the next market over arrived. The reporter from the other station put together a story and went live. After the live shots, WMBF's reporters dispersed to go get more video and stories from other areas.

The meteorologist stayed behind at the satellite truck, and so did the reporter from the other station. His station apparently wasn't asking him for much new content for the next newscast.

A few minutes later, that reporter and his photographer were in the front yard throwing a football to each other. Their truck operator soon joined in on the fun. So there they were having a good ol' time, yards away from where homeowners were dealing with a devastating natural disaster.

The meteorologist was outraged. Afraid his anger would get the best of him if he asked them to stop, he instead apologized to the homeowners on behalf of all the journalists there—and everywhere. It's easy to become jaded in this business. We implore you to remember that you're reporting news—often bad news—about the lives of real people. Journalism ethics demands that we treat our story subjects with respect—both during the interview AND afterward.

As a young reporter, you *will* face similar challenges. There are going to be uncomfortable things you just have to do. When you knock on those doors, some people might slam them in your face. But every once in a while you'll find someone who wants to tell the victim's story, and when you're able to share that story with viewers, it makes your report much more touching and worthwhile. It isn't another crime story that so many people seem desensitized to.

Remember: Compassion is part of fairness. Ordinary people thrust into extraordinary circumstances will be more inclined to let you tell their stories, even after suffering a monumental loss, if you put their grief above the demands of radio or television news. Television conveys emotions more powerfully than any other medium can. People have to trust that you're not going to exploit their loss. The most compelling interviews come from a genuine interest in and empathy for the person, regardless of the subject. Be a person first, then a journalist.

Knowing the Power of Listening

As baseball great Yogi Berra once put it, "You can observe a lot just by watching." You can also learn a lot just by listening. Reporters can sometimes concentrate so much on the questions they're asking that they forget to *listen* to what their interviewees are saying. So this is a reminder to listen to the words your interviewees use. Listen carefully to the language they use to describe something. And remember also to *wait* during those "pregnant pauses." If you ask someone a question and she doesn't answer it right away, stay quiet and continue to look at her. Don't be too eager to jump in with the next question just to fill the silence and to keep the conversation going. Let the person you're interviewing pause and think for a moment, and then let her finish speaking. Sometimes the silences and the pauses themselves are as telling as the answers you thought you'd get. Sometimes the nonanswers and the evasions are more informative than the answers are. In a memorable Barbara Walters interview with one of O. J. Simpson's attorneys, there was an excruciatingly long pause before the attorney finally answered Walters' question about whether he believed O. J. Simpson is an innocent man. He never answered yes or no, but instead made a long statement that sometimes the guilty go free to prove a greater point and to right a greater wrong. As "Nightline" anchor Ted Koppel once said of ABC correspondent John Donvan, "The reason you're a great reporter is because you know when to shut up and just listen."

Checking Your Bias

The people you'll be interviewing are who they are: They look the way they look, and they are the age they are. Don't assume every business tycoon is a man. Don't assume every nurse practitioner is a woman. Don't make similar assumptions about race or age or anything else. Don't derail your interview by making inappropriate opening remarks, such as "I had no idea you would be. . . ." That says more about you than it says about the person you're supposed to interview. Just ask your questions. And don't assume that all men or women or teenagers or Christians or motorcyclists think alike about any given topic. You're interviewing *this* person about what *this* person thinks or saw or experienced.

Marium Chaudhry had been working in Karachi, Pakistan as a current affairs producer for about two years when her bosses asked her to make a documentary about different areas of Karachi and their ethnic groups. She was dreading going to Lyari, a small slum of Karachi known for its violent gangs. Every month or so there are police operations in Lyari and shoot-outs between the police and gang members, shoot-outs the police don't always win. She had been driving past Lyari once when she got stuck in a traffic jam. Two men came up to her car, knocked on her window with a gun and took her cell phone. A seasoned reporter told her if she was going back to that area, she needed to take someone with her who was a resident—for protection.

The man who worked in the office kitchen was from Lyari. He agreed to accompany Marium and the crew. They entered Lyari on foot and walked through the dirty, tiny streets, surrounded by walls riddled with bullet holes. They came to a small open-air shop where men and boys were playing pool. They looked at the journalists suspiciously and then, after talking to the guide, started chatting with the crew about their problems, the people and the police. Marium stood back, letting the reporter do the talking while she scouted for other people they could interview. A group of young girls came walking down the muddy street and surrounded her, asking if she could take their picture. They had just returned from school, in their bright clothes, all smiling. They grabbed Marium's hand and showed her their school. After a brief tour, she returned to find the reporter and camera crew dancing with the boys to loud music and cheering on two men who were playing pool. The guide said that once the people of Lyari accepted outsiders, they were family.

Marium lives in, arguably, the most dangerous country in the world. She has never come face to face with terrorism, but was always afraid she might. But as journalists it's our job to go to places, cover stories and discover truths that we might not even know exist. It's our job to go to dangerous places and find out how dangerous they truly are, what's really going on and how we can report it. When she went into Lyari, she thought she'd be surrounded by guns, gunmen, and possibly the guys who stole her cell phone. But people met her with smiles, music and laughter. She says it's necessary that you try to put your biases aside and go in thinking, "I don't know this story right now but by the time I leave here, I will know—and report—the real thing."

Reading between the Lines

As we alluded to before, people in the spotlight who are frequently interviewed sometimes develop a style of answering questions that allows them to use the media for their own purposes. You might find yourself in the position of asking a politician, for example, what he or she plans to do about a specific situation. Rather than answering the question, the person might respond with a sound bite about a totally different (but favorite and popular) subject and might then leave the room, pleading time constraints. This leaves you in the position of having only the one sound bite the person gave you, a sound bite that is completely off the subject but one the politician wants on the air.

Also, listen to what politicians don't say. The politician might say, "I categorically deny being in Laos on July 17." The truth might be that the senator was in Laos on July 16, and you'll have to read "between the lines" for your answer. So be prepared, be persistent, and pay attention to what the interviewee is saying to you. Remember that there's a difference between persistence and rudeness. You want to be persistent in searching for answers. Being rude won't help you find them. You want to be *assertive but not abrasive*. You'll be working in this market for some time, and you don't want to burn too many bridges before moving on to another market, if that's the career path you follow. You're in a high-profile job. People will remember how you treat them, or someone close to them, or they'll hear about someone else's experience from neighbors or friends. You don't want a bad interview to go viral online, and some people will record you recording them.

"The Get"

In the 1990s, an aggressive style of interview pursuit appeared, and veteran reporters quickly dubbed it "the get." This term describes the aggressive pursuit of someone—the get—for an exclusive interview. In this situation, there's ferocious competition from other reporters in the market or at the other networks.

Jill Rackmill knows how tough it can be to get an interview that everyone is after. She's a producer for ABC's investigative unit. One of the most sought-after groups following the 9/11 terrorist attacks—as much as family members and friends of those who lost their lives and the police officers and firefighters who survived rescue attempts—were the air traffic controllers handling the doomed flights. Jill's knowledge about the profession and professional contacts with controllers helped her get one of the most compelling interviews to come out of the months of coverage that followed the tragedy.

Unknowingly, seven years earlier she began laying the groundwork that resulted in that interview. One of her first assignments as a green 24-year-old was to attend a national convention of air traffic controllers in Tampa, Florida, and gather information about their safety and equipment concerns. At the time, she knew next to nothing about aviation. The only advice she got was that air traffic controllers are an intense bunch with a notoriously high tolerance for stressful situations. She says that as a journalist who shares some of the same personality traits, she was in heaven.

She spent four days interviewing dozens of controllers from across the country. A "tough-guy" attitude permeated the smoke-filled convention rooms as they swapped one harrowing story after another about radar blackouts, weather disturbances, pilot errors, and worst of all, near midair collisions because of faulty equipment.

But beneath all the controllers' tough talk was a passionate and deeply personal commitment to a job in which a single wrong decision could mean life or death for strangers flying at 30,000 feet. Sure, they made a lot jokes about "pushing tin" around the sky and getting paid for "playing a video game" but they realized the gravity of their mission and took pride in their skills and training. The "controllers" were just that: control freaks whose worst nightmare was losing sight of a plane—even for a split second—because of mechanical or human error.

Soon, she began to speak their jargon and laugh at their inside jokes. During the next seven years Jill stayed in touch with many of the controllers. Sometimes she called for off-the-record guidance or background about an aviation story, but often, it was just to say hello.

On September 11, 2001, like most Americans, Jill watched as the horror unfolded live on television. And, like most journalists, she recognized instantly that this would be the biggest story of our time. Because of her past reporting experience, her thoughts immediately turned to the air traffic controllers who were working the hijacked flights. Someone somewhere in a darkened room had watched the events unfold on a radar scope, had lost radio contact with the pilot, had seen the green blip go off course. The controllers *had* to know before the rest of the world that something had gone terribly wrong— but for once, it was beyond their "control" to do anything but watch. The thought was chilling.

Immediately she knew in her heart that she would tell this story. She knew controllers; she understood their mentality. They had a story to tell and she would be the one to tell it. And maybe in some small, small way, she says, she could contribute to our shared national understanding of what had happened.

By 10:30 A.M., she was driving to Boston, where two of the four hijacked flights had originated, with the hope of meeting the controllers directly involved in handling those flights. All of New York City's bridges and tunnels were shut down, and she spent nearly five hours sitting in traffic, listening to radio reports and wondering if the car trip had been such a good idea. The phone lines were jammed, but after repeated efforts, she finally reached one air traffic controller who, in the years since they had met, had been elected to an office in the national union representing controllers. The source was furious, telling her that thousands of people were dead, we were in the middle of an intense law enforcement investigation, many of the nation's controllers were in hysterics and, finally, that her call was *not* appreciated. (Only the source didn't say it quite so nicely.)

Still she drove on. Late that night she arrived at the Boston Air Route Traffic Control Center, which is actually in Nashua, New Hampshire. The facility, which even in normal times is highly secured, was under full alert. Police cars surrounded the building and it appeared that no one was coming or going. So she sat in the bar right next door to the center, hoping some controllers would wander in for a beer. No luck.

She stayed in Boston for five days helping ABC News with other reporting, but she struck out with the Boston controllers. The national union had decided that no controllers would speak to the media.

When she returned to New York, she redoubled her efforts and was one of many journalists trying desperately to get the same story. (In fact, the National Air Traffic Controllers Association logged 475 interview requests.)

Through sheer desire and persistence, long-established contacts, and a sincere respect for the controllers' profession, she finally managed to get an interview with a remarkable woman named Danielle O'Brien, who on the morning of September 11 handled American Flight 77, the plane that hit the Pentagon.

Jill is quick to point out that the Danielle O'Brien interview, which aired on "20/20," was much more than "a get" for her. It was a labor of love, born in a time of tragedy. She says there's no substitute for the hard work of cultivating sources, combined with a true, heartfelt sincerity of wanting to be a responsible and thoughtful conduit for someone else's voice. Through the years, she had gained the respect and trust of air traffic controllers by learning how to speak their language and by consistently honoring their needs for confidentiality when they spoke on background. And most important, she had maintained regular contact with her sources, even when there was no "big get" to get. That's what made the difference.

Conclusion

As a reporter, you'll find there are competing values within your newsroom. Think about them when considering whom to interview and how to go about it. Here's a list of news values that most can agree with: integrity, accuracy, fairness, responsibility, sensitivity, and accountability. But these news values compete and conflict with others that are equally important and valid to your news director: being competitive, being timely, being compelling, being commercially successful in the ratings, being marketable, being promotable. If your organization has a mission statement, it might provide some guidance to you about what's really important at your station. If the mission statement declares, "We will seek every opportunity to destroy our competitors," you'll be moving in one direction with your interviews and your reports. If the mission statement pledges the newsroom "will bring to light the good news, so we can celebrate, and the bad news, so we can work together to correct the problems we encounter," then you'll be going in a different direction and can explain to your interviewees the reasons behind some of your questions.

Get out in your community and listen to what "real" people are saying when they're standing behind you in the grocery store checkout line. You can listen to what people are saying when they're talking with each other at high school basketball games. You can listen to what people are saying when they're talking with each other at the gym, at the gas station, at the table next to yours in the restaurant or coffee bar, or in the chair next to you in the beauty salon or the barber shop. Many people complain that media types rarely go out to community events to find out what average people are up to. You get the idea. Get out there, and wherever you are, listen. You'll learn what's important to people in your community. And you'll increase your list of people in the middle, not just those on the fringe or in "official" positions, whom you can call for interviews. You'll then have enterprise story ideas and interview subjects for your newscast, stories that will differentiate your station, and you, from competitors.

News directors and assignments editors love enterprising reporters who come up with many of their own story ideas. Let people in the community help in this regard. In big markets, the community isn't just the city of license. It might be the surrounding beach communities, or communities of commuters, or certain demographic communities. As a reporter, you're a contact person, a conduit to put informed people in your community on the air so that others can hear their voices, thoughts, and opinions. You have the power to do that. Use it wisely.

Also, don't forget to listen to the people who work at your own station in departments other than news. Ask the receptionist, members of the sales staff, the engineering staff, or the housekeeping staff about news story ideas and interview possibilities. These people have most likely been at your station and in your community much longer than you have. They all have networks of family and friends and business associates. As a group, they're most likely more diverse than your circle of friends. They can help you decide whom to interview and what questions to ask, especially when you're just getting started in a market.

As a tech-savvy young journalist, you have many new ways to find sources to interview. You can google "professors who contributed to presidential candidates in 2012," for example, and find a list of potential sources and contact information about a political campaign. You can use social media to look for contacts and story angles. You can use Twitter to "crowd source" a story. For example, you can put a question on Twitter at the start of the day; your followers can answer with contacts, angles, or opinions; and you, the reporter, get targeted feedback from people with relevant life experience. This works better than random person-on-the-street interviews. It's still important to get out and talk to people in the flesh. But using social media might help you find the type of people you're looking for more efficiently. Reporters have successfully used Internet social media platforms such as Twitter in settings in which government authorities have shut down more traditional means of communication in an effort to censor the truth.

Such was the case in Iran in early 2009. Various media outlets were receiving e-mails, tweets, and camera phone video from protesters angry about what they termed a rigged presidential election. CNN editorial director Richard Griffiths says, "These are not journalists. These are people coming at it with a point of view. So we have to evaluate the material." But, he adds, the social networking sites give CNN and other mainstream media another newsgathering tool. It's then up to the news operation to provide context to what viewers are seeing. All the old rules apply; Griffiths says, "You have to be careful and thorough. The fundamentals of journalism remain the fundamentals of journalism," regardless of the technology you use to gather the material.

We've covered a number of points in this chapter, from planning the interview to managing the interviewee to actively listening to what your interviewee is saying. Here's a quick checklist of things to remember when you're getting ready for and conducting a news interview.

DOs and DON'Ts When Interviewing

Do

- Think ahead.
- Be organized and prepared.
- Research the topic and the people.
- Dress appropriately.
- Be courteous.
- Maintain eye contact.
- Interview in a conversational tone.
- Leave editing space after answers.
- Attribute charges to the person making them.
- Read between the lines (especially when interviewing politicians).
- Listen.

Don't

- Ask yes or no questions, especially of children.
- Be "married" to your questions.
- Give up control.
- Show agreement or disagreement.
- Tell the interviewee what your specific questions will be.
- Forget to ask for clarification.
- Ask really tough questions right away.

Questions

1. What are some of the elements of being prepared?
2. What are some of the mechanics to consider in interviewing?
3. What does it mean to be in control of the interview?
4. What's the objective information in a story and who delivers it?
5. What's the subjective information in a story and who delivers it?
6. Explain "the get."

Writing Radio News

Radio is a fast and widely dispersed mass medium. Because you can listen to the radio in places where you can't watch TV, surf the Web or read a newspaper, it's the medium through which much of the public is first informed when big news breaks. The style of writing is short, simple, conversational. It's writing meant to be heard. And in these days of social media messaging and text alerts, radio reporters might be expected to text message their friends and followers and to post audio, video and photos to their station's Web site.

Listening to radio reports is how many people first heard of the September 11, 2001, terrorist attacks against the United States. Beth Fertig is a reporter for WNYC Radio in New York City. She was two blocks north and one block east of the World Trade Center complex when the first tower collapsed on September 11. She remembers, "I heard this huge rumbling noise like an elevated train above my head. . . . I just held my microphone out to get the sound of it and, after a few seconds, started narrating what I was seeing" (see *Women Journalists at Ground Zero: Covering Crisis* by Judith Sylvester and Suzanne Huffman). Beth worked all day and through the night of September 11. She did a feature that **NPR** (National Public Radio) ran of her tape and colleague Marianne McCune's tape, just recounting their experiences at Ground Zero. Beth's feature was recorded off-site under very trying circumstances. The audio of her story is archived on the WNYC Web site for September 12, 2001. It's titled "Witness to Collapse" and runs 4:14. Listen online at http://www.wnyc.org.

When you listen to that piece or others like it, you'll notice how the background noises in the recorded interviews add to the sense of mood and place. Sound is the driving force of radio, and good-quality audio is very important. The voices of the reporters and anchors, the natural sounds from the scene of events, and the eyewitness sound bites with those who are there are the essential ingredients of radio news.

It's important for the radio journalist to remember that sound itself attracts. Just ask any eavesdropper. Sounds have a romance. Consider how the sound of a cricket at night establishes mood in a radio drama. Or think about the sound of thunder or of rain. (See "Empire of the Air [video recording]: The Men Who Made Radio"; a film by Ken Burns; a production of Florentine Films; produced by Ken Burns, Morgan Wesson, Tom Lewis; written by Geoffrey C. Ward; PBS Home Video; Turner Home Entertainment, 1991, 1996.) Radio is a medium that employs the magic of sound. Radio made America a land of listeners in the early 1920s. And America remains a nation of listeners today, a captive audience commuting to and from work each day.

High-Energy News

Radio news is a high-energy production of highly condensed information. Some radio newscasts might run only four minutes, but contain a dozen to 15 stories.

"Hyperkinetic" best describes radio news on many commercial stations these days. Short, rapid-fire stories, a high story count, and a driving rhythm are what one hears most often on the car radio during morning and evening drive times. Radio news at the top of the hour often precedes traffic and weather reports, sports updates, medical reports, commentary, possibly a syndicated piece or a business report, and then the cycle repeats itself on the quarter-hour and the half-hour. Most stories are only a few seconds long on commercial stations.

KFWB (980 AM) is an all-news radio station in Los Angeles. This station was one of the pioneers of the all-news radio format. Listen online at http://www.kfwb.com. here's a script from one of KFWB's newscasts. It's a straight "reader"—to be read live by the newscast anchor. Its **slug**—or title—is Dog Mauling and it runs :26.

SLUG: DOG MAULING

COPY: 0:26

THE MONTEREY COUNTY DISTRICT ATTORNEY'S OFFICE SAYS CRIMINAL
CHARGES WILL MOST LIKELY NOT BE FILED AGAINST A WOMAN WHOSE
GRANDDAUGHTER WAS MAULED BY THE FAMILY DOG. SPOKESMAN RANDY
TAYLOR SAYS THE ATTACK WAS A SURPRISE AND THERE WERE NO
INDICATIONS OF PREVIOUS NEGLIGENCE. THE GRANDMOTHER WAS WALKING
WITH HER 5-YEAR-OLD GRANDDAUGHTER, HER 10-YEAR-OLD GRANDSON,
AND THE FAMILY'S TWO ROTTWEILERS WHEN THEY WERE STARTLED BY A
LIZARD. IN THE COMMOTION, ONE OF THE DOGS ATTACKED THE GIRL, WHO
DIED HOURS LATER. THE DOGS ARE IN THE IMPOUND.

Notice that the writing is short. It's written to be read out loud. So it's helpful to first say the story in your own words and then write it down.

Technology and Terminology

Technology and terminology can vary from station to station. Radio newsrooms are moving to computer work stations where reporters write stories, record audio clips and arrange the newscast lineup at their own desks. The script formats can vary, too. Some are written in all caps, some in caps and lowercase. In some stations, one story is an entire paragraph. In others, each sentence is a paragraph. Some writers indent; others don't. Some double-space their copy, some single-space. So you have to be flexible and willing to learn. You're going to have to adapt to your station's format, news "style," and audience.

There are two basic kinds of radio news stories: **reader/actualities (RAs)** and **wraps.** An RA will be read by the anchor, who will read the opening copy, play the audio recording of the actuality or sound bite, and then read the closing copy. A wrap includes the anchor lead and a voiced report from the reporter along with an actuality (sound bite); a wrap is the equivalent of a news package in television. In some newsrooms, a reader or "R" means the anchor reads the copy, a sound bite or "S" means the anchor reads a story that includes a sound bite, a voicer or "V" means a reporter delivers a story that includes a sound bite or bites and is prerecorded with the reporter's voice. Most stations are digital now and play the audio cuts out of a computer.

Most radio news stories on commercial stations are *very* short. As a writer, think in terms of 30 seconds for each story; that's about five sentences long. A story that runs 35 seconds will raise an eyebrow at the editor's desk in some stations. Generally speaking, each radio news story opens with a couple of sentences of copy, followed by a sound bite or clip of natural sound that runs between 5 and 10 seconds, and ends with a closing sentence or two. Write the bare minimum you need. You have to be clear, and you also have to be concise. Remember that broadcast writing is "writing for the ear to hear." It's writing that's meant to be spoken out loud, clearly and easily. In radio, words and sounds alone are your tools. You want to use carefully chosen words and sounds to attract and hold a listener's interest and attention. The stories are linear; they go by only once, in a straight line. You want to make the stories interesting for your listeners to hear.

Here's a script Barbara Schwarz wrote for KRLD news radio (1080 AM) in Dallas. The anchor introduced it and the reporter read the copy and played the audio clips. Notice how succinct the writing is, how informative the audio clips are, and how tightly she has woven them into the story.

##GREENER SIDE## 12/23

RECYCLE RECESSION

TOUGH ECONOMIC TIMES MEANS RECYCLABLES AREN'T WORTH WHAT THEY USED TO BE . . . AND RECYCLERS AREN'T MAKING MUCH MONEY. HERE'S 1080 KRLD's BARBARA SCHWARZ WITH THE GREENER SIDE.

[CLIP] RUNS 1:49 WITH SOC

LOOK AT HOW THE PRICES OF OIL AND GOLD HAVE FALLEN . . . PRICES FOR OLD CARDBOARD, GLASS AND METAL HAVE PLUNGED AS WELL. DALLAS RECYCLING'S JILL McHAG SAYS CARDBOARD FETCHED 120 DOLLARS A TON BACK IN MAY.

[CLIP] <FOR THE MONTH OF DECEMBER, THE HIGH SIDE IS 25 DOLLARS.>

THE CITY OF IRVING'S FRAN WITTY SAYS THERE'S PLENTY OF THIS STUFF OUT THERE . . . AND NOT ENOUGH TAKERS.

[CLIP] <DO WE HAVE A GLUT OF THIS? I WOULD SAY THAT THERE IS AN ACCUMULATING GLUT RIGHT NOW BUT AH YOU KNOW IT'S IT'S LIKE ANYTHING ELSE, WHEN YOU'RE IN A RECESSION IT'S CERTAINLY GOING TO AFFECT JUST ABOUT EVERY COMMODITY OUT THERE.>

RECYCLERS HAVE TO MAKE MONEY TOO . . . AND MANY ARE HANGING ON TO TONS OF CORRUGATED CARDBOARD AND GLASS BECAUSE THEY DON'T WANT TO SELL FOR PENNIES ON THE DOLLAR.

[CLIP] <THEY'RE LIKE ANY, LIKE THE AUTO MAKERS TO SOME DEGREE. THEY'RE NOT SUFFERING AS BIG, OR LET'S JUST SAY THEY HAVEN'T GONE TO THE LEGISLATORS YET ABOUT IT, BUT YOU KNOW THEY'RE LOOKING FOR HOMES AND MORE HOMES AND MORE HOMES FOR THE MATERIALS THAT THEY ARE COLLECTING OUT THERE.>

McHAG TELLS ME IT'S NOT JUST RECYCLING COMPANIES HURTING, THIS AFFECTS THE MILLS THAT BREAK THE PRODUCTS DOWN . . . THEY'RE SHUTTING DOWN LINES . . . AND NOW RECYCLERS ARE HAVING TO BE PICKY ABOUT WHAT THEY TAKE.

[CLIP] <AND IF IT'S MIXED LOADS WE NO LONGER HAVE THE STAFF TO BE ABLE TO SORT THROUGH ALL THAT. UNFORTUNATELY WHAT IS HAPPENING IS A LOT OF THOSE LOADS ARE HAVING TO GO TO THE LANDFILL.>

SHE SAYS THE MARKET WILL BOUNCE BACK.

[CLIP] <SOME PEOPLE ARE PREDICTING YOU KNOW THREE TO SIX MONTHS AND SOME OTHERS ARE PREDICTING YOU KNOW IT WON'T COME BACK FOR THE WHOLE YEAR OF 2009 BUT NOBODY REALLY KNOWS, THAT'S THE PROBLEM.>

WITTY EMPHASIZES THE IMPORTANT THING IS TO KEEP RECYCLING . . . NO MATTER WHAT.

[CLIP] <THEY MAY HEAR SOMETHING THAT SOUNDS NEGATIVE OUT THERE IN REGARD TO RECYCLING AND MARKETS AND MILLS, BUT PEOPLE NEED TO KEEP RECYCLING BECAUSE THOSE MARKETS WILL REBOUND AND THEY'LL REBOUND FAIRLY QUICKLY.>

WITH THE GREENER SIDE . . . I'M BARBARA SCHWARZ ON NEWS RADIO 1080 KRLD.

Life in the "Biz"

Radio news keeps its writers and reporters busy. One reporter says, "It's like feeding a shark. You keep feeding it, or it eats you." It's a high-energy job, and you need lots of stamina to do it. The hours are long, and there are constant deadlines. You have to be fast, you have to be organized, and you have to write short.

Writing short is a challenge. It's much tougher than writing long is. It takes practice because there's so much you have to leave out. That increases the burden of deciding what the important details are that you must put in. A radio story is reminiscent of the old "Dragnet" Sergeant Friday statement: "Just the facts, ma'am." There's no time for any more than that.

The radio news writer needs to remember: (1) to write in the present or future tense—the listeners are hearing this news in the current moment; (2) to write with a sense of urgency or a sense of the event itself; and (3) to choose the sound bite with the most "zing." The shorter the sound bite in commercial radio, the better. Three seconds is long enough *if* the bite delivers the message. For example, the opening copy reads "U.S. Senate candidate Ron Kirk is pleased." Then bring up the sound bite: "Boy! Howdy!" Then continue the copy for the story and explain why the candidate is so happy.

As is the case in television, a good lead can make a radio news story. It's what gets the listener's attention in the first place. So think carefully about the words and sounds you're planning to use at the beginning of each story.

It's almost always necessary for the radio news writer to identify the person speaking in the sound bite or actuality. For example, write "Former President Bill Clinton says the devastation in Haiti is almost too much to take in" leading into his sound bite. In radio, the idea is to let the listeners hear the voices and the sounds in the news. It's up to the writer to explain to the listeners why those voices and sounds are important.

Radio reporters work in relative anonymity compared with television reporters, because a lot of radio interviewing is done using the phone. If you can get someone on the phone, you can probably get that person to agree to a recorded interview. Radio reporters can locate possible interview subjects by using city directory cross-referencing systems. If a man is holding children hostage at a day care center in town, the radio reporter can cross-reference the address of the house across the street from the day care center, look up the phone number and name of the people living in that house, call them up, and ask them to describe for the listening audience what activity they can see going on across the street. Most people are willing to do this. If these eyewitnesses don't want their names used on the radio, the reporter can identify the person speaking as a "neighbor" or "someone who lives directly across the street from the day care center."

In a large-market commercial radio newsroom, there are news editors, news reporters, and anchors/personalities. In other radio stations, one or two people might wear all the hats, serving alternately as anchors, reporters, and editors. The news editors are similar to assignments editors and producers in television. They're concerned with the newscast itself, the individual stories in it, and how the stories fit together. They're also consciously concerned with getting and keeping listeners, the audience for their advertisers. The editors both assign stories and produce the newscasts. Producing includes putting the stories in order, lining them up so that they flow together naturally. News editors are interested in story count; the more stories in the newscast, the better. That means the shorter the stories, the better. Editors will edit reporters' copy to make the newscast as a whole flow together; they'll add segue lines to some stories; they'll rewrite and cut where necessary.

Managers assign some radio news reports, some come from the "futures" file, and others come from reporter enterprise. Radio news is a team effort; it's collaboration. Radio reporters have to produce a lot of copy. They have to "crank it out" on deadline. This pressure to produce, to get stories on the air as quickly as possible, is enormous. And it's relentless, because the clock is always ticking.

Radio reporters at commercial stations often have to write four or five different news stories a day. And they often have to write multiple versions of each story, using different audio clips or sound bites. This might add up to 20 different stories a day. That's 20 different pieces of copy. So radio reporters have to be able to write fast and to write a variety of leads for their copy. Their days are long and unpredictable. It's hectic, concentrated work. There are few breaks, and there are no long lunch hours. Radio news reporters often eat while they work, or they eat while they drive. As they drive between assignments, they're rethinking the story they just covered, deciding about definitive leads and choosing which audio clips to use.

Radio reporters rarely know what they're going to be doing as the day progresses. When spot news happens, they go there, and they *stay* until they get the story—whether it's to the river where searchers are looking for a body or to a day care center where a gunman is holding children hostage and police are set up to wait him out. Reporters can call in live reports from the scene of such events using a phone, so most reporters call in their daily radio spot news stories using a landline phone or a cell phone or by e-mailing an MP3 or iTunes file.

To help keep up with what's going on in the world, news editors and reporters listen constantly to the police scanners in the newsroom, and they keep an eye on the television monitors on the wall. The newsroom phones are set on speed dial for calls to the police dispatcher, the sheriff's office, the fire department, or other agencies when a story breaks.

Radio reporters say they love "being in the know" about news events. They have access to the rich, the famous, and the infamous for interviews. They travel and have front row seats at many history-making events. And the job is different every day. After all, the "unexpected" is what makes news. Radio reporters meet world leaders, national leaders, and celebrities. They go places, see people, and have access to people and places they normally wouldn't have. If you like to observe, it's the perfect place to be. It's fun, it's creative, it's interesting, it's exciting, and there's not as much equipment to lug around as in TV. The everyday tools of the trade are portable: a writing pad or laptop computer, audio recorder, cell phone, beeper, and "patch" cords for audio jacks on public address systems. Other helpful equipment includes an umbrella, a ball cap, extra shoes, sunscreen, and a big water jug. (The umbrella can even serve as a makeshift sound booth on the scene.)

NPR–Style News

Although many commercial radio stations do a rapid-fire, high-story-count brand of news with very short stories at the top of the hour, there are alternatives for those who want more. The fastest-growing segment of the radio market is NPR and local affiliates using the same style and format.

Here's the entire script of one morning's two-minute newscast from the NPR station (KUAF, 91.3 FM) at the University of Arkansas in Fayetteville.

GOOD MORNING, THIS IS KUAF. I'M KYLE KELLAMS WITH THIS NEWS . . .

UTILITY COMPANIES SAY MORE THAN ONE-THOUSAND CUSTOMERS ARE STILL WITHOUT POWER A WEEK AFTER A DEVASTATING ICE STORM HIT NORTHWEST ARKANSAS. SOUTHWESTERN ELECTRIC POWER COMPANY SAYS 99 PERCENT OF CUSTOMERS HAVE HAD POWER RESTORED. SWEPCO OFFICIALS ARE ASKING THOSE STILL WITHOUT POWER TO CONTACT THE COMPANY. NEARLY 11-HUNDRED UTILITY WORKERS FROM SEVERAL DIFFERENT STATES ARE STILL WORKING ON DOWNED LINES AND SNAPPED POLES IN ISOLATED PARTS OF WASHINGTON COUNTY. THE SWEPCO REPORTING LINE IS XXX-XXX-XXXX.

THE COST OF THE ICE STORM TO BENTON COUNTY COULD BE IN EXCESS OF FOUR MILLION DOLLARS. COUNTY JUDGE DAVE BISBEE TOLD JUSTICES OF THE PEACE LAST NIGHT THAT HE WANTS 2-MILLION DOLLARS ALLOCATED SOON FOR TREE AND LIMB REMOVAL. REPRESENTATIVES FROM THE FEDERAL EMERGENCY MANAGEMENT AGENCY TOURED THE HARDEST HIT PARTS OF THE COUNTY YESTERDAY. OFFICIALS WITH FEMA SAY THEY SHOULD HAVE A DETERMINATION ABOUT POSSIBLE FUNDS FOR STORM CLEANUP WITHIN A WEEK.

AT LEAST ONE SITTING REPUBLICAN LEGISLATOR IS OFFERING PUBLIC SUPPORT OF GOVERNOR MIKE BEEBE'S PROPOSED CIGARETTE-TAX INCREASE. REPRESENTATIVE RICK GREEN OF VAN BUREN ATTENDED A RALLY YESTERDAY IN SUPPORT OF THE 56-CENT TAX HIKE TO PAY FOR A STATEWIDE TRAUMA SYSTEM IN ARKANSAS. THE GOVERNOR SAYS HIS PLAN WOULD RAISE 88-MILLION DOLLARS ANNUALLY TO PAY FOR THE TRAUMA SYSTEM. THE MEASURE REQUIRES SUPPORT FROM 75 OF THE 100 MEMBERS OF THE ARKANSAS HOUSE TO PASS IN THAT CHAMBER. THERE ARE 28 REPUBLICANS IN THE HOUSE, BUT SPEAKER ROBBIE WILLS, A DEMOCRAT, SAYS HE'S CONFIDENT THE 75 VOTES FOR PASSAGE CAN BE FOUND.

ARKANSAS' SALES TAX COLLECTIONS ARE DOWN, BUT STILL BETTER THAN THE FORECAST. THE STATE'S DEPARTMENT OF FINANCE AND ADMINISTRATION SAYS SALES TAX NUMBERS FOR JANUARY WERE NEARLY 23-MILLION DOLLARS BELOW COLLECTIONS A YEAR AGO. HOWEVER, THE 452-MILLION DOLLARS IS STILL 7-MILLION DOLLARS ABOVE THE FORECAST. STATE OFFICIALS SAY BETTER-THAN-EXPECTED CORPORATE INCOME TAX FIGURES HELPED PUSH THE JANUARY TOTAL HIGHER THAN EXPECTED.

THE UNIVERSITY OF ARKANSAS GYMNASTICS TEAM IS LEAPING TO THE SQUAD'S HIGHEST RANKING IN PROGRAM HISTORY. THE RAZORBACKS ARE TIED WITH GEORGIA FOR THIRD IN THE LATEST GYMINFO COACHES POLL. ARKANSAS IS 5-1 THIS YEAR AND TRAILS ONLY UTAH AND UCLA IN THE NATIONAL POLL. ARKANSAS' NEXT TWO MEETS ARE ON THE ROAD AGAINST RANKED OPPONENTS. THE RAZORBACKS FACE NUMBER 31 KENTUCKY FRIDAY AND THE FIFTH-RANKED AUBURN TIGERS ON FEBRUARY 13TH.

MORE SUNSHINE IS IN THE FORECAST TODAY AND AFTERNOON HIGHS ARE EXPECTED TO REACH THE UPPER FORTIES FOR MOST OF THE REGION. CLEAR CONDITIONS ARE EXPECTED TO CONTINUE TONIGHT WITH LOWS IN THE LOWER TEENS.

IT'S 25 MINUTES BEFORE SEVEN, I'M KYLE KELLAMS FOR KUAF.

Kyle says, "Our daily newscasts are no more than 2½ minutes long so we're limited in terms of the information we can present and leave the longer-form news for our weekend news magazines. We rarely use wrecks, fires, or crime stories . . . those are well covered by other outlets in the market. We tend to concentrate on education, environment, business and political news. We also try to do a good job of presenting news in the morning that's useful for the listener; 'today voters in Fort Smith go to the polls to determine the fate of a penny sales tax . . .' or '. . . a public hearing on a new waste water treatment plant in Fayetteville will be held tonight. . . .' We don't often do kickers or smilers to end a 'cast but do often end with a brief university or local sports bit. Almost all of our news deals with the listening area . . . on slow days we'd include items from other parts of Arkansas. We use social media to share stories on Facebook and Twitter and send out daily teases on both services as well. I certainly use Twitter to keep an eye on what events/stories are breaking or are scheduled. Facebook, too. Radio news is perhaps as important as ever . . . at least the longer form news we do. Public radio is the only broadcast medium to actually gain audience over the past decade and with newspapers shrinking, the responsibility is with us more than ever to dig deeper and provide quality, reasoned coverage of news. I think more people seek out validation of opinions rather than information than ever before. We need to be there for the people still wanting to make decisions on their own."

Sam Baker is an assistant news director and morning host for KERA (90.1 FM), an NPR station in Dallas, Texas. He writes his own scripts and anchors the station's "Morning Edition" program. Here are two versions of a story he wrote about a nationwide system that's been developed to help find missing children.

> YOU'VE HEARD A NUMBER OF RECENT STORIES ABOUT THE SUCCESS OF THE AMBER ALERT PROGRAM IN FINDING CHILDREN IN OTHER STATES. BUT THE TEXAS OFFICER WHO HELPED SET UP THE PROGRAM WORRIES THAT AUTHORITIES ACROSS THE COUNTRY MIGHT OVERUSE THE RESCUE TOOL. TARRANT COUNTY SHERIFF DEE ANDERSON TOLD THE DALLAS MORNING NEWS THE PLAN WORKS, BUT IT'S NOT EASY. HE SAID AGENCIES NEED TO UNDERSTAND THE POWER OF IT, AND THAT IF YOU USE THE AMBER PLAN TOO OFTEN, YOU CAN LOSE IT. ANDERSON WAS SPOKESMAN FOR ARLINGTON POLICE WHEN THE ALERT PROGRAM WAS CREATED TO TRY TO HELP FIND NINE-YEAR-OLD AMBER HAGERMAN. AUTHORITIES LATER FOUND HER DEAD. NORTH TEXAS POLICE HAVE ISSUED ABOUT 50 ALERTS SINCE 1997, AND HAVE CREDITED THE PLAN WITH SAVING EIGHT CHILDREN FROM HARM.

> THE AMBER ALERT SYSTEM THAT BEGAN IN TEXAS IS BEING CREDITED FOR THE SAFE RETURN OF TWO TEENAGERS IN CALIFORNIA. THE STATE IMPLEMENTED THE SYSTEM LESS THAN A MONTH AGO, AND USED IT FOR ONLY THE SECOND TIME YESTERDAY TO ANNOUNCE THE GIRLS HAD BEEN ABDUCTED AT GUNPOINT FROM A REMOTE AREA OF LANCASTER, CALIFORNIA. AUTHORITIES FOUND THEM LATER THE SAME DAY. AN AMBER PROGRAM SPOKESMAN IN THE D-F-W AREA SAID THE ALERT SYSTEM HAS BEEN CREDITED WITH THE RETURN OF 17 YOUNG PEOPLE ACROSS THE COUNTRY SINCE 1997.

"Most stories in a newscast begin with what happened. For example, 'The mayor resigned today' or 'The Texas Legislature today will consider an increase in Medicaid funding.' The following story could have begun as follows:

"'The National Trust for Historic Preservation has chosen Fort Worth as one of America's Dozen Distinctive Destinations for 2009.'

"Instead, I backed into the 'what' to clearly explain why it was important . . .

> EACH YEAR, THE NATIONAL TRUST FOR HISTORIC PRESERVATION PUTS TOGETHER A LIST OF WHAT IT CALLS AMERICA'S DOZEN DISTINCTIVE DESTINATIONS. THEY'RE COMMUNITIES THAT OFFER CULTURAL AND

RECREATIONAL EXPERIENCES DIFFERENT FROM THE TYPICAL VACATION
SPOT. FORT WORTH MADE THIS YEAR'S LIST. THE TRUST DESCRIBED FORT
WORTH AS A "CITY OF COWBOYS AND CULTURE" WITH THE STOCKYARDS;
WORLD-RENOWNED ART MUSEUMS; THE NATIONAL COWGIRL HALL OF FAME;
AND THE ENTERTAINMENT DOWNTOWN AT SUNDANCE SQUARE. OTHER 2009
"DISTINCTIVE DESTINATIONS" INCLUDE ATHENS, GEORGIA; SANTA FE, NEW
MEXICO; AND LAKE GENEVA, WISCONSIN. . . .

###

"Along with the verb 'to be,' I also try as much as possible to avoid the word 'that.' It's a convenient crutch. You don't need it most of the time."

National Public Radio stations feature long-form, thoughtful pieces that might run eight to 10 minutes in length. If NPR reporters can make it a good "sound" story, they can turn in a long piece with lengthy interviews and lots of natural sound. For example, a bridge in Austin, Texas, has become known for the colony of bats that lives in its girders. A reporter for NPR once did an eight-minute piece about the bats and the bridge. He included the natural sound of the bats beating their wings as they flew out of the bridge at sunset, interviews with people who had come to watch the bats fly out, interviews with bat experts, and interviews at the bridge with T-shirt vendors selling a variety of books, bat caps, and other bat paraphernalia. The reporter was able to create a "word picture" of the scene for radio listeners. Such word pictures are what radio journalists strive to create. Good writing is in the details, the language, and the choice of words.

Adam Hochberg is an award-winning news correspondent for NPR. He says, "The most important radio writing advice I have is to write conversationally. Never use a word in a radio script that you wouldn't say in normal conversation. (Yes, that means striking all the "journal-eeze" from your scripts such as "blaze," "suspect," "lawmakers," "amid," "probe," etc.) Write short easy-to-understand sentences. Pretend you're explaining the story to a friend . . . or to your Mom. I know some reporters who actually begin reading their scripts by saying 'Mom' or the name of a friend, as in, 'Mom, you can't park on Main Street anymore.' Of course, they edit the word 'Mom' out of the audio file before they broadcast their finished story. But the technique makes it almost impossible to write a sentence like, 'Mom, a revision of the city's motor vehicle ordinances has expanded enforcement zones along heavily traveled highways.' You can almost see the perplexed look on your mother's face when you read that out loud! As for the importance of radio (and other ways we distribute audio material, such as podcasts and live streams), audio remains the most intimate of all media. We invite radio into parts of our lives where television is too intrusive and the web is impractical—our

Taken by Robert Willett/News & Observer

Adam Hochberg (crouching, left foreground) joins a throng of reporters interviewing former presidential candidate John Edwards.

cars, our bedside tables; some people even have radios in their showers. Radio is inexpensive, portable, and easy to use; everybody from my four-year-old daughter to my 80-year-old mother can operate it without any practice or training. And from a broadcast journalist's perspective, you can be on-the-air live from anywhere just by making a simple phone call back to the studio."

Here are five examples of Adam's work. In the scripts, SFX stands for "sound effects." Some people write it as NAT or NAT SD for "natural sound." The first two scripts are 35-second news spots. Adam says, "These scripts aren't pretty; typically, they're just thrown together in a hurry and filed from the field."

Next is a standard three-minute news story filed from the field about Queen Elizabeth's visit to Virginia. (Here's a link to the audio of the finished story: http://www.npr.org/templates/story/story .php?storyId=10000214)

That's followed by an in-depth feature about jobs and the economy. (Audio: http://www.npr.org/templates/story/story.php?storyId =103380942)

And finally, there's what NPR calls a "2-way," which is a live conversation between an anchor and reporter about a breaking news story. Writers draft out a rough script for these, so that the anchor and reporter have a rough idea what each other is going to say. But the conversation is then ad-libbed based on this rough outline. (Audio: http://www.npr.org/templates/story/story.php?storyId=106131971)

Adam says, "NPR stories are mixed by a producer or engineer in Washington, using raw audio gathered by the reporter. So you'll see detailed mixing instructions on some of these."

VIRGINIA TECH1

HOCHBERG

TRT: 0:35

OFFICIALS AT VIRGINIA TECH SAY THE GUNMAN IN MONDAY'S SHOOTING HAD SEVERAL PREVIOUS ENCOUNTERS WITH CAMPUS POLICE. SEUNG-HUI CHO (SUNG HE CHO) HAD CAUSED SO MUCH CONCERN ON CAMPUS THAT HE WAS TAKEN TO A MENTAL HEALTH FACILITY IN 2005. NPR'S ADAM HOCHBERG REPORTS FROM BLACKSBURG.

IN A TWO MONTH PERIOD IN LATE 2005, CHO WAS THE SUBJECT OF TWO COMPLAINTS FROM WOMEN ON VIRGINIA TECH'S CAMPUS—WHO ACCUSED OF HIM HARASSING THEM WITH WHAT THE POLICE CHARACTERIZE AS "ANNOYING" CALLS AND EMAILS. AT ABOUT THE SAME TIME, A FRIEND OF CHO'S TOLD POLICE CHO SEEMED SUICIDAL. CHO WAS TAKEN TO A MENTAL HEALTH FACILITY, BUT RETURNED TO CAMPUS SHORTLY AFTERWARD. THE HEAD OF THE UNIVERSITY'S COUNSELING SERVICE SAYS HARASSMENT COMPLAINTS ON CAMPUS ARE NOT ESPECIALLY UNUSUAL. HE SAYS IF UNIVERSITY OFFICIALS HAD ANY WARNING ABOUT POSSIBLE VIOLENCE, THEY WOULD HAVE ACTED TO PREVENT IT.

ADAM HOCHBERG, NPR NEWS, BLACKSBURG, VIRGINIA.

VIRGINIA TECH2

HOCHBERG

TRT: 0:35

POLICE IN BLACKSBURG, VIRGINIA SAY THE GUNMAN WHO KILLED 33 PEOPLE MONDAY PREPARED A WRITTEN MANIFESTO THEY RECEIVED TODAY. THE PACKAGE OF DOCUMENTS WAS RECEIVED BY NBC NEWS. NPR'S ADAM HOCHBERG REPORTS FROM BLACKSBURG.

ACCORDING TO POLICE, THE SHOOTER IN BLACKSBURG—SEUNG-HUI CHO (SUNG HE CHO)—PREPARED A PACKAGE OF MATERIAL AND SENT IT TO NBC NEWS. POLICE RELEASED FEW DETAILS ABOUT THE PACKAGE—EXCEPT TO SAY IT CONTAINED WRITINGS AND IMAGES. ACCORDING TO NBC, THE PACKAGE WAS MAILED BETWEEN THE TWO SHOOTINGS MONDAY

MORNING—AFTER TWO PEOPLE WERE KILLED IN A VIRGINIA TECH
DORMITORY, BUT BEFORE CHO OPENED FIRE IN A CLASSROOM BUILDING . . .
KILLING 31 PEOPLE INCLUDING HIMSELF. NBC TURNED THE INFORMATION
OVER TO THE FBI. THE NETWORK CHARACTERIZED THE MATERIAL AS
DISTURBING—AND SAID IT INCLUDED A WRITTEN COMMUNICATION,
PHOTOGRAPHS, AND A VIDEO. VIRGINIA TECH OFFICIALS AND STATE
POLICE CUT SHORT A SCHEDULED NEWS CONFERENCE ON THE
INVESTIGATION—SAYING THEY NEEDED TO ANALYZE THE NEWLY RECEIVED
MATERIAL.

ADAM HOCHBERG, NPR NEWS, BLACKSBURG, VIRGINIA.

QUEEN VISITS

HOCHBERG

TRT: 3:03

ANCHOR: QUEEN ELIZABETH THE SECOND WILL TOUR JAMESTOWN AND
WILLIAMSBURG, VIRGINIA TODAY (FRIDAY)—PART OF A WEEKLONG STATE
VISIT THAT WILL ALSO INCLUDE STOPS AT THE WHITE HOUSE AND THE
KENTUCKY DERBY. YESTERDAY, THOUSANDS OF VIRGINIANS TURNED OUT TO
CATCH A GLIMPSE OF THE BRITISH MONARCH AS SHE—AND HER HUSBAND
PRINCE PHILIP—MADE THEIR FIRST U.S. APPEARANCE SINCE 1991. FROM
WILLIAMSBURG, NPR'S ADAM HOCHBERG REPORTS.

THIS WEEK'S VISIT MARKS THE THIRD TIME QUEEN ELIZABETH HAS BEEN
TO VIRGINIA DURING HER FIFTY-THREE YEAR REIGN. THAT'S MORE THAN
SHE'S VISITED ANY OTHER STATE—PERHAPS SUGGESTING SOMETHING OF A
FASCINATION WITH THIS FORMER COLONY THAT PLAYED SUCH A PIVOTAL
ROLE BOTH IN THE EXPANSION OF THE BRITISH EMPIRE, AND IN THE
AMERICANS' EVENTUAL REBELLION AGAINST IT. (SFX: SNEAK UP CARRIAGE
SOUND UNDER) BUT EVEN IN THIS STATE THAT WAS HOME TO
REVOLUTIONARY LEADERS LIKE PATRICK HENRY AND THOMAS JEFFERSON,
VIRGINIANS PROVED YESTERDAY THEY'RE STILL INFATUATED WITH ROYALTY.

CUT #1/WHITE: HERE SHE COMES, HERE SHE COMES. OKAY, AND THERE'S
PHILIP; OH GOOD, SHE'S ON OUR SIDE, PHILIP'S ON THE OTHER SIDE.
YEA, YOHOO (FADE UNDER) :11

VIRGINIANS SUSAN AND JERRY WHITE JOINED THOUSANDS OF PEOPLE
WHO LINED A WILLIAMSBURG STREET AS THE QUEEN AND PRINCE PHILIP
RODE PAST IN A HORSE-DRAWN CARRIAGE.

SFX: BRING UP CARRIAGE SOUND SO WE HEAR THE HORSE WHINNEY, AND A COUPLE OF HOOF BEATS, THEN FADE UNDER.

THE ROYAL RIDE LASTED LESS THAN TEN MINUTES, BUT YVONNE HABIS— WHO CAME FROM TAMPA TO SEE IT—SAYS SHE'LL ALWAYS REMEMBER HER BRIEF GLIMPSE OF THE QUEEN.

CUT #2/HABIS: IT'S THE CHANCE OF A LIFETIME. EVERY DAY, YOU DON'T SEE THE QUEEN OF ENGLAND COME DOWN THE STREET, AND IT WAS JUST SUCH A WONDERFUL OPPORTUNITY. :07

SFX: FADE OUT CARRIAGE SOUND UNDER THIS TRACK:

THE ROYAL VISIT TO VIRGINIA IS TIMED TO COINCIDE WITH THE FOUR-HUNDREDTH ANNIVERSARY OF JAMESTOWN—THE FIRST PERMANENT ENGLISH SETTLEMENT IN AMERICA. IN A SPEECH YESTERDAY TO THE STATE LEGISLATURE, THE QUEEN PRAISED WHAT SHE CALLED THE "INGENUITY AND IDEALISM" THAT LED TO THE SETTLEMENT'S FOUNDING IN 1607— UNDER THE REIGN OF KING JAMES-THE-FIRST—ELIZABETH'S GREAT-GREAT-GREAT, GREAT-GREAT-GREAT, GREAT-GREAT-GREAT-GREAT GRANDFATHER.

CUT #3/QUEEN: WE CAN SEE IN THAT EVENT THE ORIGINS OF A SINGULAR ENDEAVOR. THE BUILDING OF A GREAT NATION, FOUNDED ON THE ETERNAL VALUES OF DEMOCRACY AND EQUALITY, BASED ON THE RULE OF LAW AND THE PROMOTION OF FREEDOM. :16

THE QUEEN ALSO MADE NOTE OF A RECENT EVENT IN VIRGINIA—LAST MONTH'S SHOOTING AT VIRGINIA TECH THAT LEFT THIRTY-THREE PEOPLE DEAD. YESTERDAY, ELIZABETH MET PRIVATELY WITH A GROUP OF TECH STUDENTS. AND DURING HER PUBLIC REMARKS, SHE EXPRESSED CONDOLENCES TO THE VICTIMS' FAMILIES AND FRIENDS.

CUT #4/QUEEN: ON BEHALF OF THE PEOPLE OF THE UNITED KINGDOM, I EXTEND MY DEEPEST SYMPATHIES AT THIS TIME OF SUCH GRIEF AND SORROW. :08

TODAY, THE QUEEN IS SCHEDULED TO TAKE A WHIRLWIND HISTORY TOUR OF JAMESTOWN AND WILLIAMSBURG—SIMILAR TO ONE SHE TOOK DURING A VISIT HERE FIFTY YEARS AGO. BUT YESTERDAY SHE RECALLED THAT THAT 1957 TRIP CELEBRATED THE ACCOMPLISHMENTS ONLY OF THE EUROPEAN SETTLERS. SHE PRAISED RECENT EFFORTS TO INCLUDE THE CONTRIBUTIONS OF AFRICANS AND NATIVE AMERICANS IN WHAT SHE CALLED A MORE CANDID REFLECTION OF THE JAMESTOWN LEGACY.

ADAM HOCHBERG, NPR NEWS, WILLIAMSBURG, VIRGINIA.

SURVIVAL JOBS

HOCHBERG

TRT: 3:58

ANCHOR: AS THE RECESSION DRAGS ON, WE'VE HEARD A LOT ABOUT THE THIRTEEN MILLION AMERICANS WHO ARE UNEMPLOYED. BUT THERE ALSO ARE PEOPLE WHO ARE UNDER-EMPLOYED . . . WORKING JOBS WELL BELOW THEIR QUALIFICATIONS. AS OPPORTUNITIES DRY UP IN FIELDS LIKE BANKING AND TECHNOLOGY, MID-CAREER PROFESSIONS HAVE BEEN FORCED TO TAKE ENTRY-LEVEL POSITIONS AT PLACES LIKE RESTAURANTS AND STORES. NPR'S ADAM HOCHBERG TALKED WITH A FEW IN NORTH CAROLINA.

FIFTY YEAR OLD JOEL LUECK HAS TWO COLLEGE DEGREES, TWO DECADES EXPERIENCE IN INFORMATION TECHNOLOGY, AND UNTIL LAST YEAR, WORKED AS A NETWORK ENGINEER FOR ONE OF THE WORLD'S LARGEST TELECOMMUNICATIONS COMPANIES. (SFX: BEGIN SNEAKING UP CASH REGISTER SOUND AT THE TOP OF CUT #1) BUT LATELY, LUECK'S CAREER TOOK A SHARP DETOUR.

CUT #1/LUECK: OKAY, TOTAL IS 34.08. PLASTIC OKAY? :04

SFX: ROLL SUPERMARKET SOUND UNDER THE NEXT THREE TRACKS:

IN JANUARY, LUECK TOOK A PART-TIME JOB AS A LATE-NIGHT SUPERMARKET CASHIER—WORKING A CHECK-OUT AT A HARRIS-TEETER STORE NEAR HIS HOME IN CARY, NORTH CAROLINA.

CUT #2/LUECK: AND YOU SAVED $12.31 USING YOUR VIC CARD THIS ORDER. THANK YOU. :05

THIS, OF COURSE, WAS NOT THE KIND OF JOB LUECK WAS LOOKING FOR AFTER HE WAS LAID OFF FROM HIS TELECOM POSITION LAST SUMMER. BUT AFTER SEARCHING FRUITLESSLY FOR SOMETHING IN HIS FIELD, HE DECIDED WORKING A CASH REGISTER IS BETTER THAN NOT WORKING AT ALL.

CUT #3/LUECK: I THINK LIKE MOST PEOPLE I WAS THINKING, "ME WORKING IN A GROCERY STORE?" BUT NOT KNOWING HOW LONG THE UNEMPLOYMENT MIGHT BE OR HOW LONG IT WAS GOING TO TAKE FOR BUSINESSES TO RECOUP, I DECIDED TO GO FOR IT. :13

TO PUT IT MILDLY, LUECK'S INCOME TOOK A BIG DROP WHEN HE TRANSITIONED FROM THE TELECOM INDUSTRY TO CHECK-OUT LANE NUMBER FOUR. AT NORTEL NETWORKS, WHERE HE USED TO WORK, HE EARNED MORE THAN EIGHTY-THOUSAND DOLLARS A YEAR. THE SUPERMARKET JOB PAYS EIGHT DOLLARS AN HOUR.

CUT #4/LUECK: I GUESS YOU WOULD SAY IT'S HUMBLING, BUT YOU END UP DOING WHAT YOU HAVE TO DO TO MAKE ENDS MEET. I COULD BE DOING NOTHING AT HOME, OR I COULD COME IN AND MAKE 100 BUCKS IN A WEEK. IT'S NOT A LOT, BUT IT HELPS BRIDGE THE GAP. :14

SFX: FADE OUT SUPERMARKET SOUND.

EMPLOYMENT EXPERTS SAY THOUSANDS OF OTHER LAID-OFF PROFESSIONALS ARE STILL DOING WHAT JOEL LUECK DID—TAKING WHAT ARE KNOWN AS "SURVIVAL JOBS" TO MAKE ENDS MEET. DAMIAN BERKEL RUNS "PROFESSIONALS IN TRANSITION," AN UNEMPLOYMENT SUPPORT GROUP.

CUT #4/BERKEL: IT CAN BE, YOU KNOW, WORKING WITH MY BROTHER-IN-LAW ON THIS, THAT, OR THE OTHER THING. OR ONE MEMBER OF PROFESSIONALS IN TRANSITION WENT TO WORK AT THE UPS STORE. PEOPLE DO WHAT THEY HAVE TO DO TO KEEP THE ROOF OVER THEIR HEAD. :15

BERKEL SAYS SURVIVAL JOBS NOT ONLY BRING IN MONEY, BUT SOME ALSO PROVIDE BENEFITS, AND HE'S SEEN A FEW CASES WHERE THEY'VE LED TO PERMANENT EMPLOYMENT. ON THE OTHER HAND, HE SAYS EXPERIENCED PROFESSIONALS MAY STRUGGLE EMOTIONALLY WITH ACCEPTING ENTRY-LEVEL POSITIONS. AND HE WARNS THAT WORKING A SURVIVAL JOB CAN TAKE TIME AWAY FROM SEARCHING FOR A BETTER ONE.

CUT #5/BERKEL: I THINK THAT YOU WILL FIND A JOB MUCH QUICKER IF YOU ARE SPENDING 35 TO 40 HOURS A WEEK ON YOUR JOB SEARCH. AND IF YOU PEPPER THAT WITH PART-TIME POSITIONS, A FULL-TIME JOB SEARCH IS GOING TO BE COMPROMISED. :16

CUT #6/SCHWARTZ: LET ME JUST GET SOME INFORMATION, AND I'LL FAX IT TO YOU RIGHT AWAY. (FADE UNDER, THEN CROSSFADE TO FLOWER SHOP SOUND UNDER THIS TRACK) :03

NANCY SCHWARTZ SAYS SHE WAS AWARE OF THE PROS AND CONS BEFORE SHE TOOK HER PART-TIME JOB AT THIS CARY FLOWER SHOP. BUT SHE'D BEEN UNEMPLOYED FOR MORE THAN A YEAR, AFTER LOSING HER MANAGEMENT POSITION AT HABITAT FOR HUMANITY. AND SHE SAYS SHE WAS GETTING DESPERATE FOR MONEY.

CUT #7/SCHWARTZ: I MEAN I NEVER THOUGHT IT WOULD COME TO THAT, BUT IT DID. SO I SORT OF HAD TO JUST TALK TO MYSELF ABOUT HOW IT'S OKAY. YOU KNOW I DIDN'T WANT TO DO IT, BUT I ALSO KNEW I REALLY DIDN'T HAVE ANY OTHER OPTIONS AT THAT MOMENT :12

SCHWARTZ NOW MAKES ABOUT NINE HUNDRED DOLLARS A MONTH TAKING ORDERS, SORTING FLOWERS, AND WAITING ON CUSTOMERS. THAT'S NOT ENOUGH TO MEET HER EXPENSES, BUT AT LEAST SHE'S NOT DRAWING DOWN HER SAVINGS AS QUICKLY. AND SHE'S TRYING TO FOCUS ON THE POSITIVE.

CUT #8/SCHWARTZ: YOU KNOW ALTHOUGH I DON'T SEE, YOU KNOW, BEING HERE FOREVER, I REALLY LIKE THE PEOPLE A LOT, AND I LOVE THE FLOWERS. AND YOU KNOW, WHEN YOU DON'T HAVE A FULL-TIME JOB, FEELING LIKE YOU'RE CONTRIBUTING IS REALLY, REALLY IMPORTANT. :11

SFX: FADE OUT FLOWER SHOP SOUND UNDER THIS TRACK.

SCHWARTZ CONTINUES TO LOOK FOR SOMETHING MORE SUITED TO HER EDUCATION AND EXPERIENCE. AT THE MOMENT, THOUGH, SHE SAYS SHE HAS NO STRONG PROSPECTS, SO SHE'S THOUGHT ABOUT PICKING UP ANOTHER PART-TIME POSITION—LIKE WAITING TABLES AT NIGHT. SHE'S COME TO REALIZE THAT AT LEAST IN THE NEAR TERM, HER CAREER MAY REMAIN IN SURVIVAL MODE.

ADAM HOCHBERG, NPR NEWS, CHAPEL HILL.

SANFORD 2-WAY

HOCHBERG

TRT: 4:10

ANCHOR: SOUTH CAROLINA GOV. MARK SANFORD REVEALED MORE ABOUT HIS EXTRAMARITAL AFFAIR YESTERDAY. SANFORD ADMITTED TO SEEING HIS MISTRESS FIVE TIMES IN THE PAST YEAR AND ALSO SAID THAT HE, IN HIS WORDS, "CROSSED THE LINE" WITH OTHER WOMEN DURING HIS MARRIAGE. THE REVELATIONS DID LITTLE TO BOLSTER THE GOVERNOR'S EFFORTS TO STAY IN OFFICE. NPR'S ADAM HOCHBERG JOINS US FROM COLUMBIA.

ADAM, TELL US MORE ABOUT WHAT THE GOVERNOR SAID YESTERDAY.

(((DID A REVEALING INTERVIEW WITH THE ASSOCIATED PRESS . . . MORE THAN THREE HOURS OF INTERVIEWS OVER TWO DAYS . . .. HE FILLED IN DETAILS ABOUT HIS AFFAIR. MULTIPLE MEETINGS WITH HIS GIRLFRIEND OVER THE PAST YEAR—SOME OF THEM IN ARGENTINA, SOME OF THEM IN

NEW YORK. ADMITTED HAVING INAPPROPRIATE RELATIONSHIPS WITH
OTHER WOMEN DURING HIS TWENTY YEARS MARRIAGE, THOUGH HE SAYS
HE DIDN'T GO AS FAR IN THOSE RELATIONSHIPS AS HE DID IN THIS MOST
RECENT ONE . . . . CALLED HIS GIRLFRIEND HIS SOULMATE; DESCRIBED
HIS AFFAIR AS "A LOVE STORY" . . . . LEFT LITTLE DOUBT THAT HIS HEART
IS WITH THE OTHER WOMAN.)))

2. WHY DOES THE GOVERNOR KEEP GIVING INTERVIEWS?

(((UNUSUAL FOR A POLITICIAN TO DO SO. HELD A NEWS CONFERENCE
WEDNESDAY, TOOK MORE QUESTIONS FRIDAY AND MONDAY, DID THIS AP
INTERVIEW YESTERDAY . . . . SEEMS TO BELIEVE THAT THE MORE HE TALKS
ABOUT THE SITUATION, THE MORE SYMPATHY AND SUPPORT HE MIGHT GET
FROM PUBLIC.)))

3. WHAT HAS BEEN THE REACTION IN SOUTH CAROLINA?

((WHEN HE FIRST ADMITTED THE AFFAIR, REACTION FOR THE MOST PART
MILD CONDEMNATION AND WELL-WISHES FOR HIM AND FAMILY . . . BUT
WITH THESE LATEST REVELATIONS, CRITICISM HAS GOTTEN LOUDER . . .
SEVERAL OF HIS FELLOW REPUBLICANS WANT HIM TO RESIGN . . .
DEMOCRATIC PARTY PUT OUT A YOUTUBE VIDEO MOCKING HIM . . . .
THE REPUBLICAN STATE ATTORNEY GENERAL WANTS A LAW ENFORCEMENT
INVESTIGATION—ALTHOUGH NO EVIDENCE HE'S DONE ANYTHING
ILLEGAL . . . . GOVERNOR IS FEELING MORE HEAT WITH EACH PASSING
DAY AND EACH NEW REVELATION.)))

4. IS SANFORD SHOWING ANY SIGNS OF PREPARING TO STEP DOWN?

(((NO. SAYS QUITTING WOULD BE THE EASY WAY OUT. HE HAS 18 MONTHS
LEFT IN HIS TERM . . . WANTS TO USE IT TO REBUILD HIS REPUTATION
AND SHOW THAT HE'S REPENTANT FOR WHAT HE DID.)))

5. WHAT WOULD HAPPEN IF HE STEPPED DOWN?

(((LT. GOVERNOR WOULD TAKE OVER . . . SANFORD CANNOT RUN AGAIN
BECAUSE OF TERM LIMITS, AND THERE IS A CROWDED FIELD OF
CANDIDATES LINING UP FOR THE JOB NEXT YEAR—INCLUDING THE
LT. GOVERNOR AND ATTORNEY GENERAL . . . LOT OF POLITICAL
CALCULATING GOING ON AND POSTURING GOING ON . . . WITH REGARDS
TO NOT ONLY THE FUTURE OF THE CURRENT GOVERNOR, BUT ALSO THE
QUESTION OF WHO WILL BE ELECTED GOVERNOR NEXT YEAR.)))

NPR'S ADAM HOCHBERG, SPEAKING TO US FROM THE STATE CAPITOL,
COLUMBIA, SOUTH CAROLINA.

Conclusion

It doesn't matter if you listen to NPR or the local all-news radio station; one of radio's strengths is that it's portable. You can take it with you and hear it while you jog or while you drive your car. Another strength is its intimacy. You can hear the person speaking, hear the inflection in the voice, the tone, the emotion. You get to use your mind's eye. A child was once asked whether he preferred radio or television. He said radio. When the father asked why, the child answered that he preferred radio because the pictures are better. (See "Empire of the Air [videorecording]: The Men Who Made Radio.")

It's up to the radio writer to create those word pictures. The best writers become "wordsmiths." They know what words mean, and they choose the appropriate words, the most descriptive words for the story they're telling to the listening audience. Some television writers and reporters have started their careers in radio and will tell you "if you want to get into television, start in radio." There, the pictures don't get in the way.

DOs and DON'Ts for Writing Radio News

Do
- Write short.
- Use descriptive language.
- Create word pictures.
- Say the story in your own words and then write it down.

Don't
- Forget to get good **ambient sound**.
- Forget to write in present or future tense.
- Let the shark get you.

Questions

1. Discuss the elements of a radio "wrap."
2. Discuss the importance of capturing and using good natural sound.
3. What does "hyperkinetic" mean? Does it apply to all radio reporting?
4. What does "ubiquitous" mean? And how does it apply to radio?
5. What are radio's strengths?
6. What are the main differences between radio and TV reports?

Television News Story Forms—The VO

In television news, there are five basic story forms: **readers** (or "tell" stories), **voice-overs (VOs), voice-overs/sound on tape (VO/SOTs),** reporter **packages,** and **donuts.** Beginning writers and associate producers are the people primarily responsible for taking information from story notes and compiling it into story form for an anchor to read it as a reader, a VO, or a VO/SOT. If a story involves no video or other visual over the face of the anchor, then we call it a reader. Sometimes, the viewers can see the anchor's face for the duration of a story and also see a graphic over his or her shoulder. That story would still qualify as a reader, because the viewers see the anchor for the entire story. Because there's not much production value associated with reader stories, they're usually quite short and might include a promise of video once it becomes available.

Anchor Shelley Basinger on desk doing the midday newscast.

A voice-over is any story the anchor reads that also incorporates video, a full-screen graphic, or some other visual. The term "voice-over" simply indicates that we hear the anchor's voice "over" some visual. The abbreviation VO usually indicates that she's talking over a piece of video. If she's talking over a graphic, many news operations label the story a VO/g to distinguish between the two. Later, we'll get to the longer story forms, such as VO/SOTs and packages. In this chapter, we'll concentrate on VOs.

Voice-over stories serve an important role in a newscast. They help the producer vary the pace of the show, while allowing us to deliver useful and interesting information in short form. VOs work very well when we cover events and a comment from someone at the event really wouldn't add that much to the story, when there's no real issue involved, or when there's only a limited amount of interesting information to impart to the viewers. A downtown street fair would probably warrant VO coverage only. It would involve nice colorful video and would be a way to highlight a part of the community; however, there's no controversy, and someone saying "I enjoyed the petting zoo" doesn't add anything, so a 20- to 30-second VO would suffice. The street fair isn't as important as other stories in the newscast are, so we'd devote less time to it.

The relative importance of the story isn't the only reason for assigning the story VO status. We might be getting late-breaking video from the satellites or from a crew in the field via FTP and have no time to put together a longer piece, so we'd quickly edit some of the compelling video and give the few details that are available. Perhaps a trial has generated a couple of important bits of interesting information, but not enough to warrant more than 20 or 30 seconds. The information might be good, but there just isn't much of it.

Also, what might be a full-blown reporter package on a slow news day can be reduced to VO status simply because other news takes precedence. A producer might feel compelled to include the story, but simply can't give up the time in a packed news show to make it a long piece. Something a reporter has been working on all day might occupy only 30 seconds of news time when all is said and done.

The flip side of that is what's known as "trying to make chicken salad out of . . ." (you fill in the rest). Some days, the news managers are sitting around trying to figure out what to cover, especially as the lead story, because it seems *nothing* is going on. On those days, a compelling VO can give the show a kick start and perhaps even lead to a short series of related reports.

Elizabeth Bynum: Picking a Lead Story

Elizabeth Bynum, the executive producer at WCTI-TV in New Bern, North Carolina, deals with show rundowns every day. The most important part of the rundown, the lead, is often a challenge that she and others in the newsroom must discuss. The Greenville/New Bern/ Jacksonville market—99th largest in the Nielsen rankings—can often experience slower news day than do larger, metropolitan markets. Plus, with limited resources, she and her colleagues have to find a way to fill the shows with content from across the market. In this DMA, Elizabeth must be mindful of news in 15 counties.

So, what makes a good lead on a slow day? There are several factors that can justify a lead story: compelling visuals, an enterprise story with wide appeal, great storytelling with an emotional character, and breaking news that needs to air at the top of the show.

Following the saying "it bleeds, it leads" isn't a good way to go about choosing a lead. Sure, there are many crime stories that will lead a show because of the details behind the incident, but do you want to be a police-crime-blotter station? Would you watch a newscast that airs only mug shots of people busted for drugs? Elizabeth says the answer is absolutely not—that's boring and doesn't affect most of your viewers' lives.

Finally, choosing the lead of a show becomes tricky when you think about different newscasts. What you'd lead with in a morning show isn't necessarily what you'd lead with for the 6 P.M. newscast. You have to think about the members of the audience—what do they want most at this time of day?

The Mechanics of a VO

Information for a VO can come from a number of sources, such as story notes compiled by a reporter or videographer, news releases, wire services, video feed services, and the like. Story notes might be very brief, requiring the writer to expand on what's provided either by incorporating related information or by contacting the reporter or videographer (who might have gone on to another story assignment) for more information. The writer might also contact a source indicated in the story notes for clarification or additional information. In the case of news releases, the writer's primary task is taking the information and boiling it down to the essential elements. In the case of a script sent by a wire service or feed service, the primary task is to rewrite the information, putting a local "angle" on the story.

Writing from Video

The basic facts gathered at the story site or from newsmakers obviously give us a good starting point for what we should write. Who, what, when, where (and when we know them, why and how) are important elements in any news story. But if that's all we write, then we've created news print with **wallpaper video** over the top of it. In television, it's vital that we write from the video. In other words, what we see on the video should lead us to mention specific things in the script.

Now, we're not talking about play-by-play, as in "here's the mayor leaving her office, and here she is entering the council chambers" kind of stuff. But there should be a definite connection between the video and the words. If we mention the mayor, we should see the mayor. Some in the business call not having a picture to go along with a mention of someone or something specific the "not-seen-here syndrome," as in, "Mayor Smith, not seen here . . . ." So if we don't have a shot of the mayor we might want to refer to the project or the meeting rather than to the mayor—whatever it is we have video of.

Likewise, if we have a shot of a child jumping up and down, we might not write "little Jane Brown was jumping up and down," but instead, perhaps we would write something about the excitement of the moment. The video and the script should always match *thematically*. So let's be sure if we mention Jane specifically we have a shot of her, and if we write about her painting a picture (or say something about artistic expression), we don't see her reading a book. If we have a shot of the coach sweeping out the dugout, maybe we could make reference to the concerns he had coming into the season "being swept away." *The visuals should drive the writing, and then how the story is written will logically drive how we edit the visuals.* We call it having stories that are high on the **SWAP** scale—working toward *synchronized words and pictures.*

Here are some examples:

Example 1

GAS PRICES—Version 1

On cam	FIGHTING IN THE MIDDLE EAST IS PUSHING UP GAS PRICES HERE IN THE U.S.
:00 Take tape snd under (VO)	(vo)
[Editor: show invasion video]	ISRAEL SENT TROOPS AND TANKS INTO THE WEST BANK DURING THE WEEKEND.
	THAT HAS SOME ANALYSTS WORRIED THE ARAB STATES MIGHT RETALIATE WITH A CUTBACK OR EVEN A SHUTDOWN OF OIL PRODUCTION.
	IT HASN'T HAPPENED YET BUT FEAR OF SHORTAGES HAS SENT PRICES AT THE PUMP SOARING.
	IN SOME AREAS THE PRICE OF GASOLINE JUMPED 25 CENTS A GALLON OVERNIGHT.
:30 Tape out	

What's wrong with this story? Our short VO about how fighting in the Middle East is affecting oil prices begins well enough with "generic" video of soldiers in battle. But it continues to show combat long after the copy has turned to what's happening at the pump. Our video has become wallpaper—pictures shown for the sake of showing pictures without a direct connection to the copy. In television, we use pictures to support the copy, but in the example above, after the third sentence the pictures actually *conflict* with the copy. What sense does it make to show video of tanks rolling through streets when we're talking about people filling their gas tanks?

Here's another example.

Example 2

FIRE ECONOMY—Version 1

On cam	AS IF PROPERTY DAMAGE WEREN'T ENOUGH . . . NOW THIS SUMMER'S WILDFIRE SEASON IS HURTING ARIZONA'S ECONOMY.
:00 Take tape	(vo)
snd under (VO)	DURING THE PAST FEW WEEKS FOREST FIRES HAVE CONSUMED THOUSANDS OF ACRES AND BURNED
[Editor: at :00 show flame video]	DOZENS OF HOMES IN SOUTH AND CENTRAL ARIZONA.
	SOME OF THOSE FIRES ARE STILL SMOLDERING.
	THE SUMMER TRAVEL SEASON IS VERY IMPORTANT TO THE STATE'S ECONOMY.
	BUT TOURISM OFFICIALS REPORT VACANCIES ARE UP BY 75 PERCENT. THE GOVERNOR HAS PROMISED DISASTER RELIEF.
:30 Tape out	

This VO begins appropriately with fire video as the copy discusses the recent history of the fires, but when the story switches gears to discuss the effects on resorts, motels, and restaurants, the video continues to show towering flames.

So how can we solve this problem? A step in the right direction is to choose the correct visuals to go with the copy. In the gas prices example, the problem began when the copy switched to prices while the viewer was still seeing video of warfare. Could the producer have solved the problem by substituting "generic" pictures of people pumping gas? Not totally. Certainly, a quick shot of people gassing up would have been appropriate—for a sentence or two. But if it drags on too long then that video, too, will become "wallpaper." What about the fire story? Would "file" video of hotels and restaurants at the appropriate point have solved the problem? Again, such video would have improved the situation—but if it drags on too long, it becomes a new problem.

The general problem in both cases is that we have only "generic" video to support the copy—generic warfare, generic gas pumps, generic hotels, generic restaurants, and so on. These "generic" pictures are like the repeat patterns on wallpaper—hence the term. The best solution is to provide *specific* video. In the gas prices example, do we have pictures of people pumping gas *today,* including shots of the *current* prices at the pump? In the fire story, do we have pictures of empty resorts, motels, and restaurants shot *today?* (And while we're at it, can we get some interviews with people today who are affected by these stories? Maybe these items are worth more than a VO!)

If we get the "fresh" *specific* video, then copy should reference it in some way, *specifically.* Below are examples of how both of these stories might look with wallpaper removed.

Example 3

GAS PRICES—Version 2	
On cam	FIGHTING IN THE MIDDLE EAST IS PUSHING UP GAS PRICES RIGHT HERE IN THE BAY AREA.
:00 Take tape snd under (VO)	(vo) ISRAEL SENT TROOPS AND TANKS INTO THE WEST BANK DURING THE
[Editor: at :00 show invasion video]	WEEKEND.
[Editor: at :03 show oil field video]	THAT HAS SOME ANALYSTS WORRIED THE ARAB STATES MIGHT RETALIATE WITH A CUTBACK OR EVEN A SHUTDOWN OF OIL PRODUCTION.
[Editor: at :09 show pump video]	THAT HASN'T HAPPENED YET . . . BUT FEAR OF SHORTAGES HAS SENT PRICES AT THE PUMP SOARING.
	WE CHECKED SEVERAL STATIONS HERE IN TOWN THIS MORNING . . .
[Editor: at :15 show price]	THE LOWEST PRICE WE FOUND WAS THREE BUCKS AT THIS SUNMART STATION AT THE CORNER OF HAWTHORNE AND FIRST IN TAMPA.
[:30 tape out] On cam	(on cam) THE OWNER TELLS US THAT'S 25 CENTS MORE THAN YESTERDAY. OTHER STATES ARE REPORTING SIMILAR HIKES.

Example 4

FIRE ECONOMY—Video Match Version

On cam	AS IF PROPERTY DAMAGE WEREN'T ENOUGH . . . NOW THIS SUMMER'S WILDFIRE SEASON IS HURTING ARIZONA'S ECONOMY.
:00 Take tape	(vo)
snd under (VO)	DURING THE PAST FEW WEEKS FOREST FIRES HAVE CONSUMED THOUSANDS
[Editor: at :00 show flame video]	OF ACRES AND BURNED DOZENS OF HOMES IN SOUTH AND CENTRAL ARIZONA.
[Editor: at :06 show last year resort video]	THE SUMMER TRAVEL SEASON IS VERY IMPORTANT TO THE STATE'S ECONOMY . . . AND LAST YEAR . . . BUSINESS WAS BOOMING AT THIS RESORT IN VISTA FLAMANTE.
[Editor: at :14 show today video, starting with empty parking lot]	TAKE A LOOK AT THAT SAME RESORT TODAY: THE PARKING LOT IS MOSTLY EMPTY.
	THE STATE SAYS IT'S LIKE THIS ACROSS THE AREA WITH VACANCIES UP 75 PERCENT.
:30 Tape out	(on cam)
On cam	THE GOVERNOR IS PROMISING DISASTER RELIEF.

In both cases, the "nonwallpaper" versions of these stories are more interesting because the copy is about specifics, not statistics. Also note that in both instances, part of our solution for getting rid of the wallpaper video was to come back on-camera for the final line. There's nothing dishonorable about an on-camera shot—and some operations prefer to end stories with an on-camera tag, particularly if a different anchor will read the next story.

Literal Video

One problem almost as bad as failing to match the copy to the images is that of taking the video *too* literally. Your pictures should support your copy, but that doesn't mean your copy has to be a slave to the pictures. You're writing a story, not a slideshow and certainly not a video catalog. For instance, if you begin your story with a shot of the sunrise, you don't have to write, "The sun burst over the horizon in a huge orange ball of flame at 5:15 this morning." You can use the picture to support in a general way the idea that your story is about a new day or what it might bring. "Sunrise was not a welcome sight to dozens of weary volunteers who faced another grueling day of battling the wildfires."

Here's another example. Imagine you have a shot of a woman crying, with tears rolling down both cheeks. You don't have to write, "Tears rolled down both cheeks as Linda Jones began her press conference." You can write, "It was with uncommon bravery that Linda Jones approached the podium this morning to share her grief with the community."

In neither case are we using the video as "wallpaper" because it's specific, and we're referencing it specifically in copy. In both examples we're using the video to support our copy thematically, rather than literally.

We can use thematic video in other ways. Let's revisit a paragraph from our fire season story:

TAKE A LOOK AT THAT SAME RESORT TODAY: THE PARKING LOT IS MOSTLY EMPTY.

THE STATE SAYS IT'S LIKE THIS ACROSS THE AREA WITH VACANCIES UP 75 PERCENT.

With the words "take a look," we began showing video of a specific item, which in this case was the empty parking lot. It's OK to continue showing video of that same specific resort to cover the next sentence, even though that sentence is general in nature, because it's about what's happening at *other* resorts. Use of sustaining video to support a general theme in this way is permissible, but don't let it drag on for too long.

The fire story also provides an example of the same process in reverse: starting general and going to the specific, as follows:

THE SUMMER TRAVEL SEASON IS VERY IMPORTANT TO THE STATE'S ECONOMY . . . LAST YEAR . . . BUSINESS WAS BOOMING AT THIS RESORT IN VISTA FLAMANTE.

In this case, we'll cover the first sentence with video of the resort packed with tourists last year. This supports the theme of "travel" in a general way. The second sentence transitions from a general statement to a very specific one about the very resort we're seeing. This is also an acceptable use of video.

The key to these examples, and what sets both of them apart from "wallpaper" video, is that both contain specific references—and we move quickly to other video once we've made our point.

Writing from File Footage

Sometimes, despite your best efforts, all you have is file footage. There's no prohibition against using file, especially if it shows something specific. Often, we have to use file because we're writing about something in the past. So if you mention last year's record snowfall, you'll have to get file footage of that. Also, even in the cases when we know the video doesn't show what the script is mentioning, there are ways to downplay the discrepancy. For example, let's assume that Johnny Famoussinger died in a plane crash half an hour before airtime, and no video of the crash site is available yet. We might choose to use file tape of a recent concert, but of course that has no direct relation to today's story. Making a reference to the specific video we have at the beginning of the story makes the use of this piece of file tape more acceptable. The story would begin something like this:

Singer
_____

	(Gayle)
On cam	POP SUPERSTAR JOHNNY
	FAMOUSSINGER IS DEAD.
:00 Take cass snd under (VO)	(vo)
	SHOWN HERE AT A CONCERT LAST
	MONTH . . . FAMOUSSINGER WAS
	RETURNING TO GOTHAM CITY FROM THE
	WEST COAST EARLY THIS MORNING . . .
	WHEN HIS PRIVATE JET WENT DOWN
	IN A REMOTE PART OF THE ROCKY
	MOUNTAINS. . . .

Making a reference to the video we're seeing makes it more acceptable for use in relation to a story that has nothing to do with the concert. It's important to write from the video throughout, but in cases like this we have no video to go with today's story other than the file tape. So, a direct video reference at the top is about the best we can do. Failing to reference the video can lead to some confusion. In this example, we'd be talking about Famoussinger returning when the footage is of him singing. Giving the viewers the visual reference at the top alerts them that what they see is what they're going to get.

Improper Use of Video—or, "When Wallpaper Strikes Back"

When a producer or reporter uses video as wallpaper, file tape frequently is part of the equation. One good cure, as we saw above, is to make specific reference within copy to the pictures. If you can't figure out a way to write such a reference into the copy, then this is a strong clue that you shouldn't be using the tape. The rule is particularly important when it comes to use of file tape containing identifiable faces.

The truth is that television news has a horrible habit of turning real human beings into objects for the purpose of illustrating general problems or issues. For instance, to cover a story involving the latest report about the number of people with sexually transmitted infections, an assignments editor might say to a photographer, "Go out and spray some video of people walking around downtown." Chances are, you've seen a story just like this: The copy mentions a general health problem such as obesity, AIDS, heart disease, or whatnot, while the video shows throngs of "generic" people. If the shot is very wide, the storyteller might get away with it (although that doesn't mean it's right). But what if it's not so wide? What if there are recognizable faces in it?

Using pictures of people in this way is a form of wallpaper video. But it's worse than other forms of wallpaper because instead of using generic pictures to illustrate a story, we're using *specific* pictures. There's no such thing as a "generic" person. Every face has attached to it a real person with a real name and a real address and real rights, who's real likely to hire a real good lawyer to hit you real hard with a real ugly lawsuit. If there's a recognizable face in your video, then that video is *specific*, not generic—and some might construe your story to be *about that individual*. So if you're using a "crowd shot" to illustrate a story about something negative or embarrassing such as STIs and Ethel Icetea recognizes herself in your video, she isn't going to be happy. If she gets a call from her neighbors kidding her about it, she's going to be less happy. You might then get a call from the law firm of Ketchum and Cheatham that will negatively affect *your* happiness.

Some assignments editors who are savvy enough to realize the danger of having specific faces in generic video might say something like this to the photographer: "We're doing a story about juvenile delinquents hanging out at the skateboard park downtown. Go spray me some pictures of some kids—but no faces." So Joe Grabbenshoot brings back video of hands, feet, and torsos, which then hits the air covering portions of your juvenile delinquent story. Trouble is, your video shows the only kid hanging out downtown today who happened to be wearing a barbed wire bracelet in combination with a Marilyn Manson T-shirt and a bicycle chain belt—and he recognized himself. So did his friends. Phone call holding for you on line two.

This kind of video misuse gets on the air in other ways, too. Imagine your medical reporter is doing a piece involving the latest statistics about the problem of babies being born addicted to crack. She says to the editor, "Grab some of that delivery room video we shot last month." In goes the video to cover part of your track, and guess what? Ethel Icetea was delivering her baby the day you shot that video, and now thanks to you her friends are calling her to ask whether she's gotten over her little crack problem.

Here's an even more common example. You're the crime beat reporter. You're doing a story about the latest crime stats. Drug arrests are way up. This doesn't surprise you because you've been on four really cool crack dealer roundups in the past year. So you say to the editor, "Cover this with some of that great arrest video we got last summer." The editor pulls up a dramatic shot of police slamming some handcuffed guy against a cruiser and slaps it into the story. Trouble is, little did you know that prosecutors dropped the charges against this particular guy a few days after his arrest. He was innocent. And by the way, the guy is in the lobby and would like to have a word with you.

It's possible to victimize businesses in this way as well. An assignments editor in one medium market reportedly once sent a photographer out to "get b-roll of banks" to support a story about financial trouble in the state's banking industry. At least one of the banks the photographer shot was in perfectly good financial shape, and its managers were none too pleased to suddenly see its sign flashed in a story about failing banks. It's said that money exchanged hands because of that one.

The cure for each of these scenarios is the same one we applied earlier in this chapter: Make a specific reference to the video. If you're showing a group of people walking down the street, then you should tell us what that specific group of people has to do with your AIDS story. If you can't make the link, then drop the video. Similarly, if you're showing some guy being thrown up against the hood of a car in handcuffs for your story about street crime, your copy should tell us who that person is and how he's related to your crime story. Chances are that a year after this video you got, you either don't know who the guy is or don't know what happened to his case, or both—which means you shouldn't use the video.

Bottom line: The viewer has a right to expect that the pictures you're showing are directly related to the words you're speaking. Such is the visual language of television. If those pictures are specific and show a particular and recognizable individual, business, or organization—then the audience will believe the story is about those individuals or institutions. It's worth noting that the word "recognizable" sits on a slippery slope. The individual doesn't have to be recognizable to the public at large—only to the individual or that person's friends.

The same is true of businesses. So check your video very carefully. Raise red flags if your pictures portray (or appear to portray) any individual or organization in a less-than-favorable way. If the story is *supposed* to be about those people or places, then proceed. But make sure the connection is deliberate, not accidental.

And by the way, the word "spray," as some people use it in newsrooms, can be an indicator that something bad is about to happen, because it usually means pointing the camera in a general direction and capturing video in a quick, sometimes indiscriminate fashion. The act of capturing video for use in a television newscast should always be very deliberate.

Poster Children

Let's say you've done your homework and you're absolutely certain of the identity of the person you plan to use in your file tape. You're also certain that the person does have a direct connection to the story you're trying to illustrate, and you plan to make this connection plain in your copy. You're free to proceed, right? Actually, you should pause for just one more question: Is it *fair* to use this person in the fashion you're proposing?

If the mayor throws an ashtray at a citizen during a city council meeting, then that video is fair game every time you do a story about the mayor's temper. But what about the guy in your arrest video? Do you really want to drag this man out and parade him around every time you do a story about street-level drug busts? Even if he was guilty, how many times does his family deserve to be subjected to those pictures of him being thrown up against that car hood? Similar considerations apply to the victims of crimes and accidents. If you've been in television very long at all, chances are you've had a discussion like this one: "Jane, we're doing another piece about the Death Ramp tonight. We'll need the pictures of that great accident from last December." So tonight on your newscast some poor schlub who spent weeks in the hospital after that accident gets to see himself being pried out of the burning wreckage of his car and then wheeled out on a gurney for the 18th time. Typically, when charity organizations choose a poster child, it's a voluntary arrangement. Releases are signed. Money might change hands. Who wants to be poster child for Fatal Accident Week? Or Crime and Violence Week? No one. But in television news, we don't ask. We just do it—and we'll use those same pictures again and again.

The next time you propose to do this to someone in a story for which you're responsible, give it some thought. How many times has this particular person been used as "file tape"? Is it really necessary? Are there viable alternatives? Approach these questions with a sense of humanity.

Graphics

But what, you ask, do I do if I need to mention something for which I have no appropriate video, file or otherwise? Graphics have become increasingly important in television news for that very reason. It's particularly difficult to visually depict a lot of numbers using video, but it's fairly easy to do so with a graphic. Your story might be about crime figures: Assaults are down, armed robberies are up, property crime is down, other types of crime have remained constant. You probably won't be able to get your hands on video of each of those crimes taking place, but you can ask a talented (and VERY valuable) graphics person to put together a **full-screen graphic (FSG)** titled "Crime Statistics" that shows the numbers of each type of crime as compared to a previous period of time. Or maybe you need to write about the effects of gas leaking out of underground storage tanks. You're probably not going to persuade your photojournalist to go dig a hole and crawl down into it to get some shots, and besides, that wouldn't be as effective as an animated graphic showing the storage system and how a leak can occur. So when you don't have video of something specific, either don't write specifically about it, or consider using a graphic as your visual support.

When you use graphics, make sure the elements match the script from top to bottom or from left to right, depending on how the graphic is designed. Also, don't try to cram too much information onto an FSG. When that's the case, the graphic is "too busy" and difficult to read. Use bullet points that the anchor might read, or elaborate on. Having each new bit of information "reveal" as the anchor gets to it also adds to the pacing and look of the piece, and keeps the viewer from "reading ahead" and thereby paying less attention to the anchor than to what's on the screen. The idea is that as the anchor is saying "the number of armed robberies in the Hooverville metro area increased 17 percent compared to last year," the viewers see something such as "ARMED ROBBERIES UP 17%" on the screen. Just as is the case when we're writing from video, what the viewers hear and what they see must match when we're using graphics. The "matching" theme applies to **over-the-shoulder (OTS) graphics** as well. You'll want to find the single frame of video (a close-up shot) that best illustrates your story for the OTS, and then make sure the wording at the bottom is wording the anchor will actually use during the on-camera lead. So if you pick a cute shot of a kitten for the OTS for your story about the animal shelter and ask someone in graphics to add the words "Furry Friends" to the bottom of the graphic, we should hear the anchor say the words "furry friends" at some point before we go to video.

Following are examples of some of the most common ways stations use graphics.

Bullet Points

A **bullet point** consists of two or three words of text summarizing a statement or point presented in copy, usually set off by an asterisk, circle, square, or some other form of demarcation at the beginning of the line. Reporters or producers typically use bullet points when they need to cover a difficult passage and no specific video is available to support the copy. For example, imagine the city council is ordering the police chief to take a series of steps to reduce expenditures. When you're explaining those steps in your copy, you can either show video of city council people sitting around or video of cops at shift change. Both would be "wallpaper" used in this way. The better option is to extract bullet points from the specific steps the council is ordering, then present those points on-screen over a color background, preferably one that an artist has composed with your station's logo and artwork or an icon to support the theme of the story.

Quotes

This technique is similar to the use of bullet points described above, except that in this case instead of extracting bullet point summaries we'll excerpt full quotes. This is useful in a number of scenarios, including:

- Presenting excerpts from a formal statement given by someone who is either unwilling or unable to go on-camera
- Pulling quotes from a document used in an investigative story
- Quoting court testimony
- Giving text support to a hard-to-understand audio track, such as a 911 tape, undercover audio introduced as evidence in court, a phone conversation, and so forth

In such instances, we would typically use quotation marks on-screen.

Charts and Graphs

When presenting complex statistics, simply flashing the numbers on-screen can be confusing. Good old-fashioned bar charts, line graphs, and pie charts often do a better job of showing the meaning of numbers in relation to one another.

Locator Graphics

Viewers often find it difficult to relate to addresses or to the names of small towns or obscure locations. Full-screen maps do an excellent job of making such locations meaningful.

General Information

When your copy contains lists, numbers, or general information such as the name of someone who's giving an interview by phone, full-screen graphics support will help the viewer grasp the information.

Weather Graphics

Weathercasts make use of a wide range of full-screen graphics, everything from maps showing weather fronts and radar images to "list" graphics supporting the forecast.

Explanatory Graphics

Sometimes you find yourself needing to explain a concept for which there just aren't any good pictures. In such cases you'll need original artwork. Probably the most common use of original artwork in local television is in the area of medical reporting. For instance, if you're giving an explanation of how a quadruple bypass works, b-roll of doctors and nurses bending over a patient on the operating table isn't going to provide much help. Quite literally, you'll need to draw the audience a diagram. It's the only good way to show the problems of restricted blood flow to the heart and how the bypass operation resolves that.

Graphics of this sort are useful in many situations when you need to provide an explanation of something about which pictures don't tell the story of the larger concept involved or where cameras can't go. All of us saw this type of graphic use in action in the days following the terrorist attacks against the World Trade Center; virtually every news organization everywhere used graphics to show how the fuel-fed fires inside the buildings weakened the support girders and ultimately caused them to fail. In a story about corrosion inside the Sunshine Skyway Bridge, WFLA-TV reporter Mark Douglas found himself needing to explain a method of construction that uses steel tendons under tension to hold concrete columns together. For this purpose he asked a graphics artist to render a cross section of a bridge column.

Sophisticated graphics suites also have animation capabilities to show effects progressing over time. Again, the more sophisticated the technique, the longer it takes to render. Reporters and producers are well advised to keep this in mind when asking for graphics.

Thematic Graphics

This category involves the use of art to establish an overarching visual "theme" for a story. This visual theme then appears on all graphics for the entire story. In many cases these "themed" graphics can support

Taken by Forrest Carr

KGUN9 meteorologist April Madison live at the chromakey wall.

the story in all the ways outlined above—extracting bullet points, giving quotes, presenting explanations, and so on. Sometimes themed graphics have no purpose other than to give visual support to the theme or tone of the story.

Branding

No discussion of graphics use would be complete without some mention of "branding." Almost every full-screen graphic has the *potential* to support the news organization's brand. Some TV newsrooms pay little or no attention to branding. Others are passionate about it.

It's also quite common for stations to use full-screen graphics or animations for the sole purpose of carrying out a branding function. Thus a station's top story might be preceded by a flashy graphic bearing the words "BIG story," often accompanied by a "swooshing" sound effect. Many stations have "franchises" of various sorts—medical, consumer, investigative, and so forth—and will often precede such reports with a full-screen "stinger" flashing the station's logo with a few notes of its station music or a sound effect of some sort. Branding style and usage vary dramatically from station to station—and as always, there's no accounting for taste. But the goal is always the same: to achieve a uniform station "look" and to impress that look on the mind of the viewer.

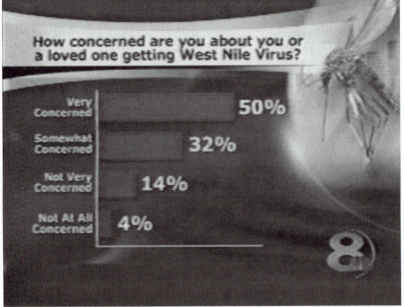

©WFLA-TV Tampa, FL

Bar chart: This graphic helps support a story about a viewer poll measuring concern about a public health threat.

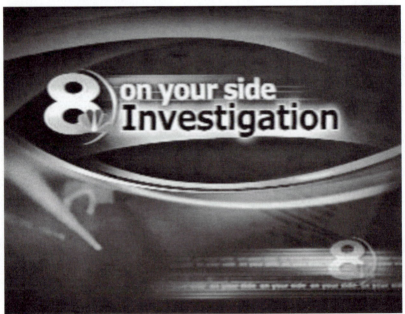

©WFLA-TV Tampa, FL

Branding graphic: The sole purpose of this visual, which was part of an animated package open or "stinger," is to brand the story.

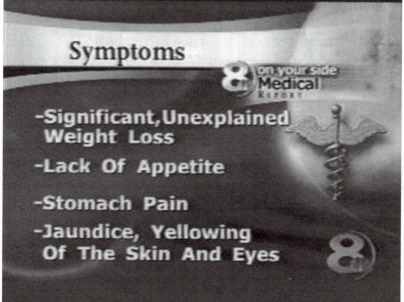

Explanatory graphic: This graphic uses bullet points drawn from the story script to provide visual support for storytelling.

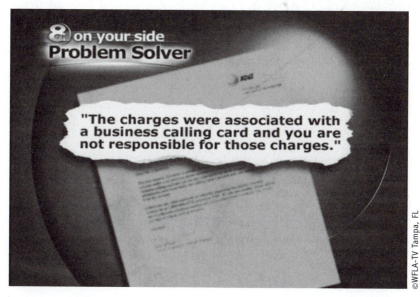

Quote graphic: This graphic excerpts an exact quote from a document referenced within the story.

A Final Thought about Graphics

Of course, we use graphics in VO/SOTs and packages as well as VOs. Good graphics are a big help when illustrating stories that are "video poor" or when we need to use numbers or other statistics, but don't use graphics as a substitute for good pictures. When you do have good video, take advantage of it. Managers tell videographers to concentrate on *tight shots of people doing things,* because that makes for compelling video. Writers need to look for those compelling pictures when **logging** tapes (making a list of the shots, including a description of each usable shot and where it's located on the tape) and let those shots drive the story. Utilize your video to its full extent, and do the same with the natural sound you have.

Use of Natural Sound

What we hear is just as important as what we see. A VO about a fund-raising concert can be more effective if the anchor pauses for a few seconds when we go to the tape to allow for some "nat SOT full" to let the viewers hear one of the bands. Then she can tell us more as the sound of the band continues "under" her voice. Pieces that have no **natural sound** are "flat." When we go somewhere, we experience sights AND sounds. The news crew serves as a surrogate for the viewers, and needs to give audience members as much of the ambiance of the scene as possible. That means incorporating natural sound, including frequent use of nats full. This is an especially important pacing element in packages, and we'll discuss it further in Chapter 9. In radio and in TV, the liberal use of natural sound makes the difference between mundane pieces and really good broadcast journalism.

A Lot to Say in 30 Seconds or Less

Although there's no set length for any broadcast story, VOs on local news programs typically run about 20 to 30 seconds. In a series of back-to-back VOs, some might be as short as 10 to 12 seconds, and in rare circumstances a VO might run as much as 40 to 45 seconds. Generally though, you can expect a VO to be about 20 to 30 seconds in length. It's not uncommon for viewers to see the anchor briefly at the beginning of a VO and perhaps again at the end. However, it's still a VO and not a reader because at some point in the story we see something other than the anchor's face.

Writing from the video is so important that we'll mention it several times throughout this book. Having the video to tell part of the story helps, but in many cases, we can't fit all the information that's available into the time limit we're given. We will leave information out. The key is not to leave out any major information. VOs are challenging because television news writers must capture viewer attention, impart the most relevant information of the story, and perhaps even transition to the next story, all in 20 to 30 seconds.

It's difficult to be very creative in such a short amount of time, and many of us making the transition to broadcast are caught in the "flowery words and phrases" mind-set we learned when writing much longer stories and essays. The creativity in broadcast writing doesn't come in how many dependent clauses and rarely used words we can stick in one sentence. Instead, creativity is often evident in the ability to tell a story so that people who don't know anything about what happened can understand what we're telling them right away. As with any good piece of broadcast writing, an informative VO gives viewers the most pertinent information and relates to what the pictures are showing.

Broadcast writers do have room to get creative with their writing, depending on the type of story they're dealing with. This is frequently the case with soft news or feature stories. We still have to use clear, understandable words and short sentences, but the English language is a wonderful tool, even when you're operating within severe time constraints. Chapter 4 contains a lot of information about writing creative news copy, but here's a quick example of how to change a lackluster story into a better one. The following very average copy is taken from an actual newscast and hit the air exactly as presented below. Note that the available video consists entirely of a giant pumpkin and the farmer who grew it. A suggested rewrite follows. We'll explain what the markings on the left side of the page mean in the "Providing Directions" section that follows the examples.

Pumpkin (Early Version)

	(Ted)
On cam	IT'S ALMOST TIME FOR HALLOWEEN . . . AND WHAT WOULD HALLOWEEN BE WITHOUT PUMPKINS?
:00 Take tape	(vo)
nat snd under (VO)	FOLKS ACROSS THE COUNTRY ARE GEARING UP FOR THE HOLIDAY . . . MAKING COSTUMES . . . BUYING TREATS . . . AND HARVESTING PUMPKINS FOR THIS SEASON.

MILTON BARBER MIGHT NOT WANT TO
BUTCHER HIS PUMPKIN BECAUSE IT'S A
WORLD RECORD PUMPKIN.

THE WINNING PUMPKIN WEIGHS A
WHOPPING 743 POUNDS.

BARBER SAYS HE'S NOT SURE WHAT
HE'LL DO WITH THE PUMPKIN BUT HE
DOES PLAN TO SELL THE SEEDS.

:40 Tape ends

The story as written contains all the pertinent information, but it certainly isn't very memorable. The following example takes the same set of facts, presents them in a different way, and still takes only 40 seconds to read. After reading both, decide which of the two you prefer.

Pumpkin (Later Version)

	(Ted)
On cam	EVERY OCTOBER SOME PERSON
OTS	PRETENDS TO HAVE PRODUCED THE
	PLANET'S MOST PRODIGIOUS PUMPKIN.
	THE PERSON MAKING THAT CLAIM
	THIS YEAR MIGHT HAVE A CASE.
:00 Take tape	(vo)
nat snd under (VO)	MILTON BARBER OF PITTSBURGH IS
	PLEASED AND PROUD TO BE THE OWNER
	OF AN OUTRAGEOUSLY OVERSIZED ENTRY.
	IN FACT . . . MILTON'S PONDEROUS
	PRODUCE WEIGHS ROUGHLY FOUR
	TIMES MORE THAN MILTON HIMSELF.
	IT'S A VERITABLE VEGETABLE ON
	STEROIDS . . . THIS PUMPKIN CRUNCHES
	THE SCALES AT A STAGGERING 743
	POUNDS.
	THAT'S ENOUGH TO GIVE A
	FOUR-OUNCE SERVING TO EACH OF
	ABOUT THREE THOUSAND PEOPLE!
	WHAT'S HE GOING TO DO WITH ALL
	THAT POTENTIAL PUMPKIN PIE?

WELL, HE COULD TURN HIS ENTRY
INTO THE JACK-O-LANTERN THAT ATE
PITTSBURGH.
BUT WHETHER HE DOES THAT OR
NOT . . . MILTON DOES HAVE ONE THING
IN MIND.
HE MAY WELL WIND UP TURNING
THE WORLD'S BIGGEST PUMPKIN INTO
THE WORLD'S BIGGEST PUMPKIN PATCH.
MILTON PLANS TO SELL THE SEEDS.

:50 Tape ends

A Few Notes about Production

By design, this book concentrates on writing. There are a number of fine texts that deal with electronic field production, and we hope by this point in your studies or career you understand the basics of shooting and editing. However, because *what you shoot should drive what you write, and how you write should drive your editing,* production is an integral part of storytelling in TV news, so let's review a few basics here.

The most compelling shots are those that involve humans or other animate beings doing something. Close-up shots of activity are best of all. We suggest that, whenever possible, you get physically close to what you're shooting, rather than zoom in. However, too many close-ups means the viewers won't get to see the big picture, so we also have to offer context by using medium and wide shots. That doesn't mean shots of the building where something occurred. Rarely is the site important visually. Instead, go right to what's happening at the site in your edited piece. There's no magic formula for how many close-ups you use, but a rule of thumb is 40 to 50 percent of your piece should be tight, compelling shots of activity. So, in a 30-second VO you'd use about 7 to 8 shots, which means 3 or 4 of them should be close-ups.

We also suggest you use few camera movements (zooms, pans, tilts), opting instead to let the action happen within the frame, rather than the frame itself moving. The reason for this is that most of the pace in news pieces comes from how they're edited. We suggest shots of three seconds in length in an edited piece. It's difficult to condense a moving shot down to that time frame. Even with shots that involve no camera movement, we suggest you shoot 15-second-long shots, in order to have some choices for the best three seconds and so you have plenty of pad on any shot you choose as your last. More about pad in a moment. The limited-camera-movement guideline is just that, and not an ironclad rule. In sports, for example, videographers zoom, pan, and tilt all the time, in order to follow the action. So sometimes we go outside the three-second range in order to let the action in a shot happen. Most likely, you wouldn't end an edited shot of the game-winning touchdown pass after three seconds. Three things guide how long a particular edit should be:

1. The length of a sentence or thought. Make edits at periods or at natural pauses in longer sentences.

2. The time it takes for the action to happen.

3. The beat of the music, if you use music in a news or sports feature story. Music is rarely appropriate in hard news stories, unless the story involves music and you recorded the music at the scene.

Here are a few other production pointers: There's nothing that screams "amateur" more loudly than unlit sound bites and stand-ups. It takes only a minute or two to set up the single light needed to light news interviews and the payoff is definitely worth the extra effort. The camera is the great equalizer. Its "eye" should be on the same level as the other eyes in the interview setting—the reporter's and the interviewee's. We call this the 5-eye rule. And of course, your shots should be steady and well composed. Production flaws distract from the story you're trying to tell.

Providing Directions

Writing a VO so that viewers can understand the story (and perhaps even get a kick out of it) is only part of the writer's responsibility. Other people in the news operation also have to understand what the writer has in mind in relation to the video or other visual elements of the story. If the story is structured so that viewers are supposed to see the anchor and an over-the-shoulder (OTS) graphic for the first sentence, the script has to indicate that.

Television news scripts are set up in split-page format. The right side of the page is what the anchor is supposed to read. It also includes a bit of information to help cue the anchors as to who reads the story and when the video appears. That information is in parentheses and isn't in uppercase, so the anchor knows not to read it. (Some stations do it differently, putting the anchor copy in upper-/lowercase and directions all uppercase. The key is to set directions and copy off from one another somehow.)

How the words appear on the page is important. Commas can be difficult to see, so we use ellipses instead. Anchors can also have trouble picking up periods, so you'll notice in the previous examples that we return and indent at the end of every sentence.

Also, let's say you have a 3-shot sequence in the edited VO. If you write "THE MARKET SPECIALIZES IN FRESH FRUIT, VEGETABLES, AND BAKED GOODS" and the anchor hasn't had a chance to preview the tape, he's going to be talking about baked goods while we're still seeing fresh fruit. So, to indicate to the anchor how he should read to that sequence, we'd write,

"THE MARKET SPECIALIZES IN FRESH FRUIT . . .

VEGETABLES . . .

AND BAKED GOODS."

Seeing it written this way, the anchor immediately understands that he's reading to a 3-shot sequence.

The left side of the page contains directions for the control room personnel. If those directions are incomplete or missing, the show director has to guess at which point to incorporate the video, or if there's even video associated with that particular story. Having the images appear too soon or too late throws off the flow of the story. Anchors can adjust their read rate when the video is a second or two early or late, but several seconds of discrepancy almost always results in noticeable errors on the air. You don't want your anchor to be talking about "this little boy" at the time the video is showing a female police officer.

In the pumpkin example above, the writer intends for the viewers to see the anchor (Ted) for a brief period of time before the video appears. That's what the "on cam" marking means. There would also be a small graphic over one of the anchor's shoulders. The director will then "take" the video at the point indicated on the script. The anchor knows his face is no longer on the screen at this point, because of the (vo) indication on the right side of the page. So, he can read directly from the hard copy of the script and keep an eye on a video monitor at the same time to make sure the script and the video are matching. If they aren't, he can vary his read rate.

We line up the directions on the left with the place in the copy at which the director is supposed to apply those directions. Go back and look at the pumpkin example. We've asked the director to take the video when the anchor is saying "folks across the country" in the "before" example and when the anchor is saying "Milton Barber of Pittsburgh" in the "after" example. We've also indicated on the script that the video is accompanied by natural sound, the sound of the people in the pumpkin patch, for example, and that the natural sound is to be played "under" the anchor's voice. When the director calls out "take VTR three" (in this example, let's say the tape in question is being played through machine three), she also indicates to the audio person to "track" it, meaning to play the accompanying sound.

All video segments start at :00, so when the director takes the video he or she also resets a timer in the control room. Writers also indicate how much time is on the video. That way, if the timer is up to :38 on a piece accompanied by 40 seconds of video and the anchor still has two sentences to read, the director knows it's time to quickly cut back to the camera shot of the anchor before the tape goes to black on the air. In an effort to keep this from happening, writers and producers time the part of the script intended to be "under" video beforehand and ask tape editors to provide 10 seconds of tape beyond what's needed.

So, if someone read the "before" pumpkin example and it took :30 to read it, the tape editor would provide :40 seconds of video. That video **pad** is critical, and we indicate the amount of video provided including the pad. This alleviates a lot of panic in the control room. A quick production note: The 10 seconds of pad isn't a new shot but a continuation of the shot that covers the final seconds of the VO. Just as we don't want the video to run out, we also don't want the shot to change just before the director punches out. So the final shot on a 40-second piece of tape would run from about :26 or :27 all the way to :40—or as close to :40 as that one shot will get you.

Also, notice where the "tape ends" marking is positioned. It comes at the bottom of the script. This indicates that once we've taken the tape, it's supposed to continue until the end of the script. If instead we had wanted to see the anchor for the final sentence of the script, we would have positioned the "tape ends" marking at the end of the preceding sentence and added an "on cam" marking at the beginning of the final sentence. It's very important to include these directions, and we'll introduce you to others as we discuss other television news story forms. Remember, television is a visual medium and news writers have to provide information to the folks on the technical side so that the pictures and the words will match up. Some playback systems give the director a warning, such as a flashing light, that the video is about to end. Whether we indicate tape time on the script or the system displays that automatically, it's up to the video editor to make sure there's a sufficient amount of video to last until the end of the script and several seconds beyond in case of anchor or control room error.

Now let's look at a few more examples.

In computer systems such as ENPS, directions in black are for the anchor, directions in red are for the director. Note that each sentence (each thought) is indented to make it easier for the anchor to read the copy from the prompter. Time cues for the director (indicating amount of video left compared to how much script the anchor still has to read) come by way of a flashing red light indicating the video is in its final seconds. In each of the first three examples below, the story begins on a shot of the anchor, followed by about 20 seconds of voice over. The fourth example is very similar, except that we switch from video to full screen graphic halfway through the story. Also, you'll notice that example three begins with an animated graphic with music (stinger) highlighting the station's emphasis on consumer news.

THE DAILY SHOW IS COMING TO NORTH CAROLINA

[TAKE: VO NATS]

{***VO NATS***}

COMEDY CENTRAL'S JON STEWART IS BRINGING THE DAILY SHOW TO THE QUEEN CITY THIS SUMMER FOR THE DEMOCRATIC NATIONAL CONVENTION.

THIS MORNING . . . THE CHARLOTTE MECKLENBURG LIBRARY BOARD OF TRUSTEES APPROVED A CONTRACT . . . ALLOWING THE SHOW TO RENT IMAGINON.

THE SHOW WILL PAY 93-THOUSAND DOLLARS TO COME TO THE QUEEN CITY . . . THAT MONEY WILL GO BACK INTO LOCAL PROGRAMS.

THE OLDEST MENTAL HOSPITAL IN OUR STATE COULD SOON BE CLOSED FOR GOOD.

[TAKE: VO NATS]

{***VO NATS***}

THIS MORNING . . .TEN ELECTED STATE OFFICIALS . . . INCLUDING THE GOVERNOR . . . VOTED TO CLOSE RALEIGH'S DOROTHEA DIX HOSPITAL IN AUGUST.

THE STATE LEGISLATURE COULD STILL BLOCK THE CLOSURE . . . WHEN LAWMAKERS RETURN NEXT MONTH.

DIX FIRST OPENED IN 1856.

ACTIVITY THERE HAS BEEN WINDING DOWN RECENTLY BECAUSE OF DECLINING FUNDS AND A NEW HOSPITAL OPENING IN BUTNER.

[TAKE: STINGER:]

{***STINGER/AMANDA***}\

WE'RE FOLLOWING AN IMPORTANT CONSUMER ALERT FOR YOU TONIGHT . . . IF YOU DRIVE A B-M-W.

THE GERMAN LUXURY CAR MAKER IS RECALLING ABOUT 367-THOUSAND FIVE AND SIX SERIES MODELS ACROSS THE U-S.

[TAKE: VO NATS]

{***VO NATS***}

THE PROBEM HAS TO DO WITH THE MOUNTING OF A BATTERY CABLE COVER ON MODELS BUILT BETWEEN 2003 AND 20-10.

IF YOU DON'T GET IT FIXED . . . YOU COULD FACE ELECTRICAL ISSUES . . . HAVE PROBLEMS STARTING THE CAR AND IN SOME CASES . . . FIRE.

THE REPAIRS ARE FREE AND TAKE ABOUT HALF AN HOUR.

NEXT TIME YOU GET YOUR DRIVERS LICENSE RENEWED, IT WILL LOOK A LITTLE DIFFERENT.

[TAKE: VO NATS]

{***VO NATS***}

TODAY THE NORTH CAROLINA DIVISION OF MOTOR VEHICLES ANNOUNCED PLANS FOR A NEW ELECTRONIC SYSTEM FOR RENEWING AND ISSUING LICENSES.

[TAKE: FS:]

{***PUSH TO FS***}

ONE OF THE NEW FEATURES IS A LASER-ENGRAVED 3-D PHOTO OF YOU.
THESE CHANGES WILL REDUCE WAIT TIME AT THE D-M-V.
THIS IS PART OF A NATIONAL PUSH TO COMBAT IDENTITY THEFT.

Example five shows us how to set up a VO when there's no video at all, just a series of full screen graphics. This station uses upper/lower case for scripts.

Campbell county deputies are investigating a theft at a local store.

TAKE MAP:

They say the break in happened at 3 a-m yesterday at the Food Lion on Timberlake Road.

The person reportedly shattered the door with a hammer . . . and stole about four thousand dollars worth of cigarettes.

TAKE GRAPHIC:

Deputies say he was wearing an orange jacket . . . dark clothing and what looks like a white dust mask and sunglasses.

They say the Bedford County Sheriff's Office responded to an identical theft at the Food Lion Moneta on February 22nd.

The person was wearing the same clothes.

If you have information . . . call the Campbell County Sheriff's Office.

The final example comes from CNN. The producer set up a series of FSGs to lead viewers into a related package putting a personal face on the cost of the war in Afghanistan.

(TJ/OC)

THE TOP U-S MILITARY COMMANDER IN AFGHANISTAN SAYS THE NUMBER OF AMERICAN CASUALITIES IN AND AROUND AFGHANISTAN IS LIKELY TO INCREASE, PARTICULARLY THROUGH THE SUMMER AND MAYBE INTO THE FALL.

IN THE WORDS OF GENERAL STANLEY MCCHRYSTAL: "WE ARE PRESSURING THE ENEMY, AND THEY ARE REACTING TO THAT."

- ANCHOR/OC—ZOOM OUT TO REVEAL VISTA WALL STATS

- (TJ/ZOOM OUT VISTA WALL REVEAL)

SINCE THE WAR IN AFGHANISTAN BEGAN IN OCTOBER 2001, 1-THOUSAND-15 AMERICANS HAVE BEEN KILLED.

(VISTA WALL/REVEAL)

- 163 HAVE DIED IN AFGHANISTAN THIS YEAR –

22 DIED THIS MONTH ALONE.

WIPE VISTA FS

U.S. TROOPS KILLED 2009

- LAST YEAR, 313 WERE KILLED . . . THE DEADLIEST YEAR OF THE WAR SO FAR FOR U-S TROOPS.

- ANCHOR OC/ VISTA WALL

DISSOLVE FS TO MONFILL

"OPERATION ENDURING FREEDOM"

(TJ/OC/VISTA FILL)

BECAUSE PRESIDENT BARACK OBAMA ORDERED MORE TROOPS INTO AFGHANISTAN, THE POSSIBILITY OF A FURTHER SPIKE IN CASUALITES IS NOT HARD TO IMAGINE.

TAKE DNT

*vid 06766244

TRT 2:16

OC: We had a bond.

DNT SCRIPT

(TRACK)

This is one of the last pictures ever taken of Sergeant Brandon Bury. This was just a week ago—in Afghanistan serving with the U-S forces. Last Sunday, two Marines showed up at his parents' home, in Texas.

(SOT)

"They just walked in the back gate and I just said, please tell me my son is alive. Please tell me he's not dead. And they said, ma'am, I can't tell you that. And I started screaming, no, no, please no."

(TRACK)

Sergeant Bury died along with two other marines in Helmand Province.

(SOT)

"With the humvee flipping over and then him drowning, that's all I kept thinking about, him gasping for air."

(TRACK)

The Burys' pain of losing a loved one serving in Afghanistan is shared by many others—and U.S. officials say there will be more.

That's because by the summer's end, there will be the largest number number of U-S soldiers in the country:—100 - thousand—as ordered by President Obama.

In March the President visited troops in Kabul. He explained to them why he put them in that country.

(SOT)

"This is the region where the perpetrators of the crime, Al Qaeda, still base their leadership. Plots against our homelands. Plots against our allies. Plots against the Afghan and Pakistani people are taking place as we speak right here. And if this region slides backwards, and if the Taliban re-takes this country and Al Qaeda can operate with impunity, then more American lives will be at stake."

(TRACK)

The top commander in Afghanistan, General Stanley McChrystal, asked for a surge of U.S. troops and believes it will work.

(SOT)

(Reporter off camera) "Can this enemy be defeated?"

(McChrystal) "Absolutely. I believe the insurgency against Afghanistan is not a unified; it's not a nationalist movement. It's not respected by the Afghan people as you see in polling and in my discussions. So I think absolutely."

(TRACK)

But winning a war has come at a great loss for many families, including Sergeant Brandon Bury's.

His father's now holding on to memories both big and small. Including something as simple as a text message conversation with his son.

(SOT)

"It might be like two o'clock in the morning and I'm watching something on ESPN. And I'd say what do you think of that play? And he'd go, awesome. And that would be it. But we had a bond."

(ANCHOR/OC)

General McChrystal says as of right now, the President and he believe the troop drawdown timeline in Afghanistan will happen as planned.

News workers at all stations in this country speak the same language; it's just that the dialects can vary. The wording for the various directions is usually a function of the newsroom computer system used in that particular station. Some of the more common software programs for writing television news are NewsStar, AP

NewsCenter, EZNews, and ENPS. In our earlier examples, we noted the place where the tape is supposed to start with the marking "take tape." Some stations use the marking "ENG NATVO." Others indicate that point by the marking "M2/VO." They all mean the same thing: This is the place to start the tape. The way we indicate the place at which the director should punch out of the tape in a story could be with the marking "ENG OUT," which means the same thing as "tape ends." In one station, "ENG" means a videotape; in another, that's indicated by "tape," and in others, it's indicated by the particular type of videotape the station uses, such as "M2," "beta," and the like.*

You'll notice that sometimes the time for the tape is indicated near the beginning of the script rather than at the end. It's simply a matter of getting accustomed to the conventions used at a particular station. Although the wording and the positioning of the director cues are sometimes a bit different, we give the director the same information: whether or not the anchor appears on-camera, if a piece of video is involved, and if so, where it starts, where it ends, and how long it is.

Conclusion

By now it should be clear that we have much more to deal with than just the words we write. The copy must support the video and vice versa, and there are other considerations as well. Some have called it writing in 3-D—having to consider the words, the pictures and the sounds we have to work with. This is true even when structuring one of the most basic television story forms—voice-overs. The challenge of incorporating those elements effectively and of providing the script cues that go along with them becomes a bit more extensive when we get to VO/SOTs and packages. The production element of what we do is also important, but the bottom line is still the ability to craft the written part of the story. Use of over-the-shoulder inserts, chroma key, wiping between pieces of video, and other production techniques can add to the presentation of stories. But no amount of jazzy production can rescue a poorly written piece.

We've provided a writing-from-video exercise, which you can find on the Web site that accompanies this book, at www.mhhe.com/tuggle5e. This exercise will allow you to practice writing VOs as described in this chapter, using video shot sheets.

---

*Even when we play stories off video servers, the markings are consistent.

DOs and DON'Ts for VOs

Do

- Write from the video.
- Grab viewer attention right away.
- Make sure everyone on the team knows what we're doing.

Don't

- Leave out times and other cues.
- Write generic copy for generic video.
- Leave out any major information.

Questions

1. What's the relationship between the available video, how we write the story, and how we edit the story?
2. What's the opposite of a high level of SWAP?
3. What are some problems that can arise when you use file footage incorrectly?
4. Which three elements make for an effective OTS?
5. Explain branding in TV news.
6. In addition to the words the anchor reads, what's the other critical part of a broadcast script?

CHAPTER EIGHT

C. A. Tuggle

Television News Story Forms—The VO/SOT

As the abbreviation implies, a VO/SOT begins as a VO, which you're quite familiar with by now. But, as also implied, the VO/SOT involves an additional element, the SOT (sound-on-tape) portion. The SOT (often called a **sound bite,** or simply a "bite") is a brief snippet of an on-camera interview a journalist selects to follow a certain amount of voice-over video. So, the VO/SOT involves more than one voice: the anchor's voice and one or more brief comments from an interview source or sources. Some news operations use the abbreviation VO/B rather than VO/SOT so they can indicate if there's more than one bite. So, a VO/B/B would include two different bites. However, many operations still use VO/SOT because the number of sound bites on the tapes isn't what's really important to the people in the control room. What's really important is the length of the SOT. More about that when we discuss marking VO/SOT scripts.

The Role of a VO/SOT

A VO/SOT lets producers vary the pacing of a news program and allows us to give a little more airtime to a story than if it were a VO, but not as much as to a package. We should use a VO/SOT when we're covering an event and something a participant or observer has to say carries some emotion or impact that we'd lose if we paraphrased the comment for an anchor to read. At times, your bites will come from public information officers (**PIOs**).

Even when you and a PIO have a good relationship, it's important to remember that an official spokesperson isn't as emotionally involved in a story as the people affected are. Many news operations are overly dependent on "official" comments. You should work to get bites from the people who are directly affected. PIOs are generally very helpful to news crews, but there's no way they can share the emotion that someone else experienced because of losing a home or suffering some other tragedy.

One word of caution: Just because you do an interview, don't think you *have* to use a portion of it on the air. If the bite isn't compelling, it's just taking up airtime. Sound is good when the sound *is good.*

Scripting a VO/SOT

When we decide to make a story a VO/SOT, there are a few more steps in the scripting process than when we're working with a VO. Because a VO/SOT begins as a VO, everything that applies to scripting and marking a VO applies to the first part of a VO/SOT. It's still very important to write from the video and to follow all the other guidelines listed in earlier chapters. But with the VO/SOT story form we incorporate an SOT, and we need to do a couple of extra things with the script. As noted in Chapter 1, we believe it isn't enough to place a super over the bite to identify the speaker. Many people are doing other things while the news is on and aren't paying close attention to the screen. If we don't verbally identify the speaker, many viewers won't know who the person is or why what that person is saying is relevant to the story. Some writers and instructors will tell you this breaks the flow of the story and, therefore, it isn't a practice followed in every newsroom; however, we think it should be for the reasons stated above.

The VO portion of the script needs to accomplish several things relevant to the SOT the viewers are about to hear. Often, the writer should identify the person who's about to speak by name and give the person's title, which usually is enough to explain why what the person has to say is relevant. In all cases, the writer should set up the bite by giving the viewers an idea of what the speaker is about to say. A super is a supplement to this spoken information, not a replacement for it.

The third item (thematically setting up the bite) is the most important, but identifying the speaker by name and title is often important as well. It's up to you to decide if the name and title are important to the story. But there's no question that an effective thematic introduction of the bite is critical for story flow.

Setting Up the Bite

The key to an effective setup of an upcoming bite is to give the viewers a sense of what to expect the speaker to say without parroting what we're about to hear. Let's say we've selected a bite from the mayor of a small town in our market. In the bite, the mayor talks about the give-and-take that occurred during an all-night bargaining session she's just wrapped up with the police union. We wouldn't lead to a bite like that by saying something about the mayor's being glad the impasse is over, because that leads the viewer to expect the mayor's comment to have something to do with her relief rather than the bargaining session itself. Equally bad is to lead into the mayor by saying something like "Hooverville Mayor Jane Smith says the deal involved concessions from both sides" if that's followed by the mayor saying "the deal involved concessions from both sides" or even "both sides made concessions." When the bite repeats what the anchor has just said, it sounds foolish indeed.

Another common mistake is to lead into a bite by writing something along the lines of "and Mayor Smith had this to say" or "we asked Mayor Smith about that" or "Mayor Smith commented about the issue." These are very weak ways to lead to a bite. We need to write something specific that sets the stage for the specific bite we're about to hear.

How do we know what to write to set up bites? Our interviewees often provide the words we need, and there's no shame in borrowing liberally from your sources to flesh out your scripts. After all, it's *their* story we're telling. Using our example with Mayor Smith, let's look at a typical question and answer from an interview about this subject.

> **Reporter:** "How would you characterize last night's bargaining session?"
>
> **Mayor:** (in typical politi-speak) "We are indeed gratified that an amicable solution has been reached and that a new contract seems imminent. We believe the union negotiators to be tough, but fair. Neither side got everything it wanted, but the deal we have arrived at proves that when people work toward a common goal and consider the ramifications of various scenarios,

agreement is possible." (At this point the mayor slips up and begins to talk like a real person.) "The bottom line is, the city wanted to come to terms before the deadline and so did the union. The officers didn't want to go without paychecks and we didn't want to face the possibility of having no police on the streets. That would have brought the city to a standstill."

Because you're a sharp reporter, your sound bite antennae immediately send a message screaming to your brain. Sound bite! The final part of the mayor's 45-second answer to the question is a nice succinct 12-second sound bite. In general, you look for bites in the 8- to 12-second range. They can be shorter but need to be at least 5 or 6 seconds long to give the people in the control room time to get the super in and out. Bites can also be longer than 12 seconds, but the information has to be truly compelling to warrant going beyond that.

The mayor has provided what we were after—a good bite of the sought-after length in the language of real people. But what about all that stuff she said before the bite? It isn't totally useless. She gave us a good phrase to use to lead to her bite when she said the agreement involved concessions from both sides. Based on the bite we've chosen and the additional information we've decided to incorporate in the VO portion of the script, we can write the story. But even after we write, we're not finished.

Marking a VO/SOT Script

Just as we have to take a few more things into consideration when writing a VO/SOT script, we also have to add some information for the director and the control room crew that we don't include on VO scripts. With a VO, all we have to do is indicate when the video is supposed to start and how long it is so that the director knows how much video remains as the anchor nears the end of the script. But with a VO/SOT, we have to indicate when the video is supposed to begin, when the audio on the tape switches from natural sound under the anchor's voice to stand-alone sound from a bite, and when the bite ends. You might wonder about the pad video that goes at the end of a VO. It's still necessary to add video pad when editing the tape, but we don't indicate the pad on the script for a VO/SOT when both the VO and the SOT are edited on the same tape. Here's why.

Let's say that we write a script that includes 25 seconds of voice-over and a 12-second bite. That tape is supposed to end at 37 seconds, regardless of when the director rolled the video or what the anchor's read rate is, because the end of the SOT determines the end of the tape. We don't want to see the interviewee just sitting there after the bite ends. We delete the audio and let the video of the interviewee continue to avoid going to black or snow just in case there are problems in the control room, but we definitely want the director to punch out of the tape right after the interviewee finishes her comment. Just in case, though, there's that silent shot (continuation of the shot of the interviewee's face) to cover us.

Reading Up to the SOT

Editing an SOT on the end of a VO creates an additional problem, because the anchor has to stop speaking at a specific time so as not to talk over the top of the SOT or leave a long pause before the SOT begins. There are two ways to keep this from happening. Someone in the control room can count down in the anchor's ear and tell her to slow down or speed up so that the VO read comes out the right length. As an alternative, many news operations place the VO and the SOT on separate playback machines. That gives the director a little more latitude for dealing with discrepancies in how long it takes to read the VO. By putting the SOT on a separate tape, we can wait until the anchor is finished reading the VO (with no one distracting her by talking into her ear while she's trying to read) and then transition to the SOT. The same guideline about including pad video is true if the SOT is on a separate machine. The first piece of video has no definitive out point, but the second one does, so we indicate the pad on the VO script but not on the SOT script. We put pad on both tapes, and on both it's a continuation of the shot with which we ended. Again, we put pad on the end of the SOT *just in case,* but the plan is for the director to punch out as soon as the bite ends, and that's the time we give the director.

Let's return to our friend Mayor Smith and look at a couple of examples of marking a VO/SOT script, followed by explanations of how we arrived at the times indicated and what the new markings mean.

New Contract

	(Dave)
On cam	HOW DOES HOOVERVILLE MAYOR JANE SMITH SPELL RELIEF? C-O-N-T-R-A-C-T.
	(vo)
:00 Take tape and snd under (VO)	AFTER AN ALL-NIGHT BARGAINING SESSION AT CITY HALL . . . THE MAYOR AND POLICE UNION REPRESENTATIVES HAVE COME TO TERMS ON A NEW CONTRACT FOR HOOVERVILLE'S FINEST. NEGOTIATIONS HAD STALLED IN PAST WEEKS AND THE JULY 1ST DEADLINE WAS LOOMING.

THE 25 COPS THE UNION REPRESENTS
THREATENED TO WALK OFF THE JOB IF THEY
DIDN'T GET A 10 PERCENT PAY RAISE AND TAKE-
HOME USE OF THEIR PATROL CARS.

THE MAYOR SAYS THE AGREEMENT INVOLVES
CONCESSIONS FROM BOTH SIDES.

:25 Tape cont. vid
and snd full (SOT)   (sot)
:26 Super: Jane
Smith/Hooverville
Mayor
:37 Tape out   Outcue: "the city to a standstill"
On Cam

IF UNION MEMBERS APPROVE THE CONTRACT
. . . OFFICERS WILL GET A FIVE PERCENT RAISE
AND WILL BE ALLOWED TO TAKE THEIR SQUAD
CARS HOME EACH NIGHT.

The first few directions on the left-hand side of the script are familiar. But at some point we transition from the anchor's voice to sound
on tape, which is new for us. We have to let the director, the audio
person, and other control room personnel know when to make those
adjustments. How do we determine that 25 seconds is the time in this
example? Simply by reading and timing the portion of the VO from
the time the tape starts until the anchor stops talking. In this example,
that goes from "After an all-night bargaining session" to "concessions
from both sides." So at 25 seconds the anchor stops reading and someone else starts speaking. As soon as possible after that transition has
occurred, we put up a super identifying the speaker. Then the director
waits to see :37 on his control room timer and to hear the final few
words of the mayor's comment, called the **outcue.** How do we figure
37 seconds? When the videotape editor got the script, the writer told
her to put down 25 seconds' worth of pictures to go along with the VO
portion of the script. The writer would then indicate the bite he'd
selected, and the editor would add that to the edited piece. In this case
let's assume the bite was 12 seconds long as indicated by the editing
machine timer, making the whole piece 37 seconds long. The editor
would end the mayor's audio at the appointed time but allow the
video to continue for an extra 10 seconds to give the director some
pad; however, the intent is to have him get out of the tape right at
37 seconds. When the director sees :37 and hears the outcue, he goes

back to a studio camera shot of the anchor, who wraps up the story by relaying one final piece of information.

It's important that the story end with the anchor and not with someone else speaking. The anchor comes back on-camera (or we could choose to add more VO after the outcue, making the piece a VO/SOT/VO) to wrap up that story and transition to something else. The stories wouldn't flow together very well if an SOT ended and the other anchor started immediately reading a different story. The anchor's role is to end one story and transition the viewers to the next one and she does so by reading either an on-camera tag or reading over trailing video.

Here's one final note about the script markings on our example. You'll notice that there's a big gap on the right side of the page. When the anchor sees nothing, that means stop reading. You'll also notice that the outcue is listed on the right side of the page. That's so the anchor can also listen for it and be ready for the next on-camera portion of the script. We also add a blank line or two after the outcue, leaving the outcue "floating out in space," to lessen the chance that the anchor might read it as part of his next line. Now, we'll set up the same story using two videotapes rather than one, which is far more common. Again, we do this so the anchor's read of the VO portion doesn't have to come out at exactly a certain time. You might have noticed that each sentence on the right side of the page is indented. This makes it easier for the anchor to know where one thought ends and another begins and makes for a smoother read.

New Contract

	(Dave)
On cam	HOW DOES HOOVERVILLE MAYOR JANE SMITH SPELL RELIEF? C-O-N-T-R-A-C-T.
	(vo)
:00 Take tape vid and snd under (VO)	AFTER AN ALL-NIGHT BARGAINING SESSION AT CITY HALL . . . THE MAYOR AND POLICE UNION REPRESENTATIVES HAVE COME TO TERMS ON A NEW CONTRACT FOR HOOVERVILLE'S FINEST.
	NEGOTIATIONS HAD STALLED IN PAST WEEKS AND THE JULY FIRST DEADLINE FOR A NEW AGREEMENT WAS LOOMING.

	THE 25 COPS THE UNION
	REPRESENTS THREATENED TO WALK
	OFF THE JOB IF THEY DIDN'T GET A
	10 PERCENT RAISE AND TAKE-HOME
	USE OF THEIR PATROL CARS.
	THE MAYOR SAYS THE AGREEMENT
	INVOLVES CONCESSIONS FROM BOTH
	SIDES.

:35 Tape out
(the remaining part of this script
would go on a separate page)
:00 Wipe to tape 2   (sot)
snd full (SOT)
:01 Super: Jane Smith/Hooverville
Mayor
:12 Tape out   Outcue: "the city to a standstill"

On cam   IF UNION MEMBERS APPROVE THE
                                CONTRACT . . . OFFICERS WILL GET A
                                FIVE PERCENT RAISE AND WILL BE
                                ABLE TO TAKE THEIR SQUAD CARS
                                HOME EACH NIGHT.

The difference between this example and the first one is that we end one piece of video and transition to another within the same story. Our VO should take 25 seconds to read, but if the anchor's read is a little short or a little long, it's not a problem because we have 35 seconds' worth of video. Whenever the anchor reaches the end of the VO, the director rolls and transitions to the next tape, which is now only 12 seconds long because it contains the SOT only. The time for the super is different because it's now based on the start time of the second piece of video, not the first one. Also, the two parts of this story appear on separate script pages.

Check Your Media

Production disasters can keep you from turning a story at all. McKinsey Harris couldn't wait to start her job as the newest reporter for WHSV in Harrisonburg, Virginia. She was lucky enough to start just one week after graduation, and to say she was ready to show them all her professors had taught her is an understatement. She was thrilled when a viewer selected her just a couple of weeks into the job to tell the viewer's story of giving back to the community.

McKinsey went into work and pitched the story. Her bosses loved it. The city of Staunton was looking to paint a firehouse that desperately needed the work. City officials allocated $35,000 for the job, but they weren't expecting one of the bids they received. Lisa Coles, a Staunton resident and painter, bid $7,500 for the job, stating that she got it as low as she could by cutting down on labor costs and not running a lot of overhead. She also planned to give $1,000 of her profit from the job back to the fire and police departments. McKinsey had Lisa on board, she had the city manager on board, and she was ready to go with the story.

McKinsey shot the b-roll and interviews and made it back to Harrisonburg about three o'clock. She ingested the video into the system and found out Lisa's interview wasn't exactly what she expected. The audio was there, the shot was white balanced, but the reporter hadn't accounted for how windy it was that day. While she was interviewing Lisa, the camera had slowly shifted from Lisa's face to McKinsey's, and showed the reporter asking questions, smiling, nodding. . . . only Lisa's nose was still left in the shot. McKinsey panicked. She brought in her news director and played the interview for him. They realized most of the SOTs she needed were at the latter half of the interview and featured none other than the station's own McKinsey Harris. The news director told her to stay calm, that this sort of thing happens, and to try to grab Lisa for a quick interview again. Staunton is about 30 minutes from Harrisonburg, but Lisa agreed to meet McKinsey about 20 minutes away and do it again. The entire time McKinsey was driving she had to convince herself that she wouldn't get fired.

Somehow, even after arriving back at the station about five o'clock and being a very "green" reporter, she still managed to get her package and a VO/SOT for a separate story ready and on the air before the six o'clock newscast. She had redeemed herself, but she also learned a valuable lesson to ALWAYS check her interviews—whether it's the shot, the audio, etc.—before she lets that person walk away and she heads back to the station. As a "one-person-band," you have to make sure of EVERYTHING because it's your reputation as a journalist that's on the line.

Stand-Alone SOTs

Let's assume that for some reason, we don't have any video to use with the VO portion of a story. We could set up the story as a straight SOT and use the same markings we used in the second half of our second example of the contract story. However, straight SOTs are pretty rare. Because this is a visual medium and head shots aren't all that compelling, the preference is to use some sort of video to get into the bite—video from the meeting, a photo opportunity with the mayor and union officials, file video of cops on the beat, or something else that goes along with our script. Still, on occasion we might script an SOT with no VO—simply an on-camera introduction from the anchor that leads directly into the bite. The same guidelines apply to that type of lead to a sound bite as to a sound bite lead accompanied by video. We still need to introduce the speaker, tell why his or her comments are important, and set up the bite.

Sometimes we'll run a straight SOT just for a bit of comic relief. When the anchor shows us why it's best not to take ourselves too seriously all the time, that's an added bonus. WSET's (Lynchburg, VA) Shelley Basinger was trying to read the following script:

Shelley Tight

A presidential tongue-twister drew some laughs at the White House last night.

President Obama had a little trouble trying to say the word "superfluous," but came up with a quick excuse.

   ((TAKE BITE)) "To many people, he wrote in his dissent, the superfla . . . let me start that over. To many people, the superfla . . . superfluous . . . it's this lip (laughter). It's hard to say. You try it when you've had 12 stitches (laughter)."

SHELLEY TIGHT

The President needed a dozen stitches after being elbowed during a pickup basketball game.

When trying to say the word the president couldn't say, Basinger couldn't say it either. So instead of getting really frustrated, she laughed, then ad-libbed and said, "Well, I guess I can't say it either. Take a listen." That pitched the story to the bite from the president, and Shelley followed up with the on-camera read to close. The whole thing went on the blooper reel. Viewers actually appreciate those human moments from anchors—just don't have too many of this type.

The Need for Good Communication

As you can tell, television news writers have a lot more to worry about than just the words they put on the page. It might seem we've placed too much emphasis on the directions you add to television news scripts, but the most beautifully written piece can quickly turn into a nightmare on the air without the correct markings. Now that we've added SOTs to the mix, the directions take on added significance. Communication with all the other people who will have something to do with how that story appears on the air is critical. Many news workers have noted that the biggest problem in the communication business is a lack of communication. Never assume that others in the news operation know how you want a story to play. You have to tell them by marking the script appropriately. The thing that stands out as a difference between TV news and all other forms of journalism is the number of people required to put a news program together. All of us must know what to expect.

Be aware that just as we might write a straight SOT story, there are variations on the VO/SOT setup to a story. We might have an SOT/VO or a **VO/SOT/VO**—starting with the bite and then going to voice-over or adding some more voice-over after the bite ends. The order of the elements doesn't matter, as long as **everyone** involved clearly understands what's going on.

Now let's look at a few more examples of how to script VO/SOTs. The first is actually a VO/SOT/VO.

Duck Folo
_____

	(Colleen)
SS: Adoption	HAVING DUCKS AS PETS IS CATCHING ON IN TUCSON.
ENG NATVO	(vo)
	THE HUMANE SOCIETY HAS ADOPTED-OUT 160 DUCKS SO FAR.
	WE BROUGHT YOU THIS STORY EARLIER IN THE WEEK.
	BIOLOGISTS ROUNDED UP THE DUCKS FROM THEIR HOME IN KENNEDY PARK.
	WE WERE THERE WHEN DONNA AVERY PICKED UP HER NEW FINE, FEATHERED FRIEND.
DISSOLVE ENG SOT	
	(sot)
ENG SOT 12 sec.	"I would take as many ducks, turkeys,
CG: Donna Avery/Animal lover	geese, anything . . . chickens. They just run wild at my house, they love it. They come to the door and beg for food and they have food outside (laugh)."

ENG NATVO   (vo)
                          CITY OFFICIALS SAY THERE WERE JUST
                          TOO MANY DUCKS AT KENNEDY PARK.
                          THEIR WASTE WAS CAUSING A VIRTUAL
                          TOXIC SOUP FOR THE FISH . . . AND WAS
                          ALSO HARMING OTHER BIRDS.
ENG OUT

In this example, we start with the anchor on-camera with a graphic from the still store machine over her shoulder. Notice that she's on-camera for only a few seconds before we go to the video. The anchor then reads over video for about 15 seconds before reaching the (sot) marking. She knows this notation means a source is about to speak, so she remains silent during the SOT.

On the left side of the page, we've told the director to dissolve (a different transition than a wipe) from the VO to the SOT at that point and have indicated the sound bite lasts for 12 seconds. We've also indicated "CG," which means character generator and is another way of saying "super." At this point we superimpose the written name of the person speaking on the lower third of the screen. We write the sound bite on the right-hand side so both the director and the anchor can follow it and listen for the outcue. Many news operations write out the bite like this for closed-captioning and also so the anchor can summarize the comment if something goes wrong with playback. The anchor knows not to read this part of the script because it's in quotes and *isn't* uppercase.

When we reach the outcue, the second video clip continues with more VO video following the SOT. When we reach the end of the SOT, the director cues the anchor, who then reads the remaining script over the video. She knows she won't have to look at the camera during the VO and will probably choose to read from the hard copy rather than from the prompter. This will allow her to pay closer attention to how her read rate is matching what we're seeing on screen. VO/SOT/VOs obviously give us an opportunity to use a few more shots than we'd use in a VO/SOT. Remember, this is a visual medium, so when you have good video, think VO/SOT/VO rather than VO/SOT/tag.

Be aware that most of the time, the two parts of a story like this are on separate pages and occupy two lines on the show rundown (see Chapter 11 about producing). So in this example, everything from "ENG SOT 12 sec." would be on a second script page. This helps the director grasp that the VO and SOT are edited separately and that the producer is calling for some type of transition between the two. The second bit of VO video is on the same playback as the SOT, so no dissolve or wipe is indicated; we merely continue with the second video clip.

Blood Testing

	(Colleen)
SS: BLOOD TESTING	A TUCSON HOSPITAL IS PIONEERING NEW BLOOD TESTING TECHNOLOGY.
ENG NATVO	(vo)
	KINO COMMUNITY HOSPITAL'S BLOOD BANK IS THE FIRST IN THE U-S TO HAVE THIS NEW TECHNIQUE . . . CALLED GAMMA REACT SYSTEM.
	NORMALLY . . . BLOOD TESTING TAKES UP TO AN HOUR AND A HALF . . . BUT THIS TECHNIQUE TAKES ONLY ABOUT 25 MINUTES.
	HOSPITAL SPOKESWOMAN BRENDA PARKER SAYS THE HOSPITAL CAN NOW CHECK FOR INCOMPATIBLE BLOOD MORE QUICKLY.
DISSOLVE ENG SOT	(sot)
ENG SOT 15 sec.	
CG: Brenda Parker/Kino Hospital	"In a crisis situation when you need blood in a hurry you've got to be able to find compatible blood fast . . . and this method enables us to identify the antibody fast and get compatible blood much, much faster than the previous method."
ENG OUT	(out)
LIVE	OFFICIALS WITH THE UNIVERSITY OF ARIZONA MEDICAL TECHNOLOGY PROGRAM PLAN TO VIDEOTAPE KINO TECHNICIANS DEMONSTRATING THE NEW TECHNIQUE FOR CLASSROOM USE.

This example is very similar to the duck folo story, except that we've set up this one to have the director punch back to the studio camera at the end of the SOT rather than having the anchor read over more VO tape. The (out) tells the anchor that the SOT has ended and she should be ready to go back on-camera. As with the previous example, everything from "ENG SOT 15 sec." will be on a separate page. Anytime there are two video clips, there are two script pages.

In the following example, we'll look at a story designed to follow a related piece about reputed drug kingpin Charles Miller. The first story details charges that Miller has threatened to harm U.S. students at a veterinary school in the Caribbean if the U.S. government continues to crack down on what it terms his illegal drug operation. That story leads us to this one:

Miller Details

	(Bob)
2SHOT	(2shot)
	TONIGHT, WE'RE LEARNING A LOT MORE ABOUT CHARLES MILLER . . . THE MAN WHO'S MAKING THE THREATS.
Gayle	(Gayle)
	HE HAS A LONG HISTORY OF VIOLENCE BUT HAS BEEN ABLE TO AVOID ARREST ON THE ISLAND OF SAINT KITTS.
SS/CG	(SS/CG)
Super: Charles Miller	AN ARTICLE IN THE WASHINGTON POST GIVES A LOT OF DETAIL ABOUT MILLER.
Add: smuggled drugs from	(add)
Miami to New York	AT ONE POINT . . . MILLER WAS SMUGGLING MORE THAN A TON OF COCAINE AND MARIJUANA A MONTH FROM MIAMI TO NEW YORK.
Add: immunity, witness	(add)
protection program	DESPITE THAT . . . HE WAS GIVEN FULL IMMUNITY AND A PLACE IN THE U-S GOVERNMENT'S WITNESS PROTECTION PROGRAM IN EXCHANGE FOR INFORMATION ABOUT A DRUG SMUGGLING RING.
Add: admitted to	(add)
participating in murders	MILLER ADMITTED IN COURT TO TAKING PART IN THE MURDERS OF FIVE PEOPLE IN A MIAMI CRACK HOUSE IN THE 1980s.

add: State Department: (add)
still dangerous

         STATE DEPARTMENT OFFICIALS SAY
MILLER IS STILL DANGEROUS . . .
THEY WANT HIM TO FACE SMUGGLING
CHARGES . . .

Add: Warning U-S citizens (add)

AND THEY'RE ALERTING PEOPLE ON
SAINT KITTS TO BE CAREFUL.

M2/SOT UP FULL (SOT)
Super: James Rubin/State ("We know of this individual and
Department Spokesman consider this threat, this person,
                                            sufficiently violent to justify taking
                                            these steps.")

RUNS: 08
TAG (tag)

         THE STATE DEPARTMENT IS HINTING THAT
U-S AUTHORITIES WILL RETALIATE AGAINST
MILLER IF HE HARMS U-S CITIZENS.
         THERE ARE 250 AMERICAN STUDENTS
AND 50 AMERICAN FACULTY MEMBERS AT
ROSS VETERINARY UNIVERSITY.

In this example, we start with a 2shot to let the anchors play off each other as they lead to this story. The news operation has no video of Miller and certainly has no video that supports the particular points to be made in this story. So the producer calls for a picture of Miller from still store (SS) and information to be superimposed over that image. That information comes from the character generator (CG). We've indicated to the director the specific places at which to add new information. The anchor has this information as well, so that she can pace herself to read something as we're adding it to the screen. The anchor reads the entire VO portion of this script over a graphic rather than over video.

When we reach the end of that section of the story, we go to a sound bite on M2 (a particular type of videotape) from a State Department spokesperson, and the director adds a super (name and title of the person speaking) on the lower third of the screen. The SOT lasts for eight seconds; then the director punches back to the studio camera for the anchor to read the **tag.** "Tag" is the term used for the final bit of information the anchor reads on-camera to wrap up a story before moving on to something else.

Conclusion

As we noted in Chapter 7, the wording of the directions we provide to the director often varies slightly from one news operation to another. But, again, the basic information we provide on VO/SOTs is the same: Do we start on-camera? Where does the VO begin? Where do we transition to SOT? How long is the bite? Does the anchor finish the story on-camera or by reading more VO copy? We reiterate a point made several other times in this book. The markings are important. Television news is *very team oriented,* and everyone on the team has to know what's coming next for the script and the visual elements to work together as we intend.

We've provided a writing-from-video exercise, which you can find on the Web site that accompanies this book, at www.mhhe.com /tuggle5e. This exercise is set up to allow you to practice writing VO/SOTs as described in this chapter, using video shot sheets and the text of sound bites.

DOs and DON'Ts for VO/SOTs

Do	Don't
• Write specific leads to bites.	• Parrot what the interviewee will say.
• Put VO and SOT on separate playback machines.	• End a VO/SOT without re-establishing the anchor.
• Leave room for error; use (pad) in case of control room mayhem.	• Assume other people on the news team know what's supposed to happen unless you tell them.
• Pick compelling bites.	

Questions

1. What type of information do we want in sound bites?
2. Why is it so important to thematically set up a bite?
3. What are the markings we use on a VO/SOT that we don't use on a VO, and why are they important?
4. Why do many stations choose to put VO/SOTs on separate tapes?
5. What's the role of the anchor at the end of a VO/SOT?
6. What are the pros and cons to verbally identifying speakers in SOTs?

CHAPTER NINE

C. A. Tuggle

Television News Story Forms—The Package

Chances are, many of you reading this book want to be on-air in some capacity, either as a reporter or an anchor. Both are worthy goals. Many viewers choose to watch particular news programs because they like the anchors, and reporting is one of the most important things we do. Gathering facts and weaving them into coherent reports is what journalism is all about. Actually, we should all be reporters, whether we're on-air or not, but for now, let's concentrate on the on-air side.

The life of a reporter seems glamorous and exciting, but that's not always the case. You can make it rewarding, though, depending on how you approach the job.

Why Beat Reporting Matters on Television

Adam Rhew covers business for News14 Carolina. He thinks a lot of young reporters expect stories to *happen*.

Sometimes, in the case of a shooting or a hurricane, they do. But more often than not, enterprise reporting is what stations, their managers and their audiences want. Indeed, Adam knows plenty of news directors who openly discriminate against "desk feeders"—that is, reporters who sit and wait for the assignments desk to dole out a story for the day.

That's why he's such a proponent of beat reporting.

The advantages of maintaining expertise in a tightly focused arena are obvious. Because you know the core issues and key players, you can spend more time digging for scoops. Nuggets of news—often overlooked by reporters unfamiliar with your beat—jump off the page.

Throughout his career, he's had the privilege of covering two specialized beats: Virginia politics and North Carolina business. After three years at the Virginia State Capitol, legislators and their staffers trusted him. They gave him access other stations didn't get. Adam developed relationships that led to exclusive stories and, he believes, unique insights for his viewers.

The principles of beat reporting are astonishingly simple:

Show up—At every meeting, every event, every photo op. Meet everyone. Hand out business cards. And read every piece of background information you can get your hands on.

Be aggressive—When you cover the same people regularly, you get comfortable with each other. Friendships develop. Trust grows. That can make it harder for new reporters to be aggressive when they need to dig for a story. Don't fall victim to this. You must be skeptical, skeptical, skeptical. Every day. There's a way to do it without being hostile. But it's your responsibility.

Treat people fairly—Your credibility is your currency. If you're honest, straightforward and fair, your reputation will open doors all on its own.

Beat reporting is especially important for television journalists. As the news cycle tightens, substantive reporting can lose out to sensationalism. Covering a beat, especially a difficult one such as politics or business, can help fulfill our mission as truth seekers.

Stories rarely *happen* for a beat reporter. But, Adam says, ferreting them out on your own is very satisfying.

It Helps to Enjoy Adrenaline Rushes

WVIR's (Charlottesville, VA) Eddie Sykes says learning in college how to work well under pressure really pays off. Less than six months into his first job, he and a co-worker were en route to one of the most exciting assignments either of them will likely ever cover—taking flight in a faithfully restored B-24 bomber that flew countless missions during WWII. Their day of high-flying excitement turned quickly into a waiting game. One of the planes was experiencing engine trouble, grounding the entire fleet for hours. They originally expected to be back at the station by two o'clock with plenty of time to write and edit; it was now 3:30, and they were on a five o'clock deadline. This was the biggest time crunch they'd ever been under, and it would take everything they ever learned to pull it off. The work started early, with Sykes logging sound on the ground before the flight. The flight itself was a rush of excitement, but by the time they touched down, the threat of not making it to air was becoming a very real possibility. The passenger's seat of the car became Sykes' writing chair, and he spent the ride back mashing his fingers into the screen of his smartphone at breakneck speed. They rolled into the station at 4:45, and with most of the work already finished, were able to edit the piece in less than an hour. It aired just after 6 o'clock. Neither of them had to say it; they knew it was the hardest test either of them had ever taken. But with a product they were both proud of, they knew they had passed with flying colors.

Now that we've gained some experience writing VOs and VO/SOTs, we can move into reporter packages. As the name implies, packages involve reporters and are "packaged," meaning they're fully self-contained pieces. You'll recall that anchors read VOs and VO/SOTs. Their involvement in a package is to set up the story in general terms and introduce the reporter. The anchor should also wrap up the story at the end with some additional fact the reporter was unable to fit into the package itself. This is called the tag. As is the case coming out of VO/SOTs, the flow from one story to another isn't what it could be if the anchor doesn't come back on-camera and wrap up a package before going on to another story. Additionally, it's important to have an anchor say something more than "Thank you, John" at the end of the package. If that's all the anchor says, he or she has no "ownership" of the story. We suggest giving anchors active roles in packages, and that would come in the package lead and the tag.

Other than the introduction and the tag, however, an anchor doesn't have anything to do with the presentation of a package. Once an anchor has introduced the reporter, the reporter takes over and relays the information relevant to the story. So, a package is the first story form we've discussed that involves a reporter's voice. A reporter might gather information for a VO and conduct the interview for an SOT, but neither of those story forms involves the reporter putting his or her voice on tape. A package does.

Stand-Ups

In most cases, a package also involves a **stand-up.** A stand-up is when the reporter appears on-camera in the field and delivers a line or two. A stand-up can appear anywhere in the package—either at the beginning or end or somewhere in the middle. When we place it somewhere in the middle, we call it a "stand-up bridge." Bridges are more common than opening or closing stand-ups. That's because we want the beginning and end of packages to be visually compelling, and the stand-up usually isn't the most compelling video we have to work with.

When a reporter does a stand-up, he or she has to have written a portion of the story so that what the reporter says in the stand-up flows with what comes before it and what comes after it. Usually that doesn't involve actually putting a portion of the story on paper; reporters quickly develop the ability to write in their heads, coming up with good 8- to 12-second stand-ups to flow with the rest of the script they'll write later.

Why Stand-Ups Are Important and How to Do Them Right

Stand-ups are important for several reasons. First, they're the reporter's opportunity for face time. News directors and other managers strive to have the viewers "identify" with newscasters, both anchors and reporters. Though it isn't essential that every package have a stand-up, it would be strange indeed to hear a reporter's voice day after day and never see that reporter's face. Also, stand-ups give you a good opportunity to talk about something for which you have limited or no video, and *when done right*, stand-ups can help draw the viewer into the story by illustrating something. We put emphasis on the phrase *when done right* because we see lots of stand-ups that are just painful to watch. When you do a stand-up, try not to look like you just had surgery to implant a metal rod in your back, and please try not to make a very unnatural turn at the waist (turning away from the mic in the process) to refer to something behind you.

Remember the Mom Rule? If you brought Mom to the scene, would you stand there in front of her, at attention, and turn *away* from her to point something out? Of course not. You'd take dear ole Mom by the hand and walk her over to something and explain what she was looking at. Though you can't literally take the viewers by the hand, figuratively that's what you need to do. Work toward involved stand-ups. If your stand-up doesn't pass the chroma key test (you might as well have been standing in front of an image of the scene projected on the chroma key wall), then why be at the scene at all? DO SOMETHING! This will require (dare we say it?) a bit of choreography to make the stand-up look and feel natural.

Think of it this way: You want your stand-ups to be interactive. The viewers can't become part of the scene directly, but can do so through you. If all you do is stand there looking and sounding stiff, you haven't done anything to engage the viewers. You want to be animated

Taken with Heather's cell phone

WSB "Hot Topics" host Heather Catlin doing a stand-up on the 17th floor balcony of the Four Seasons hotel in L.A. as part of the "Man On A Ledge" junket.

Screen grab from WVIR-TV

Ed Sykes steps through the cramped quarters inside a restored B-24 bomber. In addition to being cramped for space, he was about to be jammed for time.

Taken by Anthony Jetter

WPXI's Brittny McGraw reports live from outside Allegheny County Police Headquarters after a shooting.

Taken by AJ Chodora

News 14 Carolina's McKinsey Harris prepares for a morning live shot in Charlotte, NC.

and make your stand-up interesting and informative, without being goofy (unless the story calls for that approach). Then, you have to match the energy level you projected on-camera when you get to the sound booth to record your package narration. If you sound uninterested or uninteresting, guess what's going to happen? Viewers will find someone who has some energy on another channel. TV news reporters write conversationally in order to sound as natural as possible when delivering those lines.

Live Stand-Ups

In Chapter 12, we discuss live reporting at length, from a producer's standpoint. The producer should be involved in how reporters plan live shots. Where will we go live? What will be happening at the time? Is there any opportunity to be interactive? The reporter and producer should discuss these and other related questions for every live shot. Keep in mind that just because your stand-up is live, it doesn't mean the rules for making it interactive don't apply. Actually, they apply even more because chances are you're doing live at both the beginning and end of a taped piece. We certainly don't want to see you twice looking like you're at boot camp and are terrified of the drill instructor.

Logging

Once he or she has a good stand-up to work with, one key thing a reporter can do to make writing a package easier and quicker is to log the video back at the station, in an edit bay in a remote vehicle at the story site or anywhere he or she happens to be if the reporter's laptop is set up to play back video. Even if the reporter has been on the scene with a videographer the whole time, the reporter still doesn't know exactly what the shots show or exactly what all the possible sound bites and natural sound segments are. The reporter's sound bite antennae might have alerted him or her to several potential sound bites during the interview, but most people can't memorize things well enough to allow them to write a good package without reviewing the video.

During logging, the reporter looks at the video to pick out specific shots to write from, specific sound bites to use in the story, and snippets of natural sound to incorporate. Natural sound is what the microphone picks up when you're not in an interview situation. It could be bells ringing, parts of a conversation, or any other naturally occurring sound. It's important for the reporter to have specific shots, bites, and natural sound in mind when writing the package. We have to write words supported by the video we have, and the sound bites are the backbone around which any package is built. The natural sound clips we incorporate give body to the story. So, a reporter has to note all

Taken by Forrest Carr

KGUN9 reporter Kevin Keen logs video in a live truck.

three elements on the story log and use that material to craft an informative and interesting story. You can write a story without going through the logging process, but chances are it won't be nearly as strong as it could have been had you taken a few minutes to familiarize yourself with what's on the video.

Leading into and out of Bites

In Chapter 8 we discussed the importance of setting up the SOT by indicating who the bite is coming from and why the speaker is important to the story, and giving the viewer an idea of what the source says. We need to do the same thing in a package every time we introduce a new speaker. If we use the same speaker more than once, all we need to do to introduce the second or third bite from the same person is give the viewers an idea of what the source will say. It's not necessary to give the person's name or title again. So getting into SOTs is the same in a package as in a VO/SOT, but because more narration follows the SOT in a package, we now have to be concerned about how we get out of the sound bite as well as how we get into it.

Let's say that several of the bites we're considering using are listed on the log sheet as follows:

Bob Jones—Concerned Citizen

25:30 "I think it's strange

25:40 no public input"

27:14 "any elected official

27:25 disservice to the constituents"

28:12 "what the city is trying to do is an outrage

28:22 we'll speak at the polls"

28:57 "in this day and time

29:05 government of, by, and for the people"

Note that during the logging process, we don't write down every word in the bites. Transcribing an entire interview takes a lot more time than news reporters typically have. Later, after we've selected specific bites to use, we'll go back and get the verbatim of those bites for closed-captioning. But there's no need to write down every word of a bite until we know we're going to use it. Also note that we've indicated the time on the video at which Jones says the first few words of each comment, called the **incue,** and the time at which the bite concludes along with the last few words he says, called the **outcue.** We do this for two reasons. First, when we time the narration parts of the package and add in the times for the SOTs and the stand-up, we know if we've hit the overall time allotted for the piece by the producer. Second, indicating the times helps the video editor find things quickly. Whenever we can save ourselves or someone else some time, we need to do so. In this example, let's say we choose to use the third bite listed. The log shows we're dealing with a 10-second bite, and the videotape editor knows exactly where to find it—28 minutes and 12 seconds from the beginning of the video. The portion of the script that would include this bite would look something like this:

> . . . To say that Bob Jones and his neighbors are concerned would be an understatement.
>
> Jones incue: "what the city is trying to do is an outrage
>
> Jones outcue: we'll speak at the polls"
>
> But we won't have city elections until 18 months from now. In the meantime, the citizens' group has other plans . . . .

We've set up the bite by letting the viewers know to expect Jones to say something about being upset, and we've led out of the bite by picking up on the voting theme. In other words, our narration is a continuation of the thought that Jones started in his bite. These types of transitions, called **tie-writing,** can be very effective in keeping the flow of the story going. Let's look at a sample package script, and see how we can work for flow into and out of bites and how we can incorporate natural sound.

JURASSIC PARK

nat snd full from movie: "Can I touch it?"

In the make-believe world of Jurassic Park, scientists used D-N-A to re-create living dinosaurs. In real life, much of the work done by the Jurassic Park scientists is possible, and in some cases, commonplace.

nat snd full: "Take a look at this strand."

Gene sequencing takes place at this lab and other sites around the country every day. Project director Rob Ferl says what happened in Jurassic Park might be possible one day.

Ferl incue: in terms of basic

Ferl outcue: very rapid rate

But not quite as fast as the fictional scientists do it. In reality, scientists can extract D-N-A . . . even that of extinct animals.

Stand-up: Reproductive biologist Tim Gross is learning a lot about the diets and reproductive systems of mastodons by analyzing ancient, well-preserved mastodon droppings. Getting D-N-A is one thing, but it's the next step that science hasn't reached yet.

Gross incue: once you have DNA

Gross outcue: form an embryo

Scientists agree that it's just a matter of time before they gain that knowledge and something like Jurassic Park is a reality.

Ferl incue: certainly, once you have

Ferl outcue: reconstructing an animal

Gross incue: 20 years ago

Gross outcue: a reality today

Still, it's easier to re-create dinosaurs in Hollywood than it is in the halls of science . . . for now. In Hooverville, I'm Joe Reporter, Newswatch One.

Working with Available Video and Natural Sound

There are several things to note about how the script above is put together. First, think about the video we have to work with. If we didn't have clips from the movie, all we'd have would be shots inside a lab filled with beakers and test tubes and other shots of scientists huddled over petrified mastodon dung. Not exactly compelling stuff. But our friends in Hollywood often send out clips (they call them "trailers") of movies they're about to release. It's good publicity for the moviemakers and good video for us to use if we have a story that lends itself to using clips from a particular movie. In this case, that's exactly what we have. After looking through the trailers, we're struck by a line from the movie as a very good way to immediately capture the viewers' attention. The two kids and their scientist friend are stuck in a tree, and the little girl asks if she can pet the friendly dinosaur that's eating some of the leaves. So, that brief clip becomes the beginning of our news story. We can then get into the facts about what real-life scientists are doing in terms of gene sequencing and the like. Notice also that we've incorporated natural sound full (nat snd) in two spots. First, there's a clip from the movie at the beginning of the story, and then a comment made by one researcher to another as she looks into a microscope. Remember that natural sound is any sound recorded other than in an interview setting. So we can use snippets of conversation, a car horn, a sheep bleating, and other sounds as pacing elements and to add body to our pieces. Use natural sound liberally, as it fits. If a horse neighing has nothing to do with the story, don't use it just because you have it. But if you're doing a story about new train service in your area, maybe you can work in the conductor shouting out "All aboard," or the wheels screeching, or the whistle blowing, or all of those things.

Tie-Writing

Now let's look at some of the transitions. We know from the preceding narration that the project director is going to talk about how his work parallels what happened in the movie "Jurassic Park." He finishes the bite by talking about how rapidly gene sequencing takes place, and we follow that up with another comparison with the movie scientists. Moving on to the second bite, we know that Gross will talk about some "second step" in the re-creation process, and we follow that up with a note about the inevitability of reaching that second step. That leads us into what needs to happen for scientists to reach the point of being able to re-create an animal. Notice that Gross' bite about that subject follows immediately one from Ferl with no narration between the two. We don't need it because one comment leads naturally into the next one. That's called "butting sound bites." We finish the story by following up on Gross' comment about things that would have been unthought of 20 years ago being commonplace today, by noting that the real scientists can't do everything the movie scientists can—at least not yet. So, the goal is to have the parts of the story flow together as seamlessly as possible to support the central theme of the package.

Two Scripts for Packages

Now this part of our script is ready to go to a video editor, who puts the pieces of narration, the nats pops, and the SOTs together and places the appropriate video over the top of the sound track. The first script we provided gives the editor the order of things, and we call it the **editing script.** The next step for the reporter is to put together what we call the show script (at some stations they call it the **producer's script**). That script includes what the anchor is supposed to say to get into and out of the piece (the lead and the tag) and the directions for the director and other control room personnel. That script would look like this.

Jurassic Park

(Anne)

On cam

IT TAKES A HEALTHY DOSE OF
SCIENCE FACT TO MAKE A GOOD WORK
OF SCIENCE FICTION

     AS JOE REPORTER TELLS US . . . THE
BOOK AND MOVIE JURASSIC PARK
MIGHT CONTAIN MORE SCIENCE FACT
THAN WE REALIZE.

:00 Take vid &
snd full (PKG)   (pkg)
Supers:
:01 Courtesy: Universal Pictures
:25 Rob Ferl, geneticist
:42 Joe Reporter, Newswatch One
1:00 Tim Gross, biologist
1:31 Tape out   Outcue: standard
On cam   THE SCIENTISTS SAY AS WE
GET CLOSER TO UNDERSTANDING LIFE
AND MAYBE ONE DAY RE-CREATING
IT . . . WE'LL NEED TO ANSWER
MANY ETHICAL QUESTIONS ALONG
THE WAY.

You can see that the producer's script contains none of what the reporter will say, only what the anchor will say to get us to the reporter's recorded piece. The director really doesn't need to know anything about the content of the piece. She just needs to know when to transition to it, when to put in supers, and when the piece ends so she can come back to an on-camera shot of the anchor.

You might be wondering how we arrive at the times listed on the producer's script. Once the video editor has finished assembling the piece, the reporter looks back at it and notes when each person first appears and, in this case, when a clip from the movie appears so that we can give credit to our Hollywood friends. Those are the times we give to the director for insertion of the supers. The reporter also notes the time at which he finishes his final piece of narration and lists the final few words that he says or, in most cases, simply writes the word **standard** (or "SOQ" for standard outcue). In this case, we've told the director to be looking for 1:31 on the control room clock and to be listening for the reporter to say the line that's standard at the end of packages. In that line the reporter gives the name of the city or location where the crew shot the story, his name, and the name of the news organization. We call that the **signature outcue,** or **sig-out** for short. We place the outcue on the right side of the page so the anchor can also be listening for it. As you can see from the editing script example, in the sig-out we say "I'm Joe Reporter" rather than "This is Joe Reporter." "I'm" is more conversational and helps convey the personal relationship we try to build with viewers.

So, in essence, a reporter is responsible for two scripts for a package. One of those goes to an editor, who assembles the story (in many small markets and even some larger markets, the reporter *is* the editor), and the other goes to the producer and director. The editor puts together the self-contained part of the story, the package itself, and the producer and director deal with the live elements of the story—the lead and tag and the supers.

The Importance of Audio

All too often, the only sound reporters think about while writing is the audio captured during the interview process. But to forget about natural sound is a mistake. The best stories always make good use of nat sound—and to make that happen, reporters must work with the photographer to capture it and write to it.

The best photographers don't leave nat sound to chance and go out of their way to make sure they do a good job of getting it. For instance, video of a quiet wooded setting will come bees, frogs, crickets, the rush of wind through the trees, and so on. If the story is about a search through the woods, then you might hear the barking of dogs, the crunch of searchers' footsteps through the leaves, the chatter of two-way radios, and so forth. We hope in *neither* case will you hear instead audio of the photographer gossiping with co-workers.

If the hallmark of the good photographer is that he or she takes care to accurately capture nat sound, then the hallmark of the good reporter is that he or she works with that photographer to use the nat sound to its maximum effect. The editor will lay in nat sound "under" the reporter's audio track, but sometimes the best use of nat sound requires more than that. It requires a nat sound break, or what some call a "nats pop." Sometimes this can be as simple as writing a pause into the script. Sometimes it requires specific showcasing in the writing. Following are examples of both.

Example 1

	DEPUTIES WERE DETERMINED TO FIND THE LITTLE GIRL. NO ONE WANTED TO GIVE UP.
nat sot up full, shot of deputy jumping off log and splashing into puddle. Runs :01	(nat sot)
	BUT BY MIDDAY . . . SEARCHERS HAD BEEN SLOGGING THROUGH THESE SOGGY WOODS FOR 14 HOURS . . . AND THE STRAIN WAS BEGINNING TO SHOW.
nat sot up full—deputy on radio. Runs :03	"Hey. We've got to get some relief out here. This is nuts."
	BUT NO RELIEF WAS COMING.

Example 2

	IT ALL CAME DOWN TO THIS PITCH IN THE BOTTOM OF THE NINTH.
	KELLY LOCKED EYES WITH THE PITCHER . . . AND HER GAZE NEVER WAVERED AS THE BALL SOARED TOWARD THE PLATE.
nat sot, crack of bat. Runs :02	(nat sot)
	KELLY DIDN'T PAUSE TO SEE WHERE THE BALL WAS GOING.
	AS SHE DASHED TOWARD FIRST THE CROWD ROSE TO ITS FEET.
	WHEN THE BALL CLEARED THE FENCE . . . IT WAS INSTANT PANDEMONIUM.

nat sot, crowd screaming
Intersperse with shots of   (nat sot)
backslapping, etc.
Runs :04

THE TEAM NOBODY BELIEVED IN
HAD DONE THE IMPOSSIBLE.

Effective use of natural sound is essential for great storytelling. Good photographers will find ways to sneak it in without being told. The great broadcast journalism teams work together to make it happen.

Other Audio Elements

Music

The use of music isn't uncommon in television news, although policies vary from station to station. A sports story about car racing might include hard-driving, high-energy music. A story about a little girl battling cancer might include sad piano music. A sweeps piece about teen drinking in an urban bar district might feature hip-hop music. The first question you should ask when proposing to use music is, "Why are we doing this?" Chances are your main interest in music will be to set a mood. In the sports story above, you're using music to say, "This is exciting." In the story about the little girl, you're telegraphing to the audience, "You should be sad." In the drinking story, the music contributes to an electric, contemporary atmosphere.

Some might ask whether it's appropriate for a journalist to suggest to the viewer how he or she should feel. You'll have to make up your own mind about that, taking into account your standards and those in your newsroom. Use of music in a sports story is probably relatively safe; sports activities are, after all, a form of entertainment. Laying sad music into a "sad" story is more problematic. You are, in essence, taking deliberate steps to create sympathy for the subject of your story. Is that appropriate? Is the subject of your story truly deserving of sympathy, and is it up to you to say so? In the case of the little girl cited above, it's probably OK. But then you also have to ask, "Is it *necessary*?" And while you're at it, be careful not to make it too sappy. The bar scene example above might be the most troublesome. Hip-hop music might indeed create a contemporary atmosphere, but the "cool" music might also suggest to the wrong people that underage drinking is cool.

Music is used most appropriately when it's a natural part of the scene you're documenting and the photographer records it as nat sound.

If you decide to use music, as with any other communication tool, make sure you know the message you're trying to deliver with it. The message must be appropriate and not subject to misinterpretation. One guiding principle to consider is this: The less "feature" the story, the less likely that it would be appropriate to add music.

The Diamond Approach

In Chapter 1 we mentioned that broadcasters don't use inverted pyramid style. For packages, we sometimes use the **diamond style.** The diamond style is especially useful when writing packages in which we're dealing with something that affects a large number of people. Some examples might be the marriage penalty tax, changes in one of the city's zoning ordinances, or a promising cancer treatment. In each case, the tendency is to hit the viewers with a bunch of numbers and statistics: Married couples pay 10 percent more in taxes than unmarried people living together do, the zoning change would result in the closing of 20 local businesses, the new treatment would help the 400,000 Americans suffering with a particular type of cancer.

Don't misunderstand. Using some supporting numbers and statistics is important. But we want to "people-ize" stories—to tell them in human terms through the eyes of an individual, a family, or a small group. We can then use the experiences of the people who are our examples to make the stories more interesting. The three stories we just mentioned might start something like this:

> BEING MARRIED COSTS MIKE AND JAN PARKER AN EXTRA 500 DOLLARS IN TAXES EACH YEAR.
>
> THIS HARDWARE STORE HAS BEEN IN KEITH ROLLYSON'S FAMILY FOR 60 YEARS. BUT A CHANGE IN A HOOVERVILLE ZONING ORDINANCE MIGHT FORCE THE FAMILY TO CLOSE THE STORE FOR GOOD.
>
> SAM SMITH PLAYED COLLEGE TENNIS . . . BUT NOW HE CAN BARELY WALK. HE HOPES A NEW CANCER DRUG HELPS HIM GET BACK ON THE COURT SOMEDAY.

Remember, we have to catch the viewers' attention right away. Personalizing the lead sentence helps us do that, and the example of how the issue affects a person, family, or small group forms the top part of the diamond. The middle (and bigger) part of the diamond is for numbers, statistics, comments from experts about the subject, and the like. The bottom of the diamond is where we come back to the person or people we're using as an illustration. Using the three

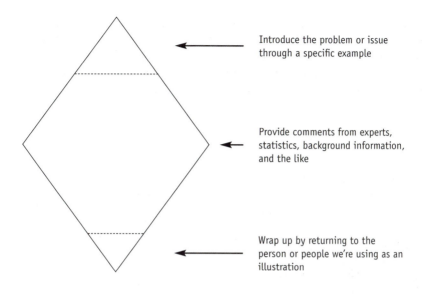

Introduce the problem or issue through a specific example

Provide comments from experts, statistics, background information, and the like

Wrap up by returning to the person or people we're using as an illustration

stories we've been talking about, that approach would allow us to close by mentioning what the Parkers hope the tax code changes would mean for them, what the future holds for the Rollyson family hardware business, or what the prognosis for Sam Smith might be and whether he'll be hitting backhands anytime soon.

Donuts

In local television news today, lots of stories include the reporter live on the scene. Sometimes, the reporter appears on-camera for a minute or more to update the viewers about a breaking story that has just occurred, and there's been no time to shoot and edit video. More often, however, the reporter has had time to put together a taped piece, which she introduces live from the field. This type of report is called a **donut** in some newsrooms and a "sandwich" in others. A donut is a special type of package and is a bit more involved than a regular package is.

With a donut, the anchor still sets up the story in general terms and introduces the reporter. But rather than introducing the reporter's taped package, the anchor "pitches" to the reporter in the field, who's live on-camera. The tone of the introduction changes a bit, and of course the script markings change some as well. The reporter further sets up the story and introduces the taped portion.

The way the package part of a donut is structured is a lot like a regular package, but there are a few differences. First, because of the extra time it takes for the live reporter segments before and after the package, the video clip will have to be a little shorter for a donut than it might be if there were no live elements. Second, because we see the reporter before and after the package, there's no reason to use a stand-up within the piece. That would mean seeing the reporter three times in one story. Some large-market stations take that approach, but we think that's too much reporter and not enough other video. Third, because the reporter is going to come back on-camera after the package, there's no need to include a sig-out at the end of the video. It would sound silly to hear "In Hooverville, I'm Joe Reporter, Newswatch One" and then switch to a shot of Joe saying something else. Let's take our Jurassic Park story and set it up as a donut. We'll assume we're airing the story to coincide with the big opening of the movie at the Hooverville Metroplex. The first showing is at 7 P.M., and by the time we go on the air with this story at 6:11, the ticket line already stretches out the door and halfway around the block. Here's how we set up the story to incorporate live reporter presence at the scene.

Jurassic Park

	(Bill)
On cam	IT TAKES A HEALTHY DOSE OF SCIENCE FACT TO MAKE A GOOD WORK OF SCIENCE FICTION.
	JOE REPORTER IS STANDING BY LIVE OUTSIDE THE HOOVERVILLE METROPLEX WHERE A LOT OF PEOPLE ARE WAITING TO SEE THE NEW MOVIE JURASSIC PARK.
	JOE . . . WE UNDERSTAND THIS MOVIE MIGHT CONTAIN MORE SCIENCE FACT THAN WE REALIZE.
Take LIVE	(Joe ad lib)
	Roll cue: "dinosaurs running loose"
:00 Take vid & snd full (donut)	(pkg)
Supers:	
:01 Courtesy: Universal Pictures	
:25 Rob Ferl, geneticist	
1:00 Tim Gross, biologist	
1:21 video out	Outcue: "halls of science . . . for now."
Take LIVE	(Joe ad lib)

On cam	THANKS, JOE. SCIENTISTS SAY
	AS WE GET CLOSER TO UNDERSTANDING
	LIFE AND MAYBE ONE DAY RE-CREATING
	IT . . . WE'LL HAVE MANY ETHICAL
	QUESTIONS TO ANSWER
	ALONG THE WAY.

The story is essentially the same as in the previous example, except that Joe is now live on-camera outside the movie theater before and after the package runs. Also, we don't write down what Joe says in the field, except for his final few words leading to the tape. The "**roll cue**" lets the director know when to roll the video. The outcue is different than in the previous example because the reporter will come back on-camera briefly after the package, so there's no sig-out. We might also include a Q and A to highlight anchor/reporter interaction.

There are two other types of packages we'll mention briefly. An anchor voices anchor packages, and because the anchor is on the set, anchor packages typically don't include a stand-up or a signature out-cue if they appear on the same show he or she is anchoring. Nat sound packages include no narration at all—just bites, natural sound, and perhaps a bit of music or other sound. Here are some more examples of package scripts.

POPULAR RESTAURANT REOPENS

{***ANCHOR***}

FOR WEEKS, CUSTOMERS HAVE BEEN WAITING FOR A POPULAR RESTAURANT TO REOPEN IN DONALDSVILLE.

"THE GRAPEVINE" HAS BEEN CLOSED SINCE HURRICANE GUSTAV HIT.

BUT AS NEWS-TWO'S DANA HACKETT TELLS US. . . . THE OWNERS AREN'T LETTING THE HURRICANE KILL THEIR SPIRIT.

[TAKE PKG]

{***PKG***}

HURRICANE GUSTAV TOOK A PRECIOUS TREASURE AWAY FROM THESE FOLKS.

[TAKE SOT

AT: 12:43:08

TO: 12:43:11

DURATION:0:03]

{***SOT FULL***}

<When I found out they were closed, I was like: what's going on?>

[TAKE SOT
AT: 12:40:12
TO: 12:40:13
DURATION:0:01]
{***SOT FULL***}
<Can't go eat. (laughs)>

NO DELICIOUS DISHES. . .
NO DAILY LUNCH GETAWAYS. . .
JUST EAGERNESS FOR THIS RESTAURANT TO REOPEN.

[TAKE SOT
AT: 12:32:19
TO: 12:32:24
DURATION:0:05]
{***SOT FULL***}
[SUPER: Cynthia Schneider, Restaurant Owner]
<They stop by our house or they call and say, "When are you going to
open?" They'll come to the door and say, "Please just cook me something!">

[TAKE SOT
AT: 12:39:14
TO: 12:39:20
DURATION:0:06]
{***SOT FULL***}
[SUPER: Cassie Ester, Waitress]
<I couldn't wait. I was telling everybody Oct. 8th, it's a Wednesday, we'll be
back.>

[SHOW VIDEO OF "OPEN" SIGN LIGHTING UP]

FINALLY . . . THEY ARE.
[TAKE SOT
AT: 12:31:07
TO: 12:31:11
DURATION:0:04]
{***SOT FULL***}
<Exciting and frustrating and scary all at the same time.>

IT'S A SEA OF EMOTIONS FOR CYNTHIA SCHNEIDER, KNOWING HOW MUCH
WORK IT TOOK TO GET THIS PLACE BACK IN SHAPE.

[SHOW PICTURES OF DAMAGE]

[TAKE SOT
AT: 12:31:12
TO: 12:31:15
DURATION:0:03]
{***SOT FULL***}
<We had roof damage during Gustav. The roof flew off into the courtyard.>

. . . LEAVING HER RESTAURANT UNRECOGNIZABLE.

[TAKE SOT
NAME: DANA STAND UP
AT: 12:51:52
TO: 12:52:02
DURATION:0:10]
{***SOT FULL***}
[SUPER: Dana Hackett, Reporting]
<They've cleaned up the courtyard and fixed their offices. But it cost them
30,000 dollars to do it. They've lost business for an entire month.>

THESE EMPLOYEES . . . LOST PAYCHECKS FOR A MONTH TOO.

[TAKE SOT
AT: 12:38:22
TO: 12:38:27
DURATION:0:05]
{***SOT FULL***}
<Especially without any other income, when this is your only thing you rely
on, it was very hard.>

[TAKE SOT
AT: 12:32:46
TO: 12:32:51
DURATION:0:05]

{***SOT FULL***}

<They're part of my family. So there's that sense of obligation that you want to be able to take care of them.>

WITH BUSINESS BACK, SHE CAN.
AND FOR ALL THE STAFF . . . SOME RELIEF.

[TAKE SOT
AT: 12:39:39
TO: 12:39:43
DURATION:0:04]
{***SOT FULL***}

<You can get your rest at night. You don't have to worry about how you're going to pay this or how you're going to do that.>

[TAKE SOT
AT: 12:34:47
TO: 12:34:52
DURATION:0:05]
{***SOT FULL***}

<To be back to our crazy restaurant routine is thrilling.>

IN DONALDSONVILLE, DANA HACKETT, WBRZ NEWS 2.

You'll notice that throughout the restaurant script the reporter has given the video editor time cues for where to find the snippets of audio, and a few suggestions about where to place certain video images based on what the reporter had in mind when she wrote particular lines. Don't be too proscriptive when asking your editor to place certain shots in certain places, because you have to allow him or her to be part of the creative process. But it is important to point out specific lines you write with specific video in mind. You'll also notice how short the snippets of sound are. Other than the stand-up, nothing is longer than five or six seconds.

At first, the example below looks quite a bit different from the previous example. This story aired on a news magazine show, so it's quite a bit longer than what you'd see on a typical local newscast. But even though it looks different, the information the writer has given to the video editor is exactly the same except that the reporter wrote in pen in the margins the information about where to find the snippets of sound. It still follows the same format, something we call the Big Mac approach. The basis of the sandwich and the story are the meat (sound bites) and the bread (reporter narration). You have to indicate the order of the bites and narration, and in some way indicate where the bites are located so the editor can find them easily. Then it's up to him or her to put the bread and the meat together, adding in other ingredients along the way, such as nats pops, specific shots, and so on. The REP/VO indication in this script simply indicates that Suzi gathered the information and voiced the narration.

STORY SCRIPT FORM

TITLE	WHO'D BE A PETITIONER?
REP/VO	**SUZI/SUZI** **DATE: July 30th** **TRT:**
LEAD IN	Earlier this week here on B-O-N we investigated the phenomenon of China's black jails—unofficial holding houses for migrants from the countryside who've come to the city to petition the central government. For those held . . . life is a nightmare. But even for those who aren't thrown into a black jail, or escorted forcibly back to their villages, life can be pretty miserable. Today B-O-N's Susan Tart takes a look at why these desperate people come to Beijing—and what their daily life is like when they get here.
SCRIPT	Life's. Not. Fair. And for the thousands of petitioners who leave their families and travel great distances to Beijing each year, this can be a hard lesson to learn. No one has learned that lesson better than Chen Zeyu. He says his local government took his land. CHEN ZEYU, PETITIONER *"The authorities told me that if I wanted compensation, they'd use the dirt-digging machines to kill me and give me four-thousand dollars for my body."* With threats like this from his local government, Chen now spends all his time and money traveling to Beijing in hopes that someone . . . anyone . . . will be able to help. B-O-N first met Chen last March, on his first trip to the city. But as with his previous trips to the local offices, it too, proved unsuccessful. CHEN ZEYU, PETITIONER *"Every time I petition, I go home and get put behind bars. I've been in prison twice. They told me I'd be sued and sentenced for a crime if I came to Beijing again."* Local governments often employ undercover means to discourage people from petitioning . . . that can mean threats, beatings, even detention—the so-called black jails. Chen says living in fear has become a way of life.

CHEN ZEYU, PETITIONER

"Rumor has it that a petitioner was killed on Friday. I didn't see it, so I don't know if it's true. I'm afraid that it could happen to me. But eventually, everyone will die, so I might as well die petitioning for my own rights."

Even a place to sleep isn't guaranteed. We went to interview Chen in a village outside Beijing. He and other petitioners pay 75 cents a night for lodging like this. But when the landowner saw the camera, she kicked us out and told Chen not to come back. Chen didn't seem fazed. In fact, he carries a burlap sack in his bag for such occasions.

STANDUP *"Chen says at times when petitioning, he's slept underneath a bridge, not too different from this one. It's far from nice, but it beats the shelter of a black jail any day. Like Chen, many petitioners come to Beijing to fight for justice. But sometimes they find themselves fighting just to survive."*

Shu Kerong is also petitioning for land rights. In her case the real estate developer who took her land is also her son's school principal.

SHU KERONG, PETITIONER

"I went to the principal to get my land back. He told me he'd seek revenge. He then took it out on my son and damaged my son's chair so that he had to stand up the entire day at school."

Shu also met with B-O-N in March. She's back to plead her case for a third time.

SHU KERONG, PETITIONER

"All I got after petitioning was a sentence of 10 days in prison when I went home. I'm sure I'll be jailed when I return again. But there hasn't been a result yet and so I have to do it. My family is waiting for me and there's no other school for my son to attend."

Petitioning like this is a constitutional right but, according to Beijing lawyer Liu Xiaoyuan, rarely successful.

LIU XIAOYUAN, LAWYER

BEIJING QIJIAN LAWFIRM

"The percentage of cases that are resolved from the central office in Beijing is extremely low. One official said to me that about 99 percent of the cases are reasonable petitions and should be resolved . . . but the number that actually gets resolved is less than 2 percent."

Desperate and with nowhere else to turn, petitioners risk it all to be part of that small two percent. Beijing doesn't want the petitioners staying here, so it can be hard for them. B-O-N contacted the national petition office in Beijing, which refused an interview. For the sake of the petitioners, we decided not to contact the local government bureaus.

	As social conflict increases, Liu says more and more petitioners are coming to Beijing. But the system is still pretty much the same system that was developed in imperial times three-thousand years ago. LIU XIAOYUAN, LAWYER BEIJING QIJIAN LAW FIRM *"The increase in petitioners has brought a lot of attention to the issue from the central government. Beijing has asked the local governments to pay more attention to their requests. But it has mainly overlooked how petitioners are punished after going back to their hometowns."* And for the petitioners that means few changes. LIU XIAOYUAN, LAWYER BEIJING QIJIAN LAW FIRM *"Sometimes I have to tell petitioners that they might as well quit. Even though the law says they deserve their rights, the legal system is undeveloped and some cases just don't have a fair ending . . . no matter how long they fight for."* China's longest petition case ended in 2008 after nearly 30 years. Chen has been fighting his case for six years. CHEN ZEYU, PETITIONER *"I have no land, no source of income, no guarantee of life. I have no idea what I'm going to do. My life at home is threatened and so I'll probably have to move. It's all gone."*
Sign Off	**Susan Tart + BON**
Talking Points	Studio chat

The next example is a feature story. At the time, the reporter was still in college and this story was part of the packet that got him into the Hearst National Championships. As with the other two examples, look for strong central characters and a defined story arc (a developed central thesis) in this piece. As with the black jails example, the reporter in this case provided time cues in pen in the margin. In all three package script examples the format is slightly different, but the information that goes to the video editor is the same.

DRIVE-IN NOSTALGIA

Track

GREGORY BRUNSKILL IS LIKE MANY MOVIE-GOERS WHO COME TO THE RALEIGH ROAD OUTDOOR THEATRE . . . WELL . . . EXCEPT PERHAPS A LITTLE MORE DEDICATED.

Brunskill

"It's a 12-hour drive from Long Island with a couple of stops in between."

Track

WHILE VISITING HIS FATHER IN HENDERSON . . . BRUNSKILL AND HIS FAMILY ARE JUST A FEW OF THOSE WHO CAN'T RESIST A TRIP TO NORTH CAROLINA'S OLDEST OPERATING DRIVE-IN THEATER . . . . . A PLACE THAT REACHES BACK TO A GOLDEN AGE.

Jim Kopp

"it's just a piece of Americana."

NATS POP

"Good evening . . . how are you doing tonight?"

Track

JIM KOPP HAS OWNED RALEIGH ROAD SINCE 2006. AFTER BUYING THE SIXTY-TWO-YEAR-OLD THEATER . . . THE FORMER LIBRARY OF CONGRESS ADMINISTRATOR AND MOVIE LOVER REMODELED THE PROJECTION ROOM AND CONCESSION STAND WITH THE DREAM OF PROVIDING AN EXPERIENCE YOU CAN'T FIND AT A REGULAR THEATER.

Kopp

"There's nothing like putting a movie on the large screen. Having the kids play on the playground. Seeing the families out in the cars. Popping the popcorn. You get all that together . . . and it's just magical.

Track

AND KOPP OFFERS THE MAGIC EVERY WEEKEND OF THE YEAR . . . WHEN HE TURNS THIS ORDINARY FIELD INTO A HOLLYWOOD ESCAPE.

Stand-Up

"And of course, once you have your popcorn and your drink . . . all you have to do is turn on your radio to listen to the show."

Track

HOWEVER . . . KOPP ADMITS THE DRIVE-IN BUSINESS ISN'T ALL THAT PROFITABLE. RALEIGH ROAD IS ONE OF FEWER THAN FOUR-HUNDRED DRIVE-INS LEFT IN THE U-S. BUT KOPP SAYS HE DOES EXPECT THE CROWDS TO KEEP HIM IN BUSINESS . . . WHICH IS GOOD NEWS FOR DRIVE-IN LOVERS LIKE BRUNSKILL.

Brunskill

It's a moment that we're creating . . . and this is one of the moments I like to create for my children.

Track

AND WITH THOSE MOMENTS . . . WHO WOULDN'T WANT A TASTE OF THIS SLICE
OF AMERICANA. IN HENDERSON . . . I'M JUSTIN PAGE.

Conclusion

Remember, when you're writing a package, your job is to provide the glue to get the viewers to the next sound bite or piece of natural sound. Get to that point as expeditiously as possible. You aren't paid on the basis of how many words you cram into your narration, but on the basis of how well you tell stories. Some of the best stories have limited narration and some (nat sound packages) include no reporter voice at all. You aren't the focus of the story. The people you're reporting about are.

Remember also that your story script is only part of what you're responsible for. The producer's script contains vital information, and the reporter is responsible for making sure that information is complete and accurate. If one person in the chain isn't "on the same page," the package you worked so hard on can wind up looking terrible on the air. Because the reporter, videographer, and editor have done most of the work on a package and it's very close to being fully self-contained, the people in the control room can take a bit of a breather while the package is rolling and "gear up" for what's ahead. But that happens only if all the needed directions are on the script.

We've provided a writing-from-video exercise, which you can find on the Web site that accompanies this book, at www.mhhe.com /tuggle5e. This exercise is set up to allow you to practice writing packages as described in this chapter, using video shot sheets and the text of sound bites.

Package DOs and DON'Ts

Do

- Give the anchor an active role.
- Work for flow from track to bites and back to track.
- Incorporate natural sound breaks.
- "Personalize" stories.

Don't

- Stand stick-straight on stand-ups.
- Leave out *any* cues on the producer's script.
- Become the focus of the story.
- Forget that reporting can be hard work.

Questions

1. What's the primary difference between a package and less involved story forms?
2. What are the purposes of a stand-up and the best way to fulfill those purposes?
3. Discuss the concept of story flow in packages.
4. Discuss the role natural sound plays in packages.
5. Why do we need two scripts for packages?
6. Discuss the diamond approach and which stories are best told through that approach.

Writing Sports Copy

Sports is the only "beat" to which we assign several news personnel on a daily basis. No other subject except weather receives as much airtime on local newscasts every day. Therefore, it's important to make the sportscast as watchable as it can be—and not just for die-hard sports fans. How we write the stories is a big part of that. As is the case with covering any beat, it's important to understand the subject and to know what you're talking about, but it's even more important to be able to impart information in understandable terms. Science and medical reporters have to "boil down" information and specialized terminology for viewers. Sports reporters should do the same.

How Writing Sports Differs

As for writing guidelines, many things about writing sports copy are the same as writing news copy. The story types are the same: VOs, VO/SOTs, packages and all the little variations of those basic TV story types and their radio counterparts. The keys to good writing are the same as well, and sports writers should follow the guidelines news writers are supposed to adhere to. There are a few differences between writing sports and writing news, and there are some guidelines that broadcast journalists covering sports should pay particular attention to.

In TV, especially with VOs, writing sports is even more driven by the available video than is news, particularly when it comes to highlights. Because it's important to identify particular players and what they did to help win (or lose) the game, highlights can almost become play-by-play in miniature. Because the pictures often speak for themselves, other than the name of the player in question and a brief description of the play, sports writers don't need to provide a whole lot of information. They can get away with dropping verbs and doing other things that would be taboo when writing a news story. For example, consider this description of a basketball play: "Pierce . . . from long range . . . good!" That's not much of a sentence in grammatical terms, but it gives the viewer everything he or she needs to know about that particular play. So when writing sports, you can get away with incomplete sentences—but never incomplete thoughts.

In addition to having some latitude with sentence construction, sports writers also enjoy some freedom when it comes to numbers and statistics. We caution news writers about trying to cram too many numbers and statistics into a story, but stats and numbers are a big part of sports, so television sports journalists use numerical information more freely. Of course, you can still overdo this. Stories containing sentences such as these actually go on the air: "Meet Joe Hoopster. The six-foot-nine-inch, 210-pound junior at Local High School averages 22 points per game, shooting a sizzling 72 percent from the floor. He pulls down an average of 11 rebounds and blocks six shots while playing only 27 minutes per contest." Only the most avid sports fan can sit through that. The problem is that people covering sports for local television or radio news sometimes get caught up in a sports culture and fail to remember that many potential viewers aren't so enamored with numbers. By falling into that trap, sports producers, reporters and anchors might actually be alienating potential viewers.

People covering sports enjoy some freedom when it comes to openly criticizing the teams they cover. Newscasters are supposed to be unbiased observers, but sportscasters are sometimes *expected* to be judges of the effectiveness of a new strategy or of a decision by team management. Opinion and commentary are part of a sportscaster's repertoire. But if you engage in commentary, label it as such.

Things to be Careful About

Although some commentary and criticism are acceptable in sports, sportscasters and writers should be cautious about being critical all the time. That just leads to charges of cynicism. But those covering sports should also avoid the other extreme—becoming shameless boosters of a team. If a team does well, it's certainly OK to say so, but when putting sports stories together you should be careful not to let a personal affinity for a team affect how you cover that team. Although writers of sports scripts do enjoy some latitude compared with their news writer counterparts, sports folks take some liberties that make the people in the newsroom think the people in the sports department could never cover serious news. Part of that comes from a marked overdependence on clichés in sports copy.

"Sports Speak"

A look at sportscasters from stations in markets of all sizes across the country would show that many sportscasters and the people who write some of their scripts for them tend to use terms that might be difficult for anyone but the most avid fans to follow. Some news directors and consultants are fond of saying "only 25 percent of the audience is interested in sports." There is some evidence to back up that claim,[1] but the question arises, "Then why are the ratings so good for the Super Bowl, the Olympics, the World Cup?" Might it be that many of our potential viewers have some interest in sports, but local sportscasters don't do a very good job of taking advantage of that interest? If so, what can aspiring television sports journalists do about it? One solution would be to write stories that don't require the viewers to have a sports dictionary handy. Currently, "sports speak" abounds on local sportscasts in all parts of the country, and it doesn't come just from the new folks in small markets trying to break into the business. Here are just a few of the terms and phrases that sportscasters overuse and the interpretations of those phrases.

"He was hacked in the act." (A basketball player was fouled while shooting.)

"He has all the tools." (Then maybe he should guest star on a home improvement show.)

---

1. See, for example, T. Atwater (1984), "Product Differentiation in Local TV News," *Journalism Quarterly*, 61, pp. 757–762; T. Wulfemeyer (1983), "The Audience for Local Television News: Getting to Know Interests and Preferences," *Journalism Quarterly*, 60, pp. 323–328.

"He's a team player." (He's not the star.)

"The team is taking things one game at a time." (It would be difficult to play two games at once, now wouldn't it?)

"They have their work cut out." (These guys don't stand a chance.)

"The team can't take anything for granted." (The team should win this game by 40 points.)

"They need to turn it up a notch." (The normal halfhearted effort won't be enough against this opponent.)

The list could go on and on and fill up several pages. In addition to using tired phrases, sportscasters also slip into sports lingo frequently. Here are some of those examples and what they really mean.

dinger, tater, round tripper—home run

ribbie—run batted in

he went yard—he hit a home run

frozen rope—an accurate football pass

laser beam—a solid base hit

reaching paydirt—scoring a touchdown

a kiss off the glass—a soft shot off the backboard

between the pipes—where a hockey goalie plays

Again, the list could go on and on, but you get the picture. The problem is that sportscasters and writers have to come up with interesting ways to say essentially the same thing night after night. Recognizing this, we still suggest that using terminology that requires viewers to figure out what the sportscaster is saying does sportscasters and producers more harm than good. It's more important to be clear than clever, and speaking in code certainly doesn't encourage those outside the culture to become a part of it. The goal is to attract viewers: It isn't to send 75 percent of the viewers scrambling for their remotes or to their computers to check scores there.

Getting Good Bites

No reporter can control what an interviewee says, but we have ultimate control regarding whether a certain comment makes it on the air. A large-market news director once told the people on his sports staff they wouldn't be allowed to use bites from coaches or athletes anymore if they couldn't come up with some people to interview who didn't speak using clichés only. On one occasion, a sportscaster even made fun of the coach he'd just quoted for saying his team could "take nothing for granted" against an opponent the better team crushed on a regular basis. The sportscaster made fun of the coach, but he used the bite. Here are some proclamations from coaches and athletes that indicate almost no thought on the part of the speaker and even less thought on the part of the person who let these comments go on the air. Again, we've provided interpretations.

"We have to put that game behind us." (We really stunk up the place, and I sure hope we don't play so poorly again this week.)

"I'm more interested in team goals than in personal accomplishments." (Yeah, right.)

"I do what I can to help the team." (If it weren't for me, these bozos would have lost.)

"We have to stay focused and give it 110 percent." (In terms of deep-thinking competition, Plato has nothing to worry about from jocks who use this line all the time.)

"We'll do our best and hopefully we'll come out on top." (Don't most sports figures hope their teams come out on top?)

If those conducting interviews would do some homework and come up with good questions, coaches and athletes might not use such tired, banal phrases all the time. Good questions frequently lead to good answers. But if you come up with really outstanding questions and still find yourself interviewing someone who's stuck in the sports-speak rut, go interview someone else. You'll be doing the viewers and the person in question a favor.

Locker-Room Interviews

Often, sports reporters interview sports figures in controlled settings. Sometimes, however, that isn't the case, such as after a big game covered by a lot of television stations, newspapers, magazines and radio stations. Semicontrolled mayhem is a fairly accurate description of what you'll find. In the locker room, it's fairly common to see an athlete surrounded by 20 or more members of the media, all trying to get a nice cogent bite for use that night or a quote for the next morning's newspaper.

There are a few "rules of the trade" to remember in these settings. First, you're not doing a documentary about the athlete in question, and he or she probably isn't in the mood (especially after a loss) to expound on the meaning of life. You're there to get a comment or two about the game that just ended and about the athlete's or the team's performance in it. Everything else can wait until another time. Asking a dozen questions tends to upset the athlete and your media colleagues. They all see it as a waste of their time.

Second, every one of your colleagues is on a deadline, and some deadlines are coming up more quickly than others. For example, the radio reporter who's in the locker room to get comments for a live broadcast is under greater pressure than the television reporter who needs to get a bite or two for a newscast that's two hours away. By deferring to the radio reporter for a few minutes, you might set the stage for a return favor sometime in the future. A little professional courtesy can go a long way in forging a relationship with someone you work alongside on a regular basis.

Third, although the audience rarely hears your questions (except when you're doing a live report), your colleagues hear everything you ask. Sometimes you have to ask something the first athlete has already addressed because you were talking to another athlete at the time and you need a particular answer from the first athlete. Asking questions that someone else has already asked is common and most athletes handle it graciously, as do other media representatives. But the truly dumb questions will hound you throughout your career, so try not to ask any. Many newspaper writers tend to think of television and radio reporters as something less than journalists anyway, and when you ask a question for all to hear that makes you sound as though you don't think before you speak, you only make matters worse.

A classic example happened in the Washington Redskins' locker room after they won Super Bowl XXII. Someone asked Doug Williams, a product of Grambling and the legendary coach Eddie Robinson: "Doug, how long have you been a black quarterback?" To his credit, Williams handled it beautifully, answering: "Since I left Grambling." (Grambling is a historically black institution.) The reporter who asked that question might never live it down.

Grammar

Just as we have to think about the questions we ask, we also have to think about the words we write. Grammar is something that gets too little attention in broadcast journalism in general, and in sports in particular. The sports department is often physically separated from the newsroom in television and radio stations across the country, and that can lead to a philosophical separation as well. It often seems that news managers don't scrutinize the sports report as carefully as they do other parts of the newscast. There's almost a sense of "as long as you fill your time" (or don't offend someone in a major way), news directors and others in news management pay little attention to what goes on the air during sports. In newsrooms in which that's the case, it's incumbent upon those working in sports to police themselves in terms of good writing, proper grammar and the like.

Two particular grammatical problems crop up all the time in sports reports. The first is the reference to "the team" as "they." The generic pronoun used in reference to a team should always be "it." For example: "The team extended *its* winning streak to 22 games," not "The team extended *their* winning streak to 22 games." There's only one team, so don't use a plural pronoun. The second problem is closely related to the first. If the team nickname is singular, then the pronoun should be singular. If you're talking about the Dolphins, the Yankees, or the Supersonics, then using "they" is correct. But if you're talking about the Heat, the Magic, or the Jazz, then the pronoun should be "it" and verbs should be singular as well.

The confusion comes because we're talking about a team that's made up of a number of players and almost all team nicknames are plural, so the tendency is to use plural pronouns in reference to all teams. But that line of reasoning doesn't follow. You wouldn't write: "Utah won their third game in a row." You'd write: "Utah won *its* third game in a row." You should also write: "The Jazz won *its* third game in a row." Likewise, you wouldn't write: "Utah are one of the best teams in the league." You'd write: "Utah *is* one of the best teams in the league." You should also write: "The Jazz *is* one of the best teams in the league." Think of the team nicknames not as references to teams but rather in terms of how we normally use the nouns, and you'll see how silly it sounds to use a plural verb with a singular noun.

David Copperfield's magic are very impressive. (Did some hick write this?)

The heat in south Florida in the summer cause electric bills to skyrocket. (English teachers cringe when they hear stuff like this from people who are supposed to know how to write.)

Jazz have been one of my favorite musical forms for a long time. (Incorrect in this context, and incorrect when you're talking about Utah's pro basketball team.)

Think of team nicknames as normal nouns and you'll be OK. If the noun is plural, use plural pronouns and verbs. But if it isn't, impress the viewers with your command of the English language.

Be Proactive

The second part of trying to attract viewers to watch the sportscast even though they might not be die-hard fans is to cover events and stories that aren't about professional football, basketball, baseball or hockey. Using what seems to be the popular approach to covering sports, we could write many 11 P.M. sportscasts on Monday and replay them each night of the week simply by inserting the names of the teams and the athletes playing today.

_____with a homer to left.

_____reaches paydirt.

_____with the monster slam.

_____with the slap shot . . . he scores!!!!!

We don't want to sound cynical here, although many sportscasts almost seem to invite cynicism. Highlights and scores are a necessary part of a sportscast. After all, you can't discard that 25 percent of the viewers and listeners who are interested in how their favorite teams did while you're trying to attract the other 75 percent of the audience. But a sportscast that consists entirely of scores, highlights and material from satellite feeds is the sign of a lazy sports department and a sure way to send people to bed early or searching for some other program to watch.

So what should sports departments cover to try to broaden the viewership base? Quite simply, anything that would be of interest to a broad cross section of the audience, sports fans and nonsports fans alike. If we cover a Little League baseball game the way we cover pro baseball games, that wouldn't accomplish anything. We might have more sports bloopers to show, but other than the skill level and size of the players, Little League games are played and won or lost the same way pro games are. People who wouldn't be interested in pro baseball highlights wouldn't be interested in Little League baseball highlights either. But let's assume that three sets of twins play for one team in the city league. A feature story about what the coach goes through trying to tell the kids apart would appeal to almost anyone in the audience because *almost anyone can relate to it.* Dan Hicken works as a sports anchor in Jacksonville, Florida. He did this very story. It won a statewide award and is still one of the most memorable sports stories this author has ever seen.

There's a river of video available on satellite feeds emanating from any number of sources several times a day. But if every sports staff in the nation uses the same basic feeds and airs the same basic video, what is it that makes a local sportscast local? Even in those markets with four, five or six professional sports teams (or, perhaps, especially in those markets), the sports department has to work to find material that's of interest to people other than those who call in to sports-talk radio programs. Some people call this approach "hyper-localism."

Teases

We cover the guidelines for writing good teases elsewhere in this book, but a quick recap is important here, because sports tease writers are among the worst in the business. The idea is to get viewers to stick with you through the commercial between the sports tease and the sports block. You do want to use your best video, but you don't want to give the story away. You also don't want to tease to information everyone in the audience already knows, such as: "find out if the Tigers won the game" when the game ended at 4 P.M. and this tease is for the 11 P.M. show. Instead, tease to what the star quarterback says was the key to the victory (as long as you didn't already cover that at 6 o'clock). There are few things about local TV sports coverage more irritating than to see exactly the same highlights and hear exactly the same script and be subjected to exactly the same bites five hours later. Was there nothing different the sportscaster could use? Even with the small staffs most stations assign to weekend sports, there has to be some way to give viewers more than they've already seen (perhaps several times) on your station, the competing stations, ESPN, the regional sports channel, the university's Web page, and so on.

Luke Notestine

In addition to covering things in your local market that aren't "big enough" for ESPN or other national outlets, sometimes you get to cover the big events that ARE going to show up on national TV and other media. Luke Notestine is a sports anchor reporter at ABC 22/ Fox 45 in Dayton, Ohio. He says sometimes the job is so much fun and so filled with excitement he has to remind himself "someone is paying me to be here." During the 2012 NCAA basketball tournament, President Obama visited Dayton for the first game of the NCAA Men's Basketball First Four. Prime Minister David Cameron joined the president on his trip to the University of Dayton arena. The station had live reports and look-live reports from the air force base where the president landed in Dayton and more reports from the arena.

Notestine's job was to sit courtside at the game, observe the crowd reaction and do live chatting with fans and viewers via social media. He's covered countless college basketball games, but says he's never felt the energy of a basketball stadium like I did that night. The excitement of the start of the NCAA Tournament coupled with the attendance of two world leaders captured not only the city of Dayton, but also the nation. The president and prime minister sat in the front row, just behind one of the baskets to Notestine's right.

Luke was sitting directly behind the announcing team of Jim Nantz, Clark Kellogg and Steve Kerr and got to observe firsthand how some of the best announcers in the business do their work. He says it was amazing how calm and collected they remained even when the games became frantic. That included Western Kentucky coming back from a 16-point deficit in the final five minutes to defeat Mississippi Valley State and BYU storming back from a 25-point deficit to defeat Iona. That was the largest comeback in NCAA Tournament history.

Notestine says being able to experience all that in one night is one of the most fun and rewarding experiences he's had in his career.

And remember, he got paid to be there.

Providing Lots of Content

But there's more to the job than just being at the big event. Especially these days, you have to share as much of that event with your viewers as you can.

It was about 4:30 P.M. on a November Sunday afternoon in New Jersey. WGRZ's (Buffalo, NY) Ben Hayes was standing in front of the locker of Buffalo Bills' star wide receiver Stevie Johnson, along with about 40 other reporters. He was working alone, with just his camera and microphone.

Johnson didn't have a good day, and Ben needed to work his way into the interview throng. Johnson had been penalized for excessive celebration after a touchdown catch and also dropped a potential game-winning touchdown pass in the final seconds. The penalty and the drop cost the Bills a critical game.

Ben found a small crack in the growing group of reporters to get a clear enough shot of Johnson's face. Contorting his arm above the crowd he got his microphone just close enough to pick up what Johnson was saying.

In the past, Hayes would have been lucky to be able to feed back the interview with Johnson in time for the 6 o'clock news. To cover an NFL road game, his station would typically have to hire a local videographer and work with the local station to use its live truck or feed point. That was expensive and time consuming.

Now, working alone, Ben shot the entire game and post-game interviews. Within 10–15 minutes everything was loaded into the editing program on his laptop computer.

By 5:55 P.M., he had written, edited and uploaded two separate packages to his station's FTP site.

Instead of giving the Buffalo viewers only one or two SOTs about the game from Johnson, Ben did two packages featuring Johnson, his coach and teammates reacting to the plays, all as a one-man-band reporter, without a live truck.

Covering sports has changed dramatically in the past 10 years. With new technologies improving every day, we can produce not only more content, but better content, faster than ever.

In addition to producing better content for on-air use, WGRZ's online coverage has grown exponentially as well. If Ben covers a story for air, it needs to be online as well. The station's Web site allows Ben and his colleagues to add even more depth to their coverage. They can post full-length interviews, extended game highlights, podcasts, and analysis segments that they don't have time to put on-air.

Sports time is limited during the news; it's unlimited online.

Fans want more than a generic game story. After a typical Bills' game, Ben's station will post up to ten different stories, all with unique multimedia content. Fans get a game recap with access to watch post-game interviews. In addition, Ben will also post a photo gallery, a podcast, a game blog, a separate game analysis story and individual commentaries.

As local news continues to change, new technologies continue to give us more opportunities to develop and create new and unique ways to cover local sports.

Conclusion

Although sports producers, reporters and anchors produce lots of content in short amounts of time, it's still as important for them as for anyone else to be clear and concise in what they write and to provide clear directions to the technical part of the team. This brings us back to the most important aspect of the communications business—a need to communicate with each other. If we don't all know exactly where we're going, we can't expect the audience to follow along. You might be a "one-person band" in the field, but putting a show on the air, or even providing comprehensive coverage on your Web site is a team effort. Often in sports, the best team is the one that's most cohesive, not necessarily the one with the most superstars. The same is true in sports media as well.

DOs and DON'Ts When Writing/Covering Sports

Do

- Look for features that would interest all viewers.
- Worry more about being clear than being clever.
- Find athletes who can talk, and ask them good questions.

Don't

- Cover only pro sports.
- Get caught up in a "sports culture."
- Fall into "sports speak."
- Think that because you're covering sports the writing rules don't apply.

Questions

1. Although sportscasters have some freedom to be critical, how do we know where to draw the line?

2. How do we avoid falling into the "sports speak" syndrome?

3. Why is "sports speak" a problem?

4. What's the difference between incomplete sentences and incomplete thoughts?

5. If there's only one pro or major college team in your area, is it OK to be a booster? Why or why not?

6. How would you define "hyper-localism" in sports?

Producing TV News

If you're reading this chapter, chances are (1) you've decided to pursue a career in TV newscast producing, (2) you're thinking about it, or (3) you're reading this as a classroom assignment. If either of the first two reasons applies, this chapter will give you a good understanding of what the job entails. We'll discuss how to carry out the basics of building a television newscast, how to fill out a production rundown, how to write leads to enhance story flow, and how to write good **teases.** If, on the other hand, you have no intention of becoming a producer, this chapter will still be of value if you plan to work in the field of television news. No matter what you do in broadcast journalism, if you aren't a producer, you'll be dealing with them. This chapter will give you a good understanding of what drives them, what their needs are, and why they act in the sometimes mysterious ways they do.

What Is a Producer?

Simply put, news producing is the art and science of filling a broadcast with news content. There's not much glamour in it and, as a consequence, most of the public at large have only a vague idea, if any, of what a producer does or even that producers exist. Yet the producer is one of the most important people, if not *the* most important person, involved with the newscast. Whereas newsroom managers hover about trying to look important, the producer is the point person responsible for getting the broadcast on the air. One good way to judge the importance of a producer is to watch what happens when one falls ill and has to call in sick: instant panic! It's guaranteed managers will call someone in as a replacement; just as a plane can't take off without the pilot, the newscast won't air without a producer.

The producer, through the decisions he or she makes, is the viewer's window to the world. It's up to the producer to decide which stories are important to the viewer, and to choose those stories and present them in a newscast in such a way as to showcase context, meaning, perspective, and, above all, relevance. This requires news judgment and a sense of mission. It also requires technical expertise. Often producers don't get much training in the latter, and it's not unusual for producers to find themselves "thrown in, sink or swim." Therefore we'll go into a great deal of technical detail in this chapter.

The producer has an alter ego and partner in crime: the director. Whereas the producer is in charge of the content and timing of the newscast, the director leads a production crew that's responsible for executing most of the technical and some of the aesthetic aspects of the plan.

Why Be a Producer?

When interviewing intern candidates, it's not unusual for news directors to hear, "I want to be an anchor." There's certainly nothing wrong with this goal. But obviously, there are only so many high-paying anchor jobs. Competition for them, or on-air jobs of any kind, is fierce.

On the other hand, competition for producer jobs isn't nearly as intense. The typical reporter opening might attract anywhere from 50 to 150 videos. The typical producer opening might attract 10 to 15 résumés. Do the math. If you're a good producer, you can write your own ticket. These days in many stations, an experienced producer of a major newscast often makes as much as, if not more than, most reporters.

If you're a good writer, have excellent people skills and excellent news judgment, enjoy leading teams of people, and prefer to be involved in the "big picture" rather than just a piece of it, then producing might be for you. But producing isn't for everybody. Most people either really like it or really hate it. There's little middle ground.

Producer Duties

The producer's shift normally begins with an editorial meeting. The editorial team consists of the newscast producers, the assignments editor, the executive producer, and other senior managers. In many (if not most) stations, reporters and photographers sit in on the editorial meetings as well. The group discusses the stories available for coverage and then assigns coverage resources. Afterward, the producer goes back to his or her desk, sorts through the local and regional news feeds, wire material, checks Internet news sites and social media, and decides which stories will go into the day's broadcast, in what form, and in what order. Producers write some or all of their own copy and also supervise other copywriters who might be assigned to the newscast. Producers edit reporter copy (at least, they're supposed to). They order or supervise the ordering of all graphics for the newscast. They sit in the control booth to time the show and deal with breaking news.

In carrying out those duties, the producer must accomplish the following tasks, arranged here in roughly descending order of priority:

- *Precisely time the broadcast.* The newscast must end at the appointed time. It can't run long, and it can't run short. Some kind of content must separate the commercial breaks; they can't "bump together!"

- *Choose the right mix of stories.* The producer, working in concert with the assignments editor and newsroom managers, must make sure coverage and newscast resources are devoted to the right stories. "Right stories" has a broad range of definitions, but normally it means those stories that are most newsworthy on the given day, in light of the community's needs and the station's coverage philosophy.

- *Place the stories in the correct order.* This is an activity also known as "filling the rundown" or "completing the lineup." The **rundown** or **lineup** (different stations use different terminology) is a spreadsheet-like form listing the stories in the chronological order in which they'll air. This information typically includes, for each story, the page number, the slug (title) of the story, the anchor who'll be reading it, the type of camera **shot** or shots to be used, the form of the story, basic production elements that will be needed, the running time, and so on. We'll discuss story placement in greater detail later.

- *Work with the director and production crew to get the newscast on the air.* A good producer never loses sight of the fact that the director is an equal partner in the newscast. Good communication and cooperation between the producer and director are absolutely essential!

- *Write copy.* Most producers write at least some copy, and some producers write *all* the copy, with the exception of reporter packages. This function varies from market to market, depending on whether writing assistance is available to the producer. Simply put, good producers must write well according to the principles outlined elsewhere in this book.

- *Edit the copy.* Good producers always carefully read any and all copy written for their newscasts. They work with the reporters to assist and help direct the development of their stories. They edit copy for accuracy, fairness, tone, coherence, and storytelling, as well as for libel and privacy concerns.

- *Order the graphics.* Generally, the more sophisticated the product, the more sophisticated the graphics. Many stations have good art departments and place a high priority on graphics. The producer orders graphics for his or her show and works with the reporters to ensure they make good use of graphics within their packages.

- *Scan for news.* Good producers continually monitor the incoming wires and feed services, and also selected Internet news sites, blogs and social media for developing and breaking news stories.

- *Work with the desk.* Good producers work closely with the assignments desk to be on top of and react appropriately to breaking news.

- *Show leadership.* The producer is a "big picture" person. He or she sees how all the individual parts fit together and, like a symphony conductor, must orchestrate everyone's efforts to achieve a satisfactory, high-quality product. In doing so, the producer works with many people whose primary responsibilities pertain to a much smaller part of the picture. In order for all of this to come together, the producer must have excellent leadership skills and must contribute to a positive and productive work environment.

Despite the "descending order" nature of this list, none of these tasks and responsibilities is unimportant. Failure to properly time a show will get you in trouble with your news director very quickly. Failure to show good leadership will get you in trouble more slowly. For a producer to be truly excellent and successful, he or she must earn an "A" in each of these categories.*

---

* For a more detailed checklist for producing a student newscast, check out Appendix C.

The Rundown

Anchors generally read their copy from scripts, which are available to them in printed form on the news set and electronically on a prompter. If the scripts are a book, then the rundown is a table of contents. But the rundown is more than that, because it also gives the director and production crew much of the information they need to execute the newscast from a technical standpoint.

Rundown design, use, and implementation vary widely from station to station. These days, most news operations are computerized. But whether the rundown is contained on a computer screen or on a printed form, its use is the same: to list the stories, story formats, running times, and other information needed to get each newscast element produced and on the air. Below is a sample of the most important columns contained in a typical rundown, followed by detailed explanation of each.

PAGE #	SHOT	RUNS
SLUG	TYPE	BACKTIME
ANC	WR	

PAGE

Most stations make use of page numbers to assist in the process of keeping the scripts in their proper order. The page number is similar to, but not exactly the same as, a page number in a textbook. Most stations label individual blocks of stories with letters of the alphabet. A news **block** is a segment of news content sandwiched between two commercial breaks. Thus the first segment of the newscast, containing all of the stories between the newscast **open** and the first commercial break, is the "A" block. The next news segment, lying between the first commercial break and the second, is the "B" block, and so on. Page numbers frequently begin with the block number. So, the first story in the newscast is generally given a page number of A1. The second story is A2. However, many stations number their stories in increments of 10—A10, A20, and so on. This allows producers to insert new stories into the middle of the rundown later without having to renumber every story.

Some stories take up more than one line on the rundown in order to accommodate production information. In such cases the page number usually is subdivided with decimals or trailing letters, depending on the capabilities of the newsroom computer system. Example 1: A10, A10A, A10B, and so on. Example 2: A10.1, A10.2, A10.3, and so on.

SLUG

The slug is a short description that serves as a daily title for the story. Different stations have different conventions for slugging stories. Some have no convention. The purpose of the slug is to make sure all scripts, graphics, videos, live remotes, and other production elements associated with the story are labeled properly and consistently. This is a critically important function. For instance, an incorrect slug on a video cassette or file can often lead to someone losing the video or miscuing it, causing major problems on the air. (Anchor: "Apparently we don't have that story. We'll try to come back to it in a moment. In other news . . .")

As mentioned, sometimes stories have more than one element, causing them to take up more than one line on the rundown. Often these different lines require individual slugs. Again, different stations have different conventions, but normally the sub-lines contain similar slugs along with a differentiating character or words. For instance, a typical package might require three scripts: the **lead** or **intro,** the package verbatim, and the package **tag.** Typical slugs for the three package elements associated with a murder trial might be:

SMITH TRIAL [Lead]

P-SMITH TRIAL [Package Verbatim]

T-SMITH TRIAL [Tag]

Depending on the limitations of the computer system or rundown form, some stations simply use the whole term, as follows:

SMITH INTRO

SMITH PACKAGE

SMITH TAG

ANC

This column would simply contain the name or initials of the anchor reading the story.

SHOT

The shot column contains information about how many people will be framed in the camera shot for a given story, and whether a graphic will be part of the camera shot. Typical basic choices might include:

- *1shot.* One anchor on camera, centered, no graphic. Sometimes known as the "head and shoulders" or "H&S" shot.
- *2shot.* Two anchors on camera, centered, no graphic.
- *OTS.* One anchor on camera, framed to accommodate a corner or side graphic positioned "over the shoulder."
- *3shot.* Three anchors on camera.
- *Wide.* All anchors on camera.
- *CK.* One anchor at the chroma key board.

- *Dblbox.* "Double box" shot, typically with an anchor framed in one box and a reporter framed opposite, for Q&A.

- *3box.* Same as above, with three boxes—typically, an anchor and two reporters or interview guests.

- *Wipe.* Not a shot at all, but rather an indication that we'll go to the next story without coming back to an anchor, by use of a production technique during which video of the preceding story will "wipe" off the screen, to be replaced by video of the next story.

There are many other possibilities, depending on the capabilities of the station and set design. In addition, terminology tends to vary from station to station. For instance, a graphic shot known as an over-the-shoulder or "OTS" in one station might be a "1box" in another. There's no universal list of terms, and producers must relearn some of these terms every time they change jobs. However, the principles are usually the same.

TYPE

A number of different terms might go here to help describe the type and format of the story. Again, specific terms used vary widely from station to station depending on technology and newsroom custom. Some basic possibilities include:

- *Intro.* Anchor- or reporter-read copy preceding a package.

- *Tag.* Anchor- or reporter-read copy following a package or VO/SOT.

- *Tossback.* Similar to a tag, but usually includes two or more people with a question-and-answer opportunity.

- *Reader.* An anchor on-camera reading copy without video support or full-screen graphics. Normally, this implies a stand-alone story, not a package or **live shot** intro.

- *VO.* For voice-over. This indicates the anchor will read copy and that for portions of the narrative, the audience will see video while hearing the anchor's narration.

- *VOB (also VO/SOT or VOBITE).* For "voice-over with sound bite" or "voice-over with sound on tape." This indicates the anchor will read copy, that for portions of it the audience will see pictures, and that the anchor will pause while the audience hears an interview excerpt with "sound up full."

- *BITE* or *SOT.* Same as above, except that no pictures will precede the interview.

- *VONATS.* Same as a VOB, except that the anchor will pause for "natural sound"—sound recorded in the field of something other than an interview (the crack of a bat, the roar of the crowd, a space shuttle countdown, and the like).

- *PKG.* For "package." Indicates a preproduced video element that typically includes interviews, pictures, and reporter narrative in one contained unit.

- *LIVE.* Indicates the use of a live remote by microwave, satellite, Internet, fiber optic line, and so forth. Some stations specify here which mode will be used: "LIVE/SAT" for a satellite shot, "LIVE/REM" for a local microwave shot, "LIVE/INET" for a Skype-style video call, etc.

- *SS/CG.* "Still store with character generator." Indicates the use of a full-screen graphic with text to be inserted electronically live on the air. Almost all SS/CGs are voiced-over live by an anchor.

- *SS/FULL.* Same as above, but the text is prepasted on the graphic rather than inserted live on the air.

- *ENG.* For "electronic news gathering." Some stations use this as a designation for whatever standard format they're using to record and play back news video; for example, eng/pkg. Some news operations list the specific format, such as "beta," "svhs," a video server or server number, and the like. Still others omit a tape or server designation for news stories, with the assumption that all such elements will be played from a standard news video machine unless otherwise designated. In our examples we'll also omit the use of this term.

WR
This column contains the name or initials of the writer assigned to the story.

RUNS
This column contains a running time for the story or story segment. (An example of a story segment, as opposed to a single story, would be "weather." Weather might contain many elements, but on most rundowns, it's listed with a single slug and running time.) Ideal running times for various story formats vary from station to station, but the following examples are typical:

Reader:	:10–:15	Pkg:	1:20–1:30
VO:	:15–:25	Tag:	:05–:10
VOB:	:35–:45	Tossback:	:05–:10, or longer if
Intro:	:10–:15		there's a Q&A session

BACKTIME
The **backtiming** column is critically important. Prior to the newscast, it shows the producer whether the show *appears* to be properly filled. During the newscast, a constant check of this column tells the producer

whether the show is light (not enough material to stretch to the off-time) or heavy (the producer might have to drop some material for the program to conclude on time). In some stations this is also described as being "short" or "long."

In the old days we used to say "all good producers can tell, add, and subtract time backward." These days most modern newsroom computer systems automatically figure the backtimes based on the information the producer enters into the "RUNS" column. If not, the producer will have to figure this information by hand (oh, joy).

Building a Newscast

Now that you have a good understanding of what kinds of story elements are available, we're ready to learn the basics of designing a newscast.

Newscast Formats

There are as many varieties of newscast as there are news organizations. The basic principles we'll discuss here apply to all formats and newscast lengths. But for the purposes of this lesson we'll build a newscast based on a typical half-hour news format.

All newscasts are defined in part by the number of commercial breaks they contain. Our sample newscast will have four commercial *breaks* of two minutes duration each. It will contain news, weather, and sports in the traditional order. It will end with an external commercial break, usually known as a "terminal break." For the purpose of this exercise, this will be a 6 P.M. newscast, and we'll title it "Rumor Has It News at Six."

Here's the format:

"Rumor Has It News at Six" with Fred Feelgood and Jane Jabberon—Basic Format

> A Block—Hard News
>
> Break One 2:00
>
> B Block—Softer News
>
> Break Two 2:00
>
> C Block—Weather
>
> Break Three 2:00
>
> D Block—Sports
>
> Break Four 2:00
>
> E Block (Kicker Block)
>
> Terminal Break 1:10

News Hole

Before we can fill our newscast, we must first determine how much time is at our disposal. The basic amount of time available for news generally doesn't vary much from night to night. The total amount of time required every night to run all the commercials, teases, sports, weather, and chitchat is sometimes called the **skeleton time** or "filler time." When you subtract this from the total available time, you're left with what is usually known, with a certain lack of elegance, as the **news hole.**

Let's figure out the news hole for our sample newscast. First, let's add in *all* the standard features that will appear every night. Typically, this will include the open, the close, the teases, the tosses, and so on.

"Rumor Has It News at Six" with Fred Feelgood and Jane Jabberon—Skeleton Rundown

Element	Running Time
Newscast Open	0:20
A Block—Hard News	
Tease One	0:20
Break One	2:00
B Block—Softer News	
Tease Two	0:15
Break Two	2:00
C Block—Weather	
Toss to WX	0:10
WX	3:20
Tossback from WX	0:15
Tease Three	0:15
Break Three	2:00
D Block—Sports	
Toss to Sports	0:10
Sports	3:20
Tossback from Sports	0:15
Tease Four	0:10
Break Four	2:00
E Block—Kicker	
Tease for 11 PM	0:25
Close	0:30
Terminal Break	1:10
Total Running Time	**18:55**

This is the "newscast skeleton"—so called because it's the bare bones that we must flesh out with news content. Adding up all of these times, we come to 18:55. Wise producers might wish to add in another 30 seconds of time for miscellaneous slippage because of package overruns, unscheduled chitchat, and the like.

Total Running Time	18:55
+ Pad Time	:30
= Skeleton Time	19:25

Thus, the skeleton time of 19:25 is the time that's already prefilled in this particular newscast before the producer even sits down to begin work. The obvious next question is, "How much work will the producer have to do?" How much time must he or she fill?

Our sample newscast begins at 6:00 P.M. and ends at 6:30, giving us one-half hour's time. We must now subtract the skeleton time from the available time to get the news hole, as follows:

Total Available Time	30:00
– Skeleton Time	19:25
= News Hole	10:35

That's our news hole: 10 minutes and 35 seconds. It ain't much, is it? Nevertheless, your job for the day is to fill it. Note: The news hole *is* adjustable. It might expand or contract depending on the length of the commercial breaks. It can also expand or contract depending on the amount of time devoted to sports and weather. For that reason, producers are known to frequently ask sports anchors and weathercasters to "donate time," which sports anchors and weathercasters really hate to do. Wise producers don't abuse the privilege.

These days it's a rare newsroom indeed that's not computerized to some extent. With most (if not all) newsroom computers, the producer has to enter and save the skeleton rundown just once. On each subsequent day, the computer prefills the daily rundown based on this stored skeleton information.

Ordering Stories—The Three Factors

Now comes the fun part, the puzzle you're paid the humongous, hairy bucks to figure out. You must choose the stories you want to put in your newscast and the order in which you'd like them to run.

The first thing you'll do is come out of the morning meeting and write down the stories assigned to your newscast. Make at least tentative decisions about the format you might like for those stories— which will be "straight packages," which will be live remotes, which will be newsroom-anchored pieces, and the like. This will leave you a certain amount of time you must fill from other sources. You'll want to spend the next hour or so scanning the wires and social media, looking at the feeds and feed rundowns, and working with the desk for updates and follow-ups in order to develop a list of potential extra stories for your newscast.

At some point you'll want to begin sketching out a rundown. How does one decide the order in which the stories should run? This is one of the most difficult tasks a producer faces. The answer will vary from individual to individual and from station to station. But every producer should have a rhyme and a reason for the order of the show. In the trade magazines you'll occasionally see job ads for producers that declare, "Show stackers need not apply." "Show stacker" is an epithet for a producer who either stacks stories seemingly at random or stacks them in the order of perceived priority without any flow from one story to the next. A good producer doesn't just stack stories, but instead takes three major factors into account when ordering them: *priority (newsworthiness), flow,* and *pace.*

Priority

Though you usually won't stack stories strictly in descending order of their importance, generally you'll *begin* with the top-priority story. Choosing the lead might well be the most important decision you make during the day. Why? News research suggests that news consumers base their viewing decisions on the lead, which they know should be the "most important story." If this most important story isn't important to them, they might switch in search of another story, and often, they don't come back. So the ratings battle for the day often is won or lost on the strength of the lead story.

It sounds simple, right? Your lead should be the most important and compelling story of the day. That shouldn't be too hard to determine, should it? Actually, it can be maddeningly difficult. You might have several stories of more or less equal importance, none of which stands out as the clear lead. Your newscast might be competing with another newscast airing on your station an hour later or earlier, leaving you to duke it out with your fellow producers about the choice of a lead. In addition, there are other factors to consider besides the basic news value of the story. In many stations producers are required to take the station's mission statement and coverage philosophy into account when choosing leads and stories. The process can get complicated. That's why in many stations this decision isn't left to the producer alone, but rather becomes a team decision.

Flow

Once you've chosen the lead, the next step is to choose story number two. This seems logical enough. You might be tempted at this point to place the *second* most important story of the day in that slot. But stop and think a moment. Placing the second most important story second isn't always the best choice. Good producers usually group stories somewhat according to theme, then group the themes in logical order, taking newsworthiness into account. Thus, if you're leading with a story about the city council raising taxes, your second story might be a VO or VOBITE about an action some other governmental body took today. Your third story should be some subject that flows logically out of the second story. It might or might not be the third most newsworthy story of the day.

This sounds difficult, but it's easy to get the hang of it. Suppose your first story is about the city council raising property taxes and the second story is about the county commission taking action to fix a problem-plagued intersection. You have a story you haven't yet placed about a bad accident. Where should it go? Chances are it will "flow" best out of the story about the intersection, flowing with the "traffic" theme. Then if you have other police- and fire-related matters, these would flow well out of the accident story, and so on.

Pacing

The third critically important factor is pacing. Many inexperienced producers make the mistake of cramming all their packages into the top of the news block, then running the "less important" VOs and VOBITEs at the end of the block. This is terrible for pacing.

Remember, your greatest enemy is the remote control. If your viewer loses interest, zap, you're the history channel. One way to keep your viewers' attention is to keep a fast pace. Ideally, something should be changing every few seconds: Reveal a new fact, change the camera shot, change the video, put in a new edit, change the graphic, and so on. Airing back-to-back packages tends to slow the pace. Break up the pace by inserting tags, VOs, VOBITEs, or readers.

A good, cheap, and easy way to keep the pace going is to tag every package on-camera, or to tag every VO or VOBITE on-camera prior to changing anchors. The latter has other benefits as well. If the anchor begins every reading sequence on-camera and ends it on-camera before the second anchor speaks, it brings a sense of closure and also boosts the anchor's image as being in control of the sequence. This enhances the authority, professionalism, and teamwork of your anchor team, which will make your news director and news consultant happy—and in the process make your newscast better and more competitive. We'll discuss tags in more detail later.

Filling the Rundown

These days most producers begin drafting the rundown by entering it directly into the computer software and then making adjustments and tweaks, a process that also continues throughout the day as news develops. That is the method we'll examine in this chapter.

So, with a list of available stories and the principles of story ordering we discussed above now firmly implanted in my mind, I'm ready to enter a proposed rundown.

"Rumor Has It News at Six" with Fred Feelgood and Jane Jabberon— Rundown Draft #1

Page#	Slug	Anchor	Shot	Type	WR	Runs	Backtime
A00	Newscast Open			vtr/sot		:20	57:20
A10	Council Taxes			live/pkg		2:10	57:40
A20	Intersection Repair			vo		:25	59:50
A30	4-Car Pileup			vobite		:40	0:15
A40	Apartment Fire			live/pkg		2:10	0:55
A50	Fire History			ss/cg		:25	3:05
A60	Housefire Update			vo		:25	3:30
A70	Robbery Attempt			vo		:25	3:55
A80	Suspect Caught			vo		:25	4:20
A90	Robbery Trial			pkg		1:40	4:45
A100	Murder Trial			vo		:25	6:25
A110	Legislature/ Crackdown			vo		:25	6:50
Alast	1-tz		2shot	vo		:20	7:15
Break One						2:00	7:35
B10	Truck Recall			pkg		1:40	9:35
B20	Recall Info			ss/cg		:25	11:15
B30	Toaster Lawsuit			vo		:25	11:40
B40	Stock Market			ss/cg		:20	12:05
Blast	2-tz		2shot	vo		:15	12:25
Break Two						2:00	12:40
C10	WX Toss		3shot			:10	14:40
C10A	Weather					3:20	14:50
C10B	Tossback		3shot			:15	18:10
C20	Waterpark Opens			vobite		:45	18:25
Clast	3-tz		2shot			:15	19:10
Break Three						2:00	19:25
D10	Toss to Sports		3shot			:10	21:25
D10A	Sports					3:20	21:35
D10B	Tossback		3shot			:15	24:55

(continued)

Page#	Slug	Anchor	Shot	Type	WR	Runs	Backtime
Dlast	4-tz		2shot	vo		:10	25:10
Break Four						2:00	25:20
E10	11 Teaze			ss/cg		:25	27:20
E20	Skiing Squirrel			vonats		:35	27:45
E30	C ya/Close			wide		:30	28:20
Terminal Break						1:10	28:50
	Totals:					32:40	6:30:00
	Over/Under					+ 2:40	

Note that the total running time is 32:40. The over/under clock confirms it: we're over by 2:40—and that figure does *not* include a safety margin. Ideally, to be "exactly" on time, we want the over/under clock to read −:30 at the *start* of the newscast, which gives us 30 seconds of "wiggle room." As the newscast progresses, however, we'll expect—and want—to burn off that pad. So, what we really have here is a 3:10 problem.

Now you begin to understand the heartbreak of producing. You can rarely, if ever, produce your ideal newscast. We're going to have to cut some content.

First I go back and re-examine my rundown. OK, I guess I don't need that house fire update that I had planned to run updating a fire from the day before. It's a shame, too, because I was going to run a "follow-up" over-the-shoulder graphic with it, and my news director loves those. Oh, well. It's toast.

Do I really need to run a bite about the water park opening? Nah. That gives me another :15 back. I'll write tight; another :25 saved.

The stock market is slow today. I'll need only :15 to give the results. There's another :05. But I'm still 2:15 too long.

My VOs are going to have to be more tightly written. I think I'm going to need the full :25 to explain the intersection story, but the rest of the VOs can be cut by at least :05 apiece. That gives me back :35. I'm still 1:40 long.

That apartment fire story has good visuals but isn't a complicated story. I'll ask the reporter to keep her lead, tag and video time tight and give me back :10.

I'm still long by 1:30.

Now, I go to sports, hat in hand, and find out how busy a sports day this has been. The sports anchor, because he's a heck of a guy, admits that there have been more active sports days, and agrees to donate :30 to the cause. So sports will run 2:50 today, instead of the normal 3:20. I'm still 1:00 long.

Second, I head to the weather office. But wait a minute. I know the weathercaster really hates giving up time even on a slow weather day, and that she always checks my rundown to verify that I really need the time. The first thing her eye is going to land on is that "Skiing Squirrel" kicker. So I change the slug to "Kicker" and knock the time down to :20 instead of the :35 I had hoped to run. This will cost me the ability to take natural sound up full within the story, but what the heck. I take those steps, walk into the weather office and make my pitch. She's unhappy about giving up a full :30 because there's a severe weather system in the Midwest she wants to talk about. But she owes me because I gave her 15 extra seconds on Wednesday and again on Thursday. She gives in and donates 30 seconds. So, weather will run 2:50 today instead of 3:20.

Inputting all these changes, here's what we now have:

"Rumor Has It News at Six" with Fred Feelgood and Jane Jabberon— Rundown Draft #2

Page#	Slug	Anchor	Shot	Type	WR	Runs	Backtime
A00	Newscast Open			vtr/sot		:20	0:15
A10	Council Taxes			live/pkg		2:10	0:35
A20	Intersection Repair			vo		:25	2:45
A30	4-Car Pileup			vobite		:40	3:10
A40	Apartment Fire			live/pkg		2:00	3:50
A50	Fire History			ss/cg		:20	5:50
A70	Robbery Attempt			vo		:20	6:10
A80	Suspect Caught			vo		:20	6:30
A90	Robbery Trial			pkg		1:40	6:50
A100	Murder Trial			vo		:20	8:30
A110	Legislature/ Crackdown			vo		:20	8:50
Alast	1-tz		2shot	vo		:20	9:10
Break One						2:00	9:30
B10	Truck Recall			pkg		1:40	11:30
B20	Recall Info			ss/cg		:20	13:10
B30	Toaster Lawsuit			vo		:20	13:30
B40	Stock Market			ss/cg		:15	13:50

(continued)

Page#	Slug	Anchor	Shot	Type	WR	Runs	Backtime
Blast	2-tz		2shot	vo		:15	14:05
Break Two						2:00	14:20
C10	WX toss		3shot			:10	16:20
C10A	Weather					2:50	16:30
C10B	Tossback		3shot			:15	19:20
C20	Waterpark Opens			vo		:20	19:35
Clast	3-tz		2shot			:15	19:55
Break Three						2:00	20:10
D10	Toss to Sports		3shot			:10	22:10
D10A	Sports					2:50	22:20
D10B	Tossback		3shot			:15	25:10
Dlast	4-tz		2shot	vo		:10	25:25
Break Four						2:00	25:35
E10	11 Teaze			ss/cg		:25	27:35
E20	Kicker			vonats		:20	28:00
E30	C ya/Close			wide		:30	28:20
Terminal Break						1:10	28:50
	Totals:					29:45	6:30:00
	Over/Under					– :15	

That 15-second "under" time is slightly less than the 30-second pad we prefer, but it's within the margins and will work provided we keep chit-chat and other slippage under control. Now that we have the basic newscast down, it's just a matter of filling out the details.

Sweating the Details of Newscast Production—Graphics, Artwork and Visual Pacing

We've decided how to fill our newscast. Now it's time to make decisions about the production of the stories. Sets, production techniques, and available artwork vary, but in every station, producers have to ask themselves questions such as:

- Where will I use wide shots?
- Where will I use 2shots?
- Where will I use 1shots?
- Which anchor intros will make use of artwork?
- How will I get into and out of live shots?
- Will I have a reporter on the set? At the chroma key board? In a debriefing area?

The answers to these questions will depend on the resources available, on your philosophy, and on the philosophy of the managers to whom you report. But one factor is nearly universal: When changing from one story to another, producers should *almost always* make a visual change as well. For instance, if an anchor is on-camera reading a story on a 1shot, don't have her begin a second story on that same 1shot! That's one of the most common mistakes inexperienced or untalented producers make. You must keep up a good visual pace.

Examples of techniques you can use to make a visual change between two stories include, but are not limited to, the following:

- Changing from a 2shot to a 1shot.
- Any change of anchors.
- Changing from a 1shot "H&S" (head and shoulders) to an "OTS" (over-the-shoulder graphic shot), or vice versa with the same anchor.
- While on an OTS shot, changing from one OTS graphic to a different graphic.
- Changing from an on-camera shot to a piece of video or graphic, or vice versa.
- Wiping or dissolving from one piece of video to another.
- Wiping or dissolving from a piece of video to a graphic, or vice versa.

How Do I Know When to Use an OTS Graphic?

Generally speaking, in any newscast, artwork and graphics are desirable. Lots of bland 1shots aren't. A newscast filled with artwork tends to look sharper and more sophisticated. Good, aggressive producers seek ways to use plenty of artwork. OTS graphics work best at the beginning of stories, during the anchor leads. Tags generally are best done on a 1shot without graphics.

That said, the artwork should have a purpose. It should add to the meaning of the story in some specific way, containing a picture or piece of art and a slug line specifically related to the story at hand. Otherwise, the graphic tends to distract from the anchor's presentation. One mistake you often see in television is the use of completely generic graphics. Thus, you'll find an anchor reading a story about a robbery and murder while sharing the camera shot with a graphic of a generic pistol and a slug that reads "Murder." It's probably the exact same graphic the audience saw in the past 57 murder stories the station aired. To add insult to injury, the pistol's probably pointing at the anchor's head. Drop the graphic. It's worse than useless; it's distracting. If, however, the graphic includes some kind of image specific to this particular case and a specific slug ("1st St. Murder"), it has more value.

If you work in a station that has strong branding, you should treat all graphics as an opportunity to express that brand. In other words, if the story is investigative in nature, the OTS graphic should include your station's investigative logo; medical news should contain the logo of your station's medical unit, and so forth.

When Should I Use a 1shot? When Should I Use a 2shot?

Another mistake inexperienced producers often make is to produce the entire newscast on a 2shot. In some cases this stems from a lack of resources—not enough cameras or camera operators on the floor. Just as often, it stems from a misguided effort to show the anchors as a "team." There are more effective ways to showcase teamwork than by always showing them on a 2shot. Remember: *The most powerful shot in television is the head and shoulders 1shot*. Why? Because it provides the best opportunity for eye contact. (This is another reason you should choose your graphics judiciously; OTS shots provide less eye contact because the anchor is, in essence, competing with the graphic for the viewer's attention.) 2shots are appropriate for establishing shots at the beginning of a newscast, as tease shots at the end of news blocks, and as transition shots.

The 2shot Transition

The 2shot transition, when used properly (and quickly), is a good tool for showcasing teamwork. The basic idea is to use the 2shot to change anchors between *related* stories.

In our sample newscast above, the Robbery Attempt story and the Suspect Caught story provide such an opportunity. Suppose we had originally planned to change anchors here, and anchor "A" is tagging the final line of Robbery Attempt on a 1shot. Make it a 2shot, and write the copy for the two stories with the transition in mind, in such a way as to enhance teamwork. The first anchor will "hand off" to the second one.

Robbery attempt tag	
2shot	(Fred reads/Jane is looking at him) THE ROBBER LEFT EMPTY HANDED BUT HE DID GET AWAY.
Suspect caught intro	
	(Jane reads, addressing Fred) NO SUCH LUCK FOR THE MAN WANTED IN YESTERDAY'S HOLDUP. (Jane addresses camera)
Push to 1shot	JUST A LITTLE WHILE AGO POLICE SLAPPED CUFFS ON A SUSPECT.

When Should I Use Tags?

Tags serve two purposes. One primary purpose is pacing. Every time you change a visual element, you add to the pacing. Tags are one more visual element you can change for the purpose of picking up the pace.

Tags also serve to bring "closure" to a story or, just as important, to a story sequence or pod. For our purposes a **pod** is a set of consecutive stories read by the same anchor. In a sense, the person reading that story pod "owns" it. Usually, he or she will begin the pod on-camera, making eye contact with the viewer, and end the pod the same way: on-camera, making eye contact with the viewer. This brings a sense of closure to the pod and underscores the anchor's ownership of it. This, in turn, serves to enhance the anchor's image and authority. Because the viewer relates to your product primarily through your anchors, anything that helps their image helps you. This is known in some circles as the "anchor in command" theory of producing. It works.

How Often Should I Alternate Anchors?

There's no hard-and-fast rule, but you should avoid anchor "ping-ponging," a technique wherein we see a different anchor every 20 seconds. Inexperienced producers use ping-ponging for the purpose of driving an audience nuts. Generally, you should *not* always alternate anchors between every story, and certainly not between every 20-second VO. A pace of alternating every 45 to 70 seconds, or between reporter pieces, is about right.

Not every newscast has dual anchors. In a solo newscast, you shouldn't alternate anchors at all. (Just checking to see if you're paying attention.)

How Do I Know When to Wipe between Visual Elements?

Another mistake inexperienced producers often make is to throw in wipes between VOs apparently at random, thinking they "look cool." Generally, they just look confusing. Wiping from one VO to a different, completely unrelated VO can throw off the audience. To be effective, wipes should take place only between related stories. For example:

- Wiping from one crime story to another
- Wiping from one fire to another
- Wiping from one consumer story to another
- Wiping from one environmental story to another
- Wiping from one weather damage scene to another
- Wiping between "thematically" related stories (back-to-back stories in state or national roundups, newsreels, or miniblocks)

Putting It on the Air

So. You've chosen your stories, filled out the rundown, written all the copy for which you're responsible, and edited all the reporter copy to your satisfaction. You're done, right? Wrong. Now you have to get your show on the air and, equally important, *off* the air *at the appropriate time.* To do so requires a skill set that's different from the one you've used so far to build your show.

Backtiming

As you'll learn, unexpected, terrible, and traumatic things can happen in the course of producing live TV. Live shots crash; playback machines eat stories or servers crash and burn; editors don't finish stories in time; reporters ad-lib information in their tags that you weren't expecting; anchors throw in ad-libbed questions you don't have time for; weathercasters go short or long; sportscasters go short or long; packages go short or long; chitchat goes short or long. Don't look now, but there are about a thousand and one things that can ruin the timing of a perfectly timed show, and you must react to all of them in the control room, while the show is live on the air. So it's crucial that you always know precisely how your show is timing out at any given moment. You do this through backtiming.

The concept is simple. Given the length of each story remaining in the newscast, at what clock time must each story begin for the newscast to end on time? In order to keep your newscast on track you must backtime every single story. Most modern news computers will take care of this function for you. If not, you'll need to do it by hand.

In backtiming a show, you begin at the end, with the off-time to the newscast. In our sample newscast the program following news begins at 6:30:00. Therefore, the off-time for news is 6:30:00. Next, look at the last element in the newscast. It's a terminal break, which runs 1:10. Subtract the running time of the terminal break from the off-time to get the backtime for the terminal break, as follows:

$$6:30:00 - 1:10 = 6:28:50$$

6:28:50 is the *backtime* for the terminal break. In other words, for the newscast to end exactly on time, the terminal break must begin at *exactly* 6:28:50. We say "exactly" because the running time of the terminal break is a "hard" time; it will run exactly 1:10, no more, no less. Now repeat this for the story element preceding the terminal break, the close, which is scheduled to run :30:

$$6:28:50 - :30 = 6:28:20$$

For your newscast to end on time, the close must roll at exactly 6:28:20. This assumes your canned close music runs exactly :30 and ends with some kind of music **stinger** or recognizable ending. However, note that just because you *roll* the close at 6:28:20 doesn't mean you have to *air* the close at that time. Chances are you don't really intend to run the full :30 of available music while sitting on a wide shot of anchors filing their nails on the set. Being up to 25 seconds "late" taking that wide shot with music up full is no problem; in fact, it might be desirable, given that you're paid to put news on the air, not music.

Now repeat the process for the kicker. The kicker runs :20 seconds:

$$6:28:20 - :20 = 6:28:00$$

The kicker must hit at approximately 6:28:00 for you to be on time. Don't forget, though, that being :15 late won't kill you because, as we discussed, the running time for the close is negotiable.

Repeat this process for every element in the newscast, and you'll find that your backtiming calls for your newscast open to roll at 6:00:15. Of course, it will actually roll at 6:00:00, a difference of 15 seconds. This is another way of saying that you are going into the newscast :15 light or short. However, remember that the computer doesn't figure in any "pad" time for you. To be perfectly on time with a desired "pad" time of :30, we'd need to go into the newscast :30 light, for a start time of 6:00:30. Our actual computed on-time of 6:00:15 might be a tad "tight," but it's in the ballpark.

By this point in our day we've "fleshed out" the rundown, using the principles outlined above to number all the pages, insert the shots, assign anchors to the stories, add in the tags and 2shots, and so on. Here's how the final rundown appears, with backtiming.

"Rumor Has It News at Six" with Fred Feelgood and Jane Jabberon—Final Rundown

Page#	Slug	Anchor	Shot	Type	WR	Runs	Backtime
A00	Newscast Open			vtr/sot		:20	0:15
A00A		f/j	2shot				
A10	Council Taxes	j	OTS	intro		2:10	0:35
A10A	p-Council Taxes			live/pkg			
A10B	t-Council Taxes	j/f	2shot	tag			
A20	Intersection Repair	f	OTS	vo		:25	2:45
A30	4-Car Pileup	f	wipe	vobite		:40	3:10
A30A	4-Car Pileup tag	f	1shot				
A40	Apartment Fire	j	OTS	intro		2:00	3:50

(continued)

Page#	Slug	Anchor	Shot	Type	WR	Runs	Backtime
A40B	p-Apartment Fire		dblbox	live/pkg			
A40B	Tossback		dblbox				
A40C	t-Apartment Fire	j/f	2shot	tag			
A50	Fire History	f	OTS	ss/cg		:20	5:50
A70	Robbery Attempt	f	OTS	vo		:20	6:10
A80	Suspect Caught	f	wipe	vo		:20	6:30
A80A	t-Suspect Caught	f	1shot	tag			
A90	Robbery Trial	j	OTS	intro		1:40	6:50
A90A	p-Robbery Trial	j		pkg			
A90B	t-Robbery Trial	j	2shot	tag			
A100	Murder Trial	f	1shot	vo		:20	8:30
A110	Legislature	f	OTS	vo		:20	8:50
A110A	t-Legislature	f	1shot	tag			
Alast	1-tz	j/f	2shot	vtr/vo		:20	9:10
Break One						2:00	9:30
B10	Truck Recall	f	OTS	intro		1:40	11:30
B10A	p-Truck Recall	f		pkg			
B10B	t-Truck Recall	f	2shot	tag			
B20	Recall Info	j	OTS	ss/cg		:20	13:10
B30	Toaster Lawsuit	j	OTS	vo		:20	13:30
B30A	t-Toaster Lawsuit	j	1shot	tag			
B40	Stock Market	f	OTS	ss/cg		:15	13:50
Blast	2-tz	j/f	2shot	vtr/vo		:15	14:05
Break Two						2:00	14:20
C10	WX toss		3shot			:10	16:20
C10A	Weather					2:50	16:30
C10B	Tossback		3shot			:15	19:20
C20	Waterpark Opens	j	1shot	vo		:20	19:35
C20A	t-Waterpark Opens	j	1shot				
Clast	3-tz	f/j	2shot	vtr/vo		:15	19:55
Break Three						2:00	20:10
D10	Toss to Sports		3shot			:10	22:10
D10A	Sports					2:50	22:20
D10B	Tossback		3shot			:15	25:10
Dlast	4-tz	j/f	2shot	vtr/vo		:10	25:25

(continued)

Page#	Slug	Anchor	Shot	Type	WR	Runs	Backtime
Break Four						2:00	25:35
E10	11-tz	f	OTS	ss/cg		:25	27:35
E10A	11-tz	f	1shot				
E20	Kicker	j	1shot	vo		:20	28:00
E30	C ya/Close		wide	vtr/sot		:30	28:20
Terminal Break						1:10	28:50
	Totals					29:45	6:30:00
	Over/Under					– :15	

In the example, we've listed the running time of each story in one lump sum. For instance, story A10, the Council Taxes live shot, should run 2:10 including lead, package, and tossback. Some producers prefer instead to time each story element individually, for example listing :15 for the lead, 1:20 for the package, :35 for the tossback, and so on. Either method is valid.

The important thing to remember about backtiming is that it's a constantly shifting target. Some newscast elements such as the open, packages, and commercial breaks have "hard" running times. But the running time of many stories or segments are *estimates.* They're soft times, not hard. It's extremely doubtful that every soft element in the newscast will run the exact amount of time you've budgeted for it. While the newscast is on the air, you must keep a constant vigil on the clock and on your backtiming, adjusting your newscast where necessary as stories go short or long.

Here's an example of how this newscast might actually play out. The perfectly timed rundown is finished, all the stories are written, and the video is ready. The open rolls, and we're on the air. Your first two live shots take more time than you allotted, and your anchors talk longer than anticipated on the 2shot at the end of the first block. Your backtiming tells you you're supposed to be hitting the first break at 9:30, but you actually hit it at 10:10. What does this mean? It means your newscast is now in a bit of trouble. The commercial break began 40 seconds later than planned, meaning you're :40 heavy. You've blown your safety margin and then some. Even if you don't roll *any* close music, at this rate you'll be :10 late hitting the terminal break. If that happens your newscast will **upcut** (run over the top of) the next program by 10 seconds. This is simply not allowed. You *must* get the show off on time, which means you're going to have to make up some time. The only course of action at this point is to begin looking for stories to drop or segments to shorten.

What if you're supposed to hit the break at 9:30, but actually hit it at 9:00? The break began 30 seconds early, meaning that you're

30 seconds light, or short. You'll need to add 30 seconds worth of content to your newscast to end on time. The easiest way to add content is to ask the sportscaster and/or weathercaster to use it. The second easiest way is to ask all the anchors to burn up a little extra time as chitchat. For really serious shortfalls, a wise producer always has a backup package in mind, such as a piece off one of the daily feeds that an associate producer can grab for you quickly. Some veteran producers are known to keep "evergreen" feature stories squirreled away for such eventualities.

Forward Timing

Forward timing is the opposite of backtiming. It's useful for newscasts in which certain stories *must* air at a certain time. It asks the question, if a particular story must air at a given desired time, at what time must each preceding story hit for the newscast to be on time?

To figure forward times, begin with the start time of the newscast, then add the running time of the first element to get the desired start time of the next element.

As an example, let's pretend the Apartment Fire story contains a live shot we'll receive by satellite, and that the satellite **window** (the time you've leased from a satellite broker) opens at 6:05 and not a second sooner. Let's see if we'll hit it.

The calculation for the forward time of the newscast open is quite simple: It begins when the newscast starts, at 6:00:00. Now let's figure the forward time of our lead story. To get it, we simply add the running time of the newscast open to its forward time, as follows:

$$6:00:00 + :20 = 6:00:20$$

So our lead story will hit at exactly 6:00:20. We know this time is exact because the running time of the open is in stone; it runs exactly 20 seconds, no more, no less.

Now let's figure the forward time of the following story, Intersection Repair. To do so we'll add the running time of the lead story to the lead story's forward time:

$$6:00:20 + 2:10 = 6:02:30$$

This tells us the Intersection Repair story will hit at approximately 6:02:30. This time is "approximate" because the 2:10 running time is the producer's estimate. The actual live shot and package could go long or short when it actually hits the air.

Repeating this process for each story preceding the Apartment Fire story, we find that Apartment Fire will hit at about 6:03:35. This is too soon; we'll miss our window. Either we must lengthen the running times of the existing content elements, or we'll have to add new content to the rundown ahead of the Apartment Fire story, thereby moving the story down in the newscast.

Writing Notes

Copywriting issues are well covered elsewhere in this book, but two bear further exploration here: story ties and teases.

The "Cheap Tie"

Having had it drilled into their heads that all good newscasts have good story flow, many producers try to create flow artificially with really bad plays on words. Thus you might see a producer lead with a story about a protest at city hall, then follow with a story about a house fire. What's the tie? There is none, but the producer vainly attempts to create one by using cute copy like this:

> WHILE HARSH WORDS ENFLAMED THE DEBATE AT CITY HALL TODAY,
> FLAMES QUITE LITERALLY ERUPTED AT ONE LOCAL APARTMENT COMPLEX.

Don't do that, please, else that strange noise you hear in the distance will be the clicking of thousands of remotes. You should almost always avoid the temptation of tying events together that weren't tied together in real life.

Another heinous producer practice involves the use of the words "while" or "meanwhile" to link unlinkable stories, *without* wordplay. Thus you might hear an anchor read the following script.

OTS = Tax Vote	THE CITY COUNCIL WILL VOTE ON THE TAX INCREASE NEXT WEEK.
OTS = Pileup	MEANWHILE IN SOUTH WHADDADUMP TONIGHT, PARAMEDICS ARE STILL ON THE SCENE OF A FOUR-CAR PILEUP.

Unless that pileup was caused by a reckless motorist madly rushing to escape the city council meeting, there's no tie and therefore no "meanwhile."

The only difference between these two forms of cheap tie is that the former is an amateurish mistake, whereas the latter is an artless amateurish mistake. Story flow is important. However, the fact is that stories don't always flow together. In such instances it's perfectly permissible to use an audible change of gears such as, "In other news." It's not creative, but it serves the purpose. Think of it as verbal punctuation for the viewer (but don't overuse it).

Conversely, if two stories *do* flow together perfectly, this might be a good place for a 2shot transition from one anchor to another, as discussed earlier.

Teases

Teases are some of the most important pieces of copy you can write for your newscast. They are, however, a double-edged sword. Research suggests people *do* base their viewing decisions on the teases—and sometimes the decision they make is to switch off. So you must make those teases compelling.

Provide Viewer Benefit

It's important to remember that teases are *not* news stories. You can't write them the same way. They're sales pitches, and you must treat them as such. In writing them you have a lot in common with any salesperson: You must try to convince the potential customer that the benefits of consuming your product are worth the price. The key word here is *benefit:* Your tease must promise the viewer benefit *without* delivering it just yet. Remember, you're trying to "make a sale" here, and the price you're asking is that the viewer stick around and devote his or her personal time to the story. That won't happen if you give your product away for free in the tease.

What is a viewer benefit? It's anything of value to the viewer. If you go to Fred's Taco Stand and shell out your hard-earned cash for a taco, you expect to get a tasty treat in return. You're trading value in the form of cash (the price) for value in the form of something nutritious, or at least enjoyable, to eat (the benefit). A similar transaction takes place between a news operation and the news consumer. The consumer pays a price by giving us his or her time and attention, an *extremely* valuable commodity for which advertisers are willing to pay top dollar. In exchange, the viewer expects to *receive* something of value. You'd better deliver if you plan to keep that viewer as a consumer. No excuses: Just cough up the viewer benefit.

Generally, for a viewer to obtain benefit from a story, the story must affect him or her in some way the viewer finds valuable. This includes a wide range of possibilities. Some examples:

- Information of any kind that is useful or which addresses a viewer need or desire
- Reassurance or resolution of a fear
- Entertainment
- A surprise
- Affirmation of personal values

- Confirmation of personal beliefs
- An emotional connection or stimulus
- Anything interesting, enjoyable or diverting

Stories without viewer benefit are, by definition, a waste of the viewers' time. If you air enough of them, the viewers will say good-bye to you and your product and, as it were, go elsewhere for their tacos. You shouldn't run stories devoid of benefit, and you *certainly* shouldn't *tease* them. An overhyped tease for a story that doesn't deliver is less than worthless; it is in fact *harmful* because it draws the viewers' attention to and might even cause them to stick around for a bad story. You've probably seen it yourself: A TV station teases a story about a basketball-shooting chimp once or twice in prime-time teases, then twice more within the newscast. When we get to the story itself, we find it's a 15-second VO showing a chimp from some roadside attraction in Dogs Barking, Mississippi, sinking one lousy basket. Further, by the time the story airs, we will have spent more airtime promoting the story than we spent airing the actual story. This really grinds your viewers' gears. They don't like being tricked. If they stick around for a story—or, in the case of a late newscast, stay up for it—and the story doesn't deliver the value the tease promised, they're going to feel used. This common practice is a sore point with viewers. They frequently complain about hyped, sensationalistic teases and promotions in viewer calls, e-mails, and focus groups.

Deliver What You Promise

Don't abuse the viewers' trust. It helps to think of it this way. Your newscast presents an array of products of varying worth. Your job, as product manager, is to set the appropriate price for each one. In TV terms, the price is the time we're asking a viewer to devote to a story. For instance, a good lead story for a 10 P.M. newscast should be worth asking the viewer to stick with us through prime time and tune in just to see it; therefore, it's a good candidate for inclusion in prime-time teases. A good third-block medical package might be worth the same price. Or maybe it's at least good enough to ask the viewer to sit through two commercial breaks to see it, and therefore would be a good candidate for inclusion in tease 1, preceding the first commercial break. We'll assess our basketball chimp story the same way: Is it worth asking the viewer to tune in at 10 o'clock just to see it? Absolutely not. Is it worth asking the viewer to sit through four commercial breaks to see it? No. Is it worth asking the viewer to sit through *one* commercial break to see it? We hope it's at least worth that, or we shouldn't run it at all. Therefore, it's a good candidate for a quick mention at the end of the preceding block, but not suitable for "deep" teasing beginning with the first commercial break. The bottom line is this: Viewers are keenly aware of the value of their time. The "price" we set for each story must accurately reflect its value. When the price and value don't match, viewers feel cheated and tend to call news directors and give them a piece of their mind, as well they should.

Don't Bore the Viewer

Teases that promote boring stories in a boring way are just as bad (if not worse) than hyped teases. Every producer tries to put together compelling newscasts, but let's face it: Not every story is tease material. Yet some producers feel compelled to tease even the most routine of stories, especially if those stories appear later in the newscast. Why would you show meeting video and write a tease to go with it that says, "AND LATER: DOZENS TURN OUT TO HEAR A TOP ACCOUNTANT SPEAK TODAY IN TOWN. WE'LL TELL YOU WHAT HE HAD TO SAY"? The viewer might rightly assume you're teasing the best story you have left to offer—and if the best you have isn't that good, why stick around? Yet you can see writers inflicting teases like this on viewers time and again in almost any TV market. It's the equivalent of our aforementioned Fred's Taco running a commercial that says, "Our tacos are as dry as dust and might even make you sick, but come on down anyway!" It's better just to say "BACK AFTER THIS" than to tease a boring story just for the sake of running a tease.

Tease the Right Stories the Right Way

In planning teases, first identify the stories still to come that have the most viewer benefit. (One important producing technique is to make *sure* you save stories for the lower news blocks that *do* provide benefit—otherwise known as "teasable" stories.) Identify that benefit. Then write to it, making the viewers understand that if they don't change the channel during the commercial break, we'll reward them with a benefit—without actually *delivering* that benefit in the tease!

Please don't make the mistake of beginning your tease copy with the words "Coming up next." This is an instant turn-off. "Coming up next" is TV-speak that, roughly translated, means "It's time for a commercial now." Start that way, and the viewer will zone out and probably leave the room to go to the bathroom or whatever. Instead, begin your tease as if it were a story. Instead of giving the full story, however, you'll hook the viewer by promising viewer benefit, thereby motivating the viewer to stay for the rest. Make use of the "you" connection wherever possible. Use narrative storytelling and/or the rhetorical question whenever possible. Use the imperative voice when appropriate to literally command attention. And we can't say it often enough: Clearly focus on the viewer benefit!

Example 1—How Not to Do It

COMING UP: THE LATEST
INFORMATION ABOUT DIABETES
FROM THE U-S GOVERNMENT.

[VO video showing doctor
examining patient]

THE STATS SHOW 25 PERCENT OF
ALL PEOPLE DON'T KNOW THE SYMPTOMS.
DETAILS WHEN WE RETURN.

The tease practically gives the story away but still manages to leave the viewer benefit unclear. Video is generic. How am I affected? Plus, the final line isn't a strong suggestion that the viewer return. Click. See ya.

How to Do It

YOU COULD HAVE DIABETES . . .
AND NOT KNOW IT.

[Video of patient with very concerned
expression listening to doctor]

THE LATEST STATS SHOW YOU OR
SOMEONE YOU LOVE COULD BE IN FOR
A FRIGHTENING SURPRISE. FIND OUT
HOW TO TELL FOR SURE . . . NEXT.

The benefit is very clear: Watching this report could improve my health. In fact, I can't afford *not* to watch it. Video and copy make the "you" connection. The imperative voice in the final line *commands* me to return in terms that show it's in my own best interests to do so. You can bet I'll hang with you. And by the way, if you promise the story is "next," don't break the promise. The story should be right there when you come back from the commercial break.

Example 2—How Not to Do It

STILL AHEAD: BRUSH FIRES
CONTINUE TO RAGE OUT OF CONTROL
IN MEXICO.

[VO video of dramatic fires]

DRAMATIC FOOTAGE WHEN THE
NEWSHOUR CONTINUES.

The benefit is weak, though I might stick around to see the pictures. But the fire is a long way away. Frankly, you don't sound like you're that interested in my watching this, anyway. Gotta go.

How to Do It

BRUSH FIRES CONTINUE TO RAGE
OUT OF CONTROL IN MEXICO.

[VO video of dramatic fires]

AND NOW THERE'S A DISTURBING
NEW DEVELOPMENT TO THE
DISASTER . . .

[Cut to VO video of asthma patient
coughing or using inhaler]

. . . ONE THAT COULD AFFECT
OUR HEALTH HERE IN THE
BAY AREA.
LEARN HOW . . . AND WHAT YOU
CAN DO ABOUT IT . . . NEXT.

Benefit is clear: Brush fires in Mexico might affect me. You're asking me to find out how and what kind of action I might need to take. I'd better listen up.

Example 3—How Not to Do It

COMING UP NEXT ON THE
NEWSHOUR:

[VO video of washing machine
in operation]

NO ONE LIKES TO DO LAUNDRY . . .
RIGHT?

[Cut to VO video of
unhappy-looking reporter
sorting clothes]

WE MADE REPORTER JANE DOE DO IT
EVERY DAY FOR A WEEK!
AND SHE MADE A SURPRISING
DISCOVERY.
WE'LL TELL YOU ABOUT IT . . .
NEXT.

Copy is semi-cute and somewhat creative—but there's no real viewer benefit other than the hint of some possible entertainment value. Yawn.

How to Do It

	DIRTY LAUNDRY. NO ONE TALKS ABOUT IT. NO ONE WANTS TO DEAL WITH IT.
[VO video of laundry going into washing machine]	
	BUT AT LEAST YOU KNOW WHAT GOES IN DIRTY . . .
[Cut to VO video of clean laundry coming out of dryer]	
	COMES OUT CLEAN . . . RIGHT? WRONG!
[Cut to VO video of germs under microscope]	
	NEW LAB TESTS PROVIDE A NASTY AND DANGEROUS SURPRISE. LEARN WHY AND WHAT IT MEANS TO YOU IN A REPORT YOU WON'T WANT TO MISS . . . NEXT.

OK, you have me. My laundry comes out dirty? This I gotta see!

Tease Tips

A question producers often ask about writing teases is, "Should I use my best video?" Photographers and reporters sometimes pressure producers not to "give away" the best pictures in a tease. Usually this is a mistake. Remember, you're *selling* the story to your audience. Your best pictures normally will be your strongest selling point. Use them! Note, this doesn't mean the package you're teasing has to begin with those pictures; sometimes narrative storytelling concerns will lead the reporter and photographer team *not* to lead off their story with the most dramatic pictures. That decision should not apply to the *tease*, however. Use your best material.

Also remember that video isn't your only option. Another effective technique you might consider is the "menu tease." Using this method, the tease writer gives a list of stories or segments and the *time* at which each will air. Example: "NEW FINDINGS MIGHT CHANGE THE WAY DOCTORS TREAT SOME WOMEN FOR

MENOPAUSE. MEDICAL REPORTER STACY STETHOSCOPE EXPLAINS WHY AT 6:18. WE'LL HAVE WEATHER AT 6:20 AND TRAFFIC AT 6:23. STAY WITH US." Such teases might or might not use video and typically will make use of on-screen text to reinforce the hit times. The idea here is that some viewers will flip around when the commercial break hits, no matter what. This style of tease gives them a reason and a *time* to come back. In essence, you're making an appointment with the viewer.

When you conclude the tease, finish in the imperative voice. Make a command. Or as a sales executive might put it, "Ask for the order." Phrases such as "find out," "learn why," "see why," and so forth, stand a much better chance of engaging the viewer than do simple declarative statements such as, "That story next."

One common tease technique is use of the rhetorical question. "Did you know you could have diabetes and not know it?" is an example of that. The power of this technique is that posing a question but not giving the answer can create a hunger for information. But don't overdo it. Not *every* tease should contain a question.

Here's a final thought and a challenge about producing teases. There's been plenty of experimentation through the years but despite that, most newscast formats remain pretty basic—30 minutes to an hour filled with news, weather, and probably some sports, punctuated by commercial breaks and teases. In many stations tease formats haven't changed in years if not decades—a 2shot of the anchors, quickly followed by video of one or two upcoming stories with "news music" slipped underneath. Often you'll find the video pre-produced with station graphics and a "coming up" banner or the equivalent, sometimes with a cute slug line, sometimes not, and you'll see them done the same way day in and day out. Weather teases are the absolute worst. How many times have you heard two anchors blabbing the following: "The weather today was really [fill in the blank] but what will it be like tomorrow? Iris Isobar is next with the forecast!" Does it really have to be that way? Which rule book says every tease must begin with a 2shot? In fact, who decreed that every tease must always involve *both* anchors? Who says every tease must have music? Or video? Through the years newscast formats have become so familiar to viewers that we've created what amounts to a visual language of sorts. When the viewer sees that tease 2shot and begins to hear the tease music, regardless of what the anchors are saying the *first* message the viewer gets is, "It's time for a commercial." To combat that, consider a technique we'll call the "stealth tease." The concept is simple: Throw away the rule book, forget format, and write a tease that best accomplishes the goal of hooking the viewer. There's no ban on the traditional 2shot tease, but it's become just one option in the tease toolbox. Other tools in that box might consist of a 1shot, or an OTS shot with a graphic, or a single anchor standing at a chroma key wall, or a single anchor standing by a monitor with video rolling, or a single anchor standing by a monitor showing bullet points or a graphic, and so on. A tease might include video. It might not. It might include music. It might not. Imagine a single anchor sitting on-set, making eye contact while holding up a piece of paper, and saying, "What's in this document could change the way doctors treat some women for menopause. Find out why and what it means to you next." The point is to sell, and to choose the tool that works best for the job at hand.

Perhaps many producers won't feel empowered to take it upon themselves to "break the format" when it comes to teasing. But you can certainly propose changes to your supervisor. Don't be shy about it. Whatever you do, don't let yourself get caught in a rut, and don't write teases just so that you can get your "tease ticket" punched.

A Final Thought about Producing TV News

We've spent several pages detailing how to produce a newscast, but we haven't addressed the question of *why* you should produce one. Only you can answer that. Every producer has a different set of drives and motivations. Some produce because they love writing. Others like the excitement of calling the shots, especially in control room environments. Still others enjoy being newsroom leaders and having the ability to shape the "big picture." One thing is certain: To do well as a producer, you must have passion. Whatever passion brings you here, don't lose sight of it. Nurture it. Cherish it. Never let it go. You'll need it to keep you going during the tough times. As we discussed in other chapters, our medium is incredibly powerful. On the best days, producing television news can be very fulfilling. Enjoy yourself. But don't squander the opportunity to do some good.

Conclusion

In this chapter we've discussed in detail how to use a rundown form to build a television newscast, time it correctly, and get it prepared for air. We've provided a producing exercise, which you can find on the Web site that accompanies this book at www.mhhe. com/tuggle5e. The exercise includes a final rundown as put together by a producer in a top-20 market. In the next chapter we'll discuss a producer's role in the booth and how to handle live shots and breaking news.

DOs and DON'Ts for Producing TV News

Do

- Remember that a producer's job is one of the most critically important in a television newsroom.
- Arrange stories to create a good story flow.
- Consider scripting an on-camera tag when changing anchors.
- Leave some pad time in your rundown.
- Understand how a computerized rundown works.
- Write teases that "sell" the viewer benefit of a story.
- Make the "you" connection when writing teases.

Don't

- Forget that being a good producer requires not only technical skills, but also leadership skills.
- Stack stories simply in order of descending priority.
- Forget that good pacing also is an essential element in ordering a rundown.
- Start a newscast "heavy" if you can avoid it.
- Blindly trust the computer to time your newscast.
- Give away the story in the tease.
- Be shy about "breaking format" or using your creativity.

Questions

1. List three attributes of a good producer.
2. Discuss the difference between skeleton time and news hole.
3. Discuss the three factors involved in ordering stories.
4. Discuss the importance of anchor tags.
5. Discuss effective versus ineffective tie writing.
6. What makes a tease a good tease?

The Care and Feeding of Television Live Shots

Being a newscast producer is like having two jobs for the price of one. Once she's completed the rundown, written the show, and checked that the video elements are finished, the producer goes to the control booth. There, the role changes completely. The producer removes the production design hat and takes on a role more like that of an airplane pilot. A good grasp of the station's technical systems and an ability to make decisions under fire are essential. In this chapter, we'll discuss two of the toughest booth challenges: the art of juggling live remotes, and coping with live, breaking news.

Live Shot Philosophy

What makes a good live shot? TV critics love to debate that point, and they often accuse stations of "going live for live's sake." To some stations and news directors, a mediocre live shot is better than no live shot at all. We won't settle that argument here. But clearly some live shots are better than others. The rule of thumb for any good live shot is similar to the standards for a good stand-up. It's not just about face time, although that's important too. Rather, all good live shots are interactive in nature. The audience can't be at the scene, so the reporter goes there for us, taking us by the hand and giving us a guided tour. He or she demonstrates something, touches something, picks something up, kicks something, opens or closes something. Walk-throughs can be effective, but not if they're "walks to nowhere." If the reporter is going to move through the scene, then there should be a point to the trip; it shouldn't simply be a journey down five feet of sidewalk. Often the reporter can give this trip purpose by simply gesturing to the surroundings and explaining what we're seeing. In general, the effectiveness of the live shot rises in proportion with its interactivity. Conversely, the less the reporter has to do on the scene of the live shot, the more it's going to seem like "live for the sake of live."

Immediacy is also a factor: Is this story legitimately late-breaking, or was it done and over with hours ago? Breaking news stories can make compelling live shots. Cold, dark crime scenes or empty buildings where something happened hours ago usually don't make good live shots. In most stations, there won't be enough live units for every reporter, so the producers have the luxury of deciding which stories are most suited for live shots on that particular day.

One element even a mediocre live shot adds to a newscast is the "people" factor. Broadcasting is all about sight and sound, to be sure,

Taken by Forrest Carr

KGUN9's Chris Moore directs the morning newscast.

Taken by Forrest Carr

Local, state and national media line up for a press conference regarding the search for a missing child in Tucson.

but it's also about *people*. It is, in fact, an intensely personal medium. Even if a live location is visually weak, the live reporter can provide that "people" connection.

For whatever reason you choose to go live, the idea is to get your live shots on the air cleanly. The best TV stations put resources and systems in place to make sure that happens.

Command and Control

Picture the following scene. It's election night. Reporter Jane Sittenfijit notices that the incumbent mayoral candidate she's covering is coming to the podium to declare victory. Jane needs to get this on the air *right this very second!* First, she tries shouting into the microphone, hoping that someone back at the station is listening to the live feed. Nothing happens. Next, she disconnects her cell phone, which she was using to monitor the station's off-air **signal,** and dials the producer's direct line. As the seventh caller, she wins a free ticket to Voice Mail Hell, where a recorded voice invites her to leave a message. With mounting panic, she calls the assignments desk, and a polite but clueless intern promptly puts her on hold and leaves in search of someone who can make a decision. Now completely desperate, Jane writes the words "PLEASE TALK TO US" in huge block letters on her reporter's notebook and begins waving it at the camera. As the mayor begins speaking, she finds herself resorting to "the jumping jacks," waving frantically and springing and bouncing in front of the camera like a poodle begging for table scraps in a desperate attempt to get someone's attention.

Meanwhile, back at the ranch, the intern talks to the assignments editor, who talks to an associate producer, who talks to the executive producer. The executive producer reads between the lines and realizes the urgency in Jane's message. She orders the associate producer to run to the control booth and tell the producer that the mayor is declaring victory and to get Jane live on the air right this very second.

In the control booth, producer Timmy Timex gets the message. He presses the **IFB** button, which pipes his voice into the anchor's ear, and orders, "Fred, toss out to Jane in the field; the mayor's at the podium."

On-air, viewers see Fred put his finger to his ear and say, "I'm told Jane Sittenfijit has some breaking news for us. Let's go live to her now." Viewers are then treated to the spectacle of Jane jumping up and down in front of the camera, waving and shouting, "Hey! Can you hear me? You guys need to come out to me now! Can you hear me? Hey! You idiots, you're not listening to me!"

This goes on for what seems like an eternity but really lasts only 10 seconds. The program cuts back to Fred, who says, "Sorry about that folks, we're having some problems. In other news tonight . . ."

The scenario described above might seem extreme, but this kind of on-air train wreck happens all the time in TV news. In live TV a certain amount of error is inevitable. But wise newspeople keep that error rate to an absolute minimum by designating a *live coordinator,* also sometimes called an *ENG coordinator* (ENG being an abbreviation for electronic news gathering). Many large-market stations have employees whose sole job assignment is to coordinate live remotes and video feeds. Smaller stations might distribute these duties among associate producers, desk assistants, or tape editors. Stations with the smallest staffs might not be able to pull anyone aside at airtime to coordinate live shots; in such cases, the producer will have to juggle live coordination along with everything else.

The live coordinator has three primary duties:

- Facilitate communication with the crew in the field, the producer, and the engineers tuning in the live shot.
- Supervise to make sure that each live remote is ready at the appropriate time.
- Make sure the producer is fully apprised of the status of all live remotes—*especially* if the live shot is in trouble.

Of those three points, the last is the most important. *The absolute number one most important task of any live coordinator is to ensure bad live remotes don't get on the air!* In a well-run station the producer never, ever attempts to air a live shot unless the coordinator has specifically pronounced the live shot ready. For a live shot to be ready, five elements must be established and verified. They are:

1. *Signal.* Is the microwave, satellite, fiber or Internet signal strong and airworthy?

2. *Video.* Obviously, we have to see a camera picture.

3. *Audio.* We must be able to hear the reporter.

4. *IFB.* The reporter must be able to hear program audio from the television station.

5. *Readiness.* The reporter and photographer must be standing by and ready for the live shot!

The concept of IFB merits further discussion. In some stations "IFB" has become a generic term used to describe all methods by which a reporter in the field can hear some or all of the television station's off-air signal. IFB is an abbreviation for "interruptible feedback." With true IFB the producer or live coordinator can open a mike, interrupt the program audio going to the field, and speak to the reporter. Stations have various ways of delivering IFB. A common method is to route all or a portion of the station's program audio to a phone line, then have the reporter dial into that line using a mobile phone. The connection is "one way"; most stations use an "auto-answer" system that connects the reporter's call to the IFB system automatically, without human intervention. The reporter can't speak, only listen. The live coordinator hears the reporter not by telephone, but rather by way of the reporter's live microphone. The disadvantage to that, obviously, is that the live coordinator can't hear the reporter's microphone unless the live signal has been established. IFB can also be delivered by way of a subcarrier on the station's broadcast signal, which is monitored in the field by way of a special receiver. Some stations deliver IFB through a two-way radio system. IFB can also be delivered by satellite signal.

In the absence of IFB, a producer can still salvage a live remote *if* he catches the IFB failure in time. **Talent** in the field sometimes can receive cues by various other methods. For instance, a field producer or photographer who's on the telephone or two-way radio with someone back at the station can relay cues by hand signal. Or talent in the field can monitor the station's on-air signal by way of a portable television receiver. None of these alternative methods is ideal because none allows the producer to communicate directly with the talent, but each will do in a pinch. In fact, the use of a TV monitor *in addition* to IFB often is necessary for sports or weather remotes, during which the talent needs to see the program in addition to hearing it.

However IFB is received, no live shot can air without it or a substitute method of communicating cues to the talent in the field. Otherwise, the reporter has no way of knowing when or whether he or she is on the air. Lack of IFB is one of the most common causes of live shot failures. In our example, the live shot crashed primarily because the reporter had disconnected her IFB line, and no one at the station noticed. It's easy to see how this can happen. A failure of live video or audio normally will be very apparent to an alert live coordinator, who will then take immediate steps to alert the producer and director not to take the shot. But a sudden failure of IFB isn't so obvious.

Live shots can also fail through *improper* IFB. With traditional IFB, the station simply feeds program audio to the reporter in the field. The reporter hears everything, including his or her own voice retransmitted by the station. This isn't a problem because the retransmission happens at the speed of light, and the reporter's words return to the reporter by way of IFB as they're spoken. However, traditional IFB will *not* work with a satellite remote. In such cases the reporter's video and audio signals travel far into space, bounce off a satellite, then return to earth. The round-trip covers tens of thousands of miles—and even at the speed of light, the journey is *not* instantaneous. There's lag. If the station feeds the satellite audio back down the IFB to the reporter, the talent's words return a noticeable fraction of a second after they were spoken. This creates an "echo" effect in the ear of the talent that can throw the reporter off balance.

Typically, the way to correct this is with a form of IFB known as **mix-minus**. Using the mix-minus method, the reporter's home station sends a special feed down the IFB line that consists of some or all of the station's program audio *minus* the reporter's microphone. Through this method, the reporter hears what's going on back at the TV station without receiving a distracting echo of his or her own words. (The "lag effect" is so distracting that some stations habitually feed mix-minus IFB for *all* live remotes as a matter of course.)

It's the job of the live shot coordinator—or, in lieu of a coordinator, the producer—to verify all five elements of a live shot, as follows:

- *Signal readiness.* Typically, a station engineer will tune in the signal and approve it as airworthy.

- *Video readiness.* The live coordinator, usually in cooperation with an engineer, will visually check the camera picture, noting stability, lighting, white balance, framing, and the like.

- *Audio readiness.* The live coordinator will listen to the audio. Usually an engineer will check it through a VU meter to make sure it's within acceptable limits.

- *IFB.* This is a simple but important task. The live coordinator merely has to open the microphone and ask, "Can you hear me?" and then listen for the reporter's response on the live feed from the reporter's microphone. A wise live coordinator asks the reporter for a *visual* confirmation, such as a "thumbs-up." Otherwise, the live coordinator can't always be sure the reporter didn't nod in response to something someone else said there on the scene. (For satellite remotes, the coordinator should verify with the audio director that the talent is receiving mix-minus IFB. If not, the problem won't be apparent until the reporter starts speaking.)

- *Readiness.* The coordinator verifies this by giving time cues to the talent. Many news operations give the field talent time warnings at 5 minutes, 2 minutes, 1 minute, 30 seconds, and 15 seconds. Some reporters like more cues, some like fewer. The practice in some stations is also to alert reporters when they're live in a double box, when they're in a VO, and to give time cues for the running times of packages or sound bites within the live shot. Most crews like to be told when the live shot has ended and they're clear to tear down.

Making Chicken Salad

Unfortunately, there's not much the live coordinator can do for the crew when everything is falling apart at the site of the live report. Ross Weidner is a special projects producer for WLS-TV ABC7 in Chicago. Some of the craziest situations he's had to manage were far from Chicago. For example, the station sent a crew to Rome to cover the Beatification of Pope John Paul II in 2011. Because the members of the crew were trying to figure out how to navigate a foreign city jammed with more than a million pilgrims for the event, the trip required them to think on their feet and get creative.

The team members didn't have workspace for most of the trip, so they had to find the closest place to St. Peter's Square where they could get a good Internet connection and a couple of tables. The café's regular patrons got a huge kick out of the crazy Americans trying to cut at least three packages a day on no sleep. Weidner says it's a good thing the cappuccinos were excellent!

On the first night the team was supposed to be live, about 10 minutes before the shot the cameraman told Weidner that his camera wouldn't feed video out. That means even though the technical people at the station could hear the anchor, they weren't going to be able to see him. That's a BIG problem. Weidner says he sure wasn't flying halfway around the world and working an eighteen-hour day to miss a live shot. He ran down from the roof live shot location to search for a working camera. Because of the time difference, it was nearly 1 A.M. in Rome and the only crew left in the building was a CNN en espanol crew and those guys didn't speak much English. After convincing the Latino videographer that he wasn't trying to steal his camera, Weidner took it and ran it up two flights of stairs to the roof live shot position and threw it on the tripod. Luckily, with about a minute to spare, they were up and running. Weidner says there's nothing like hearing someone in master control say, "We can see you in Chicago." That and similar stories have led Weidner to the conclusion that this is the best business in the world to be in and it's one of the greatest times in history to be a journalist.

Special Live Coverage

On certain big coverage days, live coordination can become very complicated. For instance, on a major election night even a small-to-medium-market television station might have four or five live shots, including some from other cities. You might need more than one live coordinator to keep track of all of them.

Ideally, each remote location will establish *two* lines of communication with the station: one line to the live coordinator, and one to the auto-answer IFB. During the live shot, the live coordinator keeps in two-way contact with the photographer or field producer on one line while also speaking to the live talent by way of the IFB. A very good rule of thumb is to set up a system ensuring that when the crews call the station to talk with the live coordinator, they never get a busy signal! One solution is to surround the live coordinator with a bank of telephones, with a dedicated phone line assigned to each remote location. Or the live coordinator might choose to have just two phones—one to be used to accept calls, the other used for a "rolling conference call." The way the latter system works is that a crew calls in on line A and then is immediately transferred to the ongoing conference call with the coordinator on line B. It's possible to pull this off with handsets, but many stations have very sophisticated communications panels set up for handling live remotes in this fashion.

In either scenario, ideally each remote crew will also have a pre-assigned number to call for IFB. This helps sort out confusion, because crews won't have to call in frantically at the last minute to learn their IFB assignments. Pre-assignment also allows the coordinator to physically label the phones or control panels with the names of the crew members who'll be using them, thus making it unnecessary for the producer to punch six buttons to discover which one is connected to Jane at the mayor's headquarters. In major coverage situations, even large-market TV stations might not have enough IFB lines to go around. Some crews will have to double up. This will require close coordination so that crews dial the right line at the appropriate time, and no one gets a busy signal.

Now let's go back to Jane Sittenfijit, covering our hypothetical mayoral race. If our system works as it should, Jane is standing by, already

KGUN9 reporter Claire Doan signals a successful IFB check prior to a live report.

Taken by Forrest Carr

dialed into the IFB line. When she frantically needs to get onto the air, all her photographer or field producer has to do is pick up the phone, alert the live coordinator, and remain on the line. The live coordinator calls the newscast producer in the control room. The producer gets the message, quickly finds a spot for Jane's report, tells the live coordinator to have Jane stand by, and within seconds, Jane is on the air—calm, collected, and kicking the competition's rear.

Extended Weather Coverage

Extended weather coverage is an example of when producers really earn their pay. Jeremy Spearman's first few weeks producing at WNCT were quite the jump into the world of local news. His first week flying solo on the 11 o'clock newscast was the same week Hurricane Irene made landfall in eastern North Carolina. He couldn't have asked for a better introduction to how a local newsroom operates. It started the week before the storm, when the news director began planning coverage. Reporters and photographers were traveling to every county in the market and doing the usual "preparation" stories and producers were calling every city, town and county Public Information Officer (PIO), establishing contacts in preparation for the weekend storm. Once Friday, August 26, rolled around (the eve of Irene's North Carolina landfall), the station went into continuing coverage for what ended up totaling 48 hours. As a rookie producer, Jeremy wasn't able to take the saddle solo in the booth, but he was responsible for setting up phone interviews with those PIOs and officials from all across the viewing area, in addition to talking with the crews in the field and sister station trucks also on the coast. At the time, it was an over-whelming situation for such a fresh producer, but the events that unfolded that week taught Jeremy more than he had learned in the previous two weeks and in his years in school. He quickly got to know officials from throughout the viewing area simply by talking with them on the phone (something that's very difficult for producers, who stay in a newsroom all day), he learned how live shots operate (SAT vs. microwave shots), and he learned the importance of communicat-ing with reporters, photographers, anchors and the director. Most importantly, perhaps, he learned how important weather coverage is to viewers and to the reputation of the news operation.

During Carly Stephenson's second day on the job at WSET in Lynchburg, Virginia, the unexpected happened. Carly looked up at the lights shaking in the studio as the ground began to move. There was silence, and then as if on cue, the phones started ringing all at once. Carly was one of many people who experienced a 5.8 magnitude earthquake that hit the East Coast. Residents called in with a lot of questions, but station staffers had only limited information in the moments after the earthquake. From that experience, Carly learned that residents truly depend on TV news operations, especially when it comes to breaking news in their backyard.

The station provided coverage on the personal and financial dam-age wrought by this natural disaster. This included coverage on the Web site and in the 7 P.M. show. The market covers Danville, Lynch-burg, Roanoke and the New River Valley, and the news crew stressed team coverage in all of the shows that day. For the 7 P.M. show, the station had a reporter live from Mineral, Virginia, the epicenter of the quake, and followed that with live reports from Lynchburg and also community reaction from Altavista. The town of Mineral sustained a lot of damage, and millions of dollars of repairs would be needed for area schools.

Twitter and Facebook also proved to be very valuable, because staffers could post instant updates as they heard from the National Weather Service and people in the communities directly affected by the quake. Carly says the importance of TV news became more real to her that day than it had ever been before.

Contingency Plans

Count on it: If your station does live shots, it *will* experience live shot failures. The main idea behind live coordination is to make sure bad live shots never get on the air and the audience never knows about your technical difficulties. Even with the best live coordination, how-ever, occasionally a live shot will go bad before your very eyes, live during your newscast: The microwave transmitter will blow a fuse, the camera will die, a short will suddenly develop in a microphone, the IFB line will disconnect without warning, a video cable will fail. A thousand and one things can go wrong with live television, and the broadcast corollary of **Murphy's Law** states that you'll experience each and every variety of live shot failure during the course of your career, probably multiple times.

There are three major steps you can take to prepare yourself. First, at all times be prepared to have your anchor apologize for technical dif-ficulties and move on. Second, *always* know what your next step will be! Never go to the control booth without a viable "Plan B" that you can execute quickly in case of live shot failure. Make sure your director and everyone else who needs to know about the plan is informed. Third, see to it that all video elements that can be fed back in advance *are* fed back in advance. That way, if the live goes south, the failure won't take every coverage element with it. (For instance, you can always roll the reporter's package even if the reporter's live signal dies at the last minute—but only if you have the package already in hand.)

One legendary coverage anecdote in Florida serves as a cautionary tale about what can happen if you don't follow the above rules. A

Taken with Ross' cell phone

Ross Weidner of WLS-TV coordinating live shots in Rome.

coastal station decided to send most of its staff to cover an approaching hurricane. The satellite truck rolled and just about everyone rolled with it—anchors, reporters, photographers, everyone except the producer and a couple of editors. All day the crew worked to cover the hurricane. The videos were to be played on the air live from the satellite truck; the crew fed back nothing in advance. Can you guess what happened? The truck croaked at the last minute. The poor producer back at the station, as legend has it, was left with 30 minutes to fill, and no way to fill it. Ow.

Now here's an example of a backup plan that worked. A Texas station rushed a crew to cover a major spot news story in a nearby city. Not long before airtime, managers learned their satellite truck was having problems. There had been no opportunity to feed back video, but another affiliate of the same network had managed to uplink about two minutes of rough-cut material. So, moments before the newscast open rolled, a producer ran a stack of Associated Press wire copy to the set and asked the anchors to ad-lib over the rough-cut video and narrate what they saw on the screen. The open rolled, and the anchors proceeded to do exactly that. While this was going on, the station managed to get in contact with its reporter and put her on the air by phone for a **Q&A** with the anchors. Shortly after that, the satellite truck operator resolved the technical problems, and the reporter went live. It wasn't elegant, but it worked, and the audience never suspected the station had encountered a major technical problem. When all was said and done, the station actually had more and better coverage than its competitors—not bad for a newscast that started with a failed live shot.

What other options might that station have employed as a backup to the satellite shot? What if there had been no video in-house at all? If you have information and an anchor, you can do television. In an absolute-worst-case scenario, you can have your anchors sit and read copy right off the wires. With a little prep time, you can prepare graphics support in the form of a map and full-screen bullet points. You can usually arrange live phone interviews with officials on the scene or at a command post. While you're doing that, you can have a producer or reporter put together a backgrounder or perspective piece using file video of similar stories from the past.

One option you definitely do *not* have: When a big story erupts, you can't hold it and push it lower down into your newscast while you get your act together. When the newscast open rolls, you *must* be there with the lead story. Period. It's your job to make sure it gets on the air with as much information as you have, in the best format you can prepare.

If you have to implement a backup plan, don't wait too late to execute it. Remember that you need time to get word of any changes to the director, anchors, editors, engineers, and everyone else affected!

Many newscasts have crashed and burned with anchors looking lost and confused on-camera, while a producer was still trying to issue instructions. Always think *two steps ahead*. In the event of live, breaking news, your audience will forgive you for all kinds of technical glitches, provided you handle them smoothly, fully explain what's going on, and step quickly to your next coverage element. The audience will *not* forgive you for looking lost, confused, or unprofessional, which is likely to happen in the absence of contingency plans or if you trigger those plans too late. Wise producers have backups for everything and know precisely when to execute them.

The Anchor Question

One hotly debated aspect of remote live shots is the anchor question. Most producers secretly (or openly, as the case may be) hate the anchor question because it takes time they'd rather devote to something else. When the newscast gets "tight," anchor Q&A often is the first thing producers toss out. Usually this is a mistake. Anchor questions provide an opportunity to showcase the expertise of both the anchor and the reporter, which is important from a competitive standpoint. Much more important than that, however, is the opportunity the Q&A provides to add context, meaning, and perspective to the story.

Until recently, conventional wisdom said no factor was more important in winning the ratings wars than a station's prowess in covering breaking news. Many believe this is no longer true. In the 21st century it's a sorry station indeed that doesn't know how to cover spot news. The future will belong to those stations doing the best job of providing context, meaning, and perspective. A well-done Q&A can accomplish this very effectively. Adding perspective is so important that a Q&A alone might be reason enough to justify a live shot. Conversely, a live shot without Q&A is a wasted opportunity.

Obviously, to get a meaningful answer, the anchor question itself has to be meaningful. Here is an example of a nonmeaningful, wasted Q&A opportunity:

[Rip N. Reed]	THAT'S THE SCENE FROM THE COURTHOUSE. BACK TO YOU, FRED.
[Fred Feelgood]	RIP . . . HAS THE DATE BEEN SET FOR THE NEXT HEARING?
[Rip N. Reed]	YES . . . FRED . . . IT WILL TAKE PLACE TWO WEEKS FROM NOW ON THE 10TH OF OCTOBER.

In the above example, the question didn't elicit any meaningful information. The anchor simply prompted the reporter to give information he would have given anyway, had he not saved it for the "question." This is an example of airing a question for the sake of airing a question.

Now, here's an example of a more meaningful Q&A:

[Rip N. Reed]	THE NEXT HEARING IS SCHEDULED FOR OCTOBER 10TH. FRED?
[Fred Feelgood]	RIP . . . IS THE DELAY NORMAL FOR A CASE OF THIS NATURE?
[Rip N. Reed]	NO . . . IT'S NOT. THE PROSECUTOR ISN'T TALKING. BUT THE DEFENSE ATTORNEY TELLS ME IT'S MORE PROOF THE CASE IS WEAK. HE BELIEVES THE PROSECUTOR IS STALLING . . . HOPING TO FIND NEW EVIDENCE IN THE WAKE OF TODAY'S SETBACK.

In the above example, the anchor asked a meaningful question, and the answer gives perspective and meaningful insight to what's happening in the trial. In the process, the anchor also comes off as a journalist who has a brain and is paying attention to what's going on.

One question that often arises in discussions about anchor questions is, "Should the question be scripted?" In most cases, it's preferable for the anchor and reporter to have a discussion prior to airtime to talk about material that might be suitable for a Q&A. This doesn't mean the question has to be precisely scripted, but both the reporter and the anchor should have an understanding of what the question will be about.

What if there's no opportunity for an advance discussion? In that case the reporter is fair game for a random question. Some reporters really hate it when anchors play "stump the reporter." But there's no shame in getting hit with a question you can't answer. Just say so— and promise an update later.

In some cases producers might decide to tightly script questions and their answers. Risky investigative reports involving lawyers who vet, approve, and lock in every word are a good example of that.

If the question is scripted in advance, it's important to write Q&A as a natural interchange. Do *not* script video, graphics, or other show-and-tell material as the answer to a question! It's amazing how often TV producers do this. Preproduced answers of this type lead to some of TV news's silliest moments. "Fred, I'm glad you asked me that question, because I just happen to have some video, graphics, and bullet points to help answer it." The audience probably suspects we prepare Q&A material in advance, but let's not be insulting about it.

Whichever method you choose, don't lose sight of your goal, which is to provide context, meaning, and relevance in a way that makes a personal connection to the viewer.

Common Live Shot Pitfalls

Live television is an incredibly complicated affair. Any successful live shot amounts to a near-miraculous escape from Murphy's Law and the dozens of pitfalls that conspire daily to defeat live reporting. Here's a list of common traps and how to avoid them.

Problem: Live reporter hears "echo" in the ear.

Cure: Make sure the live coordinator flags any satellite remotes for the audio director so that he or she will send a "mix-minus" IFB signal to the field. Even better, the station should feed mix-minus IFB for *all* remotes.

Problem: Live crew gets a busy signal when trying to call the live coordinator.

Cure: When juggling several live remotes, designate phone lines for each crew. Or, use a conference call system.

Problem: Live crew gets a busy signal when trying to dial IFB.

Cure: The live coordinator should pre-assign IFB numbers for each crew. If there aren't enough lines to go around, the crew should contact the live coordinator to request clearance before dialing IFB. Some systems require a technician to manually reset the IFB line after the crew disconnects; the live coordinator should help ensure this happens promptly.

Problem: The reporter in the field has lost IFB and isn't in immediate contact with the live coordinator by phone or radio.

Cure: The reporter should step away from the camera. Otherwise, if the producer and director see the reporter standing by looking ready, they might be tempted to punch up the shot.

Problem: You're going live in five minutes, you have a two-minute piece of video to feed, but when you call the station, you find some other crew is feeding video via the same microwave receiver you need to access.

Cure: This problem is incredibly common in breaking news situations. The station will have three or four live vans out in the field gathering news, and each crew will expect to feed video at 4:55 P.M. for a 5:00 P.M. broadcast using the same microwave receiver. The only solution is for the live coordinator to anticipate this problem and work with crews to pre-assign their video feed **windows.** Crews that miss a window get dropped from the newscast. The live coordinator might allow some live crews to feed video from the van *during the live report,* but this is very risky, requiring close coordination and the right equipment in the field.

Problem: You're producing a newscast and you learn as the open is rolling that your lead live shot isn't ready.

Cure: This problem is also very common. It represents a total breakdown in communications on the part of everyone. Sometimes producers, having heard nothing to the contrary, will sail along "assuming" the live shot is OK. Good producers *never* do that. The only correct assumption until you hear to the contrary is that the live shot is *not* ready. Further, don't be passive in your live communications. Set a deadline by which you expect confirmation—say, five minutes before airtime—and hold the live coordinator and field crews to it. Always have a contingency plan in case the live shot fails and make sure everyone understands what it is. Don't wait until too late to implement it! If you're a reporter, photographer, or producer in the field, realize that a good producer and director can handle almost any live emergency, but last-second live surprises are the hardest to deal with smoothly. If you run into technical problems in the field that jeopardize the live shot, call in to report them immediately—*even if you'd rather spend the time working on the problem.* The producer and live coordinator *must* know what's going on, and to learn that they have to hear from you. No other consideration is more important.

Problem: You're on the air live giving a report from the State Fair when a drunk stumbles into the camera and knocks it off the tripod.

Cure: There isn't one. Welcome to live TV.

Are You a Breaking News Warrior?

Compared with any other medium, local television news has two major strengths: pictures and immediacy. Combine them, and you have a live shot. The most successful television station will be the one prepared to go live with breaking news at the snap of a finger.

Are you prepared to win in this game? Let's find out. Consider the following scenario. You're sitting in the control booth a few minutes into your newscast when you get a frantic call from the assignments desk: one of your live weather cams has caught a tornado on the ground! You punch up the remote on your router and sure enough, there it is—no audio, but spectacular live pictures of a huge black tornado now looming over the downtown skyline. You check the program monitor and find that your anchor is now reading the lead to a long medical report, which your station has been promoting heavily all day.

Which of the following would you do?

1. Climb under the control desk and whimper.

2. Get on the IFB and tell the anchor to stop reading and listen. When she stops reading, tell her to toss to live pictures of a tornado on the weather cam and ad-lib over it.

3. Allow the anchor to continue reading the lead to the packaged medical report. Once the report is on the air, use the time to find out more information about exactly where the tornado is and where it's going, and to get the weather-caster to the set.

4. Do nothing; wait for the National Weather Service to issue an official tornado bulletin.

5. Run outside and roll up your car window.

If you answered 3, your heart's probably in the right place but not your posterior, which is about to be kicked by the competition. If you answered 2, you're the one who will be doing the posterior kicking.

"But wait a minute," you object. "I can't talk to my anchor while she's on the air. She can't handle it. She'll choke on-air, then hunt me down and harm me!"

If it's true your anchors can't handle breaking news, it's not neces-sarily their fault. Anchors can handle breaking news situations such as the one described above if they're trained for it and, more impor-tant, if they understand you'll ask them to do it this way. It's up to the news managers to set the tone and direction. Stations that can handle such situations are ready to do battle in the TV news wars of the 21st century.

A Final Word: What If It All Goes to Hell, or "Why Are We in This Handbasket, and Where Are We Going So Fast?"

If there's one universal factor about live television, it's that occasion-ally it will crash and burn. Count on it. Murphy's Law has several television corollaries, including:

- If a live shot can crash, it will.

- If an editing machine can jam, or a server can crash, it will.

- If this is the worst possible day for one more spot news story to erupt, it will.

- If a piece of video might not make it, it won't.

- If the president of your company's broadcasting division is in town, all of the above will occur simultaneously.

Your only defense is to remember the Boy Scout motto. If the lead story is in jeopardy of not being finished in time because the reporter was late with the copy, you'd better have a Plan B that's better than "I'm going to kill the reporter." As discussed above, have a backup plan and don't hesitate to use it.

Even with good contingency plans, the worst will sometimes happen even to the best of producers. When it does, don't lose sleep because of it. Simply learn from the experience, and come back fighting the next day. Don't let the occasional TV production tragedy get you down. No matter how bad it was, tomorrow is another day. And the same can be said in the aftermath of excellent newscasts as well! An often-heard saying in this business is, "You're only as good as your most recent newscast," and there's a great deal of truth to that. The best way to cope with that reality is to try to bring a fresh sense of energy, enthusiasm, and determination to the beginning of every day.

Conclusion

The best live shots are those in which the reporter is able to interact with the surroundings in some way. Live shots require strong communications support from the television station. The producer must verify that the signal is strong; that the remote has good video, audio, and IFB—and that the talent is ready. A good producer always has a contingency plan ready in case the live shot fails. The best producers are aggressive in their handling of breaking news and can get live shots on the air quickly and seamlessly.

Live Shot DOs and DON'Ts

Do

- Make live shots interactive.
- Have a strong and reliable system for communication with crews in the field.
- Seek Q&A opportunities that add context and perspective.
- Realize the importance of breaking news.
- Trust and expect your anchors to be able to stop what they're doing to handle breaking news.

Don't

- Just stand there!
- Air a live shot without verifying its full readiness.
- Go into the booth without a live shot backup plan.
- Let a fear of production mistakes make you timid about getting breaking news on the air.
- Let a bad live shot or on-air mistake get you down.

Questions

1. Discuss "live for the sake of live."
2. When the show is on the air, the producer switches to "command and control mode." What does that mean?
3. Discuss the importance of contingency plans.
4. What is the "anchor question"?
5. What defines a breaking news warrior?
6. What's the role of a live shot coordinator?

CHAPTER THIRTEEN

Forrest Carr

Why We Fight

My father was 25 years old when Japan bombed Pearl Harbor. He and most of his generation went to war. I graduated from college in 1980. Most of my generation went to work. During World War II the government gave director Frank Capra the job of explaining the war effort to Americans and getting them behind it. The result was the famous *Why We Fight* documentary series. There's no similar effort to motivate modern Americans to fight the office wars of the 21st century. But that doesn't mean we don't need it—*especially* in the field of journalism.

In the post–9/11 world, our job is more difficult than ever—and more important. The question people have asked many times of journalists since the attacks is: "What has 9/11 taught us?" There's probably no consensus and some believe it taught us nothing. But at the local news level, arguably the stations that had established strong reputations for honesty and credibility were the ones that fared the best. In the post–9/11 world, people came to television news looking for reliability and for context, meaning and perspective—not for the car crash or shooting of the day. To those viewers, the craft of journalism was suddenly important again. Those of us who'd never lost faith in our craft were glad to welcome them back. Another high point came during Hurricane Katrina, when reporters aggressively demanded answers about the government's lack of preparedness and poor first response. As we're preparing this edition, viewers and online users are relying on the media to steer them through an economic crisis. We must continue to serve viewers well in the future. And that will require a firm commitment to the concept of ethics.

Up to this point, this book has been largely technical in nature. We've discussed the mechanics and style of broadcast copywriting, news gathering, and news producing at length, but we haven't delved as much into its substance or purpose. For the next few pages we'll put aside the *how* of journalism and concentrate on the *why*. It's our intention to give a broad overview and summary of the ethical process at both the newsroom and the individual levels. We'll also explore a topic not often addressed in the available literature about ethics, and that's the motivational challenges, professional disappointments, and on-the-job frustrations that can adversely affect a journalist's ethical focus, commitment, and quality of work.

Although you might be tempted to think of ethics as a "given" in the profession, something all experienced journalists know how to do as second nature, even a quick glance at the recent track record of journalism shows this is not the case. Such venerable institutions as the *New York Times,* the *Los Angeles Times,* CBS News, and NBC News (to name a few) have fallen victim to grave ethical scandals in recent years. Ethics is never a "given," no matter how veteran the journalist or how steeped in tradition the news organization might be. Further, ethics isn't a virtue, something you have because you're good-hearted, honest and kind to children and animals. Ethical behavior takes training, hard work and eternal vigilance.

It's also true that in today's rapidly changing media environment, television news jobs are harder to get, and more demanding on those who do get them, than ever before. These stresses can lead to disillusionment, resentment, and even anger. We'll talk about that, too.

In discussing ethics we'll rely heavily on work, wisdom, and inspiration from the Poynter Institute and on the expertise of Poynter faculty members Bob Steele, Al Tompkins, and Jill Geisler.

Building the Ethical Newsroom

Let's assume for a moment that you work in an average newsroom. Most if not all the journalists within consider themselves ethical. They probably have above-average intelligence and abilities and at least average motivation. Now, imagine an ugly episode plays out in the community, a news coverage challenge that strains emotions to the breaking point and severely tests the newsroom's decision-making processes. Would your newsroom rise to the occasion?

On Tuesday, April 20, 1999, two heavily armed students walked into Columbine High School in Littleton, Colorado, and opened fire. More than a dozen people died. With no warning, local media found themselves having to cover what turned out to be the bloodiest school rampage in U.S. history. Some stations performed better than others. Many made mistakes, some of them spectacular. Consider the following:

- While the gunmen were still presumably roaming the halls, some stations aired live cell phone interviews with students. One anchor went so far as to urge students to call the TV station instead of 911 (advice the station quickly retracted). One purported student cell phone call, which also aired live on a network news service, turned out to be a hoax.

- By contrast, at least one other local TV news producer took such a student call and handled it far differently. Realizing she wasn't trained as a crisis counselor or hostage negotiator, she didn't even consider putting the caller on the air. Instead, she urged the student to call 911 and then disconnected the call.

- Stations aired emotional interviews with extremely distraught juveniles at their most vulnerable moments, interviews that wound up being replayed again and again on the national news media.

- Almost every station showed, to at least some degree, live helicopter pictures of police positions and student escape routes, which of course might have been of extreme interest to the gunmen inside the school, who did have access to televisions.

Clearly, different ethical and decision-making processes were at work among the various newsrooms and journalists. In the aftermath of Littleton, the local and national media endured intense criticism. But there was some praise as well for the self-restraint and balance some of the journalists showed.

Now picture this happening in your newsroom. Would your team handle it well? Even if the people in your newsroom are ethical, if your newsroom has had no training in ethical decision making, the outcome is doubtful. A newsroom filled with ethical people isn't necessarily an ethical newsroom! The Poynter Institute's Bob Steele says our individual ethical principles "compete with each other and may compete with other people's principles. So we have to have the skills of ethical decision making, the process and tools to work through conflicting principles and colliding values."

Geisler, Tompkins, and Steele of Poynter speak frequently about the issues of ethics and decision making. Their view is that ethics isn't something you *have;* it's something you *do.* Ethics isn't simply an injunction to "do right." It's a process for achieving that goal. According to Steele, Tompkins, and Geisler, the decision-making processes in most newsrooms come in three flavors. They are:

- Gut reaction
- Rule obedience
- Reflection and reasoning

Reliable, ethical decision making is likely to take place only on that third level.

Gut Reaction

It's probably safe to say that most journalists consider themselves ethical. If pressed to justify that claim, many of them might say they "go with their gut" or "trust their instincts." But according to Steele, Tompkins, and Geisler, gut-level reactions, though important, are just the first step. The problem with your "gut" is that it's unique to you. It's shaped by an entire lifetime of personal experiences and past incidents, both pleasant and unpleasant. Your gut feelings can be emotional, prejudicial, unreasonable, strongly set, even irrational. Steele puts it this way: "Too strong of a gut reaction can prevent reflective and reasoned thinking. Too strong of a gut reaction can keep us from hearing the contrarian thoughts of others. Too strong of a gut reaction can trap us in the rigidity of rules and keep us from seeing the gray that always exists between the black and the white." Steele says you *should* listen to your gut, but don't completely trust it. Your gut reaction *will* have value, though, if it gets a conversation going—provided that conversation doesn't stop at the "gut level."

Rule Obedience

If you're talking about an ethical issue, you're already ahead of some newsrooms. What sometimes happens, however, is conversation proceeds to the next level, rule obedience, and stops there. According to Steele, Tompkins, and Geisler, at this level the participants recognize there's an issue, but they're not sure how to proceed. So, they open the station's policy manual—or, if there isn't one, they discuss the issue in light of the station's known rules, regulations, and precedents. They pick the rule or regulation that seems to fit (examples: "We don't cover suicides" or "We don't show bodies") and then proceed accordingly. The problem with this, of course, is no rule book can possibly cover every situation. Blind obedience to rules precludes reflection and reasoning. At this level the best courses of action might never even come up for discussion.

Reflection and Reasoning

In healthy newsrooms most rules are really *guidelines* meant to provoke further discussion, not end it. In such a newsroom, the decision-making process will now proceed to the third level. At this stage, participants attempt to find the proper course of action in light of the given facts while taking into account the station's guidelines and policies. Such discussions work best if they include a wide range of viewpoints, especially when you're working through major crises. Participants must ask certain questions, and the discussion might make use of formal guidelines for ethical decision making, which we'll discuss in a moment.

What Is Ethical? A Case Study

So how does one decide whether a given course of action is ethical?

One of the best ethical codes is the one adopted by the Society of Professional Journalists (SPJ), http://www.spj.org. It contains four basic points. Ethical journalists should:

- Seek the truth and report it
- Minimize harm
- Act independently
- Be accountable

When newsrooms fail to act ethically, often it's because the decision-making process either got hung up on or never got to that second point. The concept of minimizing harm suggests the end does *not* always justify the means, and not every fact or fact-gathering tactic is worth the collateral damage it might cause to people or organizations. Working these problems through isn't easy. It requires a *process*. Mistakes are likely to occur when the process fails or none is in place to begin with.

In a workshop presented by the Radio-Television News Directors Foundation (RTNDF), Geisler, Tompkins, and Steele discussed a fascinating case study that shows how this can happen. A station in Denver wanted to interview a victim who had suffered burns and other injuries in a building explosion. First the reporter tried an open front-door approach; she sought the interview through the hospital's public relations department. A spokesperson denied permission for the interview, telling the reporter the family didn't wish to talk. The reporter contacted the family directly and discovered, as she had suspected, this wasn't true; the victim and his wife very much wanted to talk. Angered that the P.R. spokesperson had misled her, the reporter decided to sneak up to the hospital room and obtain the interview on the sly. Accordingly, the photographer stuck the camera under his coat. The two of them made it up to the hospital room unchallenged, grabbed the interview, and presented a compelling exclusive story on the next newscast.

Would you have a problem with this course of action? At this point none of the 40 or so participants in the RTNDF workshop, which included some veteran news managers, objected. Many said if the reporter and photographer were in the hospital room at the invitation of the patient, they had a legal right to be there.

The problem with the law is it tells you what you can get away with, not what you *ought* to get away with. Or, as Tompkins put it, "The law tells you what you can do. Ethics tells you what you *should* do."

In this case, the television station's actions might have been different had the decision makers stopped to thoroughly discuss the proposed course of action before taking it and had asked any of the following questions during that discussion:

- Will the crew's presence in the room interfere with the patient's medical treatment?
- Will the crew's presence in the room adversely affect the patient in any way?
- Is this the type of environment where the crew would need to be wearing caps and gowns?
- What if the crew plugs in its lights and blows a circuit?
- Are there any considerations we should be thinking of or might be missing because of lack of expertise? Is there someone who can guide us on this?

As it turns out, burn patients require special germ-free environments. The crew's entry into the room *was* potentially dangerous for the patient. In the aftermath, the hospital raised a hue and cry. This led to a public relations problem for the TV station, which had to apologize for its actions. The journalists weren't aware of the medical danger, of course, in part because they didn't have the expertise to know about it. In cases like this, newsrooms are wise to seek what Geisler likes to call a "rabbi," a teacher or expert who can advise the decision makers.

The concepts of seeking the truth and minimizing harm go hand in hand. But of the two, the duty to seek the truth and report it is primary. As Steele puts it, the idea is to minimize harm while maximizing truth-telling. Decision-making processes fail if they don't include prudent steps to reduce the harm a story might cause. But they fail even worse if they minimize harm by eliminating needed truth-telling.

In the case study above, the television station would have been well served to consider other options. Among the possibilities:

- Confront the P.R. spokesperson with the truth about the family's willingness to talk and enlist her help in setting up a safe interview.
- Consider a phone interview with the hospitalized patient.
- Interview the wife separately outside the hospital.

These options might have preserved the station's ability to tell the truth of what happened while minimizing the harm getting the interview might have caused.

Doing Ethics: Excerpts from the Poynter Guidelines

In a healthy newsroom environment one or more people, perhaps making use of a gut reaction, will red-flag ethical issues or challenges for discussion. The discussion will proceed to that third level, reflection and reasoning. Steele has a list of questions participants should ask. Among them, paraphrased below, are:

- What do we know? What more do we need to know?
- What is our journalistic purpose?
- What are our ethical concerns?
- Which organizational policies and professional guidelines must we consider?
- Which other voices, people with diverse perspectives and ideas, should we include in the decision-making process?
- Who are the stakeholders—those who will be affected by our decisions? What motivates them? How would we feel if we were in their shoes?
- What are the possible consequences of our actions?
- What are our alternatives?
- Will we be willing—and *able*—to publicly explain our actions?

One might reasonably question whether there's *time* to go through all of these steps in a crisis situation, given the deadlines a typical television or radio news operation faces. The answer is yes. A station's news operations do not have to grind to a halt during the decision-making process. The desk can still dispatch crews and begin the process of getting the news on the air. It's possible even in such situations to convene quick meetings, either in a nearby conference room or in the middle of the newsroom, to seek staff input for identifying issues and discussing options. Nor does the process have to stop when the formal planning meeting ends. Some stations have ongoing ad-hoc conferences, in the news director's office or some other central location, which people can join and leave as their deadlines permit. Regardless of the method, if a news organization believes ethical decision making is important, it will find a way to do it.

Acting Independently

The SPJ's admonition to "act independently" isn't as complicated or hard to interpret as the injunction to "minimize harm." Though the code contains several bullet points of advice under this heading, the gist of it is simply this: The only item on your news-gathering agenda should be the intent to gather the news. You should steer clear of any influences that might call that agenda into question. Hordes of people are out there trying to influence your reporting and swing you over to their point of view with tactics ranging from the subtle to the extreme. Land mines and pitfalls litter the journalistic landscape. If you step in one, the best course is to simply back out of it—and, if necessary, disclose the conflict, apologize for it, and take corrective action.

Accountability

That fourth ethics point—"be accountable"—is relatively new to the SPJ code, having been added in 1996. The RTDNA's (Radio Television Digital News Association) revised code of ethics, adopted in 2000, contains similar language. Journalists are still struggling with it. Most television and radio stations do a fairly poor job with it.

The text of the code itself speaks of abiding by high standards, promptly correcting mistakes, and the like. But it also urges journalists to "invite dialogue with the public over journalistic conduct." Television and radio stations are in the position to do this much better than any newspaper is; after all, we're actually *capable* of the speech the word "dialogue" implies. Some television stations have viewer mailbag segments that include comments from the public received by way of telephone and e-mail. This is a good start. Segments that specifically solicit viewer feedback about the station's news coverage decisions are better. Segments that invite such feedback and respond to it sincerely are the best. Very few television or radio stations have such segments. Fewer still—as of this writing, only two or three—have viewer representatives to facilitate this process.

If a television station, radio station, or network news operation truly wishes to hold itself accountable to the public, it should clearly state what it stands for and provide a mechanism for soliciting, airing, and, most important, *responding* to public feedback openly and sincerely.

It takes a bit of courage to do this. A commitment to public feedback implies a commitment to own up to mistakes. Journalism is difficult; few of us are completely without ethical sin. Mistakes are inevitable. History suggests the public can be very forgiving—*if* forgiveness is requested. On the other hand, the public has nothing but contempt for people and institutions that ignore or deny their mistakes or, even worse, defend them as if they were some kind of virtue.

Many in our industry don't feel we should have to explain ourselves. That attitude is evident in the reply a network news executive once gave to a reporter when the executive said that yes, the network does have a policy about privacy but no, it's not going to share it. Journalists frequently wrap themselves in the First Amendment, but don't always stop to recall where those First Amendment rights came from. They came from the American people, who decided to give our industry constitutional protections granted to no other. In return we owe it to our public to share and explain our methods and motivations.

Remember that final point on Steele's questions for ethical decision making: Has the newsroom reached a decision it's able and willing to explain? Newsrooms and journalists unwilling or unable to explain themselves cannot claim to be ethical. It's really that simple.

An Ethics Barometer

We've seen that newsrooms can't rely on the collective gut instincts of their employees for ethical decision making. They need a process, and that process requires training, implementation, and maintenance. Newsrooms with such a system in place will create a culture characterized by some or all of the following:

- Training in and frequent discussion of the ethical decision-making process within the newsroom.
- Frequent "red-flagging" of ethical issues by employees or managers for discussion.
- Management and rank-and-file attitudes that cultivate, encourage, and respect "contrarian" viewpoints. Such an atmosphere is characterized by employees who aren't afraid to speak up, and by managers who encourage them to do so.
- Special in-house workshops or staff discussion groups to talk about ethical questions the station might have encountered or case studies of ethical issues other stations have encountered.
- Regular staff meetings, one-on-one or in groups, to critique stories and discuss the issues.

- Frequent dialogue with members of the public affected by coverage decisions.
- On-air acknowledgment of viewer feedback and public discussion of major coverage decisions.

Summary

Why is all of this so important? According to Steele, Geisler, and Tompkins, when faced with a crisis such as Littleton, television news can't merely be good. We owe it to our viewers to be *excellent*. Says Tompkins, "It is not possible to be ethical without being excellent."

And vice versa.

Building the Ethical Journalist

To conduct yourself ethically on a personal level, you'll need two items. The first is your bag of decision-making tools as described above, which you'll put together and continually sharpen through training and experience. The second is that most elusive ingredient of all: a good attitude, made up of energized spirits, respect for your co-workers, a determination to make a positive difference for your viewers and community, and a passion for what you do for a living. Many authors have written about the basic tools for ethical decision making, but much less is available about the subject of how to keep your personal energies properly focused. In the pages ahead we'll talk about both: how to keep a good ethical balance in the face of the tough personal and professional challenges you'll encounter, and how to keep yourself focused, motivated, and energized.

Practice, Practice

In the first part of this chapter, we noted that without the proper training, a newsroom filled with ethical journalists nevertheless might fail to act ethically. The same is true at the individual level.

Ethical challenges and choices big and small face individual journalists every single day. Each choice you make—ranging from the stories you elect to pursue, the people you choose to interview, and the way you treat the people you encounter—has ethical implications and potential pitfalls. Sometimes the choices aren't clear. More frequently, it's not always clear there *are* choices. You might find yourself blindly pursuing a course of action without having stopped to even question whether there might be alternatives. In such cases you might traipse along blindly, not worried about anything—until you suddenly step on an ethical land mine. At that point, of course, the damage is done and the only real question is how to make repairs and clean things up.

How can you steer through the sometimes treacherous terrain of journalism? A heart of gold isn't enough. Even if you're a swell person, pay your taxes, and don't rob banks, this doesn't mean you're ethical. If you want to play the piano well, you have to practice, practice, practice. The same is true of journalism. To hone your ethical sense you'll need training in the art of ethical decision making and critical thinking, and experience doing it.

We hope that, by the time they've landed their first job, most journalists will have had some exposure to ethics concepts in college. If not, they'll have to learn the ethical process on the job. But even if you *have* had some training in ethics, you can't stop there. Says Steele, "Journalists should be in a life-long learning mode." Some have pointed out that journalists get less continuing education than members of any other profession. Chances are you'd be shocked if you were to discover that a surgeon who's about to perform heart surgery on you hasn't brushed up on the subject since leaving medical school 20 years ago. Journalists are no different. According to Steele, "You should always be searching for new information. We should always be challenging our own assumptions by adding knowledge to our noggins. We should be constantly sharpening the tools in our professional bag, including the skill-based tools of writing and interviewing and reporting, but also the decision-making tool."

The single best way to learn every day is through interacting with your colleagues, asking many questions, looking for mentors, and, as Steele puts it, for "models of excellence in our colleagues and in other newsrooms." You should constantly observe and analyze the effects of your actions and words on colleagues and on the public. Another good learning tactic is to read books and trade publications to discover the ethical challenges others have faced and how they've dealt with them. Finally, formal ethics training is available through seminars and workshops sponsored by the RTNDF, the Poynter Institute, and others.

If the process works as it should, you'll still be learning about journalism and ethics the day you retire.

The Importance of Being Earnest

When you get that first job, chances are you'll be excited, pumped, filled with good intentions, and eager to get to work. You might assume your new co-workers feel the same way. If so, you could be in for a shock. It's probably true that most journalists begin the same way: We're optimistic, determined, eager, and idealistic. But here's a disturbing truth: Often, something ugly happens along the way. We start out as people not too different from our viewers and listeners. But after a few years many of us are profoundly different.

Some of us become cynical, jaded, distrustful, and bitter. We don't react to stories and situations the same way our public does. We develop an attitude of "Been there, done that." Stories have to be bigger, more sensational, and more splashy to get our attention. We begin to think we're smarter than our viewers and listeners and have a right to decide for them what is and isn't worthy of public discourse. We're less respectful of people and of each other. Of course, this isn't true of all journalists. But you can walk into almost any newsroom in the country and see these forces in action—forces that do little to create a healthy environment for good journalism or ethical behavior.

It doesn't have to be this way. Plenty of journalists find a way to keep themselves energized and their spirits renewed in the face of the inevitable on-the-job frustrations, disappointments, and disagreeable bosses. The probability that you'll be a capable and ethical journalist rises in direct proportion to your success in keeping a healthy attitude and maintaining your ability to enjoy your work.

Journalism isn't just a job. It shouldn't be something you decided to do because it sounded more appealing than becoming an accountant or a tax attorney or a meter reader. Journalism is a calling. As with most callings, the only truly successful players will be those who have a passion for it. Why else would you be willing to work holidays? Or be on call 24 hours a day, seven days a week? Or work the long hours we're often required to work? If you don't have a passion for it, not only will you not succeed, but you might be standing in the way of someone who does have that passion.

So, you've arrived on the journalistic scene, fresh out of college, with a microphone in one hand, a notepad in the other, a heart burning with enthusiasm, and a passion for the business. How are you going to keep those fires burning? All professions sometimes lead to burnout, but ours—with its unique combination of high ideals, grueling deadlines, and profit pressure—is more susceptible than many. The most ethical journalists will also be those who've done the best job of coping with these forces and remaining true to their ideals.

How to Immunize Yourself against Disillusionment

That first disillusionment can come very quickly. Newsrooms are filled with cynics, and pretty soon you find they're having an effect on you. You notice no one around you seems to be working as hard as you feel you're working. You further notice that management doesn't seem to care. Then you begin to examine your station's news product with a more critical eye. What news is the station covering, and why? Is there a larger meaning or purpose to what the newsroom is doing? Does anyone in management articulate an overall vision, or does the news product seem to you to be a random bag of car chases, shootings, and petty crimes? Who's paying attention? Budget issues begin to bug you. Lack of leadership begins to bug you. The daily confusion begins to bug you. Pretty soon you've concluded that no one cares but you, that managers and co-workers are just phoning it in, and that the company ownership cares about nothing but the bottom line. The day arrives when you suddenly decide you can't stand it for another moment.

What are you going to do about that?

You basically have two choices. One, you can give up. "Giving up" can take the form of quitting outright, but more likely such mental surrender will manifest itself in the form of you deciding to join the cynical masses, adding to the group bitterness while going through the motions of doing your job. Giving up is really easy to do.

The second choice is more difficult. You can vow a mighty oath *never* to give up, to keep slugging, and to always do your part to make a positive difference, no matter how small that difference might seem on a daily basis. So management is driving you nuts? Become what Steele sometimes refers to as a "contrarian," someone who makes it a point to be the "loyal opposition" in challenging (diplomatically, if possible) management and co-workers. Network. Let co-workers and managers hear from you. Find ways to express yourself and to nudge people in a different direction.

For this second choice to work, you'll need to focus on the positive. Don't let yourself fall into the pit of relentless negativism where many cynics dwell. The best way to immunize yourself against disillusionment is to concentrate your attention on the things you enjoy that drew you here to begin with. Did you get into the business because you love to write? Guess what—even on the worst possible day, you're still writing, and you're still getting paid for it. Are you doing this because you like the excitement of having your finger on the pulse of the world? The world is still there, it still has a pulse, and your finger is still on it. Did you become a journalist because you want to make a difference? No matter what you do in a newsroom—every time your fingers dance across a keyboard, or your hands adjust a camera or an editing machine, or you clear your throat to begin tracking a package, or you pick up the phone to talk with a contact or source, you have a chance to change the world, if only a little bit. Focus on what you enjoy. Throw your arms around it. Don't let the negatives distract you from the realization that you fought hard to be here for a reason, and that those reasons haven't gone away.

Many have written about "youthful idealism." But idealism doesn't have to be the province of the young. There's no reason you can't hang onto your ideals and fight the disappointment and disillusionment that strike so many. But to be successful, you must not be so idealistic that you can't cope with the reality of the daily grind. More important, you have to cope with the fact that others have ideals, too, and they're likely to be different from your own. Says Steele, "I think we can be both idealistic and pragmatic. I believe that high ideals help us search for excellence. But I also believe that we have to search for the common ground that allows for differences, that respects and tolerates opposing ideas, that accepts that there is a great deal of gray between the black and white of ethical decisions."

Disillusioned journalists tend to think no one cares. An idealistic journalist knows that if he or she cares, that's one, and it beats the hell out of none. One caring journalist can find or inspire others. It just takes persistence and a little faith.

You and the Stockholders

Disillusionment was a common, if not universal, newsroom problem even in the days when an FCC television license amounted to a permit to print money. In today's world, it's worse. Local television news is under attack on all sides. Jobs are tougher to get. Staff sizes are shrinking. Salaries are coming down, especially on the high end. Survivors of newsroom purges find themselves having to take on additional duties, usually for the same or even less pay. Managers love to justify this with proclamations such as, "We must learn to do more with less." This tends to really annoy overworked employees who perceive, rightly or wrongly, that the newsroom is really doing less with less. In addition to blowing out people, some stations pad the bottom line with actions that are less than ethically defensible, such as giving advertisers favorable treatment within the news. In such environments, it's hard not to get really angry with the stockholders and disgusted with the profit motive that guides the station's efforts.

One key to coping with these feelings is to resist the temptation to indict the profit motive in general in reaction to specific questionable actions that stations sometimes take in pursuit of revenue and ratings. Such actions might constitute bad management, but they aren't necessarily an indication that something is wrong with capitalism or the profit motive. Profit is a perfectly honorable motive for any business. In fact the profit motive, and the underlying work ethic that makes it possible, form the bedrock of our society. If you work for a commercial television or radio station, then you're in the business of providing news and information for profit. You expect to be paid for your services, do you not? So do the owners and investors who make it possible for you to do your job. It's a simple equation: Resources for journalism tend to rise or fall in direct proportion to profit. A money-losing newsroom eventually will go belly-up, leading to no journalism at all. (Even if you work for a public broadcaster, then contributions and taxes from people and institutions who work for a profit fund your efforts.)

Chances are you didn't get into television or radio news because you have a burning desire to make stockholders rich. Conversely, it's a good bet the stockholders didn't invest in your station because they wanted you to have a job, two cars and a nice house in the burbs. It's possible that many of them don't give a rat's patoot about journalism, though doubtless many of them do. Yet the two of us—journalists and investors—can't live without one another. Maybe it's a shotgun marriage, but it's a marriage just the same. We can make it work—*only*—if we create value for one another.

Good journalism is one way to increase shareholder value. But in today's drastically changing media environment, that alone isn't enough. Journalists must work more closely with business owners than ever before to innovate new ways to keep profit flowing. Few are immune, and it's not a comfortable process. In fact it's stressful as hell, because the outcome isn't certain. Television newsrooms are now becoming more like any other business: Success is no longer guaranteed, and some will fail. For many journalists, it's a sad fact that the love of this business won't be strong enough for them to endure those pressures. But many others will do what it takes to evolve with the industry and stick with it precisely because of their passion for what they do.

Bottom line: Yes, you should resist bad management, to the extent you're able. But don't let contempt for stockholders and investors adversely affect your attitude, performance or ethical balance. Your ability to continue in the occupation that (we hope) you love depends entirely on your effectiveness in bringing value to your company, and on your willingness to adapt as necessary in finding new ways to do that.

The Ratings and You

The popular media, especially those in Hollywood, like to portray journalists as evil, ratings-grubbing sensationalists. This tends to paint an honorable aim, the pursuit of ratings, with the brush of a dishonorable tactic, sensationalism. Too many of us journalists tend to agree with the critics that the pursuit of ratings is somehow wrong or at least distasteful, and because of that we lose respect for our industry and, in essence, for what we do for a living. To say the least, this is *not* a morale booster. You can see the detrimental effects of this constant criticism on the morale and attitude of journalists every day in trade magazines, on the Internet, in journalism forums, and in electronic publications such as *ShopTalk*.

But as with the pursuit of profit, there's nothing wrong in and of itself with seeking to enhance ratings. For one, you want your station to be profitable, for all the reasons we've already discussed. Second, you want your journalism to be *effective*. If a storyteller shouts to the woods and no one hears, did the message get out? No. The best story in the world will have no effect if no one sees or hears it.

It *is* true that the thoughtless pursuit of quick ratings sometimes leads broadcasters to take actions that are unethical or, at the very least, tasteless, silly, and counterproductive. This is where journalists need to be on guard. But don't sneer at the basic desire to grow ratings and profit, not unless you're willing to show you mean it by giving up your paycheck and working for free. An honest craftsperson provides honest value for payment received. An honest broadcaster provides honest benefit for viewership or listenership received. Ratings and profit are the measures by which we're judged, and in a free market society, this is as it should be. Concentrate on providing the viewer and listener benefit, and have faith that your viewers and listeners will reward you.

Your Public Covenant

No matter how discouraged you might sometimes become on the job, and no matter how much respect you might lose for your employer, there's one key factor that ought to keep you going: your viewers or listeners.

A colleague once described to me his frustration caused by poor conditions at the competing station where he worked—few resources, questionable ethics, little leadership. But he claimed he still did the best job he could day in and day out *despite* his feelings. "My viewers are counting on me," he explained. "I can't let them down."

He's exactly right. Your viewers count on you. If you can't motivate yourself to do a good job for your employer, then do it for your viewers or listeners.

Some (if not most) newsrooms have a thinly veiled contempt for news consumers. How many assignments desk personnel refer to the newsroom's published telephone number as the "nut line" or "idiot phone"? To be sure, members of the public can be quirky, cranky, and sometimes downright abusive. Often they ask dumb questions. Still, we're there for them. They're our reason for being. If you can't embrace that concept, then you really should find something else to do in life.

A respect for members of the public and compassion for their feelings in your personal conduct should be a basic part of your ethical makeup. In an interview situation, which do you prefer: a confrontational question designed to show how aggressive and smart you are, or an even-toned question designed to elicit information? Which is better: to jump out of the bushes with microphone in hand and ambush someone on-camera, or to make an attempt to schedule an appointment to interview that person? Which would you rather do: ask, "How do you feel?" or say "Tell me about yourself"? If you picked the second answer to each of these questions, you're beginning to get the idea.

Broadcast journalism, especially at the local level, is all about serving people and serving the community. The best reporters seek out the unheard voices, listen hard, and tell those people's stories. The best television and radio stations reach out to all segments of the community. They establish a dialogue with community members and might even formalize it on the air through a feedback segment or community reporting beat or both. Their reporting will address community needs and reflect community values.

You'll face many ethical challenges in your career. Sometimes the process of weighing your journalistic duty against the potential harm a story might cause is very difficult. The options can be murky. Your ethical compass stands the best chance of remaining true and pointing you in the right direction if you energize it with the goal of providing service and value to your viewers or listeners and to the community. Though public distrust of the media continues to grow, the basic presumption still is that journalists should be telling the truth and serving the public interest the best they know how. It's the covenant our industry, and you personally, have formed with the public. Take it to heart.

When You and the Boss Disagree

It's bound to happen sooner or later, and odds are it won't be later: You and the boss will disagree. Like individuals, organizations tend to have a personality of sorts, and like people, some organizations are more skilled and likable than others are. There are as many different news philosophies as there are journalists. The chances of your personal news philosophy being in perfect harmony with that of your employer aren't great. Perhaps you're a "high-road" producer working for a "flash and trash" newsroom, or vice versa. Perhaps you find that you're a conservative working in a liberal environment, or vice versa. How are you going to cope while keeping your sanity, your sense of ethics, and, we hope, your job?

Realize that no matter what kind of environment you find yourself in, on-the-job clashes are inevitable. Don't expect to win every battle. Do make sure your voice is heard. You *do* have influence. Have the courage to present your ideas. Most important, work to develop the skills you need to *properly* present them. Says Steele, "A young journalist will have a much better chance of achieving her own ethical standards if she can make clear, concise principled arguments to her boss as well as to her colleagues." The good news, according to Steele, is that the best news organizations not only listen to their youthful members but also value them. "The most thoughtful counterintuitive idea might come from one of the youngest and newest members of the organization, those fresh eyes and new perspectives that might drive the decision-making process. The chance of that happening is enhanced when the young and/or new person makes a clear, concise argument that will get other people saying, 'Uh, huh, I hadn't thought of that.'"

It must be acknowledged, however, that even in the best newsrooms your voice won't be as strong and respected or have as much leverage as those of the more experienced journalists. To make yourself heard, you'll need to network with people and form alliances. Says Steele, "Even if you don't have a stripe on your sleeve because of your youth or shortness of tenure, you can influence people through your intelligence, through your commitment, and through the questions you ask and the knowledge you bring to the discussion." And he adds, if you want change, "you can only get the change through influence."

What if you have an urgent problem or a strong ethical objection in a given situation? First of all, do *not* be a hothead. Don't pitch a fit. Don't storm out of the room or seek some big confrontation. Steele says the proper tactics are essential. "There are a number of ways for a young journalist to raise concerns with a news director or executive producer. You can pose it in writing, raising three or four questions about a particular dilemma and how it's being handled. You can ask for a private conversation in which you raise some questions and state your beliefs." It does take a little courage to speak up. It also takes patience. It's not reasonable to expect that you'll be able to single-handedly change your newsroom's policies, ethics, and values. It is reasonable to expect to be able to *influence* them, however, and have an effect on your newsroom's culture over time.

What if, despite your best, patient efforts, you find yourself in a job environment that's unethical or in some other way intolerable? According to Steele, you have three basic options. They are:

- *Survival.* A situation in which you've more or less given up, are just marking time, and are pretty much miserable.
- *Coping.* A step up from survival. You haven't totally given up and are still trying to have a positive influence, but you're pessimistic and unhappy.
- *Influence.* You refuse to give up and are determined to make a difference, through the tactics we've just discussed.

Of the three, Steele much prefers the third. But he acknowledges some situations really are intolerable. "If you are convinced it is impossible to influence things for the better, then leaving and finding a better situation is a reasonable alternative."

Even in such cases, don't be in a hurry. As satisfying as it might be to tell your boss precisely what he or she can do with the job, you'll still be dealing with the consequences of your action long after the satisfaction has faded. Don't make career decisions in anger or haste. Unless you're the target of abuse or sexual harassment, even if you feel you "just can't take it another second," you probably can. Don't let an on-the-job crisis or setback push you into taking a rash action that you might regret. Think about it long and hard. As we've discussed, remember what got you into the business to begin with, reflect on your passions, and consider your viewers or listeners. Above all, be honest with yourself and make sure *you* aren't the problem. If that's the case, leaving isn't the solution. As the saying goes, "No matter where you go, there you are." Your personal problems always follow you. Deal with them first. Says Steele, "You don't want to leave a bad professional relationship only to have it re-created elsewhere."

That said, if after careful thought you decide the current environment doesn't allow you to pursue the things you enjoy and doesn't allow you to serve your viewers or listeners, then it's time to vote with your feet. Do it on *your* terms. And while you're searching for a new job, continue to do your best in the one you have. Act ethically, serve your viewers and listeners, and give good value to your employer for the paycheck you're drawing. If you have a job in journalism, then regardless of what's happening between you and your employer you have an obligation to the public. Fulfill it. When it comes to your viewers and listeners, never say die, and never give up.

The Work-Life Balance

Commitment to never give up, you might have to make some difficult choices. The news business can be highly rewarding, but it can be cruel and heartless too. You might have to work weekends, overnights, or some other shift that ruins your social life. You might end up a newsroom in which the managers proudly tell you that at your age, you don't have the right to even ask about work-life balance. To some news directors, it's all work. You might have to find a roommate to help pay the rent during your first couple of years on the job. You might have to extend your college diet of Ramen noodles three nights a week into your professional life because in many places, they'll try to pay you less than you'd make babysitting. You might work your tail off and receive little or no praise, while those around you do just the minimum and seem to be faring better, or at least not worse, than you are. Lots of young people leave the business after only a few years because they find the payoff just isn't worth the pain. Sometimes, though, it is. A LOT depends on the type of newsroom culture you enter, and a lot of that depends on who the bosses are.

Amid the everyday hustle of broadcast news, there come times when we have to make decisions about our careers. As Andrea Blanford found out, those are decisions you can't make on the fly.

It was her first job out of college. Andrea had been working as a general assignment reporter at WNCT, the local CBS affiliate in Greenville, NC, for about two years when one Monday her news director called her into his office. He said the morning anchor position was opening up and he wanted Andrea to take it. He gave her the details about the job and told her to go home and sleep on it.

Andrea's first instinct was to turn it down. She loved working as a reporter, getting out in the field every day, meeting new people and honing her skills. On top of that, she had a plan. She always thought she'd finish out her three-year contract at WNCT and move on to be a reporter in a bigger market. This new job opportunity with its contract extension was a curve ball she didn't see coming.

Several nights went by. Andrea talked with her parents; they told her they would support her either way and she slept on it. She called up her former professors at her alma mater, they imparted their wisdom about the lifestyle changes she'd have to make, and she slept on it some more. By the end of the week, she had changed her mind. She took the job.

The first month as morning anchor flew by. Andrea knew she'd made the right decision. Her role as an anchor brought new challenges, lessons to be learned, and a skill-set to master. Anchoring the morning news wasn't part of Andrea's original career plan. But people believed in her and instead of missing out on a great opportunity, she took the leap.

Andrea learned that good decision making takes courage. She didn't think she was ready to be an anchor, but her trusted mentors, family and managers knew she was. Andrea says when you're faced with a career-changing decision, it's best to take the plan you wrote down and copyedit like crazy. There's no rule for what it takes to get to where you want to be. When opportunity is within your reach, grab it or it will pass you by. Turn to trusted advisers for clarity in your decision making. And most importantly, she says, sleep on it.

Also, keep in mind that the skills you learn in classes like this one are transferrable. You're not locked into local news and there's a world of other possibilities. Brynne Miller always hoped that one day she'd own her own production company, she just never thought it would be when she was in her 20s. She went to one of the best journalism schools in the country and really fell in love with writing and producing, so it was a natural fit for her to work for a local news organization after graduation. Plus, who could complain about getting a full-time producer gig in market 28 right out of college? But as it turns out, although she loved the writing and producing aspects of her job, the hours for a morning producer (working overnight) weren't the best fit for her. She's proud she stuck it out for two years before deciding she couldn't take the lack of sleep anymore. She went back for a masters degree in interactive media. While she was in grad school, she took a business class, and the big project was writing a business plan. She and her project partner just wanted a good grade, but with encouragement from their professor and others in university administration, they decided they could make something out of the plan. They figured they had nothing to lose, and decided they could find a niche market with the different skills each brought to the partnership. They expanded their business plan and Firefly Interactive Media was born. They found that small businesses and nonprofits that had been affected by the slow economy the most were really in need of their services, which range from audio and video production to Web site design. These are the organizations that don't have the financial strength to pay full-time marketing/communications staff members. The need was there; someone just had to go after it. Their passion is bringing a voice to the voiceless and "illuminating the endless possibilities" that visual media bring to an organization's message and mission. Brynne and her partner get to write, shoot, edit, create—all the things they could do working for a legacy media company—so in a day and age when jobs are hard to come by and even harder to keep, being her own boss at a job that really doesn't feel like work is the best work-life balance she can imagine.

Despite winning the SPJ National Championship for In-Depth Reporting, Bethany Parker knew early on that the grind of local TV news wasn't for her. But she also knew that the skills she learned in her broadcast journalism classes would serve her well. As her professors always told her, the ability to communicate with people using text, audio, video, and graphics, along with the ability to work in a group and produce a product, is something almost any profession would value. In college, Bethany took great interest in the creative form of storytelling. Her favorite type of story was the kicker, or human-interest story at the end of a newscast. She enjoyed being creative in her writing and editing, using both to not only tell the story, but to also incorporate humor and allow the audience to have fun along with her. Once she graduated, Bethany and her family stepped into documentary filmmaking. Their story is about an Argentinean group of women looking for the grandchildren they believe were stolen during the military dictatorship in Argentina from 1976–1983. Bethany was the primary editor for the film. During the nearly year-long process of editing the hour-long documentary, Bethany realized her love for editing as a creative part of the storytelling process even more. In school she learned that pictures always speak louder than words, and the importance of SWAP. Coming up with an idea of how you want to tell your story and then going out and getting video that matches what you want to say is the first step. Watching your video and writing a script that closely matches the images you've captured is the second step. And the third step is something Bethany learned and appreciated so much more during her work on the documentary, which is putting the pictures and words together creatively in order to drive the message of the story. You see, hearing words and seeing pictures on a screen is good, having those pictures and words working together is even better, but telling a story with those words and pictures by the way you put them together and allowing the audience to learn something AND feel something is the best of all. Good communicators who can do that will ALWAYS be in demand whether it's in business, law, sports, government, advocacy, independent video production, or the wacky world of TV news.

One Day, You Might BE the Boss

If you wind up in TV news (or management in any other line of work), remember as you advance in the business what it was like to deal with difficult bosses. Jenelle Shriner is the executive producer at KVUE-TV in Austin, Texas. Shriner worked as a morning news producer for seven years before landing her first job as executive producer. She says the two are entirely different. As a producer, you organize the stories, make sure your writing is active, and constantly look for breaking news. You go in the control room and sweat through hours of continuing coverage when news strikes. You live it, and you breathe it.

As an executive producer, Shriner is looking to preserve journalistic values. Hers are the final eyes overseeing the stories that go out over the air. She's on the prowl for writing that incriminates people before they're convicted. She's on the lookout for accuracy. She's making sure her station is naming the right people, airing the correct mug shots, and making sure the station doesn't get sued. She's also pushing the producers to be better.

Shriner says some people don't like being pushed, but she reminds us that being good isn't about being liked. It's about being respected.

She's had managers who are condescending. She's had managers who screamed so loudly someone had to call security. And when she looks back on the years she spent at those stations, that's what she remembers, the angst about coming to work because you don't feel appreciated. She vowed she would never treat anyone with disrespect. In this business, we all work on holidays. We drive to work in ice storms and conditions we advise people to avoid. We wake up in the middle of the night to go to work. And we're all doing it for the same reason; to help our community.

One day you might consider going into management. And you'll have to make a decision about how you'll treat the people you work with. Shriner encourages you to be kind and fair, and to teach not through fear but by example. Make decisions but be open to ideas. Realize you're never going to be right all the time, but your co-workers will appreciate your efforts to be as fair as you can.

Conclusion

There are several sayings TV news professionals use to console themselves when their efforts go down the toilet. My personal favorite is, "No one ever died from bad TV." Probably the most common is, "Thank God it's not brain surgery." Indeed it's not. *It's more powerful and important than that.* Television news has the ability to build reputations or destroy them, to guide society to noble or ignoble action, to calm riots or start them, to start wars or end them, to make kings or dethrone them, to inspire the heart or depress the soul, to give hope or destroy it. The power we hold is incredible—so much so that people are always trying to take it away from us or limit it. The First Amendment to the U.S. Constitution was designed in part to protect Americans from such attacks, but it isn't always up to the challenge. Protection in other countries is even more uncertain. It's therefore incumbent upon us to wield this impressive power with sensitivity, responsibility, humility, a sense of ethics, and respect for the individual. Fewer and fewer news consumers believe we do that. Is that assessment justified? What do you think? And more important, what do you intend to do about it?

Television news is one of the few occupations available that allow you to have a wide impact on people's lives, for better or worse, while having more fun than the law allows. Do have fun. But never lose sight of the power in your hands.

Additional Readings

This chapter has been brief and introductory in nature. We hope your study of ethics won't stop here. Poynter ethics director Bob Steele recommends the following additional reading:

Sissela Bok, *Lying: Moral Choice in Public and Private Life* (Vintage Books, 1999. ISBN: 0375705287).

Jack Fuller, *News Values: Ideas for an Information Age* (University of Chicago Press, 1997. ISBN: 0226268802).

Al Tompkins, *Write for the Ear, Shoot for the Eye; Aim for the Heart: A Guide for TV Producers and Reporters* (Bonus Books, 2002. ISBN: 1566251761).

In addition, as of this writing two important codes of ethics can be found at the following Web sites:

Radio Television Digital News Association Code of Ethics: http://www.rtdna.org/pages/best-practices/ethics.php.

Society of Professional Journalists Code of Ethics: http://www.spj.org/ethics_code.asp.

Ethical DOs and DON'Ts

Do	Don't
• Plan now for how you'll deal with the next ethical challenge.	• Forget that ethics isn't a set of virtues but rather a process for making decisions.
• Pay attention to your "gut feelings."	• Let your gut have the final word.
• Involve others in ethical discussions.	• Try to tackle tough ethical problems on your own.
• Seek more information and identify alternatives.	• Let blind obedience to "the rules" make your decisions for you.
• Be willing and able to publicly explain your decisions.	• Be timid about speaking up in editorial discussions.
• Network with friends and colleagues to gain influence.	• Forget that the first loyalty of journalism is to the public.
• Focus on what you enjoy about journalism.	• Ever give up!

Questions

1. List and discuss the three levels of ethical decision making.
2. What are the four basic points of the SPJ Code of Ethics?
3. How do you "practice" being ethical?
4. Discuss immunizing yourself against disillusionment.
5. Discuss your public covenant.
6. Discuss various ways to handle disagreements with your managers.

CHAPTER FOURTEEN

C. A. Tuggle and Forrest Carr

Effectively Utilizing Social Media

Eric Kuhn has held several titles: new media consultant, audience interaction producer, and social media agent among them. None of those jobs or titles existed before Eric filled them. Throughout his young career (he worked with NBC, CBS, the NBA, CNN and United Talent Agency before he was 23), people have wondered what his various job titles actually mean. In short, he helps legacy media (and now Hollywood stars) figure out how to use social media effectively. Kuhn's journey started in high school and carried into his college years at Hamilton College, where, as a freshman, he hosted a talk-radio program about news and politics. His guests included Eliot Spitzer, former NYC mayor Ed Koch, Rev. Al Sharpton and NBC News anchor Ann Curry. Even at that time, Kuhn was giving advice to fellow journalists. That advice still applies.

1. Pursue guests through the proper channels.

2. Be persistent. (One e-mail request is almost never enough to get a big newsmaker to talk to you. Eric's approach was to politely keep calling until someone said yes.)

3. When interviewing the guest, ask the question that everyone thinks you shouldn't ask, but do it with courtesy and respect.

4. Do your homework.

Eric hoped his zeal and work ethic would eventually lead him to a job as a television news anchor, but that was way back in 2006. Instead, he started his career as a new media consultant at CBS (while still in college) before moving to the other organizations listed above. He helped launch the Twitter-happy show Rick's List at CNN with host Rick Sanchez, which Kuhn described as an on-air "continuation of Rick's Twitter page."

He doesn't see social media as a way to supplant legacy media, but as a way to supplement and inform traditional radio and television news and information. He says it's important to consider the mind-set of people who have multiple screens available to them, who are eager to provide instantaneous and unfiltered feedback, and who want to be engaged in the process. He says reporters and anchors who use social media only to encourage listeners and viewers to watch/listen to the next scheduled newscast are missing the boat because the social media phenomenon is about much more than the old-fashioned one-way delivery of information—it's about engaging marketing and inviting people to "join the conversation." He says the audience can be "an amazing focus group" in a world that's "no longer two-dimensional," requiring that we talk less and listen more. We can use social media as an amazing newsgathering tool.

Kuhn does advise caution in one area, and that's the tendency to let technology drive content. I've seen numerous posts that are so full of links that I have no idea of where to start. I call this phenomenon indiscriminate linking, and Kuhn says it's important to use technology, not just because you can, but because of the ways in which it helps push stories forward. The fundamental rules of journalism still apply in this brave new world of 140-character limits. Great content is still great content, and Kuhn thinks it's a really fabulous time to be a content provider. Your list of potential sources is nearly endless and more diverse than ever, and it's never been so easy to get noticed by using your interactions (interactivity is the key) with those sources to craft great content.

Here are Kuhn's rules of the road for journalists working for legacy media outlets who are trying to maximize the reach and impact of their journalism by also being very active and interactive through social media.

1. Dive in headfirst and use more than just Facebook, YouTube and Twitter. Check out Foursquare, Pinterest, Instagram, SocialCam, Flickr, Digg, Metacafe, SlideShare, Google+, Reddit, Orkut, and so on.

2. Push your boundaries and learn how to record and edit audio and video, post links, and take compelling photographs.

3. Remember that really good stuff can go viral, but so can really bad stuff. It's exciting to be a content provider to the world, but it's also a bit scary.

4. So, never tweet or post something you wouldn't say on air with Grandma, or the head of Standards and Practices, watching.

5. Look for forward-thinking mentors, either within your own organization or online (they might be easier to find on Facebook).

6. Above all, listen to your audience.

UNC-Chapel Hill journalism student Melissa Abbey covered the Democratic National Convention in 2012 using only social media. Although she was interning with the local metro newspaper, the lessons she learned are applicable for broadcast entities as well.

Social media is more than just a tool for newsgathering and dissemination, she says. It's a tool for storytelling. Writing for Poynter .org, Abbey said:

ONE OF THE WAYS I USED SOCIAL MEDIA AS A STORYTELLING TOOL DURING THE CONVENTION WAS TO COMPILE TWEETS THAT TOLD A LINEAR STORY. YOU CAN DO THIS BY USING STORIFY OR BY EMBEDDING TWEETS IN THE HTML OF AN ARTICLE PAGE.

TWEETS ARE GREAT FOR ILLUSTRATING HOW AN EVENT UNFOLDED. HALF AN HOUR BEFORE MY SHIFT ENDED MONDAY NIGHT, A COLLEAGUE TURNED TO ME AND ASKED, "HEY, DID YOU SEE THAT TWEET ABOUT A PROTEST HAPPENING?" I HADN'T, BUT IT DIDN'T TAKE LONG TO FIND IT. WITHIN A COUPLE OF MINUTES, I'D FOUND A LINK TO A USTREAM ACCOUNT FROM WHICH 23-YEAR-OLD NATHAN GRANT WITH (@OCCUPY EYE) WAS BROADCASTING THE MARCH.

BY THAT TIME, SEVERAL TWEETS HAD APPEARED RELATING TO THE LATE-NIGHT PROTEST. THERE WAS A LIVE VIDEO OF PROTESTERS IN BLACK MARCHING ARM IN ARM. SOMETHING WAS HAPPENING. WE TOLD THE WRITERS NEARBY. WHILE THEY TRIED TO REACH SOURCES BY PHONE, I COMPILED TWEETS IN STORIFY AND PREPARED A NEW POST IN BLOGGER. WITHIN TWO TO THREE MINUTES OF THE FIRST TWEETS ANNOUNCING THE

PROTESTERS HAD RETURNED TO THEIR CAMPSITE, WE PUBLISHED BLOG
POST (WITH THE STORIFY) HIGHLIGHTING TWEETS THAT SHOWED HOW THE
PROTEST UNFOLDED.

THE POST WASN'T A REPLACEMENT FOR THE TRADITIONAL STORY TO
FOLLOW; THE STORY IN THE PAPER HAD CONFIRMED DETAILS AND
INCLUDED A POLICE PERSPECTIVE. BUT MY POST TOLD READERS
ESSENTIALLY WHAT HAPPENED, AND IT WAS ALMOST IMMEDIATE.

Abbey knows that same Storify post could appear on any news organization's Web site. Including tweets or videos from the community isn't just a creative and immediate way to tell a story, it's a way to show consumers you're paying attention to what they're saying on social media. A Storify makes for a great placeholder until you can publish a written story or a package—and when you do, embed that Storify at the bottom of the post.

Aggregating tweets also works as a reaction piece. In the same story for Poynter.org, Melissa wrote:

YOU CAN ALSO USE TWEETS TO CAPTURE REACTIONS. AROUND 10:15 P.M.
WEDNESDAY NIGHT, I SITUATED MYSELF AT A DIMLY LIT TABLE ON THE TOP
FLOOR OF THE TIME WARNER CABLE ARENA. AS THE DELEGATES ERUPTED
WITH DELIGHT AT BILL CLINTON'S SPEECH, I QUIETLY DRAGGED AND
DROPPED TWEETS INTO A STORIFY THAT SHOWED VIEWERS' REACTIONS TO
THE FORMER PRESIDENT'S WORDS.

THE RESULT WAS AN ENTERTAINING POST THAT GAVE READERS A SENSE OF
THE KINDS OF REACTIONS PEOPLE WERE POSTING ON TWITTER. THE POST
SAVED THEM FROM HAVING TO SORT THROUGH HUNDREDS OF THOUSANDS
OF TWEETS THEMSELVES.

Consider doing this both for reactions to the news event and to your coverage. Are you going to post a package online after it airs? Great. Abbey suggests you get on Twitter and find out what viewers said about it. Below your video clip and text description, write something like: "Here's what locals are saying about the story. Join the conversation and tweet at @ournewsorganization with your thoughts." Then embed a Storify with tweets relating to the story and/or your coverage.

Regina McCombs is on the faculty of the Poynter Institute. She says part of making the transition to the professional world is deciding what you want your social media presence to be. In some cases, she says, it might be best to start fresh. The big questions are, "How have you presented yourself in the past, and how do you plan to present yourself in the future? Questions that follow on that are: "What does it mean to be a public person?" (Journalists, especially those on camera, are definitely public people). And "What do you want to be public about, and what do you not?" In addition to privacy issues, there are also potential safety concerns to consider. If you don't want to attract stalkers, Regina suggests posting after you've done something or gone somewhere, rather than before.

Additionally, your social media presence, once you become a professional, has to be more than "here's who I hung out with last night, and what we did. You have to ask, what am I adding to the community? Are you providing additional valuable information, giving your followers access to people they normally wouldn't have access to, creating or at least joining important conversations?" And you should play on your strengths. Perhaps there's not room for a regular slot on your broadcast for information about adoptable pets or the local music scene, but if that's a passion of yours, create a blog or engage in those conversations, from your perch as a professional storyteller, adding to your and your organization's standing in the community.

One caution in this regard: Your social media presence shouldn't be just a method to add to your local celebrity or even solely to generate more viewers for your TV newscast. Journalism has to be part of the mix. Regina says she can't blame journalists when they use social media primarily as a promotional tool, however, when their managers offer prizes to anchors and reporters simply for generating more followers, with no measure of the quality of the journalism involved.

Quality can be an issue when you use material you've gathered through social media (or online platforms) in your newscast. Even network news operations are using Skype for interviews, and sometimes the quality is lacking. Regina has mixed emotions about that. She says if that's the only way you can get an important interview, no problem. But if it's an excuse to be lazy or save a few bucks, instead of going to where the interviewee is, she's less forgiving. One good thing is the quality gets better all the time, and she's seen some reporters do some very interesting things with Google+ Hangouts, with no related video quality concerns.

Embracing the Conversation

As a journalism student, you've probably heard your professor stress a thousand times the importance of being conversational. We certainly stress that in this book. Being conversational doesn't end when you hit your deadline. That's just the beginning. The media landscape is changing, and journalism is evolving. Your reports won't always break news, but they will be a part of someone's discussion. As a journalist in this ever-evolving landscape, you have a responsibility to find out what people are saying. So how do you do that? Simple. Know your audience.

As the weekend editor of CNN Digital, Kristi Ramsay is responsible for planning the content that appears on CNN.com's weekend edition. The weekend readers are different than the Monday through Friday audience.

Most of them aren't reading from a cubicle at a 9 to 5 job.

These readers are choosing to come to CNN.com and spend part of their weekend there.

It's Kristi's job not only to present the news they need to know, but to also offer content that's provocative and engaging.

You have to be aware of what people are saying—and where they're saying it. If your content appears on a Web site, you likely have the privilege of instantly gauging reader feedback via the comments. Your story might also spark debate on social media, blogs or topical Web sites.

Once you've identified the audience members and what they're saying, it's up to you to figure out what to do with that information. This is your chance to show the audience you're listening, to turn a simple comment into a more meaningful dialogue about the issues of the day.

Kristi frequently jumps into the comments section and weighs in with the readers. If they question why CNN.com is running a story, she tells them. If they point out a typo, she fixes it and thanks them. If the comments get vitriolic, she tries to tamp that down by engaging the commenters and asking what they think about different aspects of the story. People enjoy intelligent and thoughtful debate, and they'll appreciate being a part of your brand.

Yet, in everything you do, you must always remember that you're a journalist first, not a commentator. Leave the opinions to the members of your audience. It's their right. Your duty is to exercise an objective perspective and keen editorial judgment. With today's technology, the conversation surrounding a story can be as important and as entertaining as the topic itself, so don't miss the opportunity.

Brooke Baldwin

Brooke Baldwin knows well the power and importance of listening to viewers. As an anchor for CNN, she loves what she does. She has what she calls "pinch me moments" often—whether it's interviewing her favorite musicians (for her weekly #MusicMonday segments) or calling out a politician or speaking with the head of NASA/going "back" to Space Camp—she says her job rocks. But, she says, journalism (as a career) is a journey. And it wasn't easy getting to where she is now, which is anchoring 2-hours on CNN Monday through Friday. It took years of working long, hard hours (including holidays) and suffering sleep deprivation in multiple TV markets before she landed at CNN. And it took her several years of reporting at CNN before she landed her very own show. And then it took her half a year to really begin to

Taken with Brooke's cell phone by a colleague

CNN's Brooke Baldwin with Dolly Parton after Brooke's MusicMonday segment.

leave an imprint—her own personality, her own touch—on the two hours of real estate she occupies each and every day on cable.

Part of that imprint comes from her relationship with her viewers vis a vis Twitter and her #WeCanDoBetter campaign. She grew angry and upset every time she'd have to tell a story about a child who was abused, neglected and often killed at the hands of his or her own parents. Kids sleeping in cages, being deprived of food, electrocuted— you name it, it's happening in our country. Brooke's not a parent, but she doesn't have to be to say: "This angers the hell out of me." So each time one of these stories would cross her desk, CNN began to tell it like this: Here's what happened in state X, here's the child who officials say was neglected and here's how we can do better—by opening our eyes to abuse that's happening next door or at school or maybe within our own family. Ergo, as a society, we can do better.

Brooke constantly tweets with her viewers during the course of her show (watch closely and you'll catch her on her computer coming back from break!) so she created this hashtag: #wecandobetter. Now people tweet her with story ideas and examples of ways they've done better. One guy called in a neighbor's abuse of a teenager, police filed charges and the caller appeared on Brooke's show—and now he's now tweeting her about all the global support he received after appearing on CNN. He's now planning to leave his day job to create a nonprofit organization to prevent child abuse. Her message to all of us is simple: Whether you're a teacher or a parent or just a guy driving by a child who looks "off"—like something might be wrong—we can all do better. And as a journalist, she's pretty proud of our power via TV or various social media platforms to relay such a powerful and important message.

The Power and Importance of Social Media

So why do mainstream news organizations post on Facebook and Twitter? The answer is simple: They're fishing where the fish are. The Pew Project for Excellence in Journalism State of the News Media 2012 report found that by the end of 2011, 133 million Americans were using Facebook and were spending seven hours a month there. By contrast, the study found that the users of the country's top 25 news Web sites spent *less than 12 minutes* a month using one of those services.

The study confirmed that Facebook and Twitter are indeed "pathways to news," but not major pathways. Only about 9 percent of users reported that they "very often" follow Facebook and Twitter-based referrals to news sites or apps. But according to the study, 36 percent of those same users "very often go directly to news organizations on one of their devices." In other words, when a news organization puts a message out on Facebook, it's talking to a large number of news consumers. And that can't be bad. For mainstream news media, then, the basic purpose of social media is very simple. While the news organization's owned platforms—in other words, the TV or radio transmitter and primary Web site—are for distributing the product (and getting paid for it), social media are for sayin' "hey" to the customers and trying to entice them into the store. Messages by a news organization on its Facebook page or its Twitter account generate traffic for Facebook and Twitter, not for the originating newsroom, which achieves no direct economic benefit at all. But the newsroom can get an *indirect* benefit if messages posted on those other platforms can generate a "buzz" and channel viewership and Web hits to its for-profit news platforms. And that's exactly what a successful social media strategy does. But—and this is a big but—merely saying "watch our report about X on tonight's news" isn't the way to go.

It's about Conversation

When Laura Kittell gets up in the morning and prepares for work, she's thinking not so much about covering the news today via the Internet, but more about how she can make a personal connection with her audience. Kittell is the Web coordinator for the Journal Broadcast Group's Tucson market. As such, it's her responsibility to help the group's various broadcasting platforms navigate the social media landscape. The largest of those platforms is KGUN9 News. The social media forum she thinks of first is Facebook.

Her strategy isn't to flood Facebook with every post that appears on KGUN9.com. Instead, she encourages the news staff to choose. "Facebook is about conversations. It is about interacting one-on-one in a huge, massive group of people. And you want to have content that is controversial, interesting, and that draws a reaction from people."

As a result, in addition to any urgent, breaking news taking place, a key tactic for Kittell and the station's Web producers is to select those stories that appear most likely to generate conversation. In most cases the post will consist of a link to a story just appearing on KGUN9.com. Sometimes, especially in the case of urgent breaking news, the Web producer might post a line or two about a topic or incident. In some cases, the posting might be a Facebook exclusive, such as a "Topic of the Day" question designed to prompt conversation for the morning news. The hoped-for result is "buzz" about the content on the station's Web site.

Why is that important? "The value of the buzz is that it keeps your brand top of mind," Kittell says. "You become their go-to person for what they are seeking. In our case, it's news. You want your followers to always think of KGUN9 as their source for all things news related."

In all cases, the writing strategy for such posts is very simple: Make it short and conversational. It's not writing as much as it is *talking*. The style is informal.

Example:

BREAKING INVESTIGATION: THE PARENTS OF A GIRL WHO WAS BULLIED AND ATTACKED AT SCHOOL SAY THEY ARE GETTING NO HELP. OUR INVESTIGATION CONFIRMS THE SCHOOL REFUSED TO CALL POLICE.

This brief description appeared beneath a link to a preview story on KGUN9.com by reporter Valerie Cavazos, describing new information in a follow-up story that hadn't yet aired. Beneath the description was a comment posted by the station containing additional information:

VALERIE HAS NOW FILED HER SCRIPT AND IT'S IN EDITING. HERE ARE A COUPLE OF MORE DETAILS FOR YOU . . . THE INVESTIGATING OFFICER ASKED ADMINISTRATORS TO CALL THEM AGAIN WHEN THE SUSPECT SHOWED UP AGAIN ON CAMPUS. BUT WHEN THE SUSPECT CAME BACK, THEY REFUSED TO DO SO. THIS STORY WILL LEAD OUR 5 PM NEWSCAST TONIGHT, AND WE'LL DEVELOP IT FURTHER FOR THE 10 PM NEWS.

The Facebook posting was a cross between a promo and a story—it contained real information, provided a link to a KGUN9 .com Web story containing even more information, and then pointed to the TV station's upcoming newscast as a source for a comprehensive, detailed report. "It can't sound like a commercial," Kittell says. "It can't sound like a news blurb. You get much better results by speaking to that person one on one, as though he or she were your friend."

At about the same time the post went up on KGUN9.com and on Facebook, the station sent out a tweet calling attention to the story. The writing style of the tweet was the very essence of simplicity, which tweets have to be given the severe character count limitation. If the story contains a headline that grabs the reader's attention, as all good headlines should, then that headline plus the URL of the Web posting should suffice. In this case, that is exactly what the station did, sending out a tweet containing the URL preceded by this text:

BULLY'S ATTACK LEAVES STUDENT BRAIN-INJURED; SCHOOL REFUSES TO TURN IN SUSPECT

If the goal was to create a buzz and also to generate clicks, it succeeded. The Facebook posting drew dozens of viewer comments within a short amount of time. Even though the story on KGUN9.com was only a "preview," it quickly vaulted to the top of the Web site's Top 5 Most Popular section. When a fully updated, detailed story appeared later, it enjoyed similar popularity. The issue drew more clicks and Facebook commentary that week than any other story featured on the station's Facebook page.

It's worth noting that this story was a follow-up to a sweeps investigation that itself had achieved success in terms of page views and ratings, through similar social media tactics.

Such reaction is no surprise to Kittell. Although it might be true that only a small percentage of Facebook users follow story links, the overall number of Facebook users is so large that even a small percentage of that total amounts to a surge of customers. "The reality is that they are following the links," she says. And further, the audience metrics show that once they arrive at the station's Web site, they tend to stay for a while. "They are not reading just one story." Kittell notes that on a daily basis social media, particularly Facebook, are the second or third top-referring domains for KGUN9.com, usually ranking just below the Google or Yahoo search engines. Kittell says one great way to create such interaction is to simply ask for it. "It's not enough for your post to be seen. It has to be commented. And the best way to do that is to give people an either/or action command."

Example

A Web producer posted an update on KGUN9.com about the aftermath of a raucous meeting at the Tucson Unified School District that had ended with someone setting off a smoke bomb. It then cross-posted the story on Facebook, with this comment:

INTERESTING NEW DEVELOPMENT IN THIS STORY: IF TUSD'S LATEST
STATEMENT IS ACCURATE, TUESDAY NIGHT'S ETHNIC STUDIES CROWD WAS
EVEN MORE OUT OF CONTROL THAN PREVIOUSLY REPORTED. CHECK OUT
THE STORY THEN COME BACK TO FACEBOOK TO COMMENT.

People did so—the post immediately attracted dozens of reader comments.

With Web media becoming more mobile by the day, more and more people consume television and social media simultaneously. Successful television newscasts tap into that. Toward that end, many newscasts, especially morning newscasts, post a "Question of the Day" or "Topic of the Day" on Facebook about issues designed to get people talking. The post might or might not be related to a story available on the station's Web site, but it should be about an issue that has "watercooler" potential—an interesting or hot-button issue that people are likely to want to discuss.

Example:

GMT TOPIC OF THE DAY: A TEXAS WOMAN IS SUING THREE AIRLINES AFTER
A TURBULENT FLIGHT. SHE CLAIMS SHE'S BEEN DIAGNOSED WITH PTSD AS
A RESULT OF A BUMPY RIDE THAT NOW CAUSES NIGHTMARES, FLASHBACKS
AND AN INTENSE FEAR OF FLYING. DOES THIS WOMAN HAVE A CASE?
CHIME IN!

The goal is to generate enough viewer feedback—a dozen or more responses will do for a start—to make the responses worth sharing within the newscast. Kittell says it's a powerful tool. "You're having people interact online, and then you're showcasing them on TV. Everybody likes their ten minutes. And if it's only 20 seconds or 10 seconds, they'll take that, too."

It's about Engagement

Conversations, even with friends, can get heated. If your friend is giving you an earful, and if you care about the relationship, then chances are you'll say something other than, "Yeah, OK, fine, and thank you for commenting." Instead, you'll engage. The result might be an argument, but you hope it won't end your friendship.

News organizations in the 21st century have a similar decision to make about the conversation that takes place on social media sites such as Facebook. Even a casual glance at the social media sites of many mainstream news organizations shows that negative viewer comments about the coverage often don't stay up for very long.

Deleting ugly comments is one way to handle public criticism. But another way is to acknowledge the criticism and tackle it head on, even if that means disagreeing with the poster.

KGUN9 had a powerful example of all these concepts combined in its coverage of a series of vicious pit bull attacks on people and pets. The station found out quickly that many pit bull owners are passionate about their animals. In one case, two days before one particular pro-moted TV story even aired, pit bull advocates began posting messages on the station's Facebook page slamming the upcoming story, calling it unfair, untrue, biased, irresponsible, sensationalistic, and so on. Word of the controversy quickly spread throughout the cybersphere. In addition to drawing a huge local crowd, "We drew pit bull lovers from all across the nation, and haters, who had absolutely no idea who KGUN9 was," Kittell says. "And we drew them in the thousands."

Many of those posters vowed not to watch the story and not to watch KGUN9 or click on KGUN9.com ever again. This comment from one pit bull partisan was typical: "I will not stand by your news channel, your channel's sponsors, or the station that airs your news channel and will encourage my social contacts to avoid supporting your station as well."

To news directors and their bosses, those are scary words. But in response, the KGUN9 News not only left the posts in place, it respond-ed. The reporter and also station management went directly to Face-book and posted comments in reaction to the criticism, using "first person" references.

First, station management wrote a KGUN9.com story about the uproar and crossed-posted a link to it on Facebook with this description:

PIT BULL ADVOCATES ATTACK UNAIRED 9 ON YOUR SIDE INVESTIGATION:
IT HASN'T EVEN AIRED YET, BUT THAT HASN'T STOPPED PIT BULL
ADVOCATES FROM ATTACKING AN UPCOMING 9OYS INVESTIGATION AS
BIASED, UNFAIR AND UNTRUE.

The story's reporter also responded, posting under her own profile. Here is an example, posted in response to a viewer comment accusing her of having edited the report at the last minute to appease pit bull advocates:

THERE WAS NO "LAST MINUTE TWEAKING" ON THIS STORY. IF WE FEEL THE
STORY IS BALANCED, WE RUN IT. CLEARLY NOT ALL OF OUR COVERAGE

PLEASES EVERYONE. THAT WOULD BE IMPOSSIBLE. WE LEAVE IT UP TO OUR
VIEWERS TO DECIDE IF THEY WANT TO WATCH.

Those posts led to more viewer commentary, both positive and negative, to which the reporter and station management posted further responses. The debate raged back and forth not for days, but for months, and attracted thousands of comments.

Although some viewers began the conversation with threats to boycott the station and its Web site, Kittell says readership analytics showed that just the opposite occurred. "It was amazing to me how these people, who had no idea who we were as an entity, continued to follow us. Even when the pit bull debate faded away, they were still clicking and coming and looking at our stories that had nothing to do with pit bulls."

That is what engagement looks like—it isn't always pretty, but if it generates a buzz, it's worth it, and the results can be dramatic. In KGUN9's case, audience metrics show that Facebook and Twitter generate a significant number of direct referrals to KGUN9.com.

The Personal Touch

News personalities, for better or worse, are celebrities of a sort. People in the community tend to want to meet them, and they like to be able to say they know them on a first-name basis. This connectivity factor drives an important aspect of social media.

KGUN9 News anchor Jennifer Waddell never got excited about blogs when they were all the rage and managers were urging anchors to create and maintain them. But she's among the KGUN9 anchors and reporters who post on Facebook, and she has learned that it's a very powerful way to connect to and interact with viewers.

For her, the key is to keep it real. "I try to make it fun but informative—not just saying, 'I am working on this story, tune in at Five.' People tune that out." Instead of posting a promo, she'll put up something that contains a personal touch. For instance, as in any other social setting, the weather is always a legitimate topic. "Whether you are talking about the fact that pollen is blowing all over the place today and I had a sneezing fit on the Five O'clock News and boy I hope that medicine kicks in by Ten, and who is suffering with me?"

Waddell has a small Web cam installed at her desk, and has been known to record and upload brief videos showing her interacting with coworkers. Sometimes she does focus on an upcoming story. "If one of our reporters who is sitting near me is working on a story, I'll pick up the camera and actually move it and show our viewers what the reporter is working on, and they'll chime in for a few seconds and talk about it." Sometimes it's not about a story, but will just consist of personal chat. For instance, she admits that she loves to catch her co-anchor, Guy Atchley, off guard. Whatever the content, she says viewers appreciate the personal touch. "Every time I do this people say, 'Oh, I love this, this is great, give us another one.'"

If such a post doesn't direct the reader to a particular story, then the benefit will be indirect, but real just the same. Waddell is building a network of contacts, people who then are that much more likely to want to watch her on the news.

And there's another benefit. This same network of contacts is likely to think of her when coming across a news tip. "I can't tell you the number of times I've either had a comment on a post, which shows up on my wall, or someone just sends me an e-mail saying, 'I've been watching the news, I like how involved you are, thanks for keeping us informed on Facebook. I've got this tip for you, here you go.'" She cited a recent example regarding the search for a missing child. The search had been the top story on all local media outlets, and had even made national news. Because of a relationship established through Facebook, on that particular day KGUN9 landed an important exclusive interview.

In addition, digital native Melissa Abbey suggests tweeting or posting to Facebook "behind the scenes" photographs. About to go on air? Post a photograph of the anchor having his or her make-up done. A reporter hard at work at the computer editing a package? Post a photograph of him or her working and briefly tease the story or provide an update. One of the reasons Facebook and Twitter are so popular, she said, is that they allow people to secretly see into others' lives (we've all heard the phrase "Facebook stalking"). As Jennifer Waddell noted, people do consider local journalists—especially those they see on TV—to be celebrities.

Story Tips and UGC

One of the beauties of Facebook is that, unlike broadcasting, the communication flows in two directions. It's not just about the news organization providing news to the community. Often just the opposite happens.

For one, viewers frequently post tips about story developments—sometimes in the form of a question. Example of such a viewer post: "Does anyone know what is going on at Craycroft and Swan?" Sometimes such questions lead to stories, sometimes not. Whatever the answer to the question, often an assignments editor or Web producer will post a response directly to Facebook in addition to covering the story in whatever fashion is appropriate.

Sometimes viewers will post detailed story suggestions. One Tucson mother posted a tragic account of her daughter's death at a crosswalk, which for some reason police had not previously reported. The mom offered to go on camera to tell her story. "I want to do something to educate people on the importance and safety of crosswalks," she wrote. An assignments editor saw the Facebook post, sent her a message asking for contact information, and scheduled an appointment. The mother then posted a follow-up comment on KGUN9's Facebook page stating that the station was going to pursue her story. When the station aired the piece, it noted that the story had come from a viewer contact.

When bad weather strikes, KGUN9's viewers share their pictures, sometimes by the dozens, many of them by way of direct posts to KGUN9's Facebook page. In the business we call such a submission "User Generated Content" or "UGC." In times of severe or unusual weather, viewer-submitted content becomes a major feature of the station's Web and TV coverage.

Viewers often submit video the same way—usually by way of a Facebook link to a You Tube posting. Sometimes the video is related to a serious story such as an accident or crime. Sometimes, it's what might be called "human interest."

Waddell's favorite example of UGC falls into that latter category. A viewer sent her a Facebook message about how the viewer's family had found a baby bunny with injured hind legs. The family built a tiny cart supporting the rabbit's hind quarters. It provided a link to a video showing the bunny getting around with the help of the contraption. "As soon as I watched the video that he had sent me, I knew that this was one of those things that would just grab people and their hearts. And it did." Jennifer wrote a TV story about Joe the Bunny along with a brief KGUN9.com story containing a link to the video. It immediately went viral, garnering more page views than any other single story for the year.

What the massive popularity of the Joe the Bunny story says about the nature of the news business, we'll leave for another day.

Melissa Abbey recommends retweeting even if you don't use the content on your Web page or in your newscast. She notes that everybody loves to be retweeted. If you publish a story online, embed related tweets or photos your viewers sent in. Not only will people be checking your Twitter and Facebook pages to see if you saw their contribution, they'll look online, too. And you can bet the farm they'll share any page on which their name appears.

Twitter

Because the Twitter format is so limited, its best use is as a news feed. While Facebook has great potential for viewer interaction and engagement, and we should carefully select its stories for that purpose, Twitter has the potential to be more like a news wire. As Kittell puts it, "Twitter is about as much information as possible, as fast as possible."

In some cases, that can mean sharing a link to stories just posted on the main Web site—which is, after all, the best way for the news organization to get a direct benefit from the tweet. In others, it can mean sending out a brief blurb of information without a link. In either case, the writing style is very simple: short, declarative, conversational sentences, with an emphasis on the present tense.

Example:

WILLCOX SCHOOL LOCKDOWN ENDS; NO STUDENT SHOT, SAYS
SUPERINTENDENT.

On that particular day this real-life tweet helped set the record straight about a story that had been widely misreported. Note that despite the character count limitations, the tweet gave a specific attribution, thereby underscoring its credibility—an important distinction that day in a landscape filled with unattributed, incorrect tweets and news reports from other media.

Twitter is also good for play-by-play-style reporting from spot news events or from certain types of proceedings, such as court cases or press conferences. Regarding the latter, there's not much room for background detail or analysis in Twitter's 140-character-count limitation. You'll have to explain and promote the purpose of the play-by-play coverage in advance on the newsroom's other platforms. The Twitter coverage itself might then contain a series of messages like these:

PROCEEDINGS NOW UNDERWAY IN JOHN SMITH MURDER TRIAL; JUDGE
FRED JONES IS NOW ON THE BENCH.

SMITH IS NOW TAKING THE STAND IN HIS OWN DEFENSE.

SMITH SAYS HE SHOT JACK THOMPSON IN SELF DEFENSE.

SMITH SAYS THOMPSON CAME AT HIM WITH A KNIFE.

JURY IS NOW COMING INTO THE COURTROOM. VERDICT EXPECTED
MOMENTARILY.

JURY: SMITH IS GUILTY OF ONE COUNT OF SECOND DEGREE MURDER.

VERDICT RESULTING IN COURTROOM TUMULT. JUDGE TRYING TO RESTORE
ORDER.

A Final Word about Style and Standards

More than ever before, in today's 24/7 always-on media world, customers want their news *now* and they want it on their platform of choice. For working journalists, the pressure to crank out the product and to be first with the news has never been greater. Because the writing style for Facebook and Twitter are so casual, it's only natural for some to adopt a casual approach to the journalism, too.

"The demand for media by the users is first and foremost that you have it first," says Kittell. "They want to be able to say, 'I just heard Michael Jackson's dead.' They don't even care if it's right. Until it's wrong."

Kittell knows what she's talking about. KGUN9 experienced a dramatic example of this effect in the aftermath of its coverage of the January 8 mass shootings in that market. Even *after* everyone knew that Congresswoman Giffords had lived, some viewers chided KGUN9 for not having reported her dead, as most other media outlets had done. In the eyes of such viewers and Web users, an unconfirmed report is better than no report at all, and they think media outlets shouldn't withhold the information.

Journalists will have to make up their own minds about how to balance accuracy against the demand for speed. Kittell is among those who believe that even today, credibility is a hugely important value, one that has the potential to set a news organization apart. The way the world works today, when rumors hit, they'll likely hit first via social media. When news organizations provide their first response, quite likely that, too, will go out via social media. It's still important to get it right, and we don't waive that no matter how casual the writing style might be.

Kittell also has this advice for today's journalism students. "Learn how to write." For social media, although the traditional forms of journalism writing style aren't as important, basic communication skills still are—and those skills must include proper spelling and grammar. "If you want to be taken seriously, you cannot have typos and errors and incorrect speech in what you post."

Conclusion

Right now Facebook and Twitter rule the social media realm. Five years ago (as of this writing) it was a different story—remember MySpace? The way media trends come and go these days, five years from now it will be no surprise if the picture has changed dramatically yet again. But whoever rules, social media are here to stay, and are likely to become an increasingly important platform for journalism.

Just as Facebook, Twitter and other social media platforms are growing in importance, so are other Internet tools that make it possible to collaborate (i.e., interact) with colleagues nationally and internationally, broadening both the reach and depth of your journalism. As an example, while working on a recent project (a 60-minute documentary about a human rights group in Argentina—searchforidentitydocumentary .com) the producers were able to work simultaneously in real time on the script by using Google Docs, could share very large audio and video files through DropBox, and could communicate regularly through e-mail and Skype. These technologies saved us untold hours of labor and thousand of dollars of expense, and even more importantly gave us the opportunity to offer each other instant feedback and suggestions that made the project much more seamless and efficient than it would have been otherwise. Think about joint projects you can participate in with one of your fellow grads who's working at another station elsewhere in the state or nation. Your bosses will love you for being innovative and taking advantage of all that technology will allow you to do. So by all means, embrace social media—and embrace related technologies as well.

DOs and DON'Ts for Using Social Media

Do

- Remember that the best use of Facebook is to generate conversation.
- Write in a conversational, casual style.
- Make it personal—talk to the user!
- Ask explicitly for viewer feedback.
- Use Twitter for a fast-paced stream of story links and updates.
- Get it right.

Don't

- Flood Facebook with a barrage of stories.
- Be afraid to attract, or to tackle, negative user comments.
- Forget to include a story link to your primary Web site, if at all possible, with your social media posts.
- Use poor spelling or grammar.
- Forget to apply the same standards of journalism as you would on any other platform.

Questions

1. How does an interactor differ from a viewer, listener or user?
2. What's the number one attribute you must have to fully take advantage of what social media use offers?
3. What's the biggest caution when it comes to your professional use of social media?
4. Is it important to keep your public presence and your professional presence separate, and if so, what are the best strategies for doing so?
5. What should be your number one motivation for utilizing social media as a professional?

© Tara Higgerson

CHAPTER FIFTEEN

Forrest Carr

Writing for the Web

The future of **convergence** isn't what it used to be. The former media buzzword of the century still has people talking, to be sure. Not quite everyone has given up on the idea of newspaper reporters writing for broadcast, and vice versa. But for most, the point of convergence has shifted. Quite simply, it's the Internet. In today's world, regardless of whether you see yourself primarily as a print journalist or as a broadcast journalist, you'll almost certainly have to function as a Web journalist.

In this chapter, we'll try to answer a simple question: "What do Web producers want?" We'll show you the basics of how to adapt broadcast copy to a style suitable for the Web. We'll do it with the assistance and guidance from a very good Web producer, KRQE.com's Bill Diven.

What style of writing do Web users demand? In large measure, the answer is, "You name it, the Web uses it." The Web can showcase a wide variety of writing styles, and it does. But one of the key strengths of the Internet is its ability to bring a broadcaster's sense of urgency and immediacy to a print reporter's in-depth, detailed approach. The new medium has the strengths of the two "legacy" media, with few of their drawbacks.

Bill Diven's career is an excellent illustration of the convergence of those newspaper and broadcasting philosophies. He works as a "new media content provider" for KRQE.com in Albuquerque—in other words, he's a Web producer. It's not something he would have dreamed of doing at the start of his career more than three decades ago. The Internet wasn't yet even a gleam in Al Gore's eye when Diven got into the business. Computers were something about the size of a luxury sedan, with which one communicated via punch cards. No one had ever heard of a home computer. Diven took his first job as a newspaper photographer before he even graduated from college. Since then, he's worked as a radio reporter, newspaper reporter, and television news photographer and editor, sometimes all at once. His background has, as he puts it, "too much print to work in broadcast and too much broadcast to work in print. Which turns out to have finally caught up to the reality of the Web."

One of the badges of honor at KRQE.com is achieving something called the "linkback." That's a link to a KRQE.com story from some other Web site with traffic, such as CBS.com or CNN.com. Linkbacks are important because they can significantly drive up page views on the local site. Diven is the reigning champ of successfully pitching linkbacks at KRQE.com. How does he do it? He has a simple answer: "I do news 101. I write a hard core newspaper story with a simple, direct, active-voice, factual lead, with some element of color to it. I write a short, punchy headline that uses an accurate, active verb. I write a simple, straightforward news story, but using the English language the best I can, to make it pop." In the next few paragraphs we'll explore in detail how he does that. We'll begin with an explanation of Web story styles and elements.

Story Styles

The Inverted Pyramid

Though, as mentioned, the Web can use all styles of writing, the most common is a form of the classic inverted pyramid, a style of writing that begins with the specific and trends toward the general, with the facts presented in descending order of importance. Chronological order is less important. In TV terms, a piece written in inverted pyramid style is more of a recitation of straight facts than it is a "story." You won't make much use of narrative storytelling and you won't use the "diamond" approach discussed in Chapter 9 at all. Conversational writing isn't as important. Complex sentences with dependent clauses are more acceptable. There's a beginning and somewhat of a middle, but not always a clear ending. You'll just give the straight facts in a straightforward fashion, and then stop.

Example

This story appeared as breaking news on TBO.com in Tampa, FL. Note its straightforward, plain, "just the facts" style.

MacDILL AIR FORCE BASE—TWO LAPTOP COMPUTERS THAT WERE REPORTED MISSING FROM A VAULTLIKE ROOM AT GEN. TOMMY FRANKS' HEADQUARTERS WERE FOUND FRIDAY AND A MEMBER OF THE MILITARY WAS IN CUSTODY, OFFICIALS SAID. THE SUSPECT, WHOSE NAME HAS NOT BEEN RELEASED, CONFESSED TO STEALING THE LAPTOPS, WHICH CONTAINED HIGHLY SENSITIVE MILITARY DATA, SAID MAJ. MIKE RICHMOND, PUBLIC AFFAIRS OFFICER WITH THE AIR FORCE OFFICE OF SPECIAL INVESTIGATIONS.

ALTHOUGH THE MILITARY RANK AND JOB CLASSIFICATION ARE ALSO NOT BEING RELEASED, RICHMOND CONFIRMED THE SUSPECT HAD OFFICIAL CLEARANCE TO THE ROOM THAT CONTAINED THE LAPTOPS.

A COMPUTER FORENSIC EXPERT MUST NOW DETERMINE WHAT DATA, IF ANY, WAS COMPROMISED OR ALTERED. PRELIMINARY INVESTIGATIONS INDICATE THAT THERE IS NO CONNECTION BETWEEN THE SUSPECT AND THE ONGOING LEAK INVESTIGATION OR ESPIONAGE.

ONCE RICHMOND'S TEAM COMPLETES THEIR INVESTIGATION, THE FINDINGS WILL BE HANDED OVER TO A COMMANDER WHO, IN CONJUNCTION WITH A MILITARY JUDGE, WILL DECIDE THE LEVEL OF PUNISHMENT FOR THE SUSPECT.

FORTY-SIX AGENTS ASSIGNED TO INTERVIEW MILITARY PERSONNEL WILL BE RETURNING TO THEIR POSTS SHORTLY, RICHMOND SAID.

In writing this update, TBO.com producer Adrian Phillips updated a story that had appeared earlier on the Web site, using new information that a WFLA-TV reporter had provided. Notice that the style is very simple and direct. It gives the salient fact right off the top—the news that the missing laptops had been recovered. The story recites those facts in descending order of priority and ends with the least important fact, that the 46 agents assigned to the investigation can go home. The style was far different from that of the story on the same topic that later aired on television.

Why do it this way? Inverted pyramid worked for 19th-century newspapers because the bottom of the copy could be lost due to a downed telegraph line—or at the hand of an irascible editor looking to trim copy—leaving the remaining copy to stand as a still-viable story. In the 21st century, transmission failure is no longer a concern, but attention failure is. Online users tend to browse with a finger poised over the mouse button, never more than a twitch away from dumping out of what they're doing and going on to the next thing. They don't want their time wasted. Online users are more likely to come back to your Web site if you respect their needs and if they know their time will be well spent with you. Inverted pyramid style makes that possible. With it, readers know they can stay a short amount of time and still get what they need, while having an option to stay longer.

The Modified Inverted Pyramid

Every Web site's managers likely will have their own ideas about writing style. KRQE.com often uses what managers call "the modified inverted pyramid." As Diven explains it, it's a hybrid that follows the traditional inverted pyramid story structure, while also embracing certain broadcast stylistic devices, such as more conversational writing, more colorful turns of phrase, and a less formal adherence to certain print conventions. "Now, you would have some editors who are from a very narrow print style who would take a sentence where you let the attribution stay at the beginning, and they would move it to the end." Diven doesn't always do that. He also allows some of an individual TV reporter's unique style to show through on occasion. "If a broadcast reporter has done a nice turn of phrase, or expressed something particularly well—something that might not be in a traditional 'just the facts ma'am' kind of print style—I'm more than happy to use it. And that would not perhaps fit into the traditional inverted pyramid style that I learned in college. But the great thing about the English language is that it's there to be played with. I will let a reporter waste a few words for flavor, for color, for voice, and for their style." He says the typical online user probably wouldn't notice the difference—but a print traditionalist certainly would. As he laughingly puts it, "In the old days you would have a copy editor come over with a pica pole, and rap you on the knuckles for writing what you wrote. These days, that's not going to happen." At least, not on his watch.

Example

The following story follows basic inverted pyramid style, but also contains some of the "flavor" of the broadcast version of the story, which devoted significant time to describing the frustrations of stymied users. Note that, true to form, if the story were to be chopped off halfway down, the reader still would have gotten the gist of it. (Note: For privacy purposes, we've changed some of the names in this article.)

JOBLESS JAM STATE PHONE LINES

AGENCY ADDS STAFF, HOURS

REPORTER: MARIA MEDINA

WEB PRODUCER: BILL DIVEN

ALBUQUERQUE (KRQE)—LOSING A JOB IS BAD ENOUGH, BUT UNEMPLOYED NEW MEXICANS ARE FINDING EXTRA FRUSTRATION IN TRYING TO GET THROUGH TO THE STATE'S UNEMPLOYMENT HOTLINE.

SO MANY PEOPLE ARE CALLING THE STATE DEPARTMENT OF WORKFORCE SOLUTIONS FOR UNEMPLOYMENT BENEFITS, MANY GET THIS RECORDED MESSAGE INSTEAD: "DUE TO HIGH CALL VOLUMES, ALL AVAILABLE PHONE LINES ARE IN USE. PLEASE TRY YOUR CALL AGAIN LATER."

JOHNNA ALVAREZ SAID SHE DIDN'T EVEN GET THAT.

"A BUSY SIGNAL," SHE TOLD KRQE NEWS 13. "A CONSTANT BUSY SIGNAL."

THE DEPARTMENT HAS EXTENDED HOURS, HIRED 15 MORE PEOPLE AND BOUGHT MORE PHONE LINES.

HOWEVER THAT'S LITTLE COMFORT FOR ALVAREZ WHO LOST HER SECRETARIAL JOB LAST MONTH.

"THERE'S BILLS TO PAY," SHE SAID.

NOW HER FULL-TIME JOB HAS BECOME LISTENING TO THAT RECORDED MESSAGE OVER AND OVER AGAIN, SHE SAID.

"THE SHOE IS NOT ON THE OTHER FOOT AT THE MOMENT," SHE CONTINUED. "THEY DON'T KNOW WHAT I'M GOING THROUGH AND WHAT HUNDREDS OR MAYBE THOUSANDS OF PEOPLE ARE GOING THROUGH IN THIS STATE."

"SOMETHING NEEDS TO BE DONE; SOMETHING NEEDS TO BE DONE."

SHE ISN'T THE ONLY ONE FED UP. IT'S BECOME A TOPIC ON A LOCAL BLOG SITE WITH ONE BLOGGER CLAIMING HE CALLED 357 TIMES IN ONE DAY.

FRED POINDEXTER TRIED TO GET THROUGH FOR A WEEK AND THEN FINALLY WENT DOWN TO THE DEPARTMENT TO TALK TO SOMEONE. INSTEAD A STAFFER TOLD HIM TO USE THE PHONE IN ONE OF THE BUILDING'S ROOMS TO CALL THE SAME NUMBER.

"IT'S BEEN REALLY HARD," POINDEXTER SAID.

WORKFORCE SOLUTIONS KNOWS MANY PEOPLE ARE TRYING TO GET
THROUGH, DEPARTMENT SPOKESPERSON CARRIE MORITOMO SAID.

"SUNDAY WE HAD ABOUT 95,000 THAT ACTUALLY CAME IN TO THE CALL
CENTER," SHE SAID. "AT THIS TIME, COMPARED TO LAST YEAR IT'S ABOUT
DOUBLE OF WHAT WE WERE PAYING LAST YEAR.

"WE REALIZE THAT PEOPLE ARE FRUSTRATED AND THAT IT CAN BE
FRIGHTENING."

SHE SUGGESTED CALLING ON THURSDAY OR FRIDAY WHEN FEWER PEOPLE
ARE DIALING IN. UNEMPLOYED WORKERS CAN ALSO TRY APPLYING FOR
BENEFITS ONLINE.

HOWEVER SOME VIEWERS HAVE TOLD NEWS 13 SO MANY PEOPLE LOG ON
THAT THE WEB SITE BECOMES TOO BUSY TO ACCESS AS WELL.

THE DEPARTMENT OF WORKFORCE SOLUTIONS WILL BE OPEN ALL WEEK
EXCEPT NEW YEAR'S DAY.

Other Story Forms

Although inverted pyramid is probably the most common style of
writing for hard news on the Web, there are other styles. In fact, the
full range of story forms that appear in newspapers also show up on
the Web. Newspapers typically do not use inverted pyramid for "feature writing." This is also true of the Web.

Feature stories, rather than stuffing the most important facts into
the top of the story, often are narrative in nature, beginning with a
specific anecdote, and then broadening the picture from there. Not
surprisingly, this type of beginning often is called an "anecdotal lead."
In some cases, not only will such a lead not contain the most important
facts, it might contain virtually *no* facts. This has a parallel to some of
the best forms of lead-writing in television; it's a style of lead that
grabs the reader's attention with a quick snippet of information.

Here's an example of an anecdotal, "attention-grabbing" lead and
its follow-up sentence: "They checked in, but they could not check out.
Two Tupelo burglars who broke into a downtown bank through a
skylight overnight learned a valuable lesson: next time, have an exit
strategy." The lead says virtually nothing; the fact that it begs explanation we hope will entice the reader to stay with the story. The writer
will move from this beginning to a logical middle and end, presenting
the story in narrative style.

Another common style of lead in feature stories is the "narrative
anecdotal" lead. With this style, the writer simply begins painting the
scene, jumping right into the narrative. Example: "Sergeant Gladys
Jones bolted forward and peered through the windshield of the squad

car, where windshield wipers were waging a losing war against swiftly accumulating snow. Had she seen some movement? Within moments, suspicion had turned to certainty. A thin crack of light had now appeared in the doorway across the street. Someone was coming out." As in the earlier example, the writer will continue to present the story in narrative style. However, within a few paragraphs from the top, the writer typically will summarize the point, or the newsworthiness, of the story in what print writers call a "nut graf." Here's an example of how a "nut graf" for this particular example might read: "This particular night marks a milestone for Jones. It's her 20th anniversary on the force. Jones was not the first woman to join the police department as a patrol officer. But she was the first to win the department's highest honor, the Combat Cross."

KRQE's Diven says he'll allow his writers to mix in some narrative style even in a hard news story. "It's different in the sense that you have the freedom to craft a completed story with a flow to it, where your hard news lead leads you into whatever the elements of your story are. But you can think in terms of actually telling a story, as opposed to, I've just got to get the facts in the first three to four paragraphs because they are going to whack the rest of it."

Points of Style

No matter the particular style you choose, some stylistic devices that are common in television and radio don't translate well to the Web. With the caveat that each site might have its own rules and peculiarities of style, here are several general pointers on some of the major differences, along with a few similarities:

Past-Tense Writing

Broadcast writers have it drilled into them not to write past-tense leads. There's no such rule on the Web. In general, with certain exceptions (such as for breaking news) past tense isn't only acceptable, it's often preferred.

Complex Sentences

Broadcasters tend to avoid them, breaking them up into separate sentences for the purpose of maintaining a conversational style. This isn't as important for the Web.

The Conversational "We"

Broadcast writers often make use of the pronouns "we," "us," and "I" when referring to the news organization or the reporter. In formal Web stories, the writers typically don't do this, instead using the formal name of the organization when such a reference is needed. Blogs, which are less formal in nature, can be an exception.

Attribution

Some Web editors still prefer to put the attribution at the end of a sentence, rather than at the beginning, as is the style in print.

Reporter Introductions

The lead sentences to reporter packages typically introduce the reporter by name. Such introductions are entirely absent from Web copy; the byline will suffice.

Branding Devices

Many of the branding devices broadcasters like to use don't translate to the Web. Example: A TV producer might choose to introduce a newscast centering on a major breaking news story with a sentence such as, "We begin tonight with full team coverage." Though the Web producer might well showcase the coverage by putting the stories together in their own box or page, there's no Web equivalent to the TV concept of "beginning" coverage, and the concept of "team coverage" might not have a specific Web component, either.

Quotes

In Web writing, the broadcast sound bite becomes a quote. Broadcasters don't always give both the name and title of a person appearing in a sound bite within the reporter copy on first reference, and often omit any identifier in copy on later references. Web writers must give full identification on first reference, and typically will need to use at least the last name of the person being quoted on later references.

Know the Style Guide

Many broadcast newsrooms have style guides dictating how names, titles, and locations should appear within copy, especially when used on-screen in a super. Web sites often have similar rules for presenting such information. For those that don't, the *Associated Press Stylebook* is widely accepted.

Active Voice

Skilled broadcasters know to write their copy in active voice (discussed elsewhere in this book). This is equally true for Web writers.

Keep It Tight

A good rule for broadcast copy is that every word of every sentence should advance new information. Writers should avoid repeating facts. This is even truer for Web writing. When editing copy for the Web, KRQE's Diven is on a mission in this regard. "My idea of editing is to go through and take out every unnecessary word. I don't want to waste the reader's time." (However, as previously noted, Diven sometimes will allow a writer to "waste words" for the purpose of stirring in a modicum of flavor—but just a few.)

Example: Broadcast vs. Web

Here's a brief example of how one commonly used broadcast style (introduction of a bite from a spokesperson) might translate to the Web:

BROADCAST VERSION

SUZIE SUEYA IS SENIOR PARTNER AT THE LAW FIRM OF PHINDEM AND FRISKHAM. SHE TELLS NEWS 13 SHE WILL FILE A NEW MOTION IN THE MORNING.

[TAKE SOUND UP FULL]

SUPER: SUZIE SUEYA/PHINDEM & FRISKHAM

"THESE PEOPLE SIGNED A BINDING CONTRACT. APPARENTLY THEY'VE FORGOTTEN THAT. IT WILL BE OUR PLEASURE TO REMIND THEM."

POSSIBLE WEB VERSION

SUZIE SUEYA, SENIOR PARTNER AT THE LAW FIRM OF PHINDEM AND FRISKHAM, PLANS TO FILE A NEW MOTION TOMORROW MORNING. "THESE PEOPLE SIGNED A BINDING CONTRACT. APPARENTLY THEY'VE FORGOTTEN THAT. IT WILL BE OUR PLEASURE TO REMIND THEM," SUEYA TOLD NEWS 13.

Story Elements

A typical TV "package" has three basic elements: the lead, usually read on camera; the story body, typically containing audio/visual elements; and a tag line, often read on camera. The number of elements for a Web story depends on the Web site itself. In fact, it's difficult to have a general discussion about story elements because presentation styles can differ, often dramatically, from Web site to Web site. Some allow for nothing more than a single headline on the home page, followed by a link to the complete story. Others allow for more, such as a headline, a dateline, and a story summary or abstract, followed by a link to the complete story and/or links to related stories. What follows is a discussion about some of the elements Web sites might require of their writers.

The Headline

As is typical in print, the headline appears at the top of the story, and contains a short summary or "story sell." The specific style of the headline will depend in large measure on the content management system (CMS) the Web site is using. The CMS is the "client end" software that writers use to compose a story and post it on the site. Some CMSs rely on the headline for keywords that Internet search engines such as Google and Yahoo can use to locate the story for a searcher. In such shops, writers will need to make liberal use of specific keywords that an online user might type into a search request. Not all CMSs have this requirement, making use of other methods besides the headline text to interface with search engines. In any case, the headline is the point of sale for the story, so for that reason Web writers and producers tend to put a lot of thought, energy and creativity into it.

KRQE's Diven prefers a strict headline structure: noun, verb, object. He likes colorful action verbs. "Your headline had better be sharp. It had better be colorful. It had better be the exact wording you want to say what you mean. It had better tell a lot in a very few words." To enforce this rule, the KRQE.com CMS imposes a 39-character limit on the headline text.

Example Scenario

A gang of criminals broke into a local school to steal computer and office equipment. To get into the school, they had to scale an outside wall, cross the roof, rappel down a courtyard wall then smash into a high library window. A typical but flat lead might read: "Burglars steal school computers." Diven's read: "High-flying burglars smash into school."

Another Example

A man commits suicide, but stages it in such a way as to make it look like murder. The details are eerily similar to an episode of a popular television crime drama. A perfectly usable headline might read: "Man fakes his own murder." Diven's headline: "Suicide mimics TV plot."

Final Example

Searchers spend two days looking for a teen snowboarder lost in the wilderness. They finally find him well after dark, guided in part by the glow of the kid's iPod. Typical headline: "Searchers rescue snowboarder." Diven's: "IPod saves lost snowboarder."

The Sub-Headline

The sub-headline fits right underneath the headline and simply adds another snippet of interesting information, if there's such a snippet to be had. The sub-headline for the snowboarder story referenced above was: "Rescuers spot tiny glow." The sub-headline for the burglary story was: "Masks, gloves hid identities."

The Byline

The byline typically consists of a few short words identifying the writer. Some Web sites also use a byline to identify the Web editor and/or other contributors. The byline might or might not contain a second line with additional information, such as a contact number or e-mail address. Some Web sites place the byline right under the headline; others place it at the end of the story.

Examples

- "By Darla Dashdigit"
- "Reporter: Darla Dashdigit, Action News 13"
- "Reporter: Darla Dashdigit ddashdigit@actionnews13.com"

Timestamp

The timestamp consists of the date the story was posted. Some timestamps also include the day of the week and the time of day. Some also indicate the date and time the story was modified or updated, if applicable. Many CMSs generate this information automatically.

The Dateline

Ironically, there's usually no "date" on the "dateline." But it likely will contain a location where the story originated, and the news organization generating the story. Example: "MUDDY WELLS, Arizona (AP)—" Some Web sites omit the reference to the originating news organization if the Web site itself generated the story; others don't. The first sentence of the story body begins right after the dash.

The Story Body

Quite simply, this consists of the story itself—typically, several paragraphs beginning with the first word of the first sentence, and concluding with the period at the end of the final sentence. Even a casual glance at news Web sites will show that story lengths can vary wildly from site to site and story to story. A breaking news brief may be very short indeed, possibly no more than one sentence. A more routine story might run 200 to 500 words. But longer news stories of 1,000 words or more aren't uncommon, either.

The Lead

The lead (sometimes spelled "lede") follows the dateline and is the first sentence of the body of the story. For the purpose of engaging the reader, it's second in importance only to the headline. In the classic inverted pyramid style, the lead should capture the most important and relevant facts in a straightforward, declarative sentence. KRQE's Diven puts it this way: "Basically what I'm looking for is a hard news lead that is concise, accurate, gets into the who, what, when, why, what's going on and all that. You're looking for a punchy factual lead that will draw people into the story."

Examples

- "Four acrobatic burglars scaled buildings and rappelled down a wire to break into Los Lunas High School escaping with computers and cameras while overlooking the camera that took their pictures."

- "The light from a portable music player helped guide airborne rescuers to a lost snowboarder facing a second frigid night on a New Mexico mountain."

- "A satellite bound for space instead ended up in an Orlando apartment where police arrested three men now charged with auto theft and burglary."

The Abstract

The story abstract is similar to the lead and serves much the same purpose. It's one declarative sentence highlighting the main facts of the story, typically appearing on the home page underneath the story headline. Its purpose is to support the headline and to continue the process of drawing the viewer into the story. In some shops, the abstract is the lead.

The laptop story referenced above again serves as a good example. The day the story broke, the headline, abstract and links to related story elements appeared on the TBO front near the masthead in the "breaking news section" framed with a picture of General Tommy Franks. The copy read as follows:

BREAKING NEWS

Missing Laptops Found; Suspect Arrested

MacDILL AIR FORCE BASE—Two missing laptop computers that were reported missing from a vaultlike room at Gen. Tommy Franks' headquarters were found Friday and a member of the military was arrested, officials said. Tune into News Channel 8 for the latest.

► **FULL STORY**

► **LAPTOP PROBE DRAWS 51 AGENTS**

▶ EXPERTS FAULT GOVERNMENT IN LOSSES

▶ MACDILL AIR FORCE BASE INSIDER

Multimedia Enrichment

As we've seen, a 500-word story written for the Internet might not be radically different in style from a similar story written for a printed newspaper. However, if the daily mission for your Web site is simply to provide a written version of your broadcast story, it's not going to be particularly competitive. The Web cries out for multimedia enrichment and user interactivity, elements that other media platforms just can't match. The brass ring will go to those sites doing the best job of seizing those opportunities.

When editing copy for the Web, producer Bill Diven hungers for ideas from reporters for providing a rich, multimedia experience. "Reporters in the field should be gathering documents that we can scan, to create PDFs. They should be gathering Web sites. They should conduct real straightforward no-bantering interviews so we can post that on the Web. . . . If they've got ideas on how something can be packaged, other elements that can be brought in, a particular map or graphic idea—they absolutely need to be thinking the Web with everything they do."

The possibilities are endless. Below is a list of some of the ideas reporters might consider. Because the technical aspects of how to create these elements can vary from site to site and system to system, we'll focus our discussion on just the broad concept.

Hyperlinks

Hyperlinks are Web site addresses, or URLs, hidden beneath highlighted copy. The highlighting typically consists of blue, underscored characters; the software usually creates the highlighting automatically when the writer creates the hyperlink. *Example:* Say you've decided to reference earlier coverage in your copy. Don't just reference it; create a hyperlink: "As News 13 **has reported for weeks**, people trying to sign up for unemployment benefits are likely to get a busy signal." In creating the hyperlink to the words "has reported for weeks," the writer uses the CMS software to insert the URL of a Web page containing a story or series of stories related to that previous coverage. When the user clicks on the link, the related coverage pops up.

Story and Additional Information Links

This is a list of links to other, related articles or information on the host Web site, or on other Web sites. The laptop theft abstract example discussed previously contains an example of this; each story slug below the abstract copy contained a hyperlink to a related story.

Contact Boxes or Links

A contact box contains e-mail and/or phone contact information—people or organizations that users can call if they want more information, would like to express an opinion to an elected official, find out how to make a donation, and so on.

Pictures

What's the old saying about the worth of a picture? A photograph or still frame can go a long way toward making the written story more understandable, powerful and memorable. A well-composed and carefully chosen picture can draw the reader's eye right to the story, and in fact form the centerpiece of an entire Web page.

Video/Audio Story Links

If video or audio reports related to the written story are available on your Web site, make sure you provide those links. Web producers will typically use a small graphic art video icon with the link.

Maps

Maps showing the location of the story can be a powerful feature. Advanced maps can be interactive in nature—users can click on them to find additional embedded information, satellite views, directions, and so on.

Graphics and Animations

A pie chart or bar graph can be very effective in helping illustrate complex numbers. A building schematic might be useful in explaining a complex chain of events in a given location. A rotating cross section of a gadget might help explain its inner workings. The variety of graphics possible is endless. And as with maps, the most sophisticated graphics are interactive in nature, allowing users to click their way to additional information.

Raw Video and Audio

When producing their reports, TV and radio journalists often must leave good material on the cutting room floor. Consider picking up some of those outtakes and putting them online. Or, you might want to edit together an extended version of your best video, or highlights of the best portions of your key interviews—or maybe even post the entire interview, unedited.

Supporting Documentation

A print reporter might reference a scandalous love letter and quote from it. The Web reporter can scan the whole thing and put it online, linked from the story itself. Supporting documentation can be a powerful enhancement to a story.

Polls

Users love to express their feelings, and to see how others feel. Consider adding a "Web poll" to your story. Example: "How confident are you that the state will resolve the unemployment hotline crisis? A: Very confident. B: Somewhat confident. C: Somewhat unconfident. D: Very unconfident."

Comment Boards

You might also consider allowing users to post comments about your story directly. (Some sites do this automatically for every story.) But beware: Some users don't play nice. If you provide a comment board, you'll want to make sure that you have the resources to police it, or at least a mechanism for reporting (and responding to) inappropriate comments.

Final Thoughts

Will newspapers survive? Will television and radio reporting be here in 10 years? Five? One? As of this writing the future of the traditional or "legacy" media is by no means certain. The woods are filled with argumentative experts armed with conflicting facts, analyses and opinions. Some of them are probably right, and therefore some have to be wrong—but which? Who knows? But despite the confusion, two facts seem crystal clear. One, as long as there are people, there will be a market for reliable news and information, and for informed, insightful opinion—and that means journalism. Second, the World Wide Web isn't going away. It therefore follows that anyone who wishes to hang out a shingle as a practicing, professional journalist should embrace the Web, and learn the skills necessary to survive—and thrive—in that environment.

DOs and DON'Ts for Writing for the Web

Do

- Understand the basics of the inverted pyramid writing style.
- Write in past tense.
- Write in active voice.
- Know what your Web editor expects from your story.
- Be prepared to continually update your Web story as needed.
- Provide ideas for multimedia enrichment.
- Know your newsroom's Web style guide.

Don't

- Treat Web writing as an afterthought.
- Forget that your deadline is *now*.
- Waste words.
- Write in passive voice.
- Use the conversational "we" or "us" in your reporting.
- Turn your back on Web innovation, or be afraid of new technology and approaches.

Questions

1. Discuss some ways writing for the Web differs from writing for broadcast.
2. Explain the modified inverted pyramid.
3. Discuss different "branding" styles for Web and broadcast.
4. Discuss the relationship of the headline and the lead in Web writing.
5. Are there ways not listed in the book to achieve multimedia enrichment?
6. Discuss ways to integrate social media into Web reporting.

So You Want a Job? The Art of the Résumé

The question people ask me most often has nothing to do with any of the gems of wisdom thus far imparted in this book. It's simply this: "How do I land a job?" Or, in its indirect form, "What do you look for in a résumé video?" This section will provide some answers to those questions and arm you with information that, we hope, will help you find, land and keep a job. The information and advice herein are based on my own personal hiring preferences, on practices I've witnessed during my time in the industry, and on feedback over time from other news directors, some of whom are quoted here. I've tailored the advice to television applications, but much of the advice can apply to other journalism platforms as well.

What Does a News Director Look For?

Of course, every news director is different. That's a good thing, or else few people would be able to land jobs! Tastes vary. What doesn't appeal to one news director might appeal to another. However, when a news director looks at a video or résumé, some factors are of great or possibly even universal importance. Primarily, these factors are talent, experience, qualifications, references and job stability.

Talent

Plainly speaking, is the candidate any damned good? Can he communicate on camera? Is she an aggressive, enterprising reporter? Does she write well? Is he appropriately dressed and groomed? Does he have an appealing personality? If the candidate is applying for an on-air position, the news director will judge talent—in most cases, rather quickly, I'm afraid—from the résumé video. Hiring managers will judge line producer, photographer and editor candidates the same way. Assignments desk and off-line producing or writing candidates normally skip this step and managers make their preliminary judgments directly from the written résumé.

Experience

Has the applicant performed this job before, or done anything that might prepare him or her for the job? If the candidate currently holds a similar job, how long has she been doing it? Did he have any major successes, as judged by ratings, blockbuster stories or professional awards?

Entry-level candidates with no professional experience aren't excused from this question. If the candidate is a recent graduate, what kind of experience did he or she gain while in college? Internships or media-related extracurricular activities are important here. Woe betide the candidate who graduates from college and starts looking for that first job without having worked as an intern or at least gained experience some other way, such as by working at the campus newspaper, Web site, yearbook, or radio or TV station.

Minimum Qualifications

When posting a job, many news directors will list the minimum qualifications required for the job—a college degree, perhaps of a specific type; thus-and-so years of experience; skills or experience with particular kinds of journalism; knowledge of particular software systems or equipment; and so on. Candidates rightly perceive that there might be some wiggle room in meeting these requirements. But you still must land close to the mark. The last time I posted an anchor opening, I'm pretty sure every TV news intern in America applied for it even though the job description was very clear that significant past experience was required. I've talked with many other news directors who've had the same experience. Every one of those applicants wasted his or her time, and that of the hiring manager. You might indeed be the next Brian Williams or Christiane Amanpour. But they didn't start at the top, and neither will you. "Everyone wants to be an anchor," says veteran news director Tauna Lange. "That is the biggest turnoff to me."

References

What kind of references does the candidate have? Here, what's important isn't the number of references, but the type and quality. It's usually a given that your cronies and friends will speak highly of you. What news directors really want to know is what your supervisors have to say about you. If a candidate doesn't list a single news manager as a reference, we distrusting, evil-minded news directors usually assume there's a reason why.

What if you don't want your supervisors to know you're looking for a job? If you must be discreet, you still should work hard to provide peer references who aren't just friends and golf buddies. For instance, producers and assignments editors, who are notoriously hard to please, make good references.

If you blew something up on the previous job and don't have any references, it's not necessarily the end. History suggests many news directors might be willing to give you a second shot if you have the talent.

Job Stability

Another factor many news directors look for is job stability. A certain amount of moving from job to job is understandable, especially if you've started out in a small-market, low-paying job. But after a job change or two, one hopes you'd stop and catch your breath for a while. If you've jumped ship every year, or even more often, the next hiring manager might wonder whether you really left voluntarily or in fact escaped steps ahead of a posse. In any case, your next prospective employer is going to want some assurance that you'll be staying around long enough to be worth the effort of hiring, moving and training you.

The Cover Letter and Résumé

A lot of candidates really sweat the cover letter. But keep in mind that news directors aren't looking for *War and Peace* or prose by Hemingway. Explain which job you're applying for (you'd be amazed how many candidates don't do that), your qualifications and experience, your contract status and timetable for availability, and say a little something about what makes you unique. That's typically all you need—unless the job ad requests more. Some also demand a statement

of news or management philosophy. Others ask for salary requirements. (If asked for the latter, keep in mind that you're not negotiating
a final figure here, but the news director needs to know if the two of
you are at least within shouting distance. Name a range, and don't say
"salary negotiable" unless you really mean it—and as a test, if you're
not willing to accept a pay cut, then you don't mean it.)

Although you usually can't go wrong with "short and sweet," you
do want to sell yourself. One effective way to do this is through narrative storytelling. Begin with a story or anecdote shedding light on
your character and talents:

> DEAR MR. CARR: I WAS DRIVING TO WORK ONE DAY LAST MONTH WHEN I
> SPOTTED A WOMAN STANDING ON A STREET CORNER, HOLDING A HAND-
> LETTERED SIGN. IT READ, "WILL TEACH FOR FOOD." LIKE MOST PEOPLE
> THAT DAY, I WAS READY TO DRIVE ON BY, AND NEARLY DID. BUT
> SOMETHING MADE ME STOP. THAT DECISION LED TO A STORY THAT DEFINES
> WHAT I STAND FOR, AND WHAT I BELIEVE IN, AS A JOURNALIST.

The example is fictional, but I've seen many cover letters that start
with a story in this fashion, and they never fail to pique my interest
and cause me to spend more time with that candidate's material.
News director Darren Richards, who typically spends little time reading cover letters, admits that he's not immune to this style, and calls it
"a great way to hook a news director." An effective customized sales
pitch will distinguish you from dozens of other applicants whose pro-
files are similar to yours—something you definitely want to accomplish. Says Lange, "One of the biggest filters for me is when someone
says, 'I have recently graduated from blah blah blah.' That goes in a
hole. I don't even look at them."

Keep the résumé itself basic: name, objective, contact information,
education, relevant experience and employment history in the field of
journalism, any relevant leadership or community service organizations or projects, and awards you've won. The ideal résumé is just one
page long and should never run more than two.

The Interview Process

If you make it through the steps above, you'll be on a "short list" of
finalists, from which the news director will choose candidates for personal interviews, conducted face to face or by phone. There's only one
secret for success in getting through the interview: Talk honestly about
your skills, your accomplishments, and your professional passions. Be
yourself! Don't try to be something you're not. In some (if not most)
organizations, personality is an important factor in the hiring process.
News directors want to know not only that you'll be good at your job
but also that you'll fit well into that particular newsroom's culture.

The last thing you want to do is to present a false face. If you do and you land the job, then both you and your employer will be unhappy, if not miserable, in the long run.

It does help if you do a little homework ahead of time to find out about the market and the newsroom's challenges, news philosophy and marketing position. Check out the station's Web site. Call ahead and speak with a few people in the newsroom. If you're feeling particularly industrious, you might even want to talk with some of the station's competitors.

During your visit, be prepared to demonstrate your skills. Many stations will give writing tests of one form or another, even for veteran candidates. Some news directors have been known to take reporting and photography candidates for a "test drive," asking them to actually go out into the field and turn a story.

Remember that the interview process is as much for you as it is for the station. As it's checking you out, check *it* out. Ask tough questions. Talk with employees. Find out whether this particular company is one for which you'd like to work. As the saying goes, look before you leap.

Negotiating

If all goes well, the news director will offer you a job. Now it's time to negotiate a salary, moving expenses, perks and the like. Probably by this point you've named a salary range. The news director might attempt to lowball you (hey, nothing personal—it's just business). Make a counter offer. If neither you nor the news director is greedy (which is by no means a given), you should be able to reach a mutually acceptable figure without a great deal of pain and suffering.

Also keep in mind that not every news director plays this "you go high, I'll go low" game. Some will tell you flat-out that the job pays such and such figure, nonnegotiable. Says veteran news director Shane Moreland, "I really, really do offer the 'final' number up front. It takes the guess work out for both parties." If the news director is adamant that she's named the top dollar figure, don't make the mistake of digging in your heels and being argumentative—especially in today's shrinking TV news job market. Instead, if you want the job, then see if there's anything else on the table to talk about, such as vacation time, clothing allowances, contract "outs" and so on.

Agents

One question a lot of people ask is, "Do I need an agent?" Here, just between us, is the truth about agents. They can be very good at helping you find a job, especially if you're not able to devote your full time and attention to a job search. If you're stepping into a new shop, an agent will usually know what the job is worth and will help see that you get a fair offer. An agent is most valuable if you're negotiating for a higher-level job, particularly with a big-market station or a network. They're less valuable for negotiating salaries in medium and smaller markets; the reality there is that the agent is less likely to be able to "squeeze" the employer enough to cover the agent's commission. But even so, a good agent will relieve you of the emotional burden of fighting for cash with your news director or GM, and will give you peace of mind that you're getting the best deal possible. Many people find those factors alone to be worth the cost of the commission.

After you sign the contract, be *very* careful about how you use the agent. Your agent isn't a shop steward. Some employees like to ask their agents to intercede for them on the job. Many managers find this inappropriate—after all, the station employs you, not your agent. The station is *not* required, under any circumstances, to talk to your agent. This is true even during contract negotiations.

The Résumé Video

If you're seeking an on-air position, then you've entered a brutally competitive arena. Here's a sobering fact for you: When the news director plays your video, you might have only about 10 seconds to get his or her attention. Most news directors have so many videos to go through for any given position that they can't possibly view every minute of every one. So, the video starts, the reporter appears, and the news director makes a very quick decision as to whether the candidate is a "keeper." The process is highly subjective. That 10-second review might seem brutal, harsh and unfair, and probably is. But as WTSP's Richards puts it, "That's also the kind of judgment the viewer is making." Ten seconds. Don't waste it.

Begin your video with a montage of live and package stand-ups— four or five of the best ones in different settings, showing a composite of your work. Says Richards, "What follows next depends on what they are applying for. If you are applying for a reporter job, don't put anchoring first." Reporters should put on four or five examples of stories *that speak to the job they're applying for*. For general assignments, this could be a couple of spot news live shots, one or two **enterprise** hard news stories, and a human interest story or feature. But an investigative reporter's reel should look different—it should contain investigative examples. As mentioned, there's a chance the news director might hit the stop button during the montage and never get around to seeing your stories. Don't make the mistake of concluding that your reporting samples therefore aren't important. If your on-camera work makes the cut, then your stories will get a fair viewing. It's certainly possible to have a decent stand-up montage and then blow your chances with poor packages!

In all cases, reporters should include good examples of enterprise reporting. Says Moreland, "Anyone can put together a good 'major house fire' story. But I'm looking for reporters who can work their sources and break stories that no one else has."

Anchors should also begin with a stand-up montage, if they report. But anchoring, not reporting, should come next. Showcase several examples of your best news reading and delivery in various circumstances—and be sure to include samples of live breaking news. Also include samples of interaction with other anchors, such as in teases and 2shots. Then put on some reporting samples as described above.

The principles for producers, photographers and editors are similar. Show examples of your best and most challenging work. News directors and EPs tend to judge producers on lead writing, story flow, use of graphics, showcasing of team or themed "big story" coverage, story pacing, and so on; pick one good newscast, or a series of samples from several strong first blocks. News directors and photo chiefs base photojournalist evaluations on composition, lighting, use of nat sound, pace of editing, and so on; include four or five varied examples showing a range of your work.

In any case, whatever you put on your video, if it makes the first cut, then be prepared for the news director to call back and ask for something else. Many like to see "what you did last night."

Which Video Format Should I Use?

Technology changes so fast that I've given different answers to this question in each of the past four editions of this book. Currently, electronic résumés submitted by e-mail linking to Web-based videos have overtaken DVDs in popularity. If the video loads and plays instantly, that method is fine *unless* the job posting specifies a different format. DVDs are still more convenient for some news directors, who like to be able to show candidate videos to other people in a meeting setting. For that reason, it doesn't hurt to send both. Some candidates send a link and offer to follow up with a DVD, and that can work, too. Any video you send by Internet should feature "click and play" simplicity. If you ask a busy hiring manager to sit and watch a file transfer protocol progress bar crawl across the screen, then you run the risk that he or she will dump it and go on to the next of the 150 other submissions that might load more quickly. Says Lange, "FTP? No, no, no. No time for that. Especially considering the number of applicants you get."

Know Your Objective, and State It

Occasionally I receive résumés from applicants who state as a job objective that they're "seeking any job" that will make use of their "skills and abilities in the communications field." If you're willing to do "anything," then it's reasonable to assume you've done nothing. Result: "Yes, we have an opening for you. And don't slam it on your way out."

By the time they graduate, serious students will have worked one or two internships in TV newsrooms and should have a good idea of what they'd like to do. Target a specialty and seek it aggressively. That's not to say you can't change your mind later. For instance, if you spend six months seeking a reporter's job and come up dry, then you might want to begin again, targeting entry-level producing or copywriting jobs instead. But as veteran KGUN9 reporter Craig Smith likes to say, "Before you can change your mind, you must first make a decision."

Should I Call?

If you're responding to a job ad that says "No calls," then don't call. Many news directors disqualify people who disregard that admonition. Why? Because they can. If your résumé gets tossed because of your failure to follow clearly stated instructions, the news director has about a hundred more just like it. News directors don't forbid calls because they're mean, antisocial and cantankerous—or at least, not for that reason alone. They do it because they can't afford to spend every waking moment yakking on the phone with job seekers.

If the ad doesn't say "No calls," then the news director is fair game. Calling won't hurt and might even help, because even if the news director doesn't find time to return the call, your name and persistence might register. But do yourself a favor: Don't call with inane, time-wasting questions. Chief among them is, "Did you get my video?" In my case, I don't have the time or inclination to paw through dozens of submissions to find yours and verify its arrival. Most package delivery and e-mail services are reliable. Assume it's here.

After you've sent your material and/or made contact, don't toss and turn at night wondering why the phone hasn't rung. The process could take a while—days, weeks, even months. Sure, it can be maddening. But your phone's silence doesn't mean you're not in the running.

Should I Send a Video Unsolicited?

If you have time to send out unsolicited résumés, do so. It can't hurt. You never know when one might strike a chord with a news director. Some agents make a very good living sending out loads of unsolicited résumés. But don't expect instant results. For you to get a job this way, a lot of random factors must work in your favor.

If you're not able to devote every waking moment to the job search, however, you'll find it's much more cost-effective to target stations that do have openings. Keep your eye on the trade magazines and TV news job Web sites. If necessary, cold-call stations (assignments editors usually are a good choice of people to call; they know everything).

Networking

We've seen the power of networking again and again. When you send out that first unsolicited video, you've begun the process of networking. When you cold-call a TV station assignments desk to inquire whether there's an opening, you've opened a door to networking. When you ask a news director if you may call again and he or she says "yes," then you're networking. The method is simple: Get to know people, keep in touch with them, and get them to introduce you to other people.

If you're a student, start with people you know—friends, instructors, faculty advisors and so on. Get them to introduce you to their friends. Find out which professional organizations are available in your area and join them. If you can afford to go to conferences and conventions, do so. If you make those aforementioned cold-calls to TV assignment desks, take names and numbers. Ask if you can call again. Here's a hint, though: Don't waste time with people who clearly don't want to be bothered. There are plenty of warm and friendly people out there.

Student Question: "What Are My Chances—Really?"

Students have often asked me to look at their work and tell them if they have what it takes to land a job in this business. I can examine a video and tell a student what he or she needs to work on to do a better job, but I've gotten out of the business of trying to tell students what their prospects for success might be. For one thing, I've discovered that my tastes are strictly my own and might not apply to other news directors. For another, if there's any factor that's as important as raw talent, if not more important, it's persistence, and that doesn't always show on a video. I've seen students whom I thought had little to no chance of landing an on-air position do just that—because they were persistent and believed in themselves. The converse is also true; I've seen students with an incredible amount of raw talent waste it through lack of ambition and effort.

Still, it's reasonable to ask how much time you should spend looking for that first job before you throw in the towel. My advice is this: Treat your job search the way an entrepreneur would approach a start-up business. Write a business plan. If you go to a bank and try to take out a loan to start such a business, the lending officer is going to want to see a business plan. How much capital do you need? How are you going to become profitable? What will it take to get there, and by what timetable? Treat your job search the same way. You decide how much time, energy and effort you'll be able to devote to searching for a job. Set a timetable. If you haven't begun to "turn a profit" at the end of that time by landing a job, then perhaps the marketplace is telling you something about your employability. Also please remember that the industry is just as hungry for good producers, assignments editors and photographers as it is for on-air talent, and those jobs aren't quite so insanely competitive.

Final Points

Stupid Applicant Tricks For every on-air job posted, most news directors will get dozens and dozens of thoughtful, well-crafted applications from qualified journalists. But a significant number of applications will be dead on arrival through one or more boneheaded, opportunity-killing mistakes. Below is a list of the most common unsmooth moves that job seekers tend to pull.

- **Spelling, typographical and grammatical errors:** Don't make these. Not one. If you're weak in this area, have a friend proof your work. Then have another friend proof your friend's proofing. The news director will expect your résumé and cover letter to be an expression of your personal best. If you can't get it right when asking for a job, is the hiring manager supposed to believe that you'll miraculously transform into a paragon of journalistic prowess afterward? My favorite applicant line of all time was this one: "You will not be able to find a better qualified candidate for the job for which I've applied for." The statement left me unclear as to whether the candidate was applying for a job or pronouncing a curse.

- **No supporting material:** If you send a DVD, check it before you send it to make sure it will play on a standard machine. If you send a video link, make sure you haven't password-protected it, and then make sure the link stays live. If you promise an attachment, check your "sent" file to make sure you actually did include the attachment. Quality control and attention to detail are huge issues on any job, and the news director's assessment of your ability in this area starts with your application. Further, a news director who is in on a Saturday or Sunday to view résumés isn't likely to be contacting job hopefuls about dead links, unplayable DVDs or missing attachments, and then waiting patiently for a response.

- **Keep it real:** Don't trick out your submission with "creative" packaging and cutesy marketing. Many applicants suffer from a strange and exotic mental condition known Resumeus Videus Sillyatus—thankfully a rare disorder that forces candidates to take extraordinarily dramatic, sometimes outright goofy, steps to call attention to their applications. News director Larché Hardy once received a huge box containing a videotape enclosed with a set of battery cables and a cover letter that began, "Let me jump start your newscast." Hardy said, "After all of that, I watched the first 10 seconds." Says Lange, "The silliest was a box of chocolates with confetti, and a little résumé rolled up like a scroll, inside a box. I read the résumé just so I would know whom not to hire." Don't be doin' that stuff.

- **Keep it simple:** Don't roll logs at the news director's feet in the form of time-wasters. If you're applying in hard-copy form, make sure your package is easy to open. If applying by e-mail, as noted above, your video link needs to be "click and play" ready. Attach your résumé. A lot of candidates like to provide links to the home page of a customized Web site, where the news director must then root around to find a résumé and video demo. Don't do that. Regardless of your method of application, make sure your material is clearly marked with your name and the job for which you're applying. And keep the packaging simple. Nothing screams "intern" like a résumé packaged in a three-ring binder complete with tabbed pockets and glossy photos.

- **Address your application to the correct person:** If you're responding to a job ad, address your application exactly as the ad specifies. But if you're contacting the news director directly, take a moment to figure out who the news director is. Do not address your letter to "News Director" then begin with the salutation, "To Whom It May Concern." You run the risk that it won't concern anyone. Remember, you're seeking a job as a professional fact-finder. Consider this your first test. And here's a hint: When seeking this information, don't rely on source books or even on official web pages. Always call the station and ask.

- **No walk-ins:** Many news directors will agree to see job hopefuls if they happen to be in town and have the courtesy and professionalism to call ahead to schedule an appointment. But don't walk into a station lobby and ask to see the news director about a job without an appointment. Not ever. People who do so might as well wear a T-shirt saying, "I'm with Stupid," with an arrow pointing up.

- **Apply for the job for which you are applying:** This sounds simple and obvious enough. But an astonishing number of résumés never state what job the applicant is seeking. Many of those who do clearly state an objective then fail to provide a cover letter and demo reel tailored to the job. Says Lange, "I might get a multitasker who can do sports and general assignments reporting or whatever. I might be looking for sports, but then I have to hunt for their sports material. Customize your reel for the job."

If you're having a tough time finding a job, don't be too quick to give up. Mainstream journalism is one of the most selective and competitive industries in the world. But like any industry, it needs good people—and the needs of the day are subject to change. If you have skills, passion and persistence, and you're willing to start small and go wherever the job takes you, then there's no reason you can't make it eventually.

Good luck.

DOs and DON'Ts for the Résumé

Do

- Make sure your cover letter and résumé are absolutely perfect—zero defects.
- Clearly state the job you're seeking and outline your qualifications for it.
- Conduct some basic research about the station before interviewing.
- Make sure your résumé video is brief and showcases a good cross section of your best work.
- Closely follow any instructions on the job advertisement.
- Make a job-seeking plan with a timetable for success.

Don't

- Address your cover letter "To Whom It May Concern."
- Get cute with your packaging and presentation.
- Try to be something you're not in the interview.
- Forget that reporter and anchor videos should begin with a montage of on-camera work.
- Call if the ad says "no calls."
- Give up too easily.

Questions

1. Discuss the importance of the cover letter.
2. How do the cover letter and résumé work together?
3. Discuss ways to make the interview a conversation.
4. Do new hires right out of college have any negotiating power?
5. Discuss ways to determine what your objective is.
6. Discuss ways to enhance your "network."

WORD USAGE AND GRAMMAR GUIDE

C. A. Tuggle

We misuse many words in the English language. What follows is a list of some of the more common problem words and phrases for broadcasters. You should supplement this guide or any other stylebook with a good, recently published dictionary, but it's important to note that dictionaries list all the ways we can use words, even in slang. Writers should stick to the definitions that are most accepted, usually the first two definitions listed. Going to the sixth or seventh definition of a word in the dictionary can cause broadcast writers problems in terms of the viewers or listeners being able to follow what you're saying. We stress again, a television or radio news writer should make sure audience members understand what she or he has written the first time they hear it.

Some Helpful Hints

In broadcasting, you can probably have a successful career without knowing the difference between a complex and a compound-complex sentence, or the difference between a gerund and a participle. But you do have to be able to recognize what the subject of the sentence is, whether verbs and pronouns agree with it, and so on. Here are three guidelines to help in troubling cases.

Using "I" or "Me"

You should use these in conjunction with other nouns and pronouns just the same as you use them when they're alone. For example, you wouldn't say "Bob went to the store with I." You also wouldn't say "Bob went to the store with Jill and I." The key is to remove the second person and the word "and" from the sentence, see if you should use *I* or *me*, and then reinsert the second person and the word "and." It would be "Bob went to the store with me," so it should be "Bob went to the store with Jill and me." Also, it would be "I went to the store," so it should be "Jill and I went to the store."

Identifying the Subject of the Sentence

This is sometimes a problem when the sentence includes a prepositional phrase. For example: "a group of students," "a herd of elephants" and "a coalition of English teachers" are all singular. The general rule is to remove the prepositional phrase, determine whether the subject is singular or plural, use an appropriate verb, then reinsert the prepositional phrase. So take out the phrases "of students," "of elephants," and "of English teachers," and you'll see that it would be "a group goes," so it should be "a group of students *goes*"; it would be "a herd charges," so it should be a "herd of elephants *charges*"; and it would be "a coalition votes," so it should be "a coalition of teachers *votes*."

There is one exception to this. If you're talking about something or someone who is one of many in a group, then the verb should agree with the group. So in situations when you're talking about one of many, don't apply the general rule of removing the prepositional phrase. For example: "She's one of the best teachers who *have* ever worked at City High." The reason you treat these differently is that if you removed the prepositional phrase, all you're left with is "She's one." One what?

Here's another way to think about it. If you lump someone or something into a group, the reference goes back to the group and is plural. However, if you pull that person or thing out of the group and consider the person or thing individually, then it's singular. For example:

"He's one of the boys who are coming to the party."

"One of the boys is coming to the party."

Subject/Verb Agreement

First, you have to determine what the subject is and whether it's singular or plural. How about "Two thousand dollars is/are enough to buy the stereo system"? That's singular, because you're talking about a quantity; so it should read "Two thousand dollars is enough. . . ." If you were referring to 2,000 individual bills, that would be plural, such as with "There were two thousand dollars stacked on top of one another." But with most quantities, the subject is singular. For example: 500 dollars, a million pounds, 2,500 square feet and so on. With most portions and proportions, the subject isn't the amount, but the noun itself. For example, "a third of our viewers," "27 percent of the respondents," and "half the supplies" are all plural.

Giving Human Characteristics to Nonhuman Things

Rescue boats can't pluck people out of the water, unless they're equipped with robotic arms. Plans can't intend to do anything; only planners can. Small craft can't exercise caution on the high seas, Mr. Weatherman; only boaters can. Storms don't *decide* to turn back out into the Atlantic; they just do it. When you write a sentence, make sure the subject is capable of the action (verb) you've assigned to it. Some things can be done only by living organisms, and the more complicated the task (reasoning, for example) the higher the life form required to do it.

Word Usage

a, the   Some writing texts advise not using "a" when referring to something that can be numbered because "a" sounds too much like "eight." However, if we write and pronounce words as we do in conversation, this isn't a problem. Pronounce the word "a" as "uh" and the word "the" as "thuh." That's how we all talk, and it sounds very stiff to say "A (long "a" sound) train derailed and spilled the (as in "thee") cargo." Also, this allows us to say "a million dollars" and not "one million dollars." The latter sounds a bit stiff, and again, that's not how people talk.

Also, don't use "the" in the first reference to something. For example, don't say "police discovered the body" if the viewers don't know which body we're talking about. Say "police discovered a body"; then on subsequent references it's OK to say "the body" because we've already established which body is the subject of the story.

about   Things happen about a certain time, not around a certain time. See **on.**

abstinent   See **celibate.**

abuse, misuse   Both words mean to use wrongly or incorrectly, but abuse often has the added connotation of physical injury or harm.

accept, except   Accept means to receive with approval; except means to exclude. For example: The club voted to *accept* everyone *except* John.

across, around   Around means encircling; therefore, it's impossible for things to be happening around a certain area. Instead, things happen across (from one side or end to the other) the state or nation. It would be around the world, because as Columbus proved, the world is round.

acute, chronic   Acute is something that's sharp, sudden, and of short duration. Chronic is of long duration and might or might not also be acute. So in most cases, acute pain differs from chronic pain.

administration   See **government.**

adopt, approve, enact, pass   Amendments, resolutions, and rules are adopted or approved. Bills are passed; laws are enacted.

adopted, adoptive   Children are adopted, making their new parents adoptive.

adversary, opponent   An opponent is anyone on the other side. An adversary is openly hostile.

adverse, averse   Adverse means harmful or unfavorable, such as with adverse weather. Averse means not in favor of or disposed against.

advice, advise   Advice is a noun, and it's what you give. Some people seem to like to give it whether they're asked for it or not. Advise is a verb and means to give advice, to suggest a course of action.

affect, effect   These words create much confusion, but that doesn't have to be the case. Both can be used as verbs or nouns, but in the most common usage affect is a verb meaning to produce a change or to influence; effect is a noun meaning the change itself, the result. For example:

How will the vote *affect* the council's stance on the proposal?
The *effect* isn't likely to be seen for some time.

affluent, effluent   Affluent typically means wealthy; effluent means liquid waste.

afterward, backward, downward, forward, toward, upward   Not afterwards, backwards, downwards, forwards, towards, or upwards.

aggravate, irritate   Aggravate means to make something worse, as in "He aggravated an old football injury." Irritate means to annoy. You can't aggravate someone nor can you be aggravated about something.

agnostic, atheist   An agnostic believes there's not enough evidence to conclude that there's a God. An atheist believes there is no such thing as God.

allude, elude   To allude is to refer to something indirectly; to elude is to escape from or avoid, often by deceitful means.

although, while   Use although when you mean in spite of the fact that or on the other hand. While means at the same time as or during the time that. For example:

Although Sarah doesn't like sleeping on the floor, she agreed to do so *while* the relatives are visiting.

alumna, alumni, alumnus   A male graduate is an alumnus, a female graduate is an alumna, and more than one graduate are alumni.

among, between   Things take place among three or more people or objects, and between two parties or objects. However, even if there are three or more people or objects involved, if they interact two at a time, it's between.

amoral, immoral   Someone is amoral if that person has no morals, and is immoral if he or she breaks an existing moral code.

annual   An event isn't considered annual until it has taken place for three consecutive years. In its first year, call it the inaugural or the first. In its second year, call it the second.

anticipate, expect   Anticipate carries the added connotation of preparing for what's expected.

anxious, eager   If you're anxious about something, you're nervous, fearful, or apprehensive. If you're eager to do something, you're excitedly anticipating it.

anybody, anyone, everybody, everyone, nobody, no one, somebody, someone   All take singular verbs. For example:

Everybody *comes* to my house after Friday night football games.
Someone *knocks* on my door every Saturday morning at seven.
No one *jumps* when the tiny cannon is fired.
Anybody *has* the right to voice an opinion.

apparently, evidently   Both mean appearing to be so. However, apparently implies some doubt as to the truth of the statement. For example:

Apparently, Jane is sincere this time. (It seems that way, but you're not sure.)
Evidently, the burglar left some clues at the scene. (In this sense, you don't doubt this is true, but you don't have firsthand knowledge of it.)

apprise, appraise   Apprise means to inform; appraise means to place a value on something. For example:

The jeweler *apprised* the couple that he had *appraised* the diamond necklace at two million dollars.

approve   See **adopt.**

arbitrate, mediate   After hearing the sides of an argument, an arbitrator comes to a decision that the parties must adhere to. A mediator helps the parties talk through and solve their differences.

around   See **across.**

as   See **like.**

assassin, killer, murderer   An assassin kills by secret assault and frequently for political reasons. Someone who kills with a motive of any kind is a killer. A murderer is someone who has been convicted of murder. However, be careful calling someone a murderer even if that person has been convicted of the crime. It's preferable to say he or she was convicted of murder, because we don't know the person did the crime unless we were there to witness it. However, we know the person has been convicted. That's a matter of record.

assure, ensure, insure   Assure means to convince or make secure or stable. Ensure means to make certain that something happens. Use insure when referring to insurance. For example:

I want to *assure* you I'll be there.
She *assured* him everything would be OK.
I'll *ensure* the package arrives on time.
Do you want to *insure* the package?

atheist   See **agnostic.**

athletics director   Not athletic director. The full title is Director of Athletics.

author   Use this word as a noun only. If you want to say someone wrote something, then say the person wrote it.

average   If you write about *the* average, it's singular. *An* average is plural. For example:

The average age of incoming students *has* risen in the past decade.
An average of 250 people *have* seen the play each night.

averse   See **adverse.**

backward   See **afterward.**

bad, badly, good, well   People feel bad or they feel good. If you say someone feels well or feels badly, it means the person's sense of touch either is or isn't well developed. However, in terms of *doing* something, people either do well or do badly. If you say someone did good, the meaning is that he or she did a good deed such as feeding the hungry or working with Habitat for Humanity. The same is true of someone who does bad. So, on a test or project you do well or do badly. Don't be confused by the difference between how you feel and how you perform. However, if asked how you feel, it's appropriate to say "I'm well." The meaning is that you're not sick. But don't say "I *feel* well."

ban, bar   Ban means to forbid or prohibit; bar means to shut or exclude. People can be banned from doing something, and things can be banned. Only people can be barred from something. For example:

My father *banned* me from seeing Jill again.
Demonstrations are *banned* on the library lawn.
I was *barred* from entering the courthouse.

bear market, bull market   A bear market means declining stock prices; a bull market indicates rising stock prices.

because   See **since.**

because of   See **due to.**

benefactor, beneficiary   A benefactor does good; a beneficiary is the one who benefits from the doing of good.

between   See **among.**

biennial, biannual, semiannual   Something is biennial if it occurs every two years. It is biannual or semiannual if it occurs twice a year.

blatant, flagrant   Something is blatant if it's very noticeable, noisy, or offensive. It's flagrant if it's overtly outrageous, that is, not just a little harmful. Something can be blatant (there for everybody to see) and not be flagrant.

both, each   Both means two things collectively; each means two or more things considered individually.

boy, girl, man, woman, gentleman, lady   Only people in their teens or younger should be called boys or girls. Some suggest only those younger than 16 years of age should be called boys or girls. Man and woman are the preferred terms used to refer to physically mature individuals. Definitely *don't* refer to a group of males as men and a similarly aged group of females as girls. Use gentleman or lady only with titled people or in very specific circumstances when that's definitely what you're trying to say (as in First Lady, Lady Diana, everyone considered him a true gentleman, and so on). Don't use lady or gentleman in a generic sense as synonyms for woman or man, because most of the time you have no way of knowing if someone is a gentleman or is a lady. Also, don't use man as a replacement for human, human being, or person.

boycott, embargo   A boycott involves a group agreeing not to purchase goods or services from another group or business until certain conditions are met. An embargo is a legal restriction of trade and usually involves not allowing goods into or out of a country. For example:

Southern Baptists said they'll *boycott* Disney theme parks and products until the company quits producing R-rated movies.
The United States will continue its *embargo* of Cuba.

bring, take   You *bring* something toward the speaker or subject and *take* it away from the speaker or subject. For example:

Grandma wanted Red Riding Hood to *bring* her some cookies.
Red Riding Hood decided to *take* cookies to her grandma.

brothers-in-law, daughters-in-law, fathers-in-law, mothers-in-law, sisters-in-law, sons-in-law   Not brother-in-laws and so forth.

bug, tap   A bug is a concealed electronic listening device used to pick up sounds in a room. A tap is a device attached to a telephone line and is used to pick up phone conversations. Hence, offices are bugged and phone lines are tapped.

bull market   See **bear market.**

bullet   See **shell.**

burglarize   See **rob.**

but, however   Both of these words indicate that what follows contrasts with what's been said or written already, but many people use them to continue a thought. For example: "Bethany went to the store but came back with groceries." One would expect that she'd come back with groceries if she went to the store, so there's no contrast. That sentence should read: "Bethany went to the store and came back with some groceries." A sentence in which "but" would be appropriate is "Bethany went to the store, but she came back without anything." There's a contrast because what happened differs from what we'd expect. Likewise, "but" doesn't work in this sentence: "He only wanted to stop crime in his neighborhood but that might have cost a Miami man his life." There's no contrast here; it's a continuation of a thought. Either replace "but" with "and" or, better yet, make it two sentences. "He only wanted to stop crime in his neighborhood. That might have cost a Miami man his life."

can   See **may.**

celibate, chaste, abstinent   Celibate means unmarried, so priests who take vows of celibacy have agreed to remain unmarried. Chaste means abstaining from carnal love, and chastity often goes along with a vow of celibacy, but they're not the same thing. Practicing abstinence also means deciding not to do something, at least for a time, and is often used in reference to a decision not to engage in premarital sex.

cement, concrete   Cement is the powder that's mixed with water to make concrete. So houses are made of concrete blocks, not cement blocks. (And the Beverly Hillbillies didn't swim in a *ce-ment* pond.)

censor, censure   Censor (as a verb) means to delete as unsuitable, to find fault with. A censor (as a noun) is the person who does those things. Censure (as a verb) means to officially criticize or reprove. Censure (noun) is the criticism. Representatives and senators who run afoul of their colleagues are censured.

Centers for Disease Control and Prevention   Considered one entity, so use singular verbs.

character, reputation   Your character is what kind of person you are; your reputation is what others think of you.

chaste   See **celibate.**

cheap, inexpensive   Both mean costing little, but cheap has the added connotation of poor quality.

childish, childlike   People who are childlike display the positive attributes of childhood, such as being innocent, trusting, loving, and the like. Childish is derogatory and means displaying negative and inappropriate traits often associated with children, such as stubbornness, selfishness, and so forth.

chronic   See **acute.**

citizen, resident   A citizen is a person who has acquired all the civil rights afforded by a nation through birth or naturalization. So, one can be a citizen of a country, but not of a state or city. Refer to Chicago residents rather than Chicago citizens. Some of the residents of any major city, we're sure, *aren't* citizens.

climatic, climactic   Climatic means having to do with the climate and is rarely used in broadcasting. Climactic pertains to a climax. So don't write about a *climatic* event unless you're talking about the weather, and be careful with *climactic*. It isn't very conversational, anyway.

coed Out of date and considered sexist. Avoid it.

cohesive, coherent Both mean sticking together, but cohesive is used in reference to people and objects, coherent in reference to ideas or other abstractions and has the added connotation of logical flow. For example:

The army platoon was a *cohesive* unit.
He made a *coherent* argument in favor of the bill.

collision, crash For there to be a collision, both objects must be moving. A car can't collide with a utility pole, but it can crash into it.

comedian, comic Use these for both males and females. Comedienne is considered out of date.

compare, contrast When you compare, you look at similarities and differences; when you contrast, you look only at differences.

comprise, compose Compose means to be the parts of; comprise means to include or contain. For example:

The 50 states *compose* the United States.
The United States *comprises* 50 states.

Make up or *includes* are preferred.

concrete See **cement.**

constant, continuous, continual Continuous means without ceasing; continual means repeatedly. If it were to rain continuously during an extended period of time, we'd all be looking for an ark in which to stay dry. It could rain continually for weeks without causing any major concern. Constant is a problem because it can mean either ceaseless or regularly recurring. Because constant is used in different ways and the viewers might not be able to figure out which way you're using the word, you're better off writing continuous or continual.

contagious, infectious Something that's contagious can be spread only by physical contact. Something that's infectious is communicable by the spread of germs, with or without physical contact.

contemporary, modern Something that's modern is recent or is happening now. Something is contemporary if it happens or happened at the same time as something else. So, something can be contemporary and not be modern.

convince, persuade You convince someone *of* something; you persuade someone *to do* something.

could See **may.**

couple   This word causes grammatical problems because it can take either singular or plural verbs. It depends on whether you're referring to the couple as a unit or as distinct individuals. For example:

The couple *has* standing dinner reservations at Bob's Steak House.
The couple *were* married at St. Vincent's Cathedral.
A couple of gang members *were* brought in for questioning.

Also, the "of" is needed. It's not a couple apples or a couple years; it's a couple of apples or a couple of years.

crash   See **collision.**

criteria, criterion   Criteria is plural; criterion is singular. For example:

The *criteria* for the contest have changed.
The primary *criterion* for membership in the club is a hefty bank account.

criticism, critique   Criticism carries the connotation of a negative evaluation; critique commonly means pointing out both the good and the bad.

cupfuls   Not cupsful.

currently, presently   Currently means now; presently means soon. Don't use presently to mean "at this time."

cynical, skeptical   Skeptical means inclined to doubt; cynical means contemptuous, quick to find fault. A good dose of skepticism is healthy in journalism. Cynicism can get you in trouble in a lot of ways.

data   Correctly used, data is a plural noun and takes plural verbs. Often when you use this word, you're doing a story involving scientists, economists, and the like, and they know the difference.

daughters-in-law   As written.

Daylight Saving Time   Not daylight *savings* time. When you're referring to a particular time zone, it's Central Daylight Time, for example.

debris   Fragments of a former whole.

defective, deficient   Defective means having a defect; deficient means lacking something. For example:

He sent the *defective* part back to the manufacturer.
He was *deficient* in the number of credit hours needed to graduate.

definite, definitive   Definite means exact or certain; definitive means conclusive or final. For example:

The incorporated area has *definite* boundaries.
The scientist's findings were *definitive.*

demolish, destroy   Both indicate doing away with something completely, so it's not possible to partially destroy something, and it's redundant to say something was completely demolished.

diagnosis, prognosis   A diagnosis tells us the state of something; a prognosis predicts the future developments related to that thing. For example:

The doctor's *diagnosis* was cancer and her *prognosis* wasn't good.

differ from, differ with   To differ from something is to be unlike it; to differ with someone is to disagree.

dilemma   A dilemma is worse than a problem or a concern. A person facing a dilemma has to choose between two unattractive alternatives.

disabled, handicapped   Disabled is preferred. However, don't use either if the disability isn't germane to the story.

disinterested, uninterested   Disinterested means impartial; uninterested means having no interest in something. You can't be disinterested in a movie, unless you're rating it.

dispute   See **rebut.**

dissociate   Dissociate means to end a connection or association with. Note that the word contains only one "a." It's not disassociate.

dived, dove   Dived is the past tense of dive. Dove is often used in this way (as in the boys dove into the water), but dived is more precise. Dove presents the additional problem that it might be pronounced as dove (a bird).

Down syndrome   Not Down's syndrome.

downward   See **afterward.**

due to, thanks to, because of   Because of is better. You certainly don't want to write a sentence like this, which we heard during one of the worst winter storms on record: "Power lines are down all across the area *thanks to* a severe ice storm." Why would anyone be thankful to be without electricity in subzero weather? The power lines were down *because of* the ice storm.

each, either, neither   Use either when referring to one or the other of two objects or people; use each when referring to both or all of two or more things or persons. However, *each* word takes singular verbs, unless either or neither is followed by both a singular and a plural noun or pronoun. Then the verb takes the form of the noun or pronoun closest to it. For example:

Each of us *needs* to make an effort to succeed.
Either of the two options *is* acceptable.
Either he or they *have* to show up.
Neither *is* suitable for the position.
Neither they nor he *wants* to leave the company.
Neither he nor they *want* to leave the company.

Also see **both.**

each other, one another   Two people look at *each other,* but more than two people look at *one another.*

eager   See **anxious.**

effect   See **affect.**

effective, efficient   Something that's effective gets the job done. Getting it done with a minimum of time and effort means you're efficient. So, something can be effective without being very efficient. You can skateboard from Chicago to St. Louis and you'd get there eventually, but you'd expend a lot of energy and use a lot of time doing so. It's an effective way to travel between the two cities, but it certainly isn't very efficient.

effluent   See **affluent.**

either   See **each.**

elicit   See **illicit.**

elude   See **allude.**

embargo   See **boycott.**

empathy, sympathy   Both words mean to share the feelings of another, but empathy goes a bit further than sympathy and means being able to imagine yourself in someone else's situation.

enact   See **adopt.**

enormity, enormousness   Enormity refers to something outrageously heinous or offensive; enormousness refers to massive size. For example:

The *enormity* of his crime was beyond belief.
The *enormousness* of the mountain was truly impressive.

ensure   See **assure.**

epigram, epigraph, epitaph, epithet   An epigram is a witty saying. Epigraphs and epitaphs are inscriptions on monuments or tombstones. An epithet is a word or phrase used to characterize a person or thing and often carries a negative connotation.

eternity, infinity   Eternity refers to endless time; infinity refers to anything that's infinite or endless.

everybody, everyone   See **anybody.**

evidently   See **apparently.**

except   See **accept.**

excite, incite   Excite means to arouse the emotions of (normally taken to mean arousing positive emotions); incite means to influence someone to act.

expect   See **anticipate.**

explicit, implicit   Explicit means clearly stated; implicit means implied or suggested. Therefore, something that's implicit is open to interpretation. In broadcast writing, we should always clearly state what we mean.

famous, infamous   Famous means widely known and popular; infamous also means widely known, but carries a negative connotation. For example, at times in his career Mohammed Ali has been famous. At one point, however, he was infamous.

farther, further   Use farther to refer to physical distance and further for all other uses. For example:

Los Angeles is *farther* from New York than from Denver.
The board members voted to study the proposal *further.*
We have much *further* to go to come to an agreement.

fathers-in-law   As written.

fewer   See **less.**

figurative, literal   Figurative means symbolic, not literal. Literal means exact.

firm   A firm is a partnership, such as a law firm. The term shouldn't be used to refer to companies or corporations, both of which are incorporated business entities. Firms aren't incorporated.

flagrant   See **blatant.**

flail   The word means to whip or beat. Some dictionaries include "a wild waving of the arms" among the definitions.

flammable   See **inflammable.**

flaunt, flout   Flout means to show disdain for; flaunt means to make a showy display of something to draw attention.

flounder, founder   As verbs, flounder means to struggle helplessly and founder most commonly refers to ships and means to sink or run aground. Ships don't flounder because inanimate objects can't struggle.

forward   See **afterward.**

further   See **farther.**

gender, sex   Use gender when you're referring to the way a group of people is viewed by society; use sex when you're talking about the biological differences between men and women.

gentleman   See **boy.**

gibe, jibe, jive   Gibe means to taunt or sneer, jibe means to agree (or, in sailing, to shift direction) and jive means either swing music or talk meant to deceive or confuse. For example:

They *gibed* him about his lack of athletic ability.
The two suspects told stories that didn't *jibe.*
The senator's speech was nothing but *jive.*

girl   See **boy.**

good   See **bad.**

got   This is one of the most overused words in the English language. Got is the past tense of get. For example:

I got an "A" on the test. Got shouldn't be used to add emphasis to the words "has" or "have." For example, it's unnecessary to say: "You have got to See Joe's new car" or "The city council has got to make a decision soon." "You've got" means the same thing as "you have got" and shouldn't be used, nor should she's got, he's got, we've got, and so forth. A television station in central Florida uses the slogan: "We've got you covered." Perhaps the promotions people think that's catchy, but the news people should never put up with that in the station's P.R. campaign. The line "I've got you babe" might be acceptable in a song by Sonny and Cher (we just admitted to having been around for a long time), but it's not acceptable when you're trying to write with precision.

government, junta, regime, administration   Governments and juntas are ruling groups. The only difference is that juntas are in power after a coup (an overthrow of the existing government). A regime is a political system, and an administration is the people who make up the executive branch of a government.

handicapped   See **disabled.**

hanged, hung   People are hanged (though not often anymore), and objects are hung. For example:

They *hanged* the horse thief at noon.
The stockings were *hung* by the chimney with care.

he, him, I, me, she, her   There's often a lot of confusion about which one of these pronouns to use when they're used in conjunction with a noun or another pronoun. The key is to remove the noun or the second pronoun and the word "and." In other words, consider the pronoun by itself. For example, look at this sentence: "Barbara went to the store with Veronica and I." It should be "with Veronica and me." Take the words "Veronica" and "and" out of the sentence. You wouldn't say Barbara went to the store with I; you'd say she went to the store with me. So, decide on the pronoun and then add the other words back into the sentence. Some other examples:

I watched the movie with Bob and *her.*
He and I are on the football team. (Here you have to use the singular verb with the singular pronoun "I" when you take "he and" out of the sentence. Considering the pronoun by itself the sentence would read: "I am on the football team." Don't be confused by the need to change from plural to singular verbs at times. The concept is the same.)

Lou's not as smart as *she*. (This type can be a little tricky. There are a couple of implied words at the end of this sentence. What we're really saying is "Lou's not as smart as she is smart." Turn the sentence around, and you'll see why it should be "she." If Lou isn't as smart as she, that means that she is smarter than Lou. You wouldn't say "Her is smarter than Lou.")

he, she   There's no gender-neutral singular pronoun in English. In the past, writers have used "he" when the sex of the subject was unknown, but this is now considered sexist. To say "he or she" sounds stiff, so in broadcast it's best to restate the sentence and use the plural pronoun "they." For example:

A student should do the best *he* can. (sexist—not all students are male)
A student should do the best *he or she* can. (grammatically correct, but sounds a bit awkward and nonconversational)
Students should do the best *they* can. (best choice)

historic, historical   Something is historic if it makes history or is significant in history. Anything that's part of history is historical. However, this distinction has virtually disappeared.

hopeful, hopefully   Use hopeful and hopefully to describe someone's feelings, not as a substitute for "I hope." For example:

I hope the professor will change my grade. (If you said "Hopefully, she will change my grade," you're saying she will change it and will be hopeful about something while she's doing it.)
Hopefully, I made my request for a grade change. (In other words, I was hopeful that my request would be honored.)
"Most Americans *hope* the tensions in the Middle East will end soon." (Rather than "Hopefully, the tensions will end soon." Tensions can't be hopeful.)

hung   See **hanged.**

I   See **he.**

illicit, elicit   Illicit means unlawful; elicit means to bring to mind. For example:

She was convicted of *illicit* use of campaign funds.
Seeing him at the reunion *elicited* memories of high school.

Note: These words are used frequently by reporters and writers trying to sound knowledgeable. Both sound somewhat nonconversational, don't they? In the first sentence "illegal" would work better, as would "brought back" in the second sentence.

injured, wounded   Both mean that a living being is hurt. But *wounded* has the added connotation of intent and, most often, through use of a weapon. So it's better to say that earthquake victims are *injured* and shooting victims are *wounded*.

immoral   See **amoral.**

impeach   Impeach means to accuse a public official of wrongdoing. It doesn't mean "to remove from office." Bill Clinton was impeached but not removed from office.

implicit   See **explicit.**

imply, infer   Imply means to suggest or indicate something without saying it directly; infer means to draw a conclusion from. For example:

The speaker *implied* that a new university president would be appointed.
I *inferred* that there had been problems with the current university administration.

impromptu   Impromptu means without planning. Anything that involves an invitation or notice to attend can't be impromptu.

incite   See **excite.**

incredible, incredulous   Incredible means unbelievable; incredulous means skeptical. For example:

When he described the ride as *incredible,* she was *incredulous.*

indict   Indict means to bring legal charges against. Don't write that someone was indicted for murder because that sounds as though you think the person did it. Say the person was indicted on a charge of murder (or bribery, arson, and so on).

inexpensive   See **cheap.**

infamous   See **famous.**

infectious   See **contagious.**

infer   See **imply.**

infinity   See **eternity.**

inflammable, flammable   Both mean capable of burning, but inflammable sounds as though it means exactly the opposite. Use flammable if you mean capable of burning, and describe something that won't burn as nonflammable. (Hyphenate words like this to make them easier to read.)

insure   See **assure.**

inter, intra   The prefix inter means between two or more items in the same category; intra means within or between two parts of the same thing. For example:

interstate—goes from one state to others
intercollegiate athletics—contests between teams from different colleges or universities
intramural sports—students on teams within the same school play against each other

invaluable, valuable, valueless   Invaluable means of immeasurably great value, and often carries the added connotation of irreplaceable. Valuable means of great value or price, but isn't as strong as invaluable. Valueless means without value.

irritate   See **aggravate.**

issue   An issue is a point in question or dispute. Therefore, all issues involve controversy; so there's no need to refer to a controversial issue, and there's no such thing as a noncontroversial issue.

itch, scratch   Itch is a noun and scratch is a verb. To relieve the discomfort caused by an itch, you scratch. You can't itch something.

jail   See **prison.**

jerry-built, jury-rigged   Jerry-built means put together hastily and with flimsy materials. Jury-rigged means assembled quickly with materials on hand. So, something might have been jury-rigged without being jerry-built. Broadcast engineers have been known to jury-rig entire remote systems that are very sturdy and work beautifully.

jibe, jive   See **gibe.**

junta   See **government.**

jurist, juror   A jurist is an expert at law; a juror is a member of a jury. A jurist might or might not be a judge.

ketchup   Other spellings aren't correct and could lead to pronunciation problems (such as catsup or catchup).

killer   See **assassin.**

kudos   The word means credit or praise for an achievement and takes singular verbs. For example:

Kudos *is* in order for your graduation with honors.

lady   See **boy.**

last, latest, past   When one says last night, there's not much room for confusion about what's meant. Everyone knows the speaker is talking about the most recent period of darkness. The same is true of last week. But when you write "*the* last week," there *is* room for confusion, as in: "John wrecked his car twice in the last week." The question that arises is, In the last week of what? John's life on earth? Don't use "the last" unless there will be no more of whatever we're talking about. Therefore, the sentence we wrote earlier should read: "John wrecked his car twice in the *past* week." So, don't write that something happened in the last month, or in the last year, or in the last decade, or in the last millennium unless the world is about to end. Also, if you write something about John's last trip to the store, the implication is that John will never again go to the store. Write "John's latest" or "most recent trip."

lay   See **lie.**

leave alone, let alone Leave alone means to depart from or cause to be in solitude. Let alone means to allow to be undisturbed. If you ask someone to leave you alone, that means you want to be by yourself. If you want the person not to harass you, you would ask to be let alone.

lend, loan Lend is a verb; loan is a noun. You lend something, such as your car or money. What you lend is a loan.

less, fewer Use less when something can't be numbered and fewer when numbering is possible. For example:

There are *fewer* oranges on the trees this season.
There is *less* fruit on the trees this season.

You can number *pieces* of fruit or specific types of fruit, but you can't number fruit. Likewise, you can number hours or minutes, but you can't number time.
Note: Although it would be very time-consuming to count grains of sand, it is possible. However, although it's possible to number grains of sand, it's not possible to number sand itself. Think about it this way, using sand as an example: Can I say, "There's one grain of sand, and there's another"? Can I say, "There's one sand and there's another"? If the answer is yes, then use fewer (as in grains of sand, pieces of fruit, lumps of coal); if the answer is no, then use less (as in sand, fruit, or coal).

less than See **over.**

libel, slander Libel is defamation in writing or printing; slander is defamation by the spoken word. In the vast majority of modern legal cases, courts haven't distinguished between whether material was broadcast or printed, and most suits brought against media outlets are libel suits. Because of the reach and permanence of broadcast, material that defames is considered to have been "published."

lie, lay Lie means to tell an untruth or to recline. Lay means to place something on something else. You *lie* down, but you *lay* something down. The problem comes with lie (recline) in the past tense, which is lay. For example:

He felt so bad he wanted to *lie* down and die.
He *lay* down and died.

Here's how to conjugate the verbs: *Lie (tell an untruth): lie, lied, lied*

I cannot tell a *lie.*
I *lied* to my mother.
I've *lied* in similar situations.

Lie (recline): lie, lay, lain

I will *lie* on the bed.
Yesterday, I *lay* on the couch until noon.
I've *lain* in bed all day when I've been sick.

Lay (place something) lay, laid, laid

I will *lay* my books on the table.
I *laid* my books on the table when I got home.
I've *laid* my books there before.

You can see that the two ways to use "lay" can create some problems. But you wouldn't want to say he lied down, because that leads to confusion. Initially, it sounds as though you're saying he told an untruth.

like, such as   Like means similar to. Use "like" when you're comparing two things and "such as" when mentioning something as an example of a broader category. For instance:

Joe is *like* Pete in many ways. (The two are similar.)
Mothers *such as* Betty Jones are in favor of the new grant for child-care facilities.
Betty Jones is among those mothers who favor the grant. If you write mothers *like* Betty Jones are in favor, what you're saying is that mothers similar to her are, but perhaps she herself isn't. Also, don't substitute like for "as" or "as if."
He studies, *as* he should. (He should study and he does.)
If you write he studies *like* he should, you're making a judgment about his particular study habits. Perhaps he studies with the CD player at full volume. Are you saying he should study in that way?

lion's share   This phrase means more than "the majority of." It means all or nearly all.

literal   See **figurative.**

loan   See **lend.**

majority, plurality   The majority is more than half the total, often referred to as 50 percent plus one. When there are more than two candidates for office, the candidate receiving more votes than any other, but less than 50 percent has received the plurality of votes. This often means there must be a runoff between the top two vote-getters.

man, mankind   Other words are preferable, such as humans, people, or humanity for mankind, and a person or an individual for man. Also see **boy.**

masochism, sadism   Masochism means enjoyment of inflicting pain on yourself; sadism means enjoyment of inflicting pain on others. The pain doesn't necessarily have to be physical. People who fall into these categories are masochists or sadists.

Mass   Priests don't say Mass; Catholics celebrate Mass.

may, might, can, could   These are often used interchangeably. They shouldn't be. The key question, as with all words used in broadcast, is, "Might the viewers take what you've written in a way that's different from how you intended it?" For example, the following sentence could be interpreted two different ways.

Jane *may* go to the park.

Do you mean Jane might decide to go to the park, or that Jane has permission to go to the park? In instances when you mean something might happen, use "might" and there will be less room for confusion. The same is true for "can." Use "can" when you mean "is able." For example:

Can Jane go to the park?

We don't know if you're asking if she has permission to (if you are, use may) or if she's physically able to. In that case, use "can." The word "could" should be used when there's a condition attached.

Jane *could* have ridden to the park if her bike weren't broken.

me   See **he.**

media   The word "media" is plural and takes plural verbs. It means all forms of mass communication considered together. A single form of mass communication, such as television, is a medium. Mediums are palm readers.

mediate   See **arbitrate.**

medium   See **media.**

might   See **may.**

misuse   See **abuse.**

modern   See **contemporary.**

moral, morale   Moral deals with right and wrong; morale refers to one's confidence, self-esteem, and the like.

more than   See **over.**

mothers-in-law   As written.

Mr., Mrs., Miss, Ms.   All are courtesy titles. See Chapter 1.

murderer   See **assassin.**

neither   See **each.**

next of kin   This is brutally nonconversational. When have you ever used that phrase in a chat with a friend? Use family or relatives, either of which would be used in a conversation, rather than next of kin, which wouldn't.

nobody, no one   See **anybody.**

none   None means not one in most uses and takes singular verbs. There are times when saying not one of something doesn't make sense, such as "not one clothes" or if you're referring to no amount of something. Read the sentence and substitute not one for none and see if it makes sense. If it does, use a singular verb. If it doesn't make sense, use a plural verb. For example:

None of the children *was* injured in the fire.

None of his clothes *are* worth much.

However, even if you know something is grammatically correct, it might sound wrong to you, and if it sounds wrong to you, it will probably sound wrong to some of the viewers or listeners. So in the first example, you wouldn't change the sentence to make it grammatically incorrect and you might not want to write it the way it's written because the word "none" is used incorrectly so often it sounds wrong when you use it the right way. So rewrite the sentence: "All of the children escaped injury in the fire."

notorious, notable   Notorious means widely but unfavorably known. Notable is a synonym for prominent or noteworthy. When one gains notoriety, he or she is *unfavorably* thought of.

number, total   "The number" or "the total" takes singular verbs; "a number" or "a total" takes plural verbs. See **average.**

obscene, pornographic   Anything that's highly offensive is obscene. Pornographic material is designed to stimulate sexual thoughts. Obscene material might or might not be pornographic.

observance, observation   An observance is the act of complying with a law or custom or of taking part in a ceremony. Observation is the act of noticing. So, to say that the couple celebrated the *observation* of their 50th anniversary would be incorrect.

occur, take place   Things that occur happen with no planning. Things that take place are planned.

Olympics   This is a plural noun: "The Summer Olympics *are* held every four years." They are considered a collection of different sports events, not a single entity.

on, about   You give a speech on a stage, about a certain topic. You get and give information about things, not on them. Use on to mean "positioned upon."

one   The question of which possessive pronoun to use with "one" or "a person" creates some problems. To say, "one's home is one's castle" sounds very stiff, but so does "one's home is his or her castle." Also, you wouldn't want to use "is his castle" or "is her castle," nor would you say "is their castle," because you're talking about a single individual and "their" is plural. Try: "People's homes are their castles." The great majority of the time, when you use the word "one," you're referring to one at a time, and that's singular.

one another   See **each other.**

opponent   See **adversary.**

oral, verbal   Oral means of the mouth; verbal means using words, which can be written or spoken. You could say "she verbalized her feelings" or "they made verbal arguments" if you mean that someone spoke; but there's some room for confusion unless you explain that you specifically mean words were uttered. Of course, you wouldn't say "she oralized her feelings." Write: "She spoke about her feelings."

over, more than, under, less than   Over and under are frequently misused. Use under and over when something is physically under or over something else. However, when you mean a greater or lesser amount or number of something, use more than or less than. For example:

The plane flew *over* the field.
The car cost *more than* 30 thousand dollars.
The car was *under* water.
The house sold for *less than* 100 thousand dollars.

Also, people don't argue *over* something; they argue *about* it. And "through the years" is preferable to "over the years."

overlook, oversee   Overlook means to ignore or to fail to see. It also means to have a view of. Oversee means to supervise. For example:

I *overlooked* the small print in this contract.
I've decided to *overlook* your latest temper tantrum.
The house *overlooks* the canyon.
I'll *oversee* the construction project.

pardon, parole, probation   A pardon results in the forgiveness of the charges against a person; he or she faces no further punishment. A pardon is granted by a chief of state. Parole means the person was let out of prison before the end of the sentence. It's granted by a parole board. A person on probation is convicted but doesn't actually serve time, if the person doesn't mess up again. A suspended sentence is the same as probation.

pass   See **adopt.**

past   See **last.**

persecute, prosecute   Persecute means to harass; prosecute means to bring legal proceedings against. Members of the legal profession aren't supposed to persecute people, but some are supposed to prosecute those accused of wrongdoing.

person, people   Use person when speaking about an individual and people when the reference is to more than one person. Avoid persons.

personal, personnel   Personal means private or pertaining to an individual. Personnel means workforce or employees. There's a big difference between a manager making personal decisions and making personnel decisions.

persuade   See **convince.**

phenomenon, phenomena   Phenomenon is singular; phenomena is plural. You wouldn't write about *a* phenomena.

plurality   See **majority.**

pornographic   See **obscene.**

possible, probable   Something that's possible might happen; if it's probable, it's *likely* to happen.

precede, proceed   Precede means to come before; proceed means to move forward. For example:

Ninth grade *precedes* tenth grade.
Let's *proceed* to the next item on the agenda.

prescribe, proscribe   To prescribe is to suggest the use of something. To proscribe is to forbid or prohibit something. For example:

The doctor *prescribed* a powerful pain killer.
The judge *proscribed* him from having further contact with his ex-wife.

presently   See **currently.**

prison, jail   Generally, people serve time in prison for committing felonies. Jails are for minor offenders or those awaiting trial or sentencing on any charge. Penitentiaries and correctional facilities are prisons.

probable   See **possible.**

probation   See **pardon.**

proceed   See **precede.**

prognosis   See **diagnosis.**

proscribe   See **prescribe.**

prosecute   See **persecute.**

prostate, prostrate   The prostate is a gland; prostrate means lying down, in a prone position. Hence, no one suffers from *prostrate* cancer.

proved, proven   Proved is the past tense of prove; proven is an adjective describing something tested and shown to be effective. For example:

The lawyer had *proved* her case.
The program is a *proven* ratings winner.

ravage, ravish   Ravage means to inflict great damage or destroy; ravish means to rape or abduct and carry away. For example:

The storm *ravaged* the town.
The attacker *ravished* the sisters.

rebut, refute, dispute   To rebut or dispute is to argue to the contrary, to debate or quarrel; to refute is to prove something wrong or false. A television station in south Florida once ran a promotional spot that said its anchor was correct about something although other media in the area *refuted* him. If he was proved wrong, how could he have been right?

remains   That which is left, typically after decomposition (note: buildings don't decompose).

recur   Not reoccur.

regime   See **government.**

reluctant, reticent   Reluctant means unwilling to act; reticent means unwilling to speak.

reputation   See **character.**

resident   See **citizen.**

revert   Revert means to go back to a former place, position, or state of being. Revert back is redundant.

rob, burglarize, steal   Rob means to strip or deprive someone of something *by force.* Burglary is a crime of stealth usually involving breaking and entering. Therefore, people are robbed and places are burglarized. Anyone who takes something dishonestly has stolen.

rubble   Rough, broken stones or bits of concrete.

ruins   Anything (but usually buildings) in a state of destruction or decay. Has the added connotation of much time having passed.

runners-up   Not runner-ups.

sadism   See **masochism.**

sanction   This word has two different meanings. It can mean to approve or to punish. If you use this word, be sure your meaning is clear.

schizophrenia, split personality   These aren't the same. Schizophrenics can't distinguish fantasy from reality. Someone with a split personality has two or more distinct personalities, each with its own character traits.

scratch   See **itch.**

semiannual   See **biennial.** Semiannual is the correct spelling, but you might want to spell it semi-annual to make it easier to read.

sensual, sensuous   Both mean affecting the senses and are often used with a sexual connotation. People are sensual and things are sensuous.

sex   See **gender.**

she   See **he.**

shell, bullet   Shotguns and some military weapons fire shells. Handguns and rifles fire bullets. The pellets from a shotgun shell are called shot.

since, because   In some instances, since can be used to indicate a causal relationship, but that's not the primary use of the word. It should be used to mean from then until now. Sometimes since can mean because, but because always means because. Why take a chance of using since incorrectly? Use because. For example:

Since she came to live here, she's been disagreeable.

Do you mean she's been disagreeable because she came to live here, or that she's been disagreeable from the time she came to live here until now? "Since" leaves room for confusion as to your meaning. "Because" does away with the confusion.

sisters-in-law   As written.

skeptical   See **cynical.**

slander   See **libel.**

somebody, someone   See **anybody.**

sons-in-law   As written.

split personality   See **schizophrenia.**

steal   See **rob.**

such as   See **like.**

sympathy   See **empathy.**

take   See **bring.**

take place   See **occur.**

tamper, tinker   Tamper means to meddle harmfully; tinker means to fuss clumsily or to idly examine.

tap   See **bug.**

than, then   Than is used to introduce the second item of a comparison. Then means at that time or next in order. For example:

John is taller *than* Bill.
Then the board voted to give the mayor a raise.

thanks to   See **due to.**

that, who, which   Use "that" when you're referring to anything other than people or animals with names. In those cases, use "who." "Which" should be used only to introduce a nonessential clause or when "that" has already been used in the sentence. For example:

How to use "that" is the rule *that* is broken most often.
John is the student *who* breaks the rule most often.
Spike is the dog *who* accompanies John everywhere.
The rule, *which* is broken often, is the subject of much debate.
The professor said *that* it's the rule *which* is broken most often.

the   See **a.**

tinker   See **tamper.**

total   See **number.**

toward   See **afterward.**

under   See **over.**

uninterested   See **disinterested.**

unique   If something is unique, it's one of a kind. Things or people can't be quite unique or very unique or one of the most unique. They're either unique or they're not.

unknown, unnamed   Everyone has a name. Assailants, robbers, and the like are unknown, not unnamed. If the police know who the bad guy is but aren't saying, he still has a name. He's just unidentified.

upward   See **afterward.**

valuable, valueless   See **invaluable.**

verbal   See **oral.**

wait on, wait for   People in the service industry (servers in restaurants, for example) are the only people who wait on others. In all other contexts, use wait for.

watch, warning   In weather, a watch means a hurricane might pose a threat to a specific area. A warning means the hurricane is expected to hit a certain area within 24 hours. With tornadoes, a watch means a tornado is possible; a warning means a tornado exists or is suspected to have formed.

well   See **bad.**

well-known, widely known   People who are famous are widely known. (Note there is no hyphen in widely known.) A fact that is known by many people is well-known. For example:

Sylvester Stallone is *widely known.*
It's *well-known* that the sky is blue.

what, which   "What" should be used when the category is unknown, but "which" should be used when referring to a specific item in a category. For example: *What* do you want to do this weekend? I want to go to a movie. *Which* movie do you want to see? It would be incorrect to say, *What* movie do you want to see?

whereabouts   Takes singular verbs. For example: The whereabouts of the robber *is* unknown. However, whereabouts isn't very conversational. Use location or something similar.

while   See **although.**

who, which   See **that.**

woman   See **boy.**

wounded   See **injured.**

wreck, wreak   Wreck means to destroy; wreak means to inflict.

wreckage   Aftermath of destruction, usually in reference to cars, boats, or planes that have been wrecked.

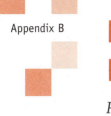

LEGAL AND PRIVACY FAQs

Forrest Carr

People used to say, "The truth is an absolute defense against libel." This might still be true, but in today's environment, journalists face many legal perils other than libel and slander. It might shock some newsmen and newswomen to learn that for some of those legal issues, not only is truth not a defense, it's actually *irrelevant*. From a legal standpoint, it's a scary world out there. And with the rise of the Internet, which presents its own legal challenges, it's scarier than ever before.

In the pages that follow, Gregg D. Thomas and Susan Tillotson Bunch will give us some pointers for surviving the legal minefields covering the 21st-century media landscape. Both are partners in the Tampa, Florida, law firm of Thomas, LoCicero, and Bralow. Combined, they have nearly half a century of experience in media law and First Amendment litigation. Together, we'll chart some of the more common legal shoals on which journalists' ships often founder and we'll address some commonly asked questions. The purpose isn't to turn you into a First Amendment and libel expert. Rather, this should serve as a quick-reference guide, showing you some obvious hazards and helping you understand when you need to raise a red flag and take precautionary steps, seek further legal advice, or both.

What Are Libel and Slander, and How Can I Avoid Them?

Libel is the publication of something untrue about a person or organization such that it damages that person's or organization's reputation, business or standing within the community. Slander is similar, but it's "oral," involving words spoken by one individual about another. In either case, Thomas says the issue is "defamation." In other words, if you tell a friend or publish a statement that Joe Blow is a lying womanizer, and it's not true, then you have defamed Mr. Blow—you've hurt his reputation and standing in the community. He's going to come after you legally. And maybe illegally.

It's worth noting that simply asking questions about someone could open you up to a slander claim. Be careful what you say to people! For instance, making phone calls to ask people if they've heard the rumors about Joe Blow's lying and womanizing is risky. Asking sources if they've heard anything unusual about Joe Blow is less risky.

A27

The defense to a libel or slander claim is pretty simple. For it to be defamation, says Thomas, it has to be false. When it comes to libel or slander, says Thomas, "The protector for every journalist is the truth." The best cure is preventative. Get your facts straight and keep them straight.

If Someone Makes an Allegation, May I Publish It?

This falls under a doctrine that says, "Quoted speech is your speech." Says Thomas, "Allegations alone if adopted by journalists can create problems because you've adopted their speech, and if it's false, you're responsible for it." This can be true even if you're simply faithfully reporting a quote. In other words, if you publish or broadcast a quote from a private individual who says Joe Blow is a lying womanizer, it's pretty much the same as if you said it yourself. You'd better be able to prove it. Such comments are very unsafe if one private individual makes them against another private individual and you repeat them. They're safer if one public figure makes them against another, especially if the comments are made in public—we'll have more about the difference between public and private figures in a moment. Also, allegations set down in court proceedings are public record. Says Thomas, "We are entitled and have a privilege to write about those matters."

Can Someone Sue Me If I or Someone I Quote Expresses an Opinion?

Thomas points out that the answer to *any* question beginning with the words, "Can someone sue me," is "Certainly. You can be sued for anything." The goal is not to give the other side a case. Happily, the truism, "You're entitled to your opinion," is still pretty much true. You may report opinions, provided that you disclose the underlying facts. Says Thomas, "There's a great quote from a Supreme Court case that says, 'There is no liability for a false idea.' No such thing as a false idea. What you want is the widest dissemination of ideas. If it's an opinion, and you disclose what the surrounding facts are, then you are protected."

However, take care to make sure the opinion is framed as just that, an opinion, not a statement of fact. Also make sure that any facts supporting the opinion are clearly stated and provably true. There's no legal principle barring a journalist from expressing an opinion; in such matters journalists should be guided by journalistic ethics and newsroom policy. The public generally accepts the idea that columnists—who are, after all, journalists—will express opinions on the editorial pages, but resists the idea that journalists should express opinions in straight news reporting. The Internet is a different animal, but experience suggests the public recognizes the difference between, say, a straight news report contained on the home page of a news site, and a blog posting—and accepts opinions and commentary as part and parcel of the latter. Likewise, viewers tend to understand the difference between a straight news report and a news talk show—although, arguably, those distinctions are becoming less and less clear all the time.

If I Make an Honest Mistake, Can Someone Sue Me?

Yes. See above comments. In this case, a jury might hold you accountable for even an honest mistake when you're reporting about a private individual. However, there are ways to soften the blow. If you move quickly to retract and correct a mistake, you might mitigate or lessen the damages. Make sure your newsroom has a policy to quickly and promptly address calls for corrections or retractions. Above all, treat the caller with courtesy. Poor treatment of a caller, says Thomas, "May not add to damages, but certainly may add to their zest to sue you."

What's the Difference between Public Figures and Private Individuals?

If you get your story wrong and damage the reputation of a private individual, that individual has only to prove that your story was wrong, that you were negligent, and that your story harmed him or her. But a public figure has a higher burden of proof. In that case, the plaintiff must not only prove the information was false, but that the broadcaster or publisher acted with "actual malice," also referred to as "reckless disregard of the truth." According to Thomas, this is *not* a heightened negligence standard. You're not guilty of "reckless disregard," for instance, just because you forgot to check with a police source that you typically consult. It means, says Thomas, "knowing falsehood, that is, you know that something is false at the time you publish it." You're guilty of reckless disregard of the truth if your facts are wrong, you knew they were wrong, and you proceeded anyway. The good news is, this is a subjective standard. To prove this, the plaintiff has to get inside your head and in essence prove what you were thinking. It's not easy.

For these reasons, the trick in every libel case is to define the plaintiff. Every defense attorney will try to show that the plaintiff is a public figure and therefore entitled to less protection. The plaintiff's side will try to show the opposite. It's a gray area, but you can generally rely on government officials, schoolteachers, police officers, firefighters, mayors, city council people and the like to be defined as public figures. Says Thomas, "Those people fall into the category where the standard is much greater, that is to encourage public debate about public matters." Celebrities usually fall into this category as well.

What's Invasion of Privacy?

Invasion of privacy is similar to libel. However, with these kinds of claims the truth isn't always a defense, and publication of a story isn't always required. According to Thomas, there are four different kinds of invasion of privacy: trespass, publication of private facts, commercial misappropriation of someone's likeness, and false light. Commercial misappropriation doesn't apply to newsgathering. We'll talk about trespass and false light in a bit. For the moment, let's concern ourselves with publication of private facts.

It's presumed that certain facts about a person are private, and that publication of those facts might be harmful to the individual's peace of mind or community standing. Says Thomas, "If you disclose something that is of an intimate personal nature about someone, you can be sued for it." But this applies only if the private facts are indeed private. You're pretty safe in reporting about anything that happens in a public place, such as a street corner or park. Facts gathered about private individuals from public sources such as court records are also fairly safe to report. But, says Thomas, "What happens inside someone's home or inside an emergency room suite or a hospital is probably their private zone." And here's something else for you to consider: When it comes to invasion of privacy, the intrusion *alone* can be actionable. In other words, merely appearing with a notepad, recorder or camera in the wrong place can get you sued, regardless of whether you broadcast or post anything.

In privacy claims, "newsworthiness" is a common defense strategy; typically, the journalist or news organization will attempt to show that publication and/or intrusion was in the public interest.

What's "False Light"?

False light occurs when a journalist or publisher paints a picture of a plaintiff so badly out of context as to give the wrong idea, especially if that idea is negative—even if the story contains verifiable facts. Example: A car crash scene photo prominently displays a broken liquor bottle in the foreground. This strongly suggests that alcohol was a factor in the crash. If that's demonstrably the case, and if the liquor bottle being shown is the specific bottle from which the guilty party drank, then the photo is safe. But if not, then the photo could place the participants in a false light, and the news organization could be liable—even if the liquor bottle was indeed present at the crash scene.

The interesting thing about false light litigation, says Thomas, is that while defamation protects reputation, "False light protects feelings." If your story uses verifiable facts stacked in such a way to give a wrong, negative impression about someone, and in the process hurts that person's feelings, you could be liable.

The good news for journalists is that the legal concept of "false light" might be falling into judicial disfavor. Not every state recognizes false light as a cause for action. In 2008 the Florida Supreme Court, ruling in the case of *Anderson v. Gannett*, rejected a "false light" tort. According to Thomas, "Basically, false light is so much like defamation, that we don't need both of them."

When Can I Go onto Private Property to Gather the News?

In general, a person's home is his castle and is presumed to be private. You're the most legally safe taking pictures of someone's home or business if you're standing on public property such as a sidewalk or street—even then, you should take care when using telephoto lenses. You're less safe walking onto someone's property, even if you're under police or fire department escort. It's legally risky to enter someone's home without the occupant's consent even if police or firefighters are momentarily controlling access and have beckoned you in. If the property is posted with a "No Trespassing" sign, you must obey it.

In places other than the private home, the laws are less clear. Says Thomas, "My rule of thumb is, go anywhere and everywhere there is not a 'No Trespassing' sign. If you are asked to leave, do so as expeditiously as possible." It can get dicey. Malls, for instance, are places where the public is welcome but reporters are not, unless you're there to cover a grand opening. Thomas says you can press the issue. "The mall of today is the city center of yesterday, and lots of things happened in city centers that were newsworthy. So my advice is, go until you are asked to leave." But here's a heads-up for you: A sign that says "No Cameras" is a no-trespassing sign for journalists and you disregard it at your peril. You can stay, but the camera must go.

If someone challenges you and you leave—can you use the material you've shot until that point? Maybe. Thomas advises, "You want to look at what you gathered, what the information is, whether it's of a private or personal nature, whether you caught someone unaware, then make a judgment call about whether to use it or not."

If a Police Officer Orders Me to Leave a Scene Where Other Members of the Public Are Present, Must I Obey?

You might be within your legal rights to stand your ground—but from a practical standpoint, the cops might also arrest you. As one police officer once famously posted, "You may beat the rap, but you can't beat the ride." If you think unfair police orders to back off are hurting your story, wait until you see what getting cuffed and stuffed does to it. Says Thomas, "Resist to the point of telling the officer that he's wrong and you shouldn't be singled out, and then retreat." Capture the conversation on camera or audiotape if you have that ability and are in a public place. Then, if you still believe officials violated your rights and you want to fight, file a complaint. Experience suggests that most police officers are duty-minded and primarily concerned with public safety, but it's certainly true that on occasion one will push the media around inappropriately for fun, sport or paybacks. Regarding the latter, says Thomas, "People who are doing that are probably jerks. And if you illustrate that to their boss, as we've done several times, the point is made much better than resisting at the lowest level."

When May I Use a Hidden Microphone or Camera?

Laws vary from state to state. Some require single party consent—in other words, you know you're recording but the target doesn't. Some require all parties to consent. Some allow hidden cameras but not hidden microphones. In most cases, it's risky to use a hidden microphone or camera in places presumed to be private, and less risky to use them in public places. A street corner is generally accepted to be very public. A business open to the public is a grayer area. A person's home is almost always presumed to be private. Don't go there.

When May I Record and Broadcast or Post a Telephone Conversation?

Federal law prohibits recording a phone call to which the person recording it isn't a party. At least one person actually participating in the call must be aware of the recording. About a dozen states impose tougher restrictions, requiring the consent of *all* parties involved in the call. According to the Reporters' Committee for Freedom of the Press (http://www.rcfp.org), those tougher states currently are: California, Connecticut, Florida, Illinois, Maryland, Massachusetts, Michigan, Montana, Nevada, New Hampshire, Pennsylvania and Washington.

Recording a call *for broadcast purposes* is a different matter. But there's one set of conditions that covers everything. As Thomas puts it, "You can record a telephone conversation anytime you have the consent of the person, and you tell them that your intent is to use the information in a news program."

What if someone else recorded the conversation and provided it to you—can you broadcast it or post it then? If you had absolutely no involvement of any kind in the act of recording the conversation—then, maybe. Federal law specifically forbids publishing an "illegal wiretap" or illegally intercepted conversation. However, in May of 2001 the U.S. Supreme Court allowed it in a case in which the participants were discussing a crime, ruling that First Amendment concerns overrode privacy issues in *that particular case*. If you're faced with such a decision, this is one of those instances when you might want to get specific legal advice.

If I Receive Photos, Audio Recordings or Documents Obtained Improperly by a Third Party, May I Broadcast or Post Them?

Possibly. Says Thomas, "If someone gives you something and they've broken the law, you are not going to be construed to be a lawbreaker." On the other hand, that doesn't mean you can just turn around and put the information on the air or on your Web site. You must still carry out your other journalistic duties, such as fact checking, taking care of fairness, privacy and libel concerns, and so on.

Must My Story Be "Balanced" with Viewpoints from Those Who Are Cast in a Negative Light?

In the legal context, Thomas defines balance as "the other side's statement—you presented the facts to them and they respond." It is *not* an equal time provision. Nor is it a legal *requirement*. Thomas describes balance as being "great to have in defending a lawsuit," but adds that it isn't utterly necessary. Nor is balance the same as fairness. "Fairness," says Thomas, "is in the eye of the beholder. Balance is trying to get the other side to respond. Balance is more important than fairness."

So what does this mean for the journalist? Seeking comment from the target of your story is a basic part of the journalistic truth-telling process. It's common for such people to refuse comment. This doesn't mean you must kill the story even though it certainly won't be "balanced" in a mathematical sense. However, it would be wise for you to show in the story that you made the attempt to obtain such comment. Juries consider such attempts to be the right thing to do and might take a dim view of reporters who don't do it.

If Someone Gives an Interview Then Later Asks Not to Be Quoted or Not to Appear on TV, Must I Comply?

This is known as "withdrawal of consent." Consent is a powerful defense to any libel or privacy claim. In other words, if someone gives permission for you to say something about him or her, or if you receive an invitation to come in, talk and record, then you can proceed. But if the person changes his or her mind afterward, you lose that defense. That doesn't always mean you must lose the story. Says Thomas, "If the person has told you things and it's clear that they knew at the time that you were a journalist and you were straight with them about that, there's no need to permit them to withdraw." On the other hand, if that person revealed some intensely private and intimate facts, says Thomas, "It's a much closer call." For instance, if you're interviewing an AIDS patient giving a first-person account of his or her ordeal, an account you wouldn't otherwise be able to obtain or report, and if the withdrawal of consent comes at a reasonable time given deadline constraints, it might be wise to comply.

When May I Use an Anonymous Source?

The question of whether and when you may publish quotes from anonymous sources is a journalistic matter and subject to newsroom policy. Many newsrooms strongly discourage the use of anonymous sources. And there are legal issues as well. First among them: If your story relies solely on anonymous sources, how are you going to defend your facts in court? Says Thomas, "You essentially straightjacket or handcuff your lawyer without someone to substantiate them at a later time." And here's another wrinkle to consider. If you promise anonymity to a source, you're entering into a contract. Even though it's not written down, says Thomas, "That contract is binding, and has to be upheld. If it's not, then the source can sue for breach of contract." But what if a judge later *orders* you to reveal the source's identity? Ouch. Now you really have a problem, one that could force you to choose between violating a promise and going to jail. Says Thomas, "A journalist's pledge is his bond. If you can't uphold that promise, then you lose credibility with the public about your ability to promise anything."

As you can see, promises of anonymity are very serious deals and you shouldn't enter into them lightly. Negotiate carefully. First, before promising anonymity to a source, it's wise to make sure that such a promise is absolutely essential to being able to break the story. If it is, then ask the source whether he or she would be willing to step forward and testify should you be sued. If the source will be appearing on-camera in an obscured fashion, never make broad promises that no one will be able to recognize the source. Instead, negotiate with the source the specific production technique to be used to obscure the identity, and get an agreement about it, preferably one you capture on video or audio. It's wise to make sure that news managers are involved and are guiding these discussions. Finally, in the wake of recent journalistic scandals some reporters are now insisting as part of the deal that they'll be allowed to reveal the source's identity if it turns out the source is lying or withholding important facts.

May I Go Undercover?

In general, anytime a reporter uses deception in pursuit of a story, it's legally risky. If you lie to anyone about your name, profession, or purpose, you might be putting yourself at risk of being sued for fraud. Juries tend to take a dim view of reporters, period. Reporters who lie or break the law, no matter the merits of the story the reporter is pursuing, get even less sympathy. News managers should keep these risks firmly in mind when considering undercover techniques. Says Thomas, "You don't go undercover if you can get the story with a little bit more work, or maybe even a lot more work."

Is There Any Easy Way to Check a Story to Assess Risk of Libel or Invasion of Privacy?

Remember, if you can't easily prove the truth of your claim in terms that would satisfy a judge or a jury, you're in legal peril. The best practice is to make absolutely sure what you're saying is demonstrably true before you say it—"demonstrably" being the operative word. Proofread every story carefully and red-flag any instances in which your story casts a person or organization in a negative light. Double-check every such instance to make sure your facts are straight and well sourced. Public documents and statements by government officials generally are the safest sources. Private individuals and other nonofficial sources are less safe; if you're relying solely on the latter, it's best to have multiple sources. Least safe of all are facts about private individuals gleaned through surreptitious methods, such as using hidden cameras or microphones. Also test everything you've red-flagged for balance and fairness—have you given that person or organization a chance to respond?

When vetting a script, Thomas looks for certain common indicators. "There are some key words that are going to make you look askance at a story. If the story says 'fraud' or 'scam' or any of those sorts of jump words, if it involves inherently private information about pregnancy or disease or something like that, then you are going to want to look at it a second time."

Should I Keep My Notes and Outtakes?

Regarding outtakes, says Thomas, "My thought is not only 'no,' but 'hell no.'" The best advice here is to have a policy and follow it. A practice of regularly recycling videotapes or of purging video files is a good idea. Outtakes, says Thomas, "only present peril, not benefit." For personal notes, Thomas urges you to develop your own personal policy and stick to it. "If you throw them out every six months then throw them out every six months." But he adds, don't have the attitude of, "'I really like this story so I'm going to hold on to the notes. . . .' Because my experience is it comes back and bites us, and you know where, every time it happens."

Deviations from habit—either in the form of carefully keeping material you don't normally keep or hurriedly destroying material you normally *do* keep—can look suspicious to a jury. However, for similar reasons, if a potential plaintiff puts you on notice to save your notes and outtakes for potential litigation, Thomas says you should do so, even if you haven't received a legally binding subpoena.

What's "Fair Use"?

Fair use is a legal doctrine under which you may take very small portions of someone else's copyrighted material and use it in your newscast or Web posting. The key is "small portion." Says Thomas, "If it's a thirty-minute interview of Strom Thurmond, his last interview ever given, and you take a minute of it, then you are probably protected doing that, particularly given the newsworthiness." However, you'd be ill advised to use 15 seconds of someone else's video if that particular 15 seconds captures the entire newsworthiness of the story.

If It's Safe to Broadcast, Is It Safe to Post on the Web?

As is so often the case with legal issues, the answer is, "It depends." In general, the legal principles we've just discussed are the same on the Internet. However, the Internet does present some unique challenges. Chief among them is the fact that your Web posting is a second publication—a second "count" if you will, for which you can be sued separately from the television broadcast, or in addition to it. Further, unlike the TV broadcast, which is aired and then gone, the Web posting typically is available online indefinitely. The good news about that, according to Bunch, is that each subsequent day that the posting is available does *not* count as an "additional publication" for litigation purposes. The first day of posting sets the clock ticking on the statute of limitations—which, according to Bunch, is a very good thing. Otherwise, "You would have eternal liability for anything published online, because anytime a viewer clicks on something, it's published."

This doesn't mean you can turn your back on "archived" stories that contain errors. Once you become aware of an error, you need to do something about that original posting. Thomas favors putting up an immediate correction, "Then correct the Web story by adding something below it."

Because the Web is a different publication platform, you need to make sure you've secured the Internet rights to anything you propose to post there. Obviously, if you or your organization created the material, it's yours. If you're purchasing amateur, freelance or syndicated video for use on the air, make sure your purchase agreement also secures Internet rights. Rare is the news director or sports director who hasn't bumped his or her nose against this issue when proposing to stream a newscast; every outside news vendor or copyright holder that's contributed to or portrayed in the television newscast must specifically agree to grant Internet rights as well. Professional sports Web rights are notoriously difficult to sort out.

If I Allow Members of the Public to Post Comments on My Web Site, Am I Liable for What They Say?

We said earlier that if you quote people, "Their speech is your speech." Thankfully, years of lawmaking and court rulings have largely cleared up the confusion about this point that characterized the early days of the Internet. If you allow the public to self-post on your Web site, you're not liable for what's posted. Thanks to the Digital Millennium Copyright Act, this is true even if you moderate or screen the site for taste, profanity, hate speech or whatnot. Self-posting is the key. According to Bunch, "You're not going to be treated as a content provider as long as all you're doing is providing a forum. Now if you get in there and you do assist in creating content, then it changes the rules." If you touch the posting in any way—such as by transcribing or retyping a comment that you've received by e-mail or by phone—then you're now deemed as the publisher of that comment, and are liable for it. This is also true if you quote the comment in a news story, or even if you move it to a different Web page. But the good news is that even if you normally screen postings and something bad slips through, you're still not liable. Bunch advises that you explicitly reserve the right to screen in your terms of use, but says the right to screen doesn't create an obligation to screen. "The law does not require the screening to be 100 percent effective." (But Bunch says that to take advantage of the Safe Harbor protections in the DMCA, the ISP must register an agent with the U.S. Copyright Office, and also post this information online. More information and the necessary forms are available at http://www.copyright.gov/onlinesp/.)

Can I Make Use of a Photo or Video a User Has Posted on the Internet?

It's a common newsroom situation: A private individual who's posted a series of photos or videos of herself on YouTube, MySpace or Facebook suddenly becomes newsworthy. Those pictures are fair game, right? Not so fast. Says Bunch, "Putting it online does not put it in the public domain for copyright purposes. Permission would have to come from the copyright holder." Even if you haven't secured the rights to the material, you still might be able to use at least a portion of it. "You have to go through the fair use analysis just like you would as if someone had mailed a copyright protected video to you." See the earlier discussion about fair use.

Bunch also points out another peril you need to consider. Some Web sites require you to create an account in order to get access, and they often come with explicit restrictions. Even if the account is free, be sure you read the terms of use before you click the "I agree" checkbox and start pulling content off that Web site left and right with gleeful abandon. Says Bunch, "They could potentially sue you for breach of contract."

Does the Internet Pose Any Unique Dangers to Journalists?

The hazard that worries Bunch the most is the habit of some journalists, particularly inexperienced ones, to believe and cite anything they find on the Internet. Not all Web postings are created equal, not by a long shot. There's a big difference, for instance, between an official report posted on a DotGov Web site and a random anonymous posting on some public bulletin board. As Bunch points out, "Anybody can publish on a Web site." About some of those postings, she says, "To me it's no different than relying on a poster taped to a telephone pole." "But Your Honor, it was posted on the Internet" is no defense against libel. At a minimum, Bunch recommends having personal knowledge of the reliability of any nonofficial postings and using double sourcing.

Summary

An understanding of the law helps journalists consider, weigh and minimize risk, but you can never eliminate legal risk in the vigorous pursuit of worthwhile journalism. Journalists are well advised to seek legal counsel when thorny questions arise. You should also remember that the law tends to set out minimum requirements for what journalists can get away with; in other words, it describes what they *can* do. Journalists should rely on a firm grounding in the ethics of their profession to understand what they *should* do.

PRODUCING A STUDENT NEWSCAST FROM BEGINNING TO END

Brynne Miller

1. As you begin to plan your show, compile the story ideas the reporters have sent in and come up with a preliminary assignments list. Then meet with the news director to discuss story selection and to finalize the assignments before the assignments meeting. At the assignments meeting, discuss the stories and their formats (VO, VO/SOT, PKG, Live, Q&A), and assign each to the appropriate reporter.

2. Producer is in charge of e-mailing reporters as a follow-up to the assignments meeting to let them know the stories they've been assigned; reporters should confirm assignment by e-mailing the producer; if they don't, the producer should follow up by sending an e-mail asking reporters to confirm they received the assignments e-mail.

3. At least 12 hours before your show (for non-breaking news), ask your reporters to send you the following information:
   SLUG:
   ERT: (estimated total runtime)
   FORMAT: (VO, VO/SOT, PKG)
   BRIEF SUMMARY:
   WHEN YOU PLAN TO EDIT:

4. No later than eight hours prior to the show, start building a rundown in your newsroom system including story format (VO, VO/SOT, PKG).

5. As you're building the rundown, start determining shot selection (1shot, 2shot) and whether or not there will be an OTS (over-the-shoulder).

6. Choose tease stories, then send an e-mail asking reporters to cut either a pre-show or in-show tease; ask them to e-mail back a confirmation. In that same e-mail, identify which stories you'd like an OTS for. Remember:
   A pre-show tease is one shot, 10–15 seconds.

An in-show tease is two shots, one 4 seconds, one 10 seconds.

**Both pre-show and in-show teases should include significant pad.

For an OTS, the reporter needs to pick a 10- to 14-letter word or words that are in the anchor lead and put that in your newsroom system to accompany the image.

7. Check to make sure stories are getting put into your newsroom system; if not, call specific reporters to get a status check and make sure their stories were or will be approved by the news director.

8. Write pre-show teases and in-show teases for A, B, C, and E blocks, and get the sports producer to write the D block tease.

9. As reporters put stories into your newsroom system, tie-write stories to make sure they flow from one to another; double-check formatting and grammar.

10. Once rundown is complete, number rundown (for example: A1, A2, A3 . . . A24) and print final rundown for director; ask someone to print director scripts.

11. Print anchor scripts on white paper.

12. Backtime prior to the show.

13. During the show, watch time closely, talk to anchors about any issues that come up (speed up, slow down, stretch toss, quick toss, and so on) and give the weathercaster time cues (2 minutes, 1 minute, 30 seconds).

14. In addition, make sure you make the news director aware of **ANY** problems that come up when you're putting your show together!

GLOSSARY

actuality   Sound or sound bite in radio.

ambient sound   The audio equivalent of b-roll natural sound in TV. Ambient sound enhances a radio story and figuratively puts the listener in the place where the story occurs.

anchor   The person who hosts a television or radio newscast.

backtime   A method of calculating the estimated "hit" time for a story within a newscast. This method calculates the hit time by subtracting the estimated running time for that story and of all remaining stories from the "end" time of the newscast. It's useful for learning whether the newscast is running long or short as the end time of the newscast approaches. See also **forward time.**

bite   A short snippet of an interview chosen for on-air presentation.

block   A segment of a television newscast, usually defined as the content between commercial breaks. The "A" block is all material up to the first commercial. The material that follows the first commercial is the "B" block. The B block ends at the second commercial break, and so on.

b-roll   Cover video.

bullet point   Two or three words of text summarizing a point, usually set off by an asterisk, circle, square, or some other form of demarcation at the beginning of the line.

chroma key (CK)   Images are electronically inserted over a wall that's a solid color, usually blue or green. Typically, an anchor or weathercaster stands in front of the wall and refers to what the viewers are seeing.

consortium   A group of stations that share video and information.

convergence   A communications industry movement wherein different forms of media, formerly in competition, cooperate and work together for mutual benefit.

cutaway   A shot related to the main action, but which doesn't show the main action. An example is fans at a sporting event.

diamond style   In a television package, telling a story about something that affects a large number of people by using a specific person or small group as an example.

donut   A short television package preceded and/or followed by live reporter presence, either in the field, on-set, or in the newsroom. A donut typically doesn't include a taped stand-up or a sig-out.

editing script   The copy of a script given to a videotape editor. For a package, this usually doesn't include the anchor lead and tag or the technical directions.

ENG (electronic news gathering)   The equipment and process of gathering video material in the field.

entermation   When information takes a back seat to entertainment.

enterprise   A type of story requiring original reporting, digging, and research—as opposed to a story involving a news release, news conference, accident, or similar material.

forward time   A method of calculating the estimated "hit" time for a story within a newscast. This method is used to calculate the hit time by adding the running time of all of the preceding stories to the start time of the newscast. It's useful for estimating whether certain stories will fall within designated time periods, such as a satellite window. See also **backtime.**

full-screen   A television visual element that takes up the entire viewing screen.

full-screen graphic (FSG)   A graphic that fills the entire screen and contains statistics, bullet points, or other information relevant to the story.

gatekeeping   The act of deciding which stories are presented in a newscast and which ones aren't.

graphic   In a television context, the word "graphic" usually refers to a full-screen presentation that is used as a substitute for video. The graphic might contain a combination of artwork and text over a color or textured background, which helps explain or illustrate a story. In a Web context, a graphic can be any combination of artwork and text laid out on the page, usually in support of a story.

IFB   An abbreviation for the words "interruptible feedback." It refers to a communications system by which an anchor or reporter can hear some or all of the television station's programming. True IFB implies that the producer is able to interrupt programming to speak to the talent, but the word is often used interchangeably with other, noninterruptible forms of audio signals to the talent.

incue   The first few words of a bite.

infotainment   Information presented in an entertaining way.

intro   Anchor- or reporter-read copy preceding a television news package.

kicker   A nonserious story positioned at the end of a television news block or newscast.

lead   1. The first sentence of a story. In television, if the story is a package, we also have a package lead, which includes an introduction of the reporter. All story leads serve to attract viewer attention. Within stories that include comments from news sources, writers lead to the comments, letting the viewers know who's speaking, why that person's comments are important to the story, and most important, "teeing up" the comment (bite) to let the viewers know what the comment will be about.

    2. The first story in a newscast.

lineup   See **rundown.**

live shot   A live camera remote, or live report from talent in the field utilizing a live camera signal, which typically is fed back to the television station by microwave, satellite, fiber, or Internet.

logging   Scanning field tapes in order to pick sound bites, listen for and list specific snippets of natural sound, and provide a brief description of usable shots and where to find them on the tape.

mix-minus   Audio fed to an anchor or reporter via IFB containing some, but not all, of the program being fed to the station's transmitter. Typically the programming is mixed without audio from live remotes, in order to prevent the talent in the field from hearing a distracting delayed feedback of his or her own words.

Mom Rule   Writing stories in the same way you'd tell the story to your mom.

Murphy's Law   A mysterious but well-documented force that requires technical malfunctions or operational mishaps to occur if there's the least opportunity for them to happen, especially if there are no contingency plans to deal with the problem.

narrative style   A style of storytelling presenting the facts in more or less chronological order with a clear beginning, middle, and end.

natural sound Any naturally occurring sound recorded in the field, other than interviews. Nat sound includes comments from people who aren't in a formal interview setting.

news hole In television: the portion of a newscast actually filled by news, minus sports, weather, commercials, bumps, teases, and other preproduced elements.

NPR National Public Radio.

open In television, this refers to the standard beginning of every newscast, typically consisting of a preproduced announcement over graphics and music.

OTS (over-the-shoulder) graphic Graphics information that appears in a box over the shoulder of an anchor.

outcue The final few words of a story element not being read by an anchor (bite, package, wrap, and so forth).

over-the-shoulder graphic See **OTS.**

package A television story filed by a reporter, which typically includes narration, a stand-up, bites, and accompanying video and natural sound. An anchor package (the anchor's voice is prerecorded, rather than that of a reporter) typically doesn't include a stand-up or sig-out. A nat sound package includes no recorded narration, just bites, natural sound, and perhaps music.

pad In a television story, a 10-second (or more) continuation of the final shot beyond the recorded track or the timed end of the copy. Used to avoid going to black on the air.

PIO Public Information Officer. A spokesperson for agencies such as police and fire departments, the sheriff's office, and so forth.

pod A group of related stories in a broadcast news block.

producer's script The copy of the broadcast script that goes to the producer. For a package, this would include the anchor lead and tag and the technical instructions.

Q&A A live appearance in which the guest doesn't deliver written copy, but rather answers questions from an anchor or reporter.

reader A short television story read by an anchor with no accompanying video or full-screen graphic. Sometimes called a "tell" story. In radio, copy being read by an anchor.

reader/actuality (RA) A type of radio story in which the radio anchor reads the opening copy for the story, plays a clip (which is the audio recording of the actuality or sound bite), and then reads the closing copy.

roll cue The final few words from a reporter doing a live introduction to a package. The roll cue lets the show director know when to roll the tape.

rundown The document that outlines the order of stories in a newscast and briefly notes how each story is to be presented. In some stations, the rundown is called the lineup.

shot Video taken from a live television camera. The term is used most often in conjunction with studio cameras aimed at talent and is frequently used in combination with the numerals one through four to designate how many anchors or reporters will be framed within the shot.

sidebar A short story directly related to a longer story.

signal A live feed of video and audio. This can refer to a station's transmitter signal but more typically is used in conjunction with live feeds sent to the station from crews in the field for use within the newscast.

sig-out (signature outcue)   The line all reporters at a given station use to end a standard package. A typical sig-out would include the location, the reporter's name, and the name of the news organization. For example, "In Waynesville, I'm Bob Strong, Newswatch 7."

skeleton time   The time in a television newscast devoted to "standard" items appearing every night, which typically include such items as commercials, sports, weather, teases, opens, closes, tosses, chitchat time, and pad time. The total news window minus the skeleton time yields the news hole.

slug   Brief title assigned to a news story.

SOT (sound on tape)   Interview sound, recorded on tape or disk, to be used in a broadcast news story.

sound bite   See **bite.**

standard   The word used on a package script to indicate to the technical staff that the package ends with a signature outcue.

stand-up   A reporter appears on-camera and delivers a line or two.

stinger   A definitive ending to a cut of music at the end of a newscast.

super   Graphics information superimposed over video. A typical identifier super contains a person's name and title.

SWAP   Synchronized words and pictures. Results from writing from the video, letting the pictures dictate how the text is structured.

tag   The anchor copy that follows a bite in a VO/SOT or follows a reporter package. The purpose of the tag is for the anchor to wrap up one story before the newscast moves on to the next story.

talent   A term referring to anyone paid to appear on-camera or behind a microphone.

tease   A short item appearing within a television newscast previewing other stories still ahead. Teases typically air just prior to commercial breaks.

tie-writing   Working to provide flow within and between stories by making smooth transitions from one thought to the next.

track   Recorded package narration.

upcut   A technical or timing mistake in a television newscast that leads to one segment sliding over on top of the next segment, causing the viewer to miss part of the audio and/or video of the following segment.

user   Short for "online user," someone who accesses an Internet Web site.

VO (voice-over)   A short television story read by an anchor accompanied by video or a graphic presented full-screen.

VO/SOT (voice-over/sound on tape)   A television story form in which an anchor reads the first part of the story accompanied by a video or a graphic presented full-screen. The anchor then pauses for a comment (bite) from a news source, before ending the story on-camera.

VO/SOT/VO   Same as a VO/SOT except that the anchor concludes the story by reading over more video rather than by reading on-camera.

wallpaper video   Video having either an indirect match or no match to the copy. This "use of video for the sake of video" usually is inappropriate.

window   A specific amount of time leased from a satellite broker for transmission of a news story or other video content.

wrap   A type of radio story that includes the anchor lead and a voiced report from a reporter along with an actuality (sound bite); a "wrap" is the radio equivalent of a news package in television.

INDEX